DAILY DOSE
of
KNOWLEDGE™

BIBLE

Publications International, Ltd.

Randy Petersen is a writer and church educator from New Jersey with more than 40 books to his credit, including *God's Answers to Tough Questions* and *100 Fascinating Bible Facts*. A prolific creator of church curriculum, he's also a contributor to the *Quest Study Bible*, the *Revell Bible Dictionary*, and the iLumina Bible software.

David W. Baker is Professor of Old Testament and Semitic Languages at Ashland Theological Seminary. He is author and editor of many books and articles and has lectured in Argentina, Canada, England, the Netherlands, South Africa, and the United States.

David A. deSilva is Trustees' Distinguished Professor of New Testament and Greek at Ashland Theological Seminary. He is the author of numerous books, including *An Introduction to the New Testament* (InterVarsity Press) and *Introducing the Apocrypha* (Baker Academic).

David M. Howard, Jr., is Professor of Old Testament at Bethel Seminary at Bethel University in St. Paul, Minnesota. He is author and editor of eight books and numerous scholarly articles on Old Testament topics.

Craig Wansink is Professor of Religious Studies and Associate Dean of Virginia Wesleyan College. He has studied in Japan, Jordan, Germany, and Israel, and he serves as Pastor of Squires Memorial Presbyterian Church.

Additional consultation by **Gary M. Burge**, Ph.D., Wheaton College and Graduate School

Facts verified by **Timothy N. Senapatiratne**, Ph.D., **Robin Shreeves, Anita K. Palmer**

Daily Dose of Knowledge is a trademark of Publications International, Ltd.

Louis Weber, CEO
Publications International, Ltd.
7373 North Cicero Avenue
Lincolnwood, Illinois 60712

ISBN-13: 978-1-4127-1541-6
ISBN-10: 1-4127-1541-5

Manufactured in China.

8 7 6 5 4 3 2 1

Library of Congress Control Number: 2008923019

Tuesday ■ Old Testament People

Wednesday ■ New Testament Events

Thursday ■ New Testament People

Mary **13** • Joseph, the Carpenter **20** • Elizabeth **27** • Zechariah, the Priest **34** • John the Baptist **41** • Caesar Augustus **48** • Herod the Great **55** • Simeon, the Messenger **62** • Anna, the Prophet **69** • Peter **76** • John, the Beloved **83** • James, the Son of Zebedee **90** • Andrew **97** • Matthew **104** • Philip, the Apostle **111** • Nathanael Bartholomew **118** • Thomas **125** • Simon, the Zealot **132** • Judas Iscariot **139** • Herod Antipas **146** • Nicodemus **153** • Zacchaeus **160** • Jairus **167** • Mary Magdalene **174** • Lazarus **181** • Martha of Bethany **188** • Mary of Bethany **195** • Caiaphas **202** • Annas **209** • Pontius Pilate **216** • Barabbas **223** • Simon of Cyrene **230** • Joseph of Arimathea **237** • Matthias **244** • Stephen **251** • Philip the Evangelist **258** • James, Brother of Jesus **265** • Barnabas **272** • John Mark **279** • Cornelius **286** • The Apostle Paul **293** • Ananias of Damascus **300** • Gamaliel **307** • Silas **314** • Luke the Physician **321** • Timothy **328** • Titus **335** • Priscilla and Aquila **342** • Apollos **349** • Lydia **356** • Philemon the Slave Owner **363** • Onesimus **370**

Friday ■ Bible Books

The Book of Genesis **14** • The Book of Exodus **21** • The Book of Leviticus **28** • The Book of Numbers **35** • The Book of Deuteronomy **42** • The Book of Joshua **49** • The Book of Judges **56** • The Book of Ruth **63** • The Books of 1 and 2 Samuel **70** • The Books of 1 and 2 Kings **77** • The Books of 1 and 2 Chronicles **84** • The Book of Ezra **91** • The Book of Nehemiah **98** • The Book of Esther **105** • The Book of Job **112** • The Book of Psalms **119** • The Book of Proverbs **126** • The Book of Ecclesiastes **133** • Song of Solomon **140** • The Book of Isaiah **147** • The Books of Jeremiah and Lamentations **154** • The Book of Ezekiel **161** • The Book of Daniel **168** • The Book of Hosea **175** • The Books of Joel and Amos **182** • The Books of Obadiah and Micah **189** • The Book of Jonah **196** • The Books of Nahum and Habakkuk **203** • The Books of Zephaniah and Haggai **210** • The Books of Zechariah and Malachi **217** • The Gospel of Matthew **224** • The Gospel of Mark **231** • The Gospel of Luke **238** • The Gospel of John **245** • Acts of the Apostles **252** • The Epistle to the Romans **259** • The First Epistle to the Corinthians **266** • The Second Epistle to the Corinthians **273** • The Epistle to the Galatians **280** • The Epistle to the Ephesians **287** • The Epistle to the Philippians **294** • The Epistle to the Colossians **301** • The Epistles to the Thessalonians **308** • The Epistles to Timothy (First) and Titus **315** • The Second Epistle to Timothy **322** • The Epistle to Philemon **329** • The Epistle to the Hebrews **336** • The Epistle of James **343** • The First Epistle of Peter **350** • The Epistles of John **357** • The Epistles of Jude and Peter (Second) **364** • The Book of Revelation **371**

Saturday ■ Miscellaneous

Know the Bible

WHEN YOU READ a mystery novel these days, you need to follow multiple story lines. It seems there are always three or four sets of characters involved in different activities. You might say the same thing about the Bible. Cover to cover, a multitude of events are occurring. After all, the Bible was written over a period of more than a thousand years by dozens of authors, using various styles of writing and multiple themes.

Thus you can follow the Old Testament saga of God's tumultuous relationship with the Israelites. Or you can trace the New Testament account of the development of the early Church. You can go step-by-step through Jesus' life and ministry or zoom in on the characters around him. Maybe you'd like to get to know the heroes of Old Testament history, such as Abraham, Moses, Ruth, David, and Esther. It's all in the pages of the Bible.

This daily reader lets you follow seven story lines at once. Every Sunday you'll read about events in the life of Jesus. Monday's entries cover significant events in the Old Testament. The focus of Tuesday is on Old Testament people. The next two days of the week swing over to the New Testament for events (Wednesdays) and people (Thursdays). The readings for Fridays cover the individual books of the Bible—their dates, authorship, situation, and purpose. Saturday write-ups are a grab bag of miscellaneous issues, mostly background articles on biblical culture. Over the course of a year, you'll have a well-rounded knowledge of this sacred text.

It's hard to overstate the significance of the Bible in history, literature, and current culture. Even those who have never cracked open this holy tome have heard of some of its phrases and characters. Have you referred to someone positively as "the salt of the earth," or negatively as a "Judas"? Have you been in a "David and Goliath" situation, or did you have to "turn the other cheek"? Were you ever tempted by a "forbidden fruit," or did you stay on the "straight and narrow"? All of these terms come from the Bible. Throughout the Western world, national constitutions have been based on biblical ideas, reform movements have been inspired by the Bible, and great works of literature have used the Bible as a symbolic treasure trove. Even if you've never been interested in the doctrines of Christianity or Judaism, it's helpful to have an acquaintance with their Scriptures.

Maybe you have always wanted to know more about the Bible but weren't sure how to go about it. Reference books seem heavy, and courses seem daunting. This book might be the answer for you. At least it will get you started, giving you basic facts as a framework on which to hang your growing knowledge. Here you have bite-size portions of Bible events, people, and background. In about five minutes a day, you'll get a working familiarity with the biblical landscape.

Daily Dose of Knowledge™: *Bible* has a devotional format, but it's not really a devotional book. Of course, many people have a daily time of devotional reading in which they seek spiritual sustenance for the day, and such discipline is laudable. But there the emphasis is on the heart rather than the head, on spiritual nourishment but not necessarily intellectual advancement. That's what sets this book apart: It's for your mind. So if you want to learn more about the Bible, you've come to the right place. Perhaps the characters you learn about will inspire you, and perhaps you'll develop spiritually as you encounter the amazing teachings of Scripture, but that's not our main aim. Pure and simple, we just want to help you know more about God's Word.

All scripture is inspired by God and is useful
for teaching, for reproof, for correction,
and for training in righteousness.

2 TIMOTHY 3:16

Christ, "the Anointed One"

DURING THE CHRISTMAS SEASON, "Merry X-mas" is a greeting frequently seen on gifts, cards, and signs. Some critics of this expression see it as heretical (they say people are taking the Christ out of Christmas). The *X* in X-mas, however, does not refer to the English letter *X*. Rather, here it refers to the Greek letter *chi*, which looks identical to the English letter *X* but is the first letter in the Greek word that we translate as "Christ." The word "Christ"

was so important to Christians that for centuries they abbreviated that word by using only the first letter of "Christ." The letter coincidentally also resembled a style of cross frequently used in Roman crucifixions.

The word "Christ" is the Greek translation of the Hebrew word "messiah." Both words mean "anointed." Kings were anointed with oil. Their anointing meant that they were called or commissioned to a particular charge. Still today the term "christening" frequently refers not to baptism but to an anointing with oil (generally on the forehead). Compared to the word "anointed," the words "messiah" and "Christ" have come to be filled with deeper, richer, and more subtle connotations. The Jews waited for a messiah—a fulfillment of prophecy. This messiah would lead them to liberation.

Jesus may have been known initially as "Jesus, son of Mary" and as "Jesus of Galilee." But his followers soon recognized something in his character and deeds that seemed to point beyond both his family and his home. When Matthew and others came to refer to Jesus as "Jesus the Christ," they were making a faith statement. They were confessing that Jesus was *the* Messiah—that he was anointed by God for a special purpose that extended beyond himself. Perhaps they would have gone so far as to acknowledge that Jesus himself put the *X* in X-mas.

POSTSCRIPT

■ The Dead Sea Scrolls offer an unusual perspective, because they speak of at least two messiahs. One messiah is a kingly figure like David who will lead in war. The other messiah is a priestly figure like Aaron who will restore the temple.

Creation of the World

THE BIBLE BEGINS with this majestically simple statement: "In the beginning God created the heavens and the earth" (Genesis 1:1 RSV). This one declaration affirms that God created all that is and all that can be known and that he is the hero and main character of this unique and wondrous book—the Bible.

The account of Creation in the first chapter of Genesis is highly regular, unfolding over six days. Moreover, it tells of a single, all-powerful God effortlessly calling his creation into being: "God said, 'Let there be...' And it was so" (verses 3, 6, 14, 30).

In the first three days, God organized, separated, and prepared the different parts of his creation to receive the special elements that would "fill" this world. These special elements were the sun, moon, stars, and creatures.

The crowning glory of all of creation was human beings. They were created male and female, both equally created in God's image. When everything was completed, the Lord declared his satisfaction with his work, pronouncing it "very good." After this, he rested on the seventh day.

The Bible's account of Creation is in marked contrast to the creation stories of the cultures that surrounded the ancient Israelites. In fact, the Bible's account appears to have been written in part as a refutation of pagan accounts. For instance, the statement that "God created the heavens and the earth" finds its opposite in the Book of Jeremiah: "The gods who did not make the heavens and the earth shall perish from the earth and from under the heavens" (Jeremiah 10:11). Or, the Mosaic statement that God "made the stars also" (Genesis 1:16 RSV) is likely a put-down of those religions (for example, in Babylon) in which the stars were powerful deities. God created even the stars; they were not his rivals. Additionally, God's effortless creation by spoken word contrasts dramatically with most ancient Near Eastern creation accounts, where creation involved titanic conflicts among the gods.

The Bible continually reiterates the message of the first chapter of Genesis, that the one, true God is responsible for all things. He is creator and sustainer of all. He alone is worthy of being worshipped—not any aspect of his creation nor the many gods and goddesses of the ancient Near East.

Adam

HUMANS—BOTH MALE AND FEMALE—were the capstone of God's creation and were created in his image. We can immediately gather from this that both men and women equally mirror God's image. One is not more godly than the other. Moreover, this indicates that humans are to live in harmonious relationship and not separated from each other.

The first human was Adam, whose name means "man" (or "red earth"), a fitting name for the first member of the human race. Adam's world was virtually limitless. God gave Adam and his wife, Eve, all things to enjoy. They were to exercise dominion over all creatures, and they were to be fruitful, multiply, fill the earth, and subdue it. Part of Adam's responsibility was to till the Garden of Eden and to keep it up. This shows the honorable nature of work; it was only after Adam sinned that work became onerous. Giving humans dominion over the rest of creation also implies proper stewardship of creation, clearly differentiating humans from animals. Humans are not, from a biblical perspective, simply the next step in the evolutionary chain.

Adam and Eve were placed in the Garden of Eden, where the Bible says, "The Lord God made to grow every tree that is pleasant to the sight and good for food" (Genesis 2:9). God's only restriction was that they were not to eat from one tree—the tree of the knowledge of good and evil. The rest was theirs for the taking.

Despite all these blessings and despite God telling Adam what not to do, why did Adam disobey? Although the serpent spoke directly to Eve, Adam himself came to the conclusion that God was a liar and did not have his best interest at heart. Rather than believing God, he trusted the words of the serpent, believing that eating the forbidden fruit would give him the power to be like God by knowing good and evil. Tragically, Adam did learn evil, but it did not make him like God. Instead, this knowledge made him ashamed of his nakedness, and not only was his relationship with God broken but his relationship with Eve was broken as well.

POSTSCRIPT

■ Adam's name is related to the Hebrew word for "ground" or "earth" *(adamah)*, since God formed him from the dust of the ground.

The Birth of Jesus

THE HEBREW PROPHETS had offered hints about the coming of a savior, a man specially anointed by God to heal and suffer and reign forever. But how would this messiah arrive, and when, and where? Daniel had presented an odd timetable made up of sevens (Daniel 9:25). Micah had identified Bethlehem (Micah 5:2) as the place of origin—fitting, since it was the home of the great King David. Isaiah had mentioned a young woman (and the Greek translation called her a virgin) who would give birth to the "God with us" child (see Isaiah 7:14).

Questions began to be answered one day in Nazareth, when an angel appeared to a teenage girl named Mary, announcing that she would be the mother of this miracle baby. At the time, she was engaged to Joseph, and it seems that they married shortly afterward.

Then there was a tax registration that required people to travel to their ancestral homes. Historically, this Roman proclamation is a mystery. No record exists of it outside of the Bible, though

Madonna and Child *by Titian*

we know the Romans had no problem ordering people around. In any case, such a decree sent Joseph and Mary to Bethlehem.

Outside the town, shepherds were working overtime—possibly fattening sheep for the upcoming Passover season—when they suddenly saw an angel announcing the birth of "a Savior, who is the Messiah" (Luke 2:11). Then an angel choir appeared singing, "Glory to God in the highest heaven" (verse 14). The shepherds rushed to the manger to see the child and returned to the fields "glorifying and praising God" (verse 20).

The Magi, who saw a star that heralded the birth of a Jewish king, arrived some time later in Jerusalem at the court of King Herod. After consulting with his own experts, Herod shared Micah's prophecy about Bethlehem, and the Magi moved on to that town, only five miles away. There they presented the child with expensive presents—royal gold, priestly frankincense, and myrrh, an embalming spice. A jealous Herod intended to kill the child, but Joseph was warned in a dream to escape. Joseph took Mary and Jesus to Egypt and returned to Nazareth after Herod's death.

Mary

MARY WAS THE MOTHER of Jesus and the wife of Joseph. A young woman from the village of Nazareth, she received a visit from the angel Gabriel, who announced that she had "found favor" with God (see Luke 1:28, 30). Though she was a virgin, Gabriel told her that she would bear a child fathered by God's Spirit. The child would be the promised Messiah. Her response to the startling announcement has been an example for Christians throughout the centuries: "Here am I, the servant of the Lord; let it be with me according to your word" (verse 38).

Head of the Virgin
by Leonardo da Vinci

Elizabeth, the mother of John the Baptist, was related to Mary, and these two women met to compare notes about the sons who were miraculously conceived in their wombs. Elizabeth was past the age of childbearing, yet she was also pregnant. Mary then erupted in a song of praise, which we know as the "Magnificat" (from the first word of her song in Latin).

Toward the end of her pregnancy, Mary traveled with Joseph to Bethlehem to register for a taxation census. There she gave birth to the Christ child, and there shepherds and Magi visited them. Mary, Joseph, and Jesus soon fled to Egypt to escape the murderous wrath of King Herod, but after his death they returned to their hometown of Nazareth, where Jesus grew up.

Mary was instrumental in Jesus' first miracle. At a wedding feast in the nearby village of Cana, Mary told her son, "They have no wine." Jesus at first rejected the implied request, saying to her, "Woman, what concern is that to you and to me? My hour has not yet come" (John 2:3–4). Nevertheless, he went on to turn water into wine. Thereafter, Mary appears only occasionally in the gospel accounts of Jesus' ministry.

Notably, she was at the cross when Jesus died. Some of Jesus' famous last words were "Here is your mother" (John 19:27), giving the Apostle John the responsibility to care for Mary. After Jesus ascended to heaven, Mary met with the disciples in Jerusalem, waiting for the arrival of the Holy Spirit. Presumably she was involved in the explosion of spiritual gifts at Pentecost (Acts 2), but the New Testament has no further record of her.

The Book of Genesis

GENESIS IS TRADITIONALLY attributed to Moses, who lived in the second millennium B.C. It describes events that occurred much earlier in history and also contains material added later by those who came after Moses. For earlier events, the author used sources such as the "list" mentioned in 5:1. Editing by later scribes accounts for mention of Israelite kings (Genesis 36:31) and later names of geographical locations (chapter 14). Nevertheless, God—the first character encountered in the book—controlled the entire writing process.

Genesis is in the form of prose narrative with pieces of embedded poetry (4:23–24; 48:15–16; 49). Genealogical lists of descendants provide a bridge between important characters in the story, such as Adam and Noah, and also provide a send-off for figures who temporarily play a key role in the story (such as Esau), but then leave the stage for those who carry forward the story line of the ancient Hebrews. The literary form indicates an interest in ordering and relationships—for example, the highly structured Creation account in the first chapter of the book—while also being interested in gripping stories, full of both heroes (Noah, for example) and villains galore. The use of poetry, as well as other literary devices, shows that care is needed in distinguishing between literal and figurative language.

Genesis moves from the creation of the good world by God to its injury through poor choices by humans and God's response to their actions. Subsequently God chooses one family, that of Abra(ha)m, through whom to demonstrate his expectations and blessings as a model for the relationship that is available to all humans (12:1–3). This sets the stage for the rest of Scripture, and of all history, by establishing what it is to be human and how to live in a responsible relationship with God, one's fellow humans, and the rest of the created world.

POSTSCRIPT

■ Among all Bible books, Genesis covers the broadest span of time (from Creation to the second millennium B.C.) and space (from Iraq to Egypt and beyond).

■ Israel's neighbors usually understood their gods as having only local control. Israel's God shows that he can work in Mesopotamia, Israel, Egypt, and the entire world.

■ Among Israel's neighbors, humans were often considered to be like slaves or even cattle, existing only to serve the gods. Israel's God elevates humanity to be like him, even as far as having responsibility for creation itself. Humans are not worthless but are valuable to God and the rest of creation.

Yahweh

AT THE BURNING BUSH, Moses experienced a divine encounter. God was sending him back to Egypt to deliver his people. But how would they know *God* was sending him? "I am who I am," God responded. Moses could tell the Israelites that "I Am" had sent him (Exodus 3:14).

Moses' initial experiences in Egypt didn't go well, and Moses complained to God. The Lord responded, "I am the Lord [*Yahweh*]. I appeared to Abraham, Isaac, and Jacob as God Almighty [*El Shaddai*], but by my name, 'The Lord' [*Yahweh*], I did not make myself known to them" (Exodus 6:2–3).

Scholars have debated at length about the full meaning of these verses. It's not that the name *Yahweh* was never used earlier with the patriarchs—it was—but the Lord seemed to be revealing a new and personal side of himself to Moses.

Elohim was the generic word for God, often shortened to *El*. Other Semitic nations used similar terms for their gods. The Hebrew Scriptures often use *Elohim*, sometimes in conjunction with other terms—including *Shaddai* (Almighty), *Elyon* (Most High), or '*Olam* (Eternal)—to define characteristics of this God.

But *Yahweh* is a personal name, unknown in other nations and not used for humans. It may be related to the Hebrew verb of being, which would explain why God could call himself "I Am" (the Hebrew word is *ehyeh*). We can understand how Yahweh might distinguish himself from the gods of other nations by saying, "I'm the one who really exists!"

Israelites treated this name of God with extreme reverence. The law says, "One who blasphemes the name of the Lord shall be put to death" (Leviticus 24:16). To avoid any hint of misuse, devout Jews would not utter this name aloud. Scribes would wash their hands before and after writing the tetragrammaton—the four letters of the divine name (YHWH). When the name occurred in Scripture readings, readers would replace it with *Adonai*, a generic term for "master."

This caused a linguistic oddity in early English Bibles. Hebrew has long been written with only consonants, but medieval scribes devised a marking system to indicate the vowel sounds, aiding with pronunciation. To ensure that people would not read *Yahweh* aloud, however, they used the vowel marks for *Adonai* with the consonants of *Yahweh*. Trying to read this concoction, translators created the name "Jehovah" (in transliteration, Y=J and W=V).

The "Word" Is Jesus

T HE GOSPEL OF MATTHEW starts with the genealogy of Jesus before describing the circumstances of his birth. The Gospel of Mark begins with Jesus as an adult and with John baptizing him in the Jordan River. The Gospel of Luke leads with a prophecy to Zechariah, the father of John the Baptist, and then goes on to speak of Jesus' birth. These three gospels are known as the Synoptic Gospels, because they present a common view of Jesus.

The Gospel of John, however, goes back—far before Jesus' birth and his baptism—to the creation of the earth. "In the beginning was the Word, and the Word was with God, and the Word was God" (John 1:1). John's

poetic introduction serves to place his gospel, and the story of Jesus in particular, in a much broader context that reaches beyond Jesus' earthly years. The opening words of John's gospel transport readers back to the opening words of the Book of Genesis, which say, "In the beginning..." Jesus' influence is presented as not being limited to approximately 30 years in Palestine but as having a cosmic impact.

Even more so, the Gospel of John sees Jesus as active in the actual ordering of the world itself. Beyond the scope of the three Synoptic Gospels, John—like the Apostle Paul—presents Jesus as intimately involved with creation. "All things came into being through him," wrote John, "and without him not one came into being" (John 1:3). Paul's first letter to the Corinthians speaks of "one Lord, Jesus Christ, through whom are all things" (1 Corinthians 8:6). In addition, Paul wrote to the Colossians, saying of Jesus, "in him all things in heaven and on earth were created, things visible and invisible" (Colossians 1:16). Thus, by understanding Jesus' own life, people come to understand something about the way the world itself is ordered and why it has meaning.

It is not enough, however, that "in the beginning was the Word." The dramatic impact for John is not just that the Word existed in the beginning. For John, the moment of reckoning comes 13 verses later, with the recognition that "the Word became flesh" (John 1:14). Indeed, creation cannot be understood without Jesus. Furthermore, John declared that this world cannot be understood unless we imagine what it means that "the Word became flesh."

Establishing the Sabbath

AFTER GOD'S SIX DAYS of creative activity, the Bible says on the seventh day "God rested from all the work that he had done in creation" (Genesis 2:3). The noun form of the verb "to rest" is *shabbat,* which is the Hebrew name for the sabbath day.

Thus we see that the observance of the sabbath as a day of rest among Jews and Christians alike has its roots in creation itself. Indeed, in the Ten Commandments, the command about keeping the sabbath day makes this explicit: "For in six days the Lord made heaven and earth, the sea, and all that is in them, but rested the seventh day; therefore the Lord blessed the sabbath day and consecrated it" (Exodus 20:11).

The sabbath day was to be unlike any other day in that all men and women were to stop their regular work. And beyond being a physical day of rest, it was to be a holy day actively "remembered" or "observed."

God did not rest because he had become tired from creating. The Bible says God "will neither slumber nor sleep" (Psalm 121:4). The idea of God resting is more that he ceased creating things. He found what he had created to be completely adequate ("very good"), and he thus finished his work.

Unlike the other six days of creation, where we read that "there was evening and there was morning" for each day (Genesis 1:5, 8, 13, 19, 23, 31), this day has no statement about its ending. This idea of God's rest extending beyond the "creation week" is further shown in both the Old and New Testaments when people enter into "God's rest"—that is, enjoy a proper relationship with God.

In the Old Testament and in Judaism, the sabbath day is the seventh day of the week, extending from sundown on the sixth day to sundown on the seventh. In Christianity, the idea of using the sabbath for remembrance led to the designation of the first day of the week as the day of rest, in remembrance of Jesus' resurrection on that day.

Jesus urged his followers not to cross over into blind legalism in trying to observe the sabbath. He said that "The sabbath was made for humankind, and not humankind for the sabbath" (Mark 2:27).

POSTSCRIPT

■ In Jewish tradition, a "sabbath day's journey" was the distance one could walk without violating the sabbath, about half of a mile.

Eve

EVE, LIKE ADAM, was created in God's image on the sixth day of creation, and, with Adam, was given dominion over the rest of creation. They both had equal value and equal standing as persons before God, and they shared equally in God's gift of dominion.

The first man and the first woman, however, were not created at exactly the same time. God created Adam first, and then he said, "It is not good that the man should be alone; I will make him a helper as his partner" (Genesis 2:18 RSV). God then brought all the animals to Adam, who gave them all names, but no "helper as his partner" was found (verse 20). This makes the important point that Adam and Eve were made to be in relationship with each other and that they would find no suitable companion in the animal world.

God then placed Adam into a deep sleep, took one of his ribs, and formed the woman from it. Delighted, Adam cried out, "This at last is bone of my bones and flesh of my flesh" (verse 23). He called her "woman" (Hebrew: *ishshah*), because she was taken out of "man" *(ish)*.

Eve's role as a "helper" for Adam meant that she was a source of strength for him. Incidentally, God himself is sometimes called a helper for those in distress. So Eve's role was not that of a servant or maid, but rather she complemented Adam perfectly. She—not any animal—was a unique "fit" for Adam. Neither was meant to live without the other. The ideal for humanity is stated thus: "Therefore a man leaves his father and his mother and clings to his wife, and they become one flesh" (verse 24).

Subsequently, the serpent entered the Garden of Eden and persuaded Eve to eat the fruit that God had forbidden. He convinced her that God had lied and that eating the fruit would make her and Adam like God. Eve did not act alone, however. The Bible says Eve took some of the forbidden fruit and gave it to her husband, "who was with her" (Genesis 3:6). Both were at fault. Indeed, the Apostle Paul stated that "sin came into the world through one man," through "the transgression of Adam" (Romans 5:12, 14). Thus Eve alone cannot be blamed for the fall of humankind.

POSTSCRIPT

■ Adam called his wife "Eve" (Hebrew: *chavvah*) "because she was the mother of all living" (Genesis 3:20).

The Wedding in Cana

WEDDING RECEPTIONS in first-century Judaea were extravagant affairs, lasting up to a week. It was up to the groom to supply the food and drink. But a problem arose at one wedding attended by Jesus, his mother, and at least some of the disciples he had just selected. Mary put it simply: "They have no wine" (John 2:3).

Let's freeze this moment and think about it. What's happening here? Of course, there's a long-standing tradition of mothers pointing things out to their sons: "The lawn needs mowing," or "We're out of milk and bread." It's their way of saying, "Please mow the lawn," or "Would you go to the store?" But what did Mary expect Jesus to do? It wasn't his responsibility. Running out of wine would be an embarrassment to the host, but it was hardly a life emergency. Did she know that he could work miracles? He hadn't performed any as far as we know. Did she think this was the time for him to start?

Jesus' answer is even odder: "Woman, what concern is that to you and to me? My hour has not yet come" (verse 4). It seems that he knew she was asking for a miracle, and he refused to do it. The time would come for such spectacles, but not yet.

Then the story takes another twist. Mary, sensing that Jesus might do *something,* told the servants to "do whatever he tells you" (verse 5). And Jesus must have rethought the situation. Maybe it wasn't the right time when he said it wasn't the right time, but the span of a few moments apparently made all the difference. He proceeded to work a miracle.

Jesus had the servants fill six large urns with water. When they ladled out some of this liquid, it was wine, and it tasted better than the wine served earlier.

What does this miracle tell us about Jesus? For one thing, it set Jesus apart from John the Baptist. John was already a popular prophet, whose parents had kept him away from "strong drink." But Jesus worked his first miracle at a *party,* celebrating a wedding. Later he was asked why John's disciples fasted and his own followers didn't. He used the image of a wedding to explain it. When the bridegroom arrives, you stop fasting and start feasting. Jesus was the groom, and at Cana, he had arrived.

Joseph, the Carpenter

HUSBAND OF MARY and stepfather of Jesus, Joseph played a crucial role in Jesus' earthly birth. Betrothed to Mary, he was shocked to learn she was pregnant. Since he knew he was not the father, he planned to break their betrothal, but he planned to do it privately so there would not be too much of a scandal. This plan was short-circuited when an angel came to him in a dream, assuring him that Mary was a virgin and that she was bearing the Son of God. Joseph was urged to go ahead with the marriage plans, and he did.

An imperial decree around this time sent people to their hometowns for registration, so Joseph took Mary from Nazareth to Bethlehem, the home of their ancestor King David. There she bore the Christ child. Another dream warned Joseph to flee to Egypt, escaping the slaughter of infants in Bethlehem. After Herod—who had ordered the slaughter—died a miserable death, Joseph moved his young family back to Nazareth, where he plied his trade as a carpenter.

The biblical term for carpenter really refers to an artisan who might work with various materials—stone and metal as well as wood. Such artisans might build houses, make tools, or repair household items. Since Jesus was called a carpenter, too, we can assume that Joseph taught him his own trade before Jesus launched his itinerant ministry around age 30.

Joseph was not involved in Jesus' public ministry, as far as we know. Apart from references to Jesus as "Joseph's son," there is no further mention of Joseph in the gospels during Jesus' adulthood. Most scholars assume he passed away before Jesus began preaching.

POSTSCRIPT

- Joseph learned of Mary's pregnancy at a unique point in the premarriage process observed among Jews at that time. They were "betrothed"—a commitment as binding as marriage—but betrothed couples did not yet live together as husband and wife. Nevertheless, it would take a divorce to dissolve a betrothal, and Joseph considered it.

- Outside of the Nativity story, the two other stories in which Joseph appears both occur at the temple: a purification ritual shortly after Jesus' birth and another visit when Jesus is 12 years old.

The Book of Exodus

MOSES, WHO LIVED in the second millennium B.C., is traditionally credited with writing not only Exodus but also the entire Pentateuch (the first five books of the Bible). As a key participant in many of the events recorded, he would have been in a good position to do so.

Exodus portrays the Israelites leaving slavery in Egypt and establishing themselves as a free people on a march through the Sinai wilderness. The book's historical narrative, its main literary genre, is interspersed with poetry (Exodus 15:1–21), laws (20 –23; 31:12–17; 34:11–26), and instructions on how to celebrate the feast of Passover and Unleavened Bread (12:1–27; 12:43—13:10) and build and stock the tabernacle (25:1—31:18).

The generation of Israelites who had migrated to Egypt to escape a devastating famine in Canaan prospered and were treated well in Egypt. But in later generations new rulers emerged in Egypt and perceived the growing number of Hebrews as a threat, so they enslaved and mistreated them. Moses, a Hebrew who was raised in the Egyptian royal court, ultimately led the Hebrews to freedom after God heard their cries of desperation. Pharaoh was persuaded to release his labor force only after ten plagues showed the superiority of the Israelites' God over those of their captors.

After releasing the Israelites, Pharaoh reconsidered, sending his army in pursuit—only to lose his soldiers in the Red Sea, where God miraculously opened a path for the Israelites but engulfed their pursuers. They celebrated this deliverance in song and then set out into the wilderness under God's protection and provision. After reaching Mount Sinai, the Israelites—through Moses—received and ratified a covenant with God, becoming a nation for the first time. They also received instruction on how to serve the Lord by obeying his laws (including the Ten Commandments; see 20:1–17) and worshipping him properly at a new worship site—the tabernacle.

The book closes with the tabernacle's completion and God descending to take up residence in it among his people. National infancy was not without problems, however. At the very time God established the covenant with Moses, the rest of the nation was turning to pagan gods and worshipping a golden calf; this threatened the nation's survival just as it was coming into being.

Nevertheless, the Book of Exodus shows God's commitment not only to the Israelites but to their descendants as well.

The Holy Spirit

WHEN THE EARTH was still a "formless void" at the beginning of Creation, the second verse of the Bible tells us that "the Spirit of God moved upon the face of the waters" (Genesis 1:2 KJV). The Hebrew word *ruach* ("Spirit of God") isn't necessarily a theological term here, but it could be. It might mean a wind or a breath, but it's also used for the spiritual life force of any being, including God. Often, however, it indicates the Lord's breath as it empowers particular people for special tasks, whether designing the tabernacle, fighting a foe, or speaking a prophetic word to Israel.

The identity and role of the Holy Spirit becomes clearer with the appearance of Jesus. "Here is my servant, whom I uphold, my chosen, in whom my soul delights," proclaimed God in one Old Testament prophecy. "I have put my spirit upon him; he will bring forth justice to the nations" (Isaiah 42:1). Those words were echoed in Jesus' baptism, as the Spirit of God descended upon him in the form of a dove, and a voice from heaven said, "This is my Son, the Beloved, with whom I am well pleased" (Matthew 3:17).

At the Last Supper, Jesus warned the disciples of his departure but said, "I will ask the Father, and he will give you another Advocate, to be with you forever. This is the Spirit of truth" (John 14:16–17). The word for advocate *(parakletos)* can be read as "counselor," "comforter," or "helper." It literally means "one who is called alongside to offer assistance." Jesus would no longer be walking beside them, but the Spirit would be present. This promise came to magnificent fruition on the day of Pentecost, when "tongues of fire" descended upon the disciples, an outward sign that they were filled with the Holy Spirit (see Acts 2:1–4).

The Pentecost *by Titian*

While such "speaking in tongues" has often dominated modern discussions of the work of the Spirit, the epistles of Paul define two additional important areas of activity—the gifts of the Spirit and the fruit of the Spirit. Each believer, he says, has at least one special ability granted by the Spirit for the good of the Church and the glory of God (see 1 Corinthians 12:7–11). And when a believer is guided by God's Spirit, the resulting "fruit" is love, joy, peace, patience, kindness, generosity, faithfulness, gentleness, and self-control (see Galatians 5:22–23).

From the Words of Isaiah

THE GOSPEL OF MARK begins abruptly: "The beginning of the good news of Jesus Christ, the Son of God. As it is written in the prophet Isaiah, 'See, I am sending my messenger ahead of you, who will prepare your way; the voice of one crying out in the wilderness: "Prepare the way of the Lord, make his paths straight."' John the baptizer appeared in the wilderness, proclaiming a baptism of repentance for the forgiveness of sins" (Mark 1:1–4).

From the very beginning of his gospel, Mark announces the fulfillment of Jewish eschatological hopes. The messenger is coming. The one who will announce the way of the Lord is here. Because John the Baptist is here, salvation is seen as imminent.

What will characterize that salvation is implied by the way Mark frames his opening quotation. The quotation itself is a combination of words from Exodus 23:20, Malachi 3:1, and Isaiah 40:3. Mark, however, introduces the quotation by attributing it only to Isaiah, thus drawing attention to the words of that prophet.

Isaiah's prophecies sometimes have been called "the fifth gospel," because they are so frequently cited and alluded to in the New Testament. In addition, within the New Testament, Isaiah is mentioned by name much more frequently than any other writing prophet, in part because he describes a suffering servant who offers himself for the sake of others. Many read these words in the light of the life and death of Jesus. "I gave my back to those who struck me," said Isaiah, placing words in the mouth of the coming Messiah, "and my cheeks to those who pulled out the beard; I did not hide my face from insult and spitting" (Isaiah 50:6). Elsewhere Isaiah said of the Messiah, "He was despised and rejected by others, a man of suffering, and acquainted with infirmity; and as one from whom others hide their faces he was despised, and we held him of no account. Surely he has borne our infirmities and carried our diseases, yet we accounted him stricken, struck down by God, and afflicted" (Isaiah 53:3–4).

When Mark began his gospel with words from Isaiah, even mentioning the prophet by name, he communicated how we should understand the one who fulfills Isaiah's prophecy. Jesus, as the Messiah, is not someone who first comes to rule. He is someone who first comes to suffer for the sake of others.

Creation of Adam

THE FIRST CHAPTER of Genesis states that God created humans as his final creative act on the sixth day, as the crowning glory of all creation. He created them in his own image and likeness, both male and female (see Genesis 1:27). And, in doing so, he gave them dominion over all of creation.

These facts suggest several things about what it means to be created in God's image. First, the male-female distinction shows that God intends humans to live in relationships. Second, all the best human attributes—whether typically "male" characteristics or "female"—have their roots in God's nature itself. Humans, both male and female, are God's image-bearers. Third, humans were placed above the animals from the very beginning and are to be wise stewards of both plant and animal life. This is what is meant by "dominion"; it denotes both authority over and wise stewardship of creation.

The second chapter of Genesis gives a more detailed account of the creation of humans. The first human's name was "Adam," from the Hebrew word *adam,* which means "humanity" in many instances. The parallel is obvious: The prototype for humanity *(adam)* was a man named *Adam.* God "formed" Adam from the dust of the ground and "breathed into his nostrils the breath of life" (Genesis 2:7). This suggests a face-to-face encounter—an intimacy between God and the first human being—that goes far beyond God's relationship with the rest of creation and that reinforces the concept of humanity as the capstone of all of creation. The language here is anthropomorphic; that is, it gives God human qualities. God is seen as an artisan sculpting the man and breathing into his nostrils.

The immediate catalyst for the creation of Adam was that there was no one to till the ground, and so God placed Adam "in the garden of Eden to till it and keep it" (verse 15). Far from being a punishment, from the very beginning work was an honored part of what it meant to be human. The entry of sin into the world resulted in a distortion of work's honorable nature, and the ground was cursed because of Adam's sin. He was sentenced to work "by the sweat of [his] face" (Genesis 3:19). Nevertheless, part of Adam's original purpose remained: He was still supposed to honorably till the ground and be a good steward over creation.

Cain

CAIN WAS THE OLDEST child of Adam and Eve. He is the ancestor of an impressive family line whose members achieved several cultural firsts. He is best known, however, for being the world's first murderer—he killed his brother Abel.

As to the cultural firsts, Cain himself built the world's first city and named it in honor of his firstborn son, Enoch. One of his descendants, Jabal, was the forefather of "those who live in tents and have livestock" (Genesis 4:20). From Jabal's brother Jubal came musicians ("those who play the lyre and pipe," verse 21). Their brother Tubal-cain was the first metalworker.

But the most notorious first was Cain's murder of his brother, Abel. Cain was a farmer and Abel a shepherd. Each brought an offering to God. Cain's offering, however, was nothing special. The Bible says it was "an offering of the fruit of the ground" (verse 3)—that is, an offering of whatever fruit was at hand. By contrast, Abel brought an offering "of the firstlings of his flock, their fat portions" (verse 4)—that is, a special offering of the best that he had. (The equivalent offering for Cain would have been the "first fruits" of his crops.)

As a result of Cain's perfunctory offering, God honored Abel's gift over Cain's, which threw Cain into a rage. He lured his brother into a field and killed him. God then pronounced a curse on Cain, sentencing him to wander on the earth as a fugitive. In an especially ironic twist, God said to this farmer, "the ground . . . will no longer yield to you its strength" (verse 12).

Cain cried out that this punishment was more than he could bear and that he feared being killed as he wandered the earth, and so God placed a mark of protection on Cain so that no one he encountered would kill him. Cain then migrated to the land of Nod, east of the Garden of Eden, and settled there.

POSTSCRIPT

■ The "mark of Cain" is often thought, mistakenly, to be part of Cain's punishment—that is, a sign of his banishment from Eden. The Bible, however, makes it clear that it was a sign of God's grace: It protected Cain, the first murderer, from being murdered himself. While many have wondered exactly what the "mark" was, the Bible is silent on this point.

Jesus Heals

O NE DAY JESUS WAS TEACHING and healing in a crowded house in
Capernaum. Houses were generally small in that culture. Maybe
20 or 30 people could cram inside, but apparently Jesus had many more
than that seeking his attention. Suddenly he heard noise from above his
head. Maybe a few clods of plaster or bits of branches came down on his
shoulders. Some enterprising people were
digging through the roof.

Four people were doing the damage. They
had carried their paralyzed friend to the
house on a mat, hoping to see Jesus. When
they couldn't get through the door, they went
to the roof. Most homes had flat roofs made
with branches and mud, and the friends
showed their dedication by clawing through
the roof to get to Jesus. When they created
an opening big enough, they lowered their
friend's bed using ropes.

Jesus looked at the paralyzed man and said,
"Son, your sins are forgiven" (Mark 2:5).

The Palsied Man Let
Down Through the
Roof *by James Tissot*

At first blush, you might think Jesus was
missing the point. The man on the bed had
a physical crisis, not a spiritual one. His friends had carted him there not
for counseling but for healing. Forgiveness was not the issue.

The religious leaders in the front row had a different problem. They
apparently had Jesus on probation, so they were taking up prime space to
watch him. "Only God can forgive sins," they murmured. "Who does this
Jesus think he is?" (see verse 7).

But Jesus had a lesson to teach. "Which is easier," he asked, "to say to the
paralytic, 'Your sins are forgiven,' or to say, 'Stand up . . . and walk'? But so
you may know that the Son of Man has authority on earth to forgive sins"
(verses 9–10). He then interrupted himself to turn and tell the man to get
up and walk. The man walked.

Anybody can say they have spiritual power, but Jesus showed his spiritual
power with an observable miracle. As a Pharisee told him later, "No one
can do these signs that you do apart from the presence of God" (John
3:2). And that's precisely the word used most often for Jesus' miracles.
They were *signs* verifying his divine identity.

Elizabeth

ELIZABETH WAS THE MOTHER of John the Baptist and wife of the priest Zechariah. She was also related to Mary, the mother of Jesus. As told by Luke, the Christmas story really starts with her pregnancy.

She was a descendant of Aaron, Israel's first high priest, and she was married to a priest who served in the temple at Jerusalem. She and her husband are described as "righteous . . . living blamelessly," but they had no children and "both were getting on in years" (Luke 1:5–7).

Then an angel appeared to Zechariah announcing that they would have a child, one who was destined to "turn many of the people of Israel to the Lord" (verse 16). Elizabeth went into seclusion for five months after becoming pregnant, and she later received a visit from her relative Mary, who was expecting a miracle birth of her own. Elizabeth responded with a heartfelt blessing that has inspired Christians ever since: "Blessed are you among women, and blessed is the fruit of your womb" (verse 42). She said that the child within her "leaped for joy" (verse 44) when Mary arrived.

Elizabeth's son was named John, and some 30 years later he became famous as a desert preacher who called people to be baptized as a sign of repentance. We know her son as John the Baptist. The angel had previously told Zechariah that this man would "make ready a people prepared for the Lord" (verse 17), and all four gospels confirm that he did exactly that. By changing the spiritual climate, by challenging the authorities, by gathering disciples, and by baptizing him personally, John the Baptist paved the way for the ministry of his cousin Jesus.

It would not be surprising to learn that John gained some of his boldness from his mother. After all, it was Elizabeth who declared his name against the objection of her neighbors and relatives (see verses 57–61).

POSTSCRIPT

■ Elizabeth was the first to hear Mary's amazing song of praise, which we know as the "Magnificat" (Luke 1:46–55).

■ We're not told exactly how old Elizabeth and Zechariah were, but the fact that they were "getting on in years" would remind many readers of Abraham and Sarah, who conceived Isaac in their old age. Isaac was a child of promise, the beginning of a new connection between God and his people. Meanwhile, John was also a child of promise, fulfilling the role of Elijah, the prophet.

The Book of Leviticus

WRITTEN BY MOSES in the second millennium B.C., Leviticus is set during Israel's stay at Mount Sinai. It consists mainly of instructions on how God's people were to worship him and preserve their religious purity by serving him through sacrifices and other ritual observances. Interspersed are narrative vignettes showing people following (Leviticus 8—9) or contravening these instructions (10). Having been raised as slaves among the pagan Egyptians, Israel needed instructions on how to truly worship God. Thus Leviticus can be seen as a manual of religious practice.

A key theme of the book is holiness—a characteristic of God that is demanded also of those who follow him (11:44, 45; 19:2; 20:7, 26). Sacrifices to maintain and reestablish holiness are outlined (1—7), demanding obedience from every level of society, from rulers to peasants, but also making this ritual accessible to all, from rich to poor. No one is either above or below the expectation to worship correctly. This is shown by the severe punishment befalling even the sons of Aaron, Israel's chief religious leader, when they violate God's instructions (10).

No part of life was exempt from holiness, so these religious instructions often include even secular areas of life. This includes discussions of food (11; 17:10–16), childbirth (12), skin diseases and growths (13—14), normal and abnormal sexual discharges (15), animal slaughtering (17:1–9), and forbidden sexual relationships (18). Even domestic economic policies such as the ownership of land or slaves are matters of interest (25—26). Religious areas of life are also explicitly discussed: Topics include priests (21), acceptable use of offerings (22; 27), and national festivals (23).

Israel did not place an artificial distinction between "Saturday" behavior and that of every other day of the week. God is God of everyone and at all times.

POSTSCRIPT

■ Leviticus 1—7 is a "Ritual Handbook for People and Priests," giving detailed instructions that are assumed in other places in Scripture, where offerings are called for but not explained.

■ The Day of Atonement, occupying a central position in the book (16), is also central to the Jewish calendar, since its solemn observance provided forgiveness from sin and allowed God and Israel to continue in their covenant relationship of worship and blessing.

The Ark of the Covenant

THE ARK OF THE COVENANT was a holy box that contained sacred artifacts of Israel's early history. Its cover was a kind of altar, where blood was sprinkled to atone for Israel's sin. And it was a powerful, mysterious symbol of the presence of the living God.

When the Lord gave Moses details for the building of the tabernacle—the massive tent where Israelites worshipped God—he included specifications for the ark of the covenant. Made of acacia wood and overlaid with gold, it measured 3¾ feet long, 2¼ feet wide, and 2¼ feet high. The lid bore two images of cherubim made of hammered gold. The ark rested inside the Holy of Holies, the innermost part of the inner sanctum of the

tabernacle, where only the high priest could enter, and he could enter only once a year on the Day of Atonement.

Inside the ark were placed two stone tablets of the law God had given to Moses on Mount Sinai, a container of manna (the bread God had rained down on the Hebrews during their wanderings in the wilderness), and Aaron's blooming rod (the staff God had miraculously brought to life to confirm Aaron's authority as high priest). Thus it was a mini-museum, commemorating the ways God provided food, leadership, and guidance to his people.

When the Israelites finally entered the promised land of Canaan, the ark of the covenant went first, parting the Jordan River. The ark also led the way as the people marched around Jericho, symbolizing God's leadership. But later the ark became more of a good luck charm. Carried into battle in one desperate attempt to turn the tide, it was captured by the Philistines—much to their misfortune. The idol of their god fell down before the ark, and their people were plagued. Finally, the Philistines returned the ark to the Israelites with gifts of gold.

Eventually, David moved the ark to Jerusalem in a great procession in which he danced joyously. When Solomon built the temple, the ark was placed in the Holy of Holies. But in 587 or 586 B.C., the Babylonians destroyed Jerusalem and the temple, carting off its treasures. It is thought that the ark was destroyed at that time, but legends abound regarding what happened to it.

The Genealogy of Jesus

TODAY WE MAY BE interested in genealogies because they can link us to past royalty, inventors, or explorers. Genealogies can help us make sense of our own lives in light of those who have preceded us. Genealogies can also let us know of potential health concerns that we ourselves may face.

The genealogy of Jesus was important to both Matthew and Luke. Each includes a genealogy in their respective gospel. Because Luke's gospel focuses on the significance and importance of Gentiles, it is not surprising that he traces Jesus' lineage beyond Judaism. The lineage goes back to Adam, and then even back to God.

Conversely, Matthew's gospel presents Jesus in Jewish terms, seeing him as the fulfillment of Old Testament prophecy. He is presented as the new Moses and—like Moses—is shown preaching on mountains while presenting a new law. It is not surprising, then, that the genealogy in Matthew also presents Jesus in Jewish terms. His lineage is traced not all the way back to Adam, but rather to the father of the Jews: Abraham.

Because biblical genealogies are patrilineal, the genealogy in Matthew's gospel would have raised eyebrows. In the opening verses four women stand out: Tamar, Rahab, Ruth, and "the wife of Uriah" (that is, Bathsheba). In many respects they are not key matriarchs within Judaism. Rather, Tamar is described in Genesis 39 as having dressed up like a prostitute. Rahab, herself, was a prostitute. At the threshing floor, Ruth engaged in behavior that could have been perceived as sexually inappropriate. And Bathsheba was known mainly as the woman in King David's sexual scandal.

Why are these women in this genealogy? Perhaps because there is also a fifth woman who appears later in the genealogy: Mary, the mother of Jesus. All of these women found themselves in questionable positions in society. Thus Matthew's genealogy argues not only that Jesus is the fulfillment of prophecy but also that God—and God's grace—works in ways that sometimes move beyond our limited views.

POSTSCRIPT

■ Although the genealogies in both Matthew and Luke trace Jesus' lineage through King David, they depart with David's offspring. From a Jewish perspective, Matthew lists King Solomon proceeding on to Joseph, thus showing that Jesus is the legal heir to David's throne. Luke goes in reverse order. He uses Mary's lineage going through David's son Nathan.

His Crowning Glory

GOD CREATED HUMANS on the sixth day as the culmination of all that he had brought into being. They were created in his image and likeness, and he gave them "dominion over the fish of the sea and over the birds of the air and over every living thing that moves upon the earth" (Genesis 1:28). Furthermore, God said to them, "Be fruitful and multiply, and fill the earth and subdue it" (verse 28). And later we learn that Adam was placed in the Garden of Eden to till the ground and to keep it.

The principal imagery associated with dominion is of royalty. God, the creator and ruler over all things, appointed humans to "have dominion" over all of his creation; that is, they are to "rule over" (NIV) creation in God's place with authority—as his vice-regents, so to speak. From this follows the critically important point that humans are not simply the next step on a never-ending creation ladder; nor are they simply a part of creation with no special status. To the contrary, humans are the crowning glory of creation: Only into the nostrils of Adam did God breathe "the breath of life" (Genesis 2:7). God deliberately placed all things under humanity's care as his royal representatives. This point is reinforced in the eighth psalm:

> "You have made them a little lower than God,
>   and crowned them with glory and honor.
> You have given them dominion over the works of your hands;
>   you have put all things under their feet" (Psalm 8:5–6).

In the Bible, benevolent kings were to rule over, protect, and care for their subjects, and so it is with humanity and creation. In other words, God intended for humans to care for creation, exercising responsible stewardship over all that he has given us. Nothing is exempt from our care: The Bible mentions animals of all kinds, as well as the ground that Adam was to till.

POSTSCRIPT

▪ The ancient Egyptian text called "The Instruction for King Meri-ka-re," dating to the end of the 22nd century B.C., uses similar language about the king's god: "He made the breath of life [for] their nostrils. They who have issued from his body are his images."

Noah

IN THE GENERATIONS AFTER ADAM AND EVE, human defiance of God increased until it reached the point where God was sorry he had ever made humans. He vowed to "blot out" all that he had made on the earth, both humans and animals.

Yet during this terrible time, one man was the exception: Noah. The Bible says Noah "found favor in the sight of the Lord," for he was "a righteous man, blameless in his generation," and he "walked with God" (Genesis 6:8, 9). For these reasons, God decided to spare Noah and his family, including his wife, three sons, and their wives.

The familiar story of Noah and the Flood then unfolded: God directed Noah to build an ark and take two of every kind of animal into the ark, including seven pairs of the clean animals so that some could be used as sacrifices. The flood waters rose, covering all the earth, and then, the Bible says, "God remembered Noah" (Genesis 8:1). The waters began to recede until the earth was dry once again.

Noah and his family offered sacrifices to the Lord, who told Noah and his sons, "Be fruitful and multiply, and fill the earth" (Genesis 9:1) in an echo of the words he had spoken to Adam and Eve. In essence, this was a "new creation," and Noah and his descendants were to exercise dominion over all of creation, just as Adam and Eve had. Because the global devastation grieved the Lord, God vowed never again to destroy his creation in this way, setting a rainbow in the sky as a sign of his promise.

Noah was a godly man through whom God saved the human race. Unfortunately, the last we read of Noah, a slightly different picture emerges: He became a man of the soil and the first to plant a vineyard, and on one occasion he became drunk, lying naked in his tent in a drunken stupor. His son, Ham, saw his father and rather than covering him, he told his brothers about their father's state, apparently deriving a perverse pleasure in seeing their father this way. His two brothers covered their father's nakedness without looking at him. When Noah discovered what Ham had done, he cursed Ham's son, Canaan, for Ham's impropriety. The Bible does not explain why Noah cursed Canaan, but his descendants would become the enemies of Israel, God's people.

John the Baptist Beheaded

W E KNOW ONLY FRAGMENTS of the relationship between Jesus and John the Baptist. We know that their mothers were cousins. Does that mean the boys grew up playing together? Well, probably not. John's father was a priest serving in Jerusalem, while Jesus grew up in Nazareth, a four-day walk away.

The gospels give us only a few direct interactions between the two men, but they seemed to be quite aware of each other. We find John the Baptist pointing out Jesus as the Messiah to some of his own followers, who then became Jesus' disciples (see John 1:29–40). There is a brief conversation between them at Jesus' baptism, when John questions whether this sign of repentance is appropriate for the Messiah (see Matthew 3:14–15). Both of these holy heroes were wildly popular among the common folk, and both earned the enmity of the elite. Yet John fully understood and freely explained that he was just a forerunner, while Jesus was the main event: "He must increase, but I must decrease" (John 3:30).

John's public exposure declined when he was arrested for speaking out against King Herod Antipas for stealing his brother's wife. In prison, he apparently had some second thoughts about Jesus, and he sent a message asking Jesus point-blank if he was the promised Messiah. Jesus coyly avoided a direct response but sent the messengers back with a report of healings and good news preached to the poor (Matthew 11:2–6). He was doing exactly what the prophet Isaiah said the Messiah would do.

Herod respected John's popularity and perhaps his holiness, so he didn't execute him immediately. But his stepdaughter, Salome, danced at a birthday party, and Herod was so smitten that he promised her anything. Coached by her mother, she asked for the head of John the Baptist on a tray. So John was beheaded.

At one point Jesus declared of John, "A prophet? Yes... and more than a prophet." He then remarked, "Truly I tell you, among those born of women no one has arisen greater than John the Baptist" (Matthew 11:9, 11).

POSTSCRIPT

■ Immediately after the account of John's death, the gospels describe the feeding of the 5,000, suggesting a sudden groundswell in Jesus' popularity. Immediately after feeding the crowd, Jesus goes off by himself to pray—no doubt weary from the crowds but probably also mourning his cousin's death (see Mark 6:14–46).

Zechariah, the Priest

ZECHARIAH WAS THE FATHER of John the Baptist. As a priest, he served in the temple at Jerusalem with his family on a regular rotation. One day, having been chosen by lot to offer incense in the Holy Place, an angel of the Lord appeared to him with a surprising birth announcement. This set in motion a chain of events that culminated in the birth of Jesus.

The angel, who identified himself as Gabriel, explained to Zechariah that his wife, Elizabeth, would bear a son. This message stunned Zechariah because his wife and he were both "getting on in years," seemingly past the age of childbearing. But even more shocking was Gabriel's prophecy about their child. "Great in the sight of the Lord" (Luke 1:15), his son would turn many people back to God, preparing their hearts for the Lord. Gabriel told Zechariah to name the baby John.

Zechariah found this all hard to believe. He expressed some doubt to the angel and asked for proof, but the proof came in an inconvenient way. As punishment for his disbelief, Zechariah was struck dumb. Until the naming of the child, he would not be able to speak. His muteness no doubt was embarrassing to Zechariah when he came out of the Holy Place of the temple to the crowd waiting outside. He had been in there a long time, but he could give no explanation. He could make only signs with his hands.

The conception happened as the angel predicted, and when the boy was born, many relatives wanted to name him after his father, but Elizabeth insisted on following the angel's instructions. Zechariah wrote on a tablet, "His name is John" (verse 63), and suddenly he could speak again. The torrent of prophecy that erupted from him included a majestic blessing of the Lord and of his newborn son: "And you, child, will be called the prophet of the Most High; for you will go before the Lord to prepare his ways" (verse 76).

POSTSCRIPT

■ The name *Zechariah* means "the Lord remembers." More than 30 people in the Bible bear this name, including the prophet who wrote the Old Testament book with the same name.

■ Some scholars have sought to use Zechariah's schedule of priestly duties to find the time of Jesus' birth. The family of Abijah, which Zechariah belonged to, had the eighth spot in the rotation (see 1 Chronicles 24:10). Those who have tried this have determined a date in the spring, around Passover, which might explain why the shepherds were tending sheep at night, because it was warm enough to be outside.

The Book of Numbers

TRADITIONALLY BELIEVED to be written by Moses in the middle of the second millennium B.C., Numbers describes Israel's preparation under Moses' leadership as they set out on their journey from Mount Sinai to Canaan—the land promised by God. Its curious mixture of narratives, laws, and lists has led to much discussion regarding its structure.

Two census lists (hence the English name "Numbers") provide a useful framework. The first chapter introduces the Sinai generation who are preparing to set out on a journey after a stay of almost a year at Mount Sinai. Able-bodied fighting men are identified and organized (1—2), as are the religious personnel (3—4). Religious rituals and laws prepare this pilgrim people for their march (5—9:14).

Almost as soon as they set out on their journey (9:15 –10:36), the Israelites begin complaining about their living conditions, rebelling against their covenant with God and against Moses, his appointed leader (11—12). They don't think they can take the land, which they have spied out (13), even though God has promised it to them. God condemns that Sinai generation, allowing almost all of the adults to die in the wilderness, never to enter the Promised Land. When the people of Israel try to take the land under their own power, they fail miserably (14).

In future years, the Israelites continue to wander in the wilderness—still rebelling and being punished by the Lord (16– 17)—as they move east and north into Transjordan (20—21), the Jordan of today. That generation engages in pagan sexual immorality, leading to severe divine punishment (25).

The second generation is introduced by its own census (26). The following events, taking place over six months in the Plains of Moab, are much more positive. A successfully negotiated legal dispute over land inheritance brackets the second half of the book (27, 36), along with a discussion of the value of the role of women in Israelite society. Worshippers are reminded of the regular religious observances (28—29), and Israel firmly establishes itself in Transjordan (31—32) before making religious and political arrangements for moving into Canaan (33—35).

POSTSCRIPT

■ One interesting structural element in Numbers is the Hebrews' geographical movement. The move from Sinai to Kadesh on the border of the Promised Land (about 120 miles) takes 20 days, while that from Kadesh to Moab (about the same distance) takes 38 years.

The Shema

MOSES DECLARED, "Hear, O Israel: The Lord is our God, the Lord alone."

That is the primary statement of faith of Jews throughout the ages, and it is found in Deuteronomy 6:4. The first word in Hebrew is *Shema* (accent on the second syllable), which means "hear." Many people have memorized this phrase in the original Hebrew, as well as other languages. It is recited every sabbath in the synagogue and several times daily in the personal prayers of devout Jews.

The passage continues with the command that Jesus (like other rabbis) called the greatest in the law: "You shall love the Lord your God with all your heart ... soul and ... might" (verse 5). Then it instructs the hearer to keep these commands in their heart and in their daily life. "Bind them as a sign on your hand ... write them on the doorposts of your house" (verses 8–9). This is why Jews often write the Shema on scraps of parchment held in small boxes on the hand (phylacteries, or *tefillin*) or by their doors *(mezuzahs)*.

The statement is succinct and powerful, employing both of the main biblical words for God: *Yahweh* (the Lord) and *Elohim* (God). It testifies to the uniqueness of the Israelites' faith in the midst of a polytheistic world. *Elohim* was the generic word for deity, used for the gods of various nations (other Semitic languages have similar-sounding words), but *Yahweh* was the personal name of the God of Israel. Virtually every other religion of the ancient world worshipped multiple gods, but the Israelites had one God. This is what set them apart. The Lord of Israel is one.

The word *hear* has an extra meaning, too. In the Old Testament the word often indicates more than the mere reception of a message, going further to suggest response and compliance (see Exodus 24:7). As verses following the prayer indicate, God's people are called to hear God's commands and also to love him fully, remember his words, and weave them into their lives.

POSTSCRIPT

- The name *Yahweh* was considered so holy that devout Israelites would not pronounce it. To this day, when the Shema is recited in Hebrew, the word *Adonai* (Lord) replaces the holy name.

- In the printed Hebrew text of the Shema, the last letters of the first and last words ("hear" and "one") are enlarged. Together they form the Hebrew word for "testimony." The Shema is the truth that followers of God testify to.

Jesus' Humble Birth

WHEN THE MAGI CAME from the East to find the newborn king, they first stopped in Jerusalem, where they visited King Herod. Perhaps they believed the birth of the new king would need to be within a place as marvelous as a palace. Of course, they soon found themselves traveling south of Jerusalem to Bethlehem. Matthew 2:11 notes that by the time the Magi arrived in Bethlehem, Mary, Joseph, and Jesus were in a house. But that was not where Jesus had been born. Some traditions say he was born in a stable; others say in a cave; still others combine the two traditions and believe it was a cave that served as a stable.

Those humble circumstances are remembered even today through religious architecture. When visiting modern Bethlehem, Christian and Muslim tourists alike visit the Church of the Nativity, a church built over the cave or stable in Bethlehem where Jesus is said to have been born. This church, one of the oldest continually operating churches in the world, was built by Helena, the mother of Emperor Constantine I.

Although the church is beautiful, ornate, and elaborate, in order to enter the church, visitors must bow or stoop down because they need to pass through a low door called "the Door of Humility." The Door of Humility is a reminder of the humble conditions surrounding the birth of Jesus.

But why was he born in the town of Bethlehem?

David, Israel's most beloved king, was both born and anointed as king in Bethlehem. The genealogy at the beginning of the Gospel of Matthew shows that Jesus—through his father, Joseph—was adopted into the lineage of David. Lest readers not understand the significance of Matthew's genealogy, Matthew is explicit when he quotes Micah 5:2 early on in chapter two: "And you, Bethlehem, in the land of Judah, are by no means least among the rulers of Judah; for from you shall come a ruler who is to shepherd my people Israel" (Matthew 2:6).

A boy by the name of David, born in Bethlehem, would watch over sheep and become king. Almost 1,000 years later, another boy would be born in Bethlehem. Born in a stable, perhaps even among sheep, Jesus would also become a shepherd and king, but of a different kind.

Creation of Woman

WHEN GENESIS STATES that God created humans in his own image as both male and female, it is clear that he intended for them to live in relationship with each other and that each one had equal value in his eyes. So, after God had created Adam, he proceeded to provide him with a suitable companion, because as he said, "it is not good that the man should be alone" (Genesis 2:18).

Accordingly, God brought all the creatures to Adam for him to give them names. When he had finished, it was clear that there was no suitable partner for him among the animals. So God put the man into a deep sleep and formed a woman from one of his ribs. When he met the woman, Adam exclaimed, "This at last is bone of my bones and flesh of my flesh" (verse 23). The creation of the woman filled a deep longing in the man that no animal could possibly fill.

He called her "woman" (Hebrew: *ishshah*), because she was taken out of "man" *(ish).* Later he called her "Eve" (Hebrew: *chavvah*), "because she was the mother of all living" (*chai,* a word related to *chavvah;* Genesis 3:20).

When Adam and Eve sinned, their relationship changed, and God said that Eve's "desire" would be for her husband. There was no romance in this "desire," as it is the same word used for sin's "desire" for Cain: that is, to master him (see Genesis 4:7). The ideal complementary loving relationship established in the Garden of Eden was tragically broken by their sin.

POSTSCRIPT

■ The term *helpmate* comes from a misunderstanding of the biblical language in Genesis 2:18 ("helper as his partner"). The King James Version states that Eve was a "help meet for him." In the English of the 17th century, "meet for" meant "suitable for" or "fit for," but as that meaning fell out of common use, people began to refer to Eve as a *help-mate* or *helpmate*.

■ Paul discusses Eve's trangression in Second Corinthians 11:3 and First Timothy 2:13–14.

■ Some people note that Eve came from Adam's side, maintaining that God intended for man and woman to live side by side as partners—and not one ahead of the other, since Eve was formed neither from Adam's head nor from his foot.

Job

JOB WAS A WEALTHY MAN. He possessed thousands of sheep, camels, oxen, donkeys, and great numbers of servants. More importantly, he was a righteous man. The Bible says he was "blameless and upright, one who feared God and turned away from evil" (Job 1:1). He also had seven sons and three daughters, and he presented burnt offerings on their behalf in case they had sinned during their youthful exploits.

A time came when various heavenly beings came before God. Satan appeared before God, too. God presented Job to Satan as a model of godliness, whereupon Satan challenged God to let him afflict Job in order to test his faithfulness. So God allowed Satan to take his property and all his children. Job grieved, but he did not turn against God. In fact, he declared, "Naked I came from my mother's womb, and naked shall I return there; the Lord gave, and the Lord has taken away; blessed be the name of the Lord" (verse 21).

Satan then upped the ante, challenging God to let him take away Job's health, which God allowed. Job suffered greatly, and even his wife advised him to "Curse God, and die" (Job 2:9). But Job retained his integrity and "did not sin with his lips" (verse 10).

Three friends of Job came and tried to commiserate with him, but they stubbornly insisted that Job must have sinned in order to invite such misfortune. Job steadfastly maintained his innocence. Indeed, he passionately cried out to God to explain why he had to suffer so grievously.

Finally, God did come and meet with Job, but he did not explain the test. Rather, he overwhelmed Job by reminding him that he was as nothing in the face of the Almighty, who had created the universe. Job's troubles were less than a drop in the bucket compared to the majesty of God.

While this may have seemed harsh, it satisfied Job. For him, his close encounter with God was life-changing. "I have uttered what I did not understand," he said. "I had heard of you by the hearing of the ear, but now my eye sees you; therefore I despise myself, and repent in dust and ashes" (Job 42:3, 5–6). Before, his experience of God had been only secondhand ("by the hearing of the ear"); now, he had actually "seen" God, and it was enough.

In a delightful conclusion, God told Job's well-meaning but mistaken friends to listen to Job and that Job would pray for them. He also restored Job's fortunes, doubly so, including seven more sons and three more daughters.

The Transfiguration

W HILE THE GOSPELS identify "the Twelve" as Jesus' close disciples, he often selected three of them to join him on special occasions: Peter, James, and John. Did Jesus choose them because they were the smartest or holiest? Probably not. Their profiles in the gospels are not especially flattering. Peter often spoke without thinking. James and John were nicknamed "the Sons of Thunder," probably because of their hot tempers. We know the disciples often quarreled over who was the most important, and these three men were in the thick of it. If Jesus could teach them how to love, he could teach anybody.

One day Jesus took Peter, James, and John up a mountain. Because they had just been in Caesarea Philippi, it's likely that this was Mount Hermon. The exact location isn't nearly as important as what happened there. Jesus was "transfigured" (from the Greek word *metamorphosis*) before their eyes. His face was shining—as Moses' face had glowed when he met with God on Mount Sinai—and his clothes were "dazzling white." Suddenly there were two other figures with him—Moses and Elijah (who represented God's laws and prophecies to the Jewish people).

In that time, the Scriptures were known as "the law and the prophets." The five books of the law were known as the Books of Moses. The other books of the Hebrew Scriptures were grouped together as "the prophets." Though Elijah never wrote a book of prophecy, he was probably the most famous prophet. And, as Moses is associated with Mount Sinai, Elijah is associated with Mount Carmel, where he called down fire from heaven to defeat the false prophets of Baal.

Peter suggested that they build three shrines on the mount. He was probably impressed that Jesus was hanging out with such great heroes of the faith; but of course Jesus was more than just another hero. A bright cloud overshadowed them—always a symbol of God's presence—and a voice from the cloud identified Jesus as "my Son, the Beloved," adding, "with him I am well pleased; listen to him!" (Matthew 17:5; this phrase echoes Isaiah's prophecy of the Servant-Messiah in Isaiah 42:1).

The three disciples fell to the ground in terror. When Jesus helped them to their feet, they realized that Moses and Elijah were gone. Jesus asked them to keep this amazing event a secret until after his resurrection.

John the Baptist

JOHN WAS THE PROPHET who prepared the way for Jesus' ministry. Like his younger cousin Jesus, John had a miraculous birth foretold by an angel of the Lord. Born to aged parents of a priestly family, John was destined to be "great in the sight of the Lord" (Luke 1:15), the angel said, echoing similar promises made about Old Testament heroes.

The last recognized biblical prophet of Israel, Malachi, had lived about four centuries earlier. In his last paragraph, he wrote God's message: "Lo, I will send you the prophet Elijah before the great and terrible day of the Lord comes" (Malachi 4:5). In many ways, John the Baptist was a new Elijah, coming out of the desert to challenge the authorities and inspire the people to live righteously. In fact, Jesus said of John, "and if you are willing to accept it, he is Elijah who is to come" (Matthew 11:14).

St. John the Baptist
by Caravaggio

Baptism was John's specialty. He lived by the Jordan River, and people flocked to him to be baptized in the water as a sign of repentance. The *mikvah* bath was a well-known ritual of purification in Judaism, but John brought new life to it. Wearing camel's hair and eating locusts and wild honey, this rough-hewn hero was phenomenally popular. "Repent," he thundered, "for the kingdom of heaven has come near" (Matthew 3:2).

Religious and social leaders came to see what the fuss was about, and John lit into them, calling them a "brood of vipers!" (verse 7). But John knew he was not the main attraction. As popular as he was, he made clear he was just a forerunner. Early on, this prophecy from Isaiah was connected to John: "The voice of one crying out in the wilderness: 'Prepare the way of the Lord'" (verse 3; see also Isaiah 40:3). He talked about someone greater who would follow him, someone whose sandals he was not worthy to untie.

John continued his ministry even after Jesus started his, though John suggested to his disciples that they now follow Jesus. Nevertheless, even John had doubts about Jesus. While he languished in prison, John sent his disciples to Jesus to ask the Lord if he was the promised one. In response, Jesus both affirmed his messianic identity and the calling of his cousin. After John was beheaded, Jesus' disciples asked him about Malachi's prophecy concerning Elijah. He replied that "Elijah" had already come and was mistreated, just as Jesus himself would be mistreated. Unmistakably, he was talking about his cousin John.

The Book of Deuteronomy

DEUTERONOMY, THE FIFTH BOOK of the Bible and last book in the
Torah, is traditionally ascribed to Moses, who lived in the second
millennium B.C. At least some of Deuteronomy, however, must have been
written later, possibly by Joshua, since it includes notice of Moses' death
(34). It is presented as a memoir, reminiscences in the form of speeches
by an aging leader as he is about to leave his followers on the eve of their
greatest moment to date—entering into the land promised by God. He is
looking back at God's actions in anticipation of God's continued work as
his people take their next step as a nation. The geographical setting is the
Plains of Moab.

The first speech remembers Israel's time in Sinai and Transjordan (1—3;
Transjordan was territory on the opposite side of the Jordan River from
the land of Canaan) and urges obedience (4). The second speech opens
with covenant instructions, including a rendering of the Ten Commandments and warnings against disobedience (5—11). It continues with
an expanded code of law (12—26), which has variations on sections
of Exodus and Leviticus. It is not just of historical interest but is also
intended for the Jews of today (26:16–19).

The third speech describes a covenant ratification ceremony (27:1–10),
with blessings for keeping the covenant (28:1–14) and curses for breaking it (27:11–26; 28:15—29:1). The last speech (29:2—30:20) shows this
covenant's ties with that at Mount Sinai. The book closes with poetic
farewell sayings of Moses (32:1–43; 33) and narratives of his final days
(32:44–52; 34).

Deuteronomy has elements somewhat parallel with those of other ancient
Near Eastern covenants. A preamble identifies the parties (1:1–5); a
historical prologue highlights previous relations (1:6—4:49); stipulations,
both general (5—11) and specific (12—26), are laid on both parties; the
covenant document is to be preserved and periodically read (27:1–10;
31:9–29); witnesses are identified (32); and blessings and curses are pronounced (27:12–26; 28:1–68). The book serves as Israel's constitution.

POSTSCRIPT

■ The ancient Near East has numerous examples of covenants between nations,
such as that between the Egyptians and the Hittites in what is now Turkey.
Israel's covenant is the only covenant between a nation and its God.

Gabriel

GABRIEL IS THE BEST known of God's angels, one of only two mentioned in the Bible by name (the other is Michael). In his four appearances in Scripture, Gabriel fulfills his role as a messenger dispatched by God to reveal God's purposes.

His first two biblical scenes occur with the prophet Daniel. "I have now come out to give you wisdom and understanding," the angel announces (Daniel 9:22). He proceeds to declare the prophecy of the 70 weeks, concerning the time before the appearance of the Messiah.

We find Gabriel's other two biblical encounters in the Gospel of Luke. First, he appears to Zechariah the priest, announcing the birth of John the Baptist. "I am Gabriel. I stand in the presence of God," he explains, "and I have been sent to speak to you and to bring you this good news" (Luke 1:19). When Zechariah doesn't believe him, Gabriel strikes him mute until the child's birth. But Gabriel's most familiar scene is with Mary, a virgin in Nazareth. The angel tells her she will give birth to the Son of God. Great artists have painted this great event, referred to as "the Annunciation," and it has been acted out in myriad Christmas pageants.

It is possible that Gabriel also appears unnamed in other biblical stories. An "angel of the Lord" speaks to the shepherds of Bethlehem, and there are angels at the resurrection and ascension of Jesus. All these events would fit with Gabriel's general task —announcing the arrival and work of the Messiah.

What did Gabriel look like? Angels are regularly described as beings of light. Sometimes they look like men in bright clothing. And people are usually terrified to see them: Gabriel told both Zechariah and Mary not to be afraid of him. Some angelic beings (cherubim and seraphim) have wings, but it's not certain that Gabriel did.

The other named angel, Michael, appears in Daniel, Jude, and Revelation as a warrior for God and a leader of angels (an archangel). Writings from between the Old and New Testaments refer to both Michael and Gabriel as archangels, two of the four (sometimes seven) highest-ranking angels. Gabriel is specifically described as one who intercedes for God's people and opposes the wicked. Later Christian writings name Gabriel as the one who will blow the "final trumpet" at Christ's return. Much of the modern fascination with angels is based on this ancient folklore rather than biblical teaching.

God Is With Us

IN DESCRIBING THE BIRTH of Jesus, Matthew alluded to Isaiah 7:14 when he wrote, "All this took place to fulfill what had been spoken by the Lord through the prophet: 'Look, the virgin shall conceive and bear a son, and they shall name him Immanuel,' which means, 'God is with us'" (Matthew 1:22–23).

These verses are just a few of the many verses in Matthew's gospel that are "fulfillment citations." Matthew clearly saw Jesus as representing the fulfillment of prophecy. He believed the words and promises spoken by the great Hebrew prophets were fulfilled in the life and person of Jesus.

One of the most significant translation debates of the 20th century involved how Isaiah 7:14 should be translated. Some Christians viewed the replacement of the word "virgin" with "young woman" by some Bible translations as a mistranslation. Some even went so far as to burn these pages from the "mistranslated" Bibles.

Apparently, this controversial phrase did not trouble Matthew, who had used the Septuagint's wording (the Greek translation of the Hebrew Scriptures). In fact, Matthew wanted his readers to understand that Jesus' birth was highly unusual. To Matthew, Mary became pregnant under extraordinary circumstances—circumstances that would be just as unbelievable and controversial had they occurred today. Ancient non-Christians made slurs about Jesus' birth, and it would be surprising if Matthew was not familiar with those charges.

When Matthew spoke of Mary, he anticipated criticism, for he hinted at how God had worked for good through all sorts of individuals, such as the women he mentions in Jesus' genealogy. More significantly, he emphasized that through Mary the truly remarkable had happened. For us today, the truly remarkable part of Matthew 1:23 may have to do with a virgin giving birth to a baby.

For Matthew, however, what was truly remarkable was the Incarnation: that God would be born on earth as a man. "God with us" is the name that is given to Jesus. When we reach the closing words of Matthew's gospel, we read Jesus' words: "And remember, I am with you always, to the end of the age" (Matthew 28:20). Thus the birth of the one named Immanuel once again gives reason for good news.

The Tree of Knowledge

THE GARDEN OF EDEN was a place of unimaginable beauty, prepared by God specifically for humans to enjoy. It had trees that were "pleasant to the sight and good for food" (Genesis 2:9), it was watered well by four rivers, and it abounded in precious metals and precious stones. All of this was for the humans whom God had placed in the garden to enjoy.

God expressed his generosity to Adam in this way: "You may freely eat of every tree of the garden" (verse 16). The only exception was that Adam was not to eat of the tree of the knowledge of good and evil. In fact, there were two special trees in the garden: this tree and the tree of life. The tree of life is mentioned elsewhere in the Bible, but its role in the Garden of Eden was minimal; the tree of knowledge is the significant one here.

What was it about the tree of the knowledge of good and evil that placed it off-limits to humans? Nothing in the Bible suggests that it was poisonous or that its physical properties were extraordinary. Most likely, it was simply an arbitrary tree designated by God to be the tree that would test Adam and Eve's obedience.

Scholars have long debated the significance of this tree. One theory is that the tree represents moral autonomy—that is, the human desire to live apart from God. Humans were created in God's image, and he provided for all their needs. They were meant to live in close relationship with him. Sadly, when Adam and Eve sinned, this relationship was broken, and they hid themselves from God.

When God prohibited Adam and Eve from eating of this tree, he was underscoring the fact that he wanted to be their God and their provider. When they violated his command, they became in a sense "like God" (Genesis 3:5); but this was a burden they could not handle, since their created purpose was to live in total dependence on him, not independently of him. For this denial of their dependence on God, Adam and Eve were driven out of the garden that was in Eden, never to return.

POSTSCRIPT

▪ Several ancient Near Eastern myths involve the eating of a plant that bestows life or immortality.

Abraham

ABRAHAM IS ONE OF the greatest figures in the Bible. God chose him to be the father of many nations, including Israel. He is the ancestor of King David and of Jesus. He had a close relationship with God, and God promised him many blessings. But he was also human, and occasionally his lack of faith got him into trouble.

In the world scene of his day, Abraham was an unknown with no special prominence. God plucked him out of obscurity in order to bless him and to bring blessing to others. He promised Abraham a great name, many descendants, the land of Canaan, and most importantly, a close relationship with himself. God, however, did not promise all of this for Abraham's sake alone. The Bible says all of this was "so that you will be a blessing. . . . and in you all the families of the earth shall be blessed" (Genesis 12:2–3).

The Departure of Abraham
by Josef Moinar

In other words, Abraham was to be the *means* of blessing others. This happened in his lifetime—he blessed many with whom he came into contact—but the ultimate fulfillment of this promise would be through his descendant, Jesus, through whom blessings on all nations would come. Abraham's original name was *Abram,* which means "exalted father." God changed his name to *Abraham,* which means "father of a multitude," a powerful confirmation of God's promises. When God assured him of a son, the Bible says, "He believed the Lord; and the Lord reckoned it to him as righteousness" (Genesis 15:6).

And yet Abraham was also on occasion capable of foolish behavior that betrayed a lack of faith in God. For a time, he did not believe God's promise that his wife, Sarah, would have a son, so he took Sarah's maidservant, Hagar, and she bore Ishmael. On two occasions he tried to pass Sarah off as his sister, fearing for their lives on account of her beauty. But Scripture's overall verdict on Abraham is a positive one.

After Abraham passed away, God affirmed that "Abraham obeyed my voice and kept my charge, my commandments, my statutes, and my laws" (Genesis 26:5). Such praise indicates how prominently Abraham is portrayed in Scripture.

The Raising of Lazarus

TOWARD THE END of his earthly ministry, Jesus heard that his dear friend Lazarus was extremely ill. Oddly, he waited two days before making the trip to see him. Lazarus died, and his sisters scolded Jesus for not coming sooner to heal him. But then Jesus asked that the tomb be opened, and he called Lazarus back from the dead, and he did come back to life. This made him even more popular with the people, but it also galvanized the opposition against him.

It's hard to think of another miracle of Jesus greater than this one. He had already amazed people with his ability to cast out demons and heal diseases. He had healed with his voice as well as his hands. He had healed someone at a distance. He had even healed someone without seemingly realizing it when an afflicted woman touched his garment. Besides the healings, there were displays of power over nature: walking on water, calming a storm, and multiplying bread. He had even brought people back to life before, but this was different. By the time Jesus arrived, Lazarus had been dead four days. This was no mere resuscitation. According to Hebrew thought at the time, it took three days for the soul to leave the body. Lazarus was dead as dead could be. As his sister Martha said of the decaying process, "Lord, already there is a stench" (John 11:39).

Many questions surround this miracle. *When Jesus heard about the sickness of Lazarus, why did he wait two days to go to see him?* Was he waiting for him to die so it would be a greater miracle? Not exactly. Assuming he was in Galilee, he was four days away when he received the news, so even if he had left immediately, he would still have arrived two days after his friend's death. (This does leave open the possibility that he waited the extra time in order to remove the idea that it was just a resuscitation.)

Another question: *If this miracle was so important in stirring up opposition that led to Jesus' death, why is John the only gospel to report it?* Many theories have been put forth in response to this. Some suggest that some of the disciples (like Peter) who were the main sources for the other gospels didn't make this trip, so they couldn't provide eyewitness testimony. Others think Lazarus might have been alive while the earlier gospels were written, and those writers didn't want to place him in danger.

And further: *Why did Jesus weep?* Didn't he know what he was about to do? Was he lamenting the disbelief of the mourners or his own impending battle against the power of death? Evidently he felt the same deep grief as his friends at the loss of a loved one.

Caesar Augustus

CAESAR AUGUSTUS was emperor of Rome at the time of Jesus' birth. One of the greatest and most powerful Roman emperors, he created conditions throughout the Mediterranean world that paved the way for the spread of Christianity.

His given name was Octavius. He was a nephew of Julius Caesar. When Julius died at the hands of assassins, there was a major power struggle, and Octavius emerged as his successor in 27 B.C. He took the name Augustus to go with the imperial title Caesar.

The land of Israel had been under the power of Rome since being conquered in 63 B.C. by Julius's colleague Pompey. Though he was not a full-blooded Jew, Herod the Great did enough schmoozing and bribing to convince the Roman Senate that he'd be an effective king over Galilee, so he was installed in 37 B.C. Though he had backed Mark Antony over Octavius after the death of Julius, Octavius (Augustus) still saw him as a strong ruler and kept him on the Judaean throne.

"In those days a decree went out from Emperor Augustus that all the world should be registered" (Luke 2:1). So begins one of the most familiar chapters of the Bible, the Christmas story in Luke 2. Outside of Luke, we have no record of such a registration, but it sounds like something Augustus would do. He was a great organizer. Though he wielded great power as the head of Rome, he also delegated power effectively to generals and governors. Under Augustus, the Romans tended to let nations rule themselves as long as they paid taxes and remained peaceful. Roman legions were stationed where necessary to keep order.

For the most part, there was peace throughout the empire. Later it was called the *Pax Romana,* the Roman peace. The Roman navy kept the Mediterranean free from piracy, and the Roman army built roads throughout the provinces to ensure rapid mobilization of troops and equipment when necessary. This made it easy to travel, and after Jesus' death, Christian missionaries took full advantage of these roads.

Augustus died in A.D. 14, having transformed Rome from a politically bickering republic to a world-dominating empire. At his death, he was hailed as a god. Meanwhile, the real God-man was learning carpentry in Nazareth.

POSTSCRIPT

■ The month of August is named after Caesar Augustus.

The Book of Joshua

JOSHUA IS A TRANSITIONAL book that moves Israel from outside the Promised Land under Moses' leadership (whose passing is noted at the beginning; see 1:1) to inside Canaan under Joshua's leadership (whose passing, along with that of Aaron's son Eleazer, closes the book; see 24:29–33). It pictures a people on the move who became an alliance of settled tribes.

Joshua follows the Pentateuch by proclaiming the fulfillment of the Promised Land. This book also begins the period of the Early Prophets (Joshua through Second Kings), which details what Israel did while inhabiting the land. No authorship claim is made in the book, and suggestions for its date of writing run from a period close to the time of Joshua himself in the middle of the second millennium B.C. to the later days of the Israelite monarchy.

The book begins with a series of speeches reminiscent of and recapitulating Deuteronomy (1:1–8). Told through a fast-paced narrative, the book's second section describes the quick conquest of the land of Canaan (2:1—12:24), starting with the occupation of its center (2:1—10:27), followed by campaigns to the south (10:28–43) and north (11), then closing with a summary of the gains in Transjordan under Moses (12:1–6) and in Canaan under Joshua (12:7–24).

The third section recounts the Israelite holdings through the use of reports and lists (13:1—21:45). Included are those Canaanite lands as yet unconquered; the holdings of each tribe, of the Levites and of Joshua himself; and a description of the cities of refuge where one could escape blood vengeance (20). The final section prepares for settlement in the land, with the Transjordanian tribes returning home and all of Israel participating in a national covenant renewal ceremony (22—24).

While battles play an important role in the book, they are not its central focus, since it is Israel's God, rather than Israel's armies, who really carries the day (10:14; 21:44; see 1:11). It is the land itself, promised to Abraham and his descendants 400 years earlier (Genesis 12:1–3; 15:7), that is the anticipated goal of the people, and its allocation forms the central part of the book itself.

The ultimate goal for the land is not its capture, but the rest from fighting to be enjoyed by Israel after the conquest and settlement is completed (Joshua 1:13, referring to Numbers 32:20–22 and Deuteronomy 3:18–20). Peace and the outflowing of God's promised blessings on a united people were Israel's hope and vision.

Cherubim and Seraphim

YOU MAY THINK of "cherubs" as pudgy children with wings. The biblical picture is very different. *Cherubim* (the *-im* ending makes it plural) are indeed a kind of angel, and they have wings, but they're usually described as hybrids of human and animal parts, and sometimes they have two faces or even four.

The prophet Ezekiel gave the most elaborate descriptions of cherubim, seeing four "living creatures," each with the face of a human, lion, ox, and eagle (see Ezekiel 1:5–14; 10:1–5). They also darted back and forth on wheels. The Book of Revelation describes the same creatures around the heavenly throne, worshipping God (see 4:6–11).

The Sistine Madonna Group of Angels
by Raphael

The first biblical appearance of cherubim occurs in Eden, where they are posted to guard the Garden of Eden after Adam and Eve are banished (see Genesis 3:24). Images of cherubim adorned the sacred lid of the ark of the covenant and were embroidered on the curtains of the tabernacle's Holy Place. They seem to have a role as guardians of God's holiness.

Seraphim are mentioned once in Scripture in Isaiah's vision of God's throne. The word means "fiery ones," which might explain why the temple was "filled with smoke" (Isaiah 6:4). They had six wings, using two to cover their faces, two to cover their feet, and two to fly. Just like the creatures/cherubim in Revelation, they sang, "Holy, holy, holy" (Revelation 4:8). In keeping with their "fiery" definition, one seraph took a burning coal and applied it to Isaiah's lips in purification.

POSTSCRIPT

Some scholars think that Ezekiel's visions of cherubim were inspired by the Egyptian sphinx and the Persian griffin, creatures that were half animal, half human. The word *cherub* might be drawn from the Akkadian *karibu,* used for a griffinlike "intercessor."

The Shepherds Visit the Baby Jesus

THE ANGEL WHO APPEARED to the shepherds is never named, although the angel Gabriel has already appeared twice in the gospel accounts up to this point of this story, first bringing an announcement to Zechariah (Luke 1:11–20) and then bringing good news to Mary (Luke 1:26–38). So perhaps it is no surprise that some have identified Gabriel as the angel who appeared to the shepherds.

The Angel Appearing to the Shepherds at Bethlehem *by Giovanni Birago*

Although the Magi from the East saw a star that led them to Jesus, the shepherds were given a less subtle sign revealing the location of his birth. After this unnamed angel revealed the good news of the birth of Jesus to the shepherds, a host of angels suddenly broke out into a song. The shepherds listened with awe to their heavenly chorus of celebration before setting off for Bethlehem, where they found Mary, Joseph, and the baby. They then left, "glorifying and praising God for all they had heard and seen, as it had been told them" (Luke 2:20).

Why bother to tell shepherds? Perhaps they were told because they represented the common people; they were not kings or military leaders. Perhaps they were told because Jesus himself would come to be understood as a shepherd. Perhaps they were told because King David had been a shepherd in this very place. Or perhaps they were told just because the angels wanted to share the news with those close by.

However much the shepherds may have marveled at this news of God come to earth, the angels seemed to marvel just as much. And that points to the good news for everyone.

POSTSCRIPT

■ Two kinds of shepherds appear in the Bible: nomadic shepherds, who migrated from pasture to pasture, and shepherds who lived in towns and tended their sheep in nearby meadows.

■ Some Egyptians held shepherds in disdain during Bible times because they had no use for sheep.

The Beguiling Serpent

THE IMAGE OF SATAN disguised as a serpent, tempting Eve with the "forbidden fruit" in the Garden of Eden, is one of the most famous of biblical images, found repeatedly in art, literature, and popular culture. The fact is, however, the Bible does not identify Satan specifically with the serpent until its final book—Revelation (see 12:9 and 20:2).

Nevertheless, the serpent in the Garden of Eden was clearly a representative of evil and obviously opposed to God and his purposes for humanity. Scripture also notes that the serpent was "more crafty" than any other wild animal. In speaking with Eve, the serpent twisted God's words, which had been sweeping and generous: "You may freely eat of every tree of the garden; but of the tree of the knowledge of good and evil you shall not eat" (Genesis 2:16–17). By asking a carefully leading question, however, the serpent depicted a cruel and anxious God who would deny his children the delights of the garden: "Did God say, 'You shall not eat from any tree in the garden'?" (Genesis 3:1). The serpent then begins to distort God's command by adding "nor shall you touch it" (verse 3), obviously appealing to Eve's physical attraction to the forbidden fruit.

Eve succumbed to the serpent's temptation and then gave the forbidden fruit to Adam. Astonishingly, the Bible states that Adam "was with her" at this time; presumably he, too, had heard the serpent's words, but apparently he did not confront the serpent. Eventually he also decided to disobey his creator, as Eve had.

In the Bible, there is no suggestion that the forces of evil are on a par with God (in contrast to many religions of the ancient Near East that describe good and evil forces as being nearly equal in power). Rather, the opposite is the case: God is far more powerful than any and all such forces. That point is made concerning the serpent this way: "Now the serpent was more crafty than *any other wild animal that the Lord God had made*" (verse 1, italics added). Even the serpent was part of the created order that God had made and over which God had absolute power.

The point of this narrative is that God chose to give humans the gift of free choice, and in this situation it was their choice how they would respond to the serpent's temptation. Would love for and trust in God motivate them to obey him, or would envy and self-interest cause them to disobey?

POSTSCRIPT

■ Even though an apple is commonly thought to be what Adam and Eve ate, in fact, the Bible does not specify what the fruit was.

Sarah

SARAH WAS ABRAHAM'S wife and the mother of Isaac, through whom God's promises to Abraham were carried forward. She possessed an uncommon beauty; even in her old age, her husband, Abraham, feared that others would take her away from him by force and kill him. Because she had been barren for many years—which she believed to be a barrier to God's fulfillment of his promises—she gave her maidservant Hagar to her husband. By ancient law and custom, any son born to Hagar would be considered Sarah's.

God, however, had plans on a grander scale. God had promised Abraham a son through Sarah, even though she was of an advanced age. Indeed, the Lord had promised descendants more numerous than the stars in the heavens. Finally, Sarah bore Isaac, whose son, Jacob, became the father of 12 sons who became the fathers of the 12 tribes of Israel. Though the mother of only one son, Sarah was critical to God's plan to establish his people, the Israelites, and ultimately to bring blessings to all peoples through them.

Nevertheless, Sarah was only human. When Hagar's son, Ishmael, was born, a fierce rivalry broke out between the two women, and Sarah dealt harshly with her servant, who eventually fled into the wilderness. Later, Sarah laughed in disbelief when a messenger from God said she'd have a son after age 90. Furthermore, it appears she went along with Abraham's misguided schemes to pass her off as his sister when he traveled to Egypt and to Philistia. (He feared he would be killed if people thought she was his wife.)

Despite her many flaws, Sarah played a key role in God's plan of reconciliation with the world. Sarah's name originally was *Sarai,* meaning "princess," but God changed it to *Sarah,* meaning essentially the same thing. Her name change, however, signified a new status, which can be understood in God's promise: "I will bless her, and she shall give rise to nations; kings of peoples shall come from her" (Genesis 17:16).

POSTSCRIPT

■ Sarah was Abraham's half sister (they shared the same father but not the same mother). Nevertheless, the times when Abraham passed her off as his sister instead of his wife showed their lack of trust in God's ability to protect them.

Triumphal Entry into Jerusalem

IT WAS THE BEGINNING of the end for Jesus' earthly ministry, but of course there would arrive a new beginning—the birth of his Church.

In Jerusalem, Jesus had enemies who were on the lookout for him. Most of the religious leaders saw him as a blasphemer, a lawbreaker, a rabble-rouser, a reformer . . . a threat to their own corrupt power. If Jesus tried to sneak into the city for the Passover celebration, they would nab him, try him, and put him to death.

But he didn't sneak into Jerusalem. Instead, he created a public spectacle, borrowing a donkey to ride into the city among hordes of adoring fans. It was the kind of victory parade a conquering general might have, or a king—except they would have rode in on a white horse. Jesus made a

Entry into Jerusalem *by Julius Von Carolsfeld*

humbler choice, fulfilling Hebrew prophecy (see Zechariah 9:9).

The crowd responded by throwing their garments on the road, waving palm branches, and singing psalms. The Book of Psalms includes a section of processional songs, and the crowd was apparently singing the last one in the series—Psalm 118, a royal psalm: "Save us, we beseech you, O Lord!" (Psalm 118:25). In Hebrew, that's *Hosanna!* Palm branches were also part of religious processions (verse 27), and the garment-tossing might have been linked with coronation ceremonies (see 2 Kings 9:13).

In any case, the point was clear. Jesus was entering the city not as a fugitive but as a victorious king. Yet he was a different kind of king—the fulfillment of prophetic hopes and dreams.

Obviously Jesus' immense popularity didn't last through the week, as another crowd called for his crucifixion on Friday. But Jesus, the master communicator, had made his point once again with meaningful imagery. He had created a motion picture in which he appeared as a humble king, hailed as the one who comes to save his people in the name of the Lord.

POSTSCRIPT

■ Hosanna—literally, "Lord, save us"—was originally a cry for help. By Jesus' time it was used as a word of praise, something like *Hallelujah*.

Herod the Great

HEROD WAS KING in Judaea when Jesus was born. He had the necessary skills at an opportune time. In the half century before Jesus' birth, Israel's power structure was in flux on account of the Roman occupation. In 47 B.C., the Romans appointed Herod governor of Galilee. Herod parlayed that position through a series of promotions and was eventually recognized as king of Judaea in 37 B.C. at age 35.

From the start, the Jews were critical of his ancestry. Herod was Idumaean. Part of the Idumaean race had descended from Esau, who was the brother of the Jewish patriarch Jacob. Thus the Idumaeans were related to the Jews but were not ethnically Jewish. Religious conservatives also repudiated his Roman ways. He seemed bent on making Jerusalem a world-class city, complete with theaters and stadiums. To a culture committed to separation from Gentiles, this was scandalous.

Yet Herod successfully ingratiated himself with his Roman overlords and politically appeased his Jewish underlings. His major building project was the temple, restored and enlarged from the structure rebuilt in Ezra's time. This magnificent building served to soften the opposition of the nation's religious leaders. He also oversaw a period of economic growth in which he actually lowered taxes a couple of times.

Paranoia, however, characterized much of Herod's reign, particularly in his early years as king when he was consolidating power and in the last years of his life when his would-be successors jockeyed for position. He executed a number of family members, including most of his first wife's family, and he survived a poisoning attempt by one of his sons, whom he also executed. In about 5 B.C., he came down with an incurable disease. Sensing the vultures circling, he began changing his will and making various arrangements for the distribution of his kingdom after his death.

This was most likely the time when the Magi showed up in Herod's court, asking about a newborn "king of the Jews." Was this another plot on his life by an impatient heir? Or was it a power play by the religious leaders to use ancient prophecy against this secular king? Herod was paranoid enough to follow up their visit with violence. Matthew tells us he ordered the slaughter of all babies in Bethlehem under two years of age. Providentially, however, Joseph was warned of this danger in a dream and fled with Mary and Jesus to Egypt, where they remained until Herod's death.

Herod the Great died in 4 B.C., leaving Judaea in the hands of his son Archelaus, who mismanaged the kingdom so badly that the Romans deposed him after about a decade.

The Book of Judges

THE BOOK OF JUDGES neatly places itself in Israel's story between the death of Joshua, Moses' successor (Judges 1:1), and the beginning of the rule of kings over Israel (21:25). This is the last part of the second millennium B.C. Judges makes no claims regarding its authorship, but its part in a continuous narrative stretching from Deuteronomy through Kings places its final form during Israel's exile in Babylon in the sixth century B.C., though most of the book comes mainly from a period much earlier than that. Judges is composed of a series of narrative vignettes, offering both short and long stories from this key period in the development of Israel as a nation.

The book opens with an overview of its historical context, with part of the Israelite territory still under foreign control, Israel being unfaithful to their covenant with God, and their military leader, Joshua, dying (1:1—3:6). The main, central section describes a succession of judges—heroic leaders of individual tribes or tribal coalitions (3:7—16:31). Due to Israel's rebellions against God, he sent armies from their neighbors to attack and plunder them. When Israel cried to God for help, he raised up "judges" to counter those forces with their own home-grown militias. When at peace, Israel soon returned to their waywardness, and the cycle of rebellion to punishment to restoration would begin again.

The last section of stories shows the sorry state to which these people once united in conquest had fallen. Two incidents involving failed religious leaders lead to conflict and ultimately to intertribal civil war (17—21). Unity had degenerated into anarchy.

The judges themselves are a motley crew, with six only briefly noted and six others more fully fleshed out. Two of the latter are among the best-known Old Testament characters. At times Gideon sought God's guidance and bravely fought on his behalf against increasing odds (6:1—8:32), while Samson did not serve as a good role model, engaging in immorality and actively consorting with Israel's enemies. Samson, however, came through for God and Israel at the end of his life (13—16). Figures such as these show that God's grace works despite human weaknesses and sin.

POSTSCRIPT

■ The name "Judges" is misleading since there are no courtrooms and lawsuits but rather battlefields and civil rule.

Lucifer

MOST OF WHAT WE think we know about the Devil doesn't originate in the Bible. It comes from writings that appeared between the end of the Old Testament period and the birth of Jesus *and* from an epic poem by John Milton. The Old Testament says very little about Satan, though its occasional references were woven together by Hebrew scholars after 200 B.C. Jesus used this general understanding as he spoke of the Devil, but he didn't fill in many details. Some Church leaders and rabbis through the centuries have come up with various ideas, but it was actually John Milton, writing *Paradise Lost* in 1667, who described Lucifer's expulsion from heaven.

As that story goes, Lucifer was one of the highest-ranking angels of God, but his pride led to rebellion, and so he was cast down from heaven, along with the angels that joined his rebellion. The story works. It explains a number of biblical hints and allusions. Still, it's surprising that the Bible itself doesn't give us better coverage of such an important event.

The most expansive scriptural discussion of this event is found in Isaiah: "How you are fallen from heaven, O Day Star, son of Dawn! . . . You said in your heart, 'I will ascend to heaven; I will raise my throne above the stars of God; . . . I will make myself like the Most High.' But you are brought down to Sheol, to the depths of the Pit" (14:12–15).

In the Latin translation, the Day Star is *Lucifer,* literally "light-bringer." It was the common term for what we know as the planet Venus, the morning star. And while this seems to describe perfectly the story of Satan's fall, the context of the passage clearly points us to the king of Babylon. Could this text have multiple meanings? Absolutely. Biblical prophecy often does. This possibility is affirmed by several New Testament passages. Jesus once said, "I watched Satan fall from heaven like a flash of lightning" (Luke 10:18). And in Revelation, "the dragon and his angels" are defeated by the forces of the archangel Michael and "thrown down to the earth." In case there was any doubt, John confirms that he's talking about "that ancient serpent, who is called the Devil and Satan" (Revelation 12:7, 9). What's more, Jesus talked about a punishment of "eternal fire prepared for the devil and his angels" (Matthew 25:41).

According to the New Testament, it seems that Satan is in transit from heaven to hell. For the time being, he prowls the earth, tempting, lying, seeking to destroy (see 1 Peter 5:8), but his doom is sure.

The Magi Visit the Baby Jesus

MOST PEOPLE KNOW the Magi largely from Nativity plays and crèche scenes. It is easy to imagine three Magi, or wise men, kneeling before the manger, bringing gold, frankincense, and myrrh to the newborn king of the Jews. In crèche scenes they may be jockeying for position, along with shepherds, lowing cattle, and donkeys.

Because these astrologers from Persia are fascinating and unusual figures, layers and layers of tradition from outside the Bible have come to surround them. Because of the number of gifts that were brought to Jesus, many traditions say that there were three Magi. At the same time, other early writers speculated that there were 12 of them, representing 12 Gentile kingdoms to match the 12 tribes of Israel.

Other traditions portray these Magi or wise men as kings. Tradition even gives them names: The names Balthasar, Caspar, and Melchior have been attached to them from the sixth century. Tradition dating from the ninth century even says each came from a different continent: from Asia, Europe, and Africa.

The New Testament, however, paints a different story, with the Magi appearing only in the Gospel of Matthew and appearing in only a few verses. They stop in Jerusalem and meet with King Herod, asking where the child is who was "born king of the Jews" (Matthew 2:2). Herod sends them on to Bethlehem, asking that they return to him with news of where this king can be found. They follow the star, enter "a house" (not a stable, as often is portrayed; see verse 11) and offer Jesus gold, frankincense, and myrrh. Then, "having been warned in a dream not to return to Herod, they left for their own country by another road" (verse 12).

The Magi stand out in part because they are presented as Gentiles who not only understand the significance of Jesus but also understand it before anyone else. Why did they bring gold, frankincense, and myrrh? The Bible itself does not say. But tradition does. The classic carol entitled "We Three Kings" offers one explanation: Gold was symbolic of Jesus' kingship; frankincense was symbolic of his divine nature; and myrrh—a resin that served as an embalming element—was symbolic of his death.

The Fall

EVE ATE THE FRUIT from the tree of the knowledge of good and evil for three reasons: (1) She saw that it was "good for food"; (2) it was "a delight to the eyes"; and (3) she thought it would make her wise (see Genesis 3:6). The fruit appealed to her physically, psychologically, and intellectually. No doubt, the most powerful temptation of them all was the serpent's promise that she and her husband would become "like God" by eating the forbidden fruit (verse 5). We do not know Adam's motivation for eating the fruit, but since he was "with her" (verse 6) when she ate, we can presume that his reasons for eating were similar to hers.

Their choice to eat from the one tree that God had placed off-limits showed that they did not trust God but instead wanted to strike out on their own and assert their human autonomy. They chose to believe the serpent rather than obey God.

The consequences of their decision were catastrophic. God sentenced Adam to work the ground at great cost, for God cursed the ground because of his sin: He would toil by the sweat of his brow in order to produce enough food to survive amidst the thorns and thistles that would spring up. Eve was sentenced to greatly increased pain in childbirth, and her relationship with Adam changed; she would now "desire" him, and he would "rule over" her as a result (verse 16).

That which was honorable and good was made into a burden because of their disobedience. Before their sin, Adam was responsible for tilling the ground; this was part of the created order, and presumably it was an easy and pleasant task. After sin, it became severely burdensome. So, too, with Eve: Childbearing was intended to be a wonderful experience for a mother, but now Eve's travail in childbirth would increase. Moreover, their relationship changed drastically: Before their sin, Adam and Eve enjoyed their sexuality without shame; after sin, they were ashamed of their nakedness. Even worse, death was now their lot, and they were driven out of the Garden of Eden.

The harshest punishment was for the serpent. God *cursed* the serpent, something he did not do with the humans. On a physical level, the serpent was sentenced to crawl on the ground. Beyond this, God promised perpetual conflict between the serpent and the woman, between its offspring and her offspring, and that, in the end, the woman's offspring would crush the serpent's head. Christians believe that the symbolism here was realized with the coming of Christ, who, in his resurrection from the dead, won the victory over death and defeated evil—thus, metaphorically, crushing the serpent's head.

Melchizedek

WHEN ABRAHAM and his nephew, Lot, settled in Canaan, Lot chose an area of the fertile Jordan Valley near the Dead Sea. Unfortunately for him, this was precisely the area where a great battle was fought between a coalition of Mesopotamian kings and another coalition of local kings. In the aftermath of the battle, Lot was captured, and so Abraham marshaled a fighting force and rescued him.

On his return from this raid, Abraham met Melchizedek, the king of Salem (that is, Jerusalem). Besides being king, Melchizedek was also "priest of God Most High" (Genesis 14:18). He blessed Abraham, and Abraham in return gave him a tithe, a tenth of his possessions.

This brief episode is the only historical reference to Melchizedek in the Bible. He is an enigmatic figure who appeared suddenly out of the blue, had a meaningful but brief encounter with Abraham, and then disappeared from history.

The Book of Hebrews, however, drawing upon Psalm 110, resurrects the memory of Melchizedek, speaking of him as a powerful symbol and forerunner of Jesus. Hebrews is sometimes called "the book of better things" because it repeatedly emphasizes that Jesus and all he stood for represented "better things" than the Old Testament system of repeated sacrifices and laws that could too easily lead to legalism.

So, in contrast to the "old" priesthood represented by Aaron, the high priest and brother of Moses, Jesus was a new kind of high priest, "a priest forever, according to the order of Melchizedek" (Hebrews 7:17). Melchizedek's name means "king of righteousness," and he was king of Salem (*Shalem* in Hebrew, which sounds like *shalom,* meaning "peace"), reminding people that he was a "king of peace." Both labels apply as well to Jesus, of course.

Precisely because he was an enigmatic figure with no ties to the Old Testament laws or sacrificial system, Melchizedek served as a good prefigurement of Jesus. The Book of Hebrews says, "Without father, without mother, without genealogy, having neither beginning of days nor end of life, but resembling the Son of God, [Melchizedek] remains a priest forever" (verse 3).

POSTSCRIPT

■ Some conjecture that Melchizedek might even have been Jesus himself.

Den of Robbers

IT WAS A RACKET. And you can bet the corrupt politicians had their hands all over it.

Devout Jews traveled to Jerusalem for the high holy days to offer sacrifices at the temple, and there were various other life situations that called for sacrifices, too. If you lived close enough to drag a lamb, ox, or dove from your own stock, you could offer that, but most travelers preferred to buy their sacrifice on site at the temple. This created a business opportunity. It also opened the door for organized corruption.

In their everyday lives, Jews used Roman money, but it was supposedly too filthy for the holy temple transactions. So buyers would have to exchange their Roman money for holy temple shekels, and the exchange rate was not fair. After a markup on the money and a markup on the sacrificial animals, the poor worshippers were getting fleeced.

No wonder Jesus said the money changers had turned the temple into a "den of robbers" (Matthew 21:13). He was quoting from the prophet Jeremiah (Jeremiah 7:11), who blasted the hypocrisy of religious leaders in his day. They hallowed "the temple of the Lord," assuming that its very presence would save them from destruction, but they woefully oppressed the poor. Jesus faced a similar situation when he saw unscrupulous merchants using the holiness of God's temple to jack up their prices.

The temple complex in Jesus' day was a sprawling campus set on an artificial plateau high on one of Jerusalem's hills. It was laid out in a series of rectangles, one inside another, creating greater degrees of holiness. In the center was the Holy of Holies where God dwelled. The surrounding areas were the Holy Place, which was only for the priests, the Court of Priests, where sacrifices were made on a huge altar, and the Court of Women, where various assemblies were held. It's likely that the money changers with their tables, coins, and animals were located in a courtyard around the temple building.

In a violent display of righteous anger, Jesus overturned those tables and drove away the merchants. This further upset the religious leaders, of course, but it might have made him even more of a folk hero. Over the next few days Jesus returned to the temple to teach and to heal.

Simeon, the Messenger

SIMEON WAS A DEVOUT Jew who saw the baby Jesus at the temple and uttered a prophecy about him. He's one of the Bible's mystery men. We don't know where he came from or what happened to him later, but for a few moments of Jesus' infancy he was on center stage, delivering an important message to Mary (Luke 2:22–35).

Mary and Joseph brought Jesus to the temple as a baby. This was probably a month or two after the birth, when Mary would go through a "purification" ritual and a sacrifice would be made for this firstborn child.

Simeon is described as a "man in Jerusalem." Was he a priest or rabbi, a religious leader? We don't know, but if he was, we would probably be given that information. Instead, he is introduced as just an ordinary citizen, "righteous and devout, looking forward to the consolation of Israel" (Luke 2:25). The Holy Spirit of God was a force in his life, and the Spirit had promised that he would not die before he saw the Messiah. That's why he came to the temple that day: The Spirit told him to.

When Mary and Joseph showed up to present Jesus, Simeon took the child in his arms and prayed. "Master, now you are dismissing your servant in peace, according to your word; for my eyes have seen your salvation, which you have prepared in the presence of all peoples, a light for revelation to the Gentiles and for glory to your people Israel" (verses 29–32).

We sense the satisfaction of a promise fulfilled. A life lived in hope has been vindicated. What's especially interesting is Simeon's reference to the Gentiles. Here in the Jewish temple, in the midst of a Jewish rite, this devout Jew speaks of the Messiah enlightening the non-Jews of the world. He didn't make this up. It comes straight out of Isaiah's messianic prophecies (see Isaiah 42:6; 49:6).

But then Simeon became a prophet himself, turning to Mary and saying, "This child is destined for the falling and the rising of many in Israel, and to be a sign that will be opposed so that the inner thoughts of many will be revealed—and a sword will pierce your own soul too" (Luke 2:34–35).

What was this "sword" that would pierce Mary's soul? We can only imagine how difficult it was to bring up the young Messiah, culminating in that gruesome scene at Golgotha, where Mary's child died for the sins of the world.

The Book of Ruth

DURING THE TUMULT and war that marked the period of Israel's judges (late second millennium B.C.), the Book of Ruth shows the lives of ordinary folk trying to live in peace. It makes no claims regarding authorship, but it must have been written during or after King David's reign (1010–970 B.C.), since his name closes the book (Ruth 4:22). The narrative is a skillfully written short story, with its focus on the problems of widowed women fending for themselves.

During the conflicts of the time and an accompanying famine, a small Israelite family was forced to migrate to neighboring Moab to find food. When the husband and sons of the family died there, Naomi and her Moabite daughters-in-law, Ruth and Orpah, were left to take care of themselves. To find family support, Naomi decides to return to Israel, and Ruth is determined to accompany her, leaving her own home and embracing Naomi's faith. Ruth looked after Naomi in Israel by gathering leftover grain. One of the fields she visited was owned by a relative, Boaz, who took an interest in her, offering protection and special treatment.

An Israelite practice sought to help the unfortunate: A near male relative (the "redeemer") was obliged to pursue the welfare of a hurting family member (see Leviticus 25:48–49), and in the case of a man dying childless, a relative would have a child by the wife, preserving the family name and inheritance (see Deuteronomy 25:5–10). Naomi's nearest eligible relative refused to help in this way (Ruth 4:1–8), so Boaz agreed to fulfill the obligations. He showed not only family loyalty but also a special love for the foreign girl Ruth. Their union was blessed with children, and they became the great-grandparents of King David (verse 17) and ultimately ancestors of Jesus (Matthew 1:5–6).

POSTSCRIPT

- Naomi's two sons who died at the beginning of the story are appropriately named *Mahlon* ("wiped out" or "sickly") and *Chilion* ("perishing" or "on his last legs").

- The grain Ruth gleaned was that which the harvesters had overlooked, making it available for those in need. This was a form of Israelite unemployment insurance to help the poor (Deuteronomy 24:19–22).

- A key concept modeled in the book is that of *chesed,* true acts of loyalty and love that should characterize every family and the faithfulness of every covenant relationship. It is shown by Ruth toward Naomi and in turn by Boaz to Ruth.

Torah

T HIS WORD FOR THE HEBREW Scriptures is often translated "law," but its meaning is much broader. We should think of it as "teaching" or "guidance."

Originally, *Torah* referred to the first five books of the Hebrew Scriptures, the books of Moses (also known as the Pentateuch). These books have a cherished position in the Jewish faith as the earliest written instruction given by God through Moses. Over time, the messages of the prophets were collected, as well as other literary works. All of these books are revered as God's Word, and in a general sense they might be referred to as Torah, but the books of Moses retained a special level of honor.

Jesus often mentioned "the law [and] the prophets" (Matthew 5:17). These were the two main divisions of Hebrew Scripture at the time—the Torah of Moses and the collection of prophetic books *(Nabiim)*. Technically, there was a third section that eventually became known as "the Writings" *(Kethubim)*, but this was often regarded as part of "the Prophets" (at the time, there was debate about which of "the Writings" should be included as Scripture).

Jesus once commented that "everything written about me in the law of Moses, the prophets, and the psalms must be fulfilled" (Luke 24:44). Considering that the psalms are the major component of "the Writings," Jesus was citing the three divisions of Hebrew Scripture that are still distinguished today.

The Torah was so respected in ancient Israel that a whole profession arose around it. By the fourth century B.C., and possibly quite earlier, scribes were employed to copy the sacred texts. They developed intricate rules to ensure the accuracy of their work, even counting the letters on each line. By Jesus' time, scribes were not only copyists but also Bible scholars.

Yet in Jewish thinking, God's instruction doesn't stop with the ancient written words. There's a rich appreciation in Judaism of the oral traditions passed down through the ages. In this sense, the word *Torah* is expanded to mean the entire Jewish faith—the way of life transmitted through the centuries. With this in mind, the term can also include the sayings of the sages and scholars collected in the *Talmud* (the authoritative body of Jewish tradition).

Herod's Reign of Terror

WHEN THE MAGI came to Herod's palace, they may well have had a large enough entourage that King Herod paid the utmost attention to them. If the "king of the Jews" were truly alive, such news would not be good in retaining his strict authority over the people in his kingdom. King Herod would need to move quickly: Any political rival would need to be killed. According to Matthew 2:16, Herod commanded his troops to murder all boys two years and younger in or near Bethlehem.

Herod the Great and his ancestors had Jewish connections, and he seems to have thought of himself as an observant Jew. He even was involved in the expansion of the temple and the Temple Mount in Jerusalem. Nevertheless, the Jews despised and distrusted him, frequently calling him a puppet king for the Romans, who had assigned him a territory over which he was allowed to rule. Because he was born around 75 B.C. and died around 4 B.C., his mention in the Gospel of Luke has raised questions among Christians and non-Christians alike as to whether the traditional dating of Jesus' life might be off by about four years.

The ruthlessness of Herod, however, has not been questioned. The "massacre of the innocents" related in Matthew 2 is not described in any sources other than Matthew, but most historians see that atrocity as consistent with the kind of actions that characterized his rule. The Jewish historian Josephus informs his readers that Herod killed some of his own children, his wife, and his brother-in-law, all of whom he saw as potential rivals to the throne. He also murdered a high priest and put to death a number of the members of the Sanhedrin.

The Gospel of Matthew says Mary and Joseph took no chances. After Joseph was warned in a dream of Herod's intentions, they took Jesus to Egypt, where they were able to avoid Herod's wrath. Shortly thereafter, Herod himself died. Jesus returned from Egypt, and a new kingdom began to emerge in ways that Herod himself never would have understood or recognized.

POSTSCRIPT

■ Herod was well known for his building projects, ranging from the second temple to fortresses (such as Masada and the Herodium) to the establishment of new cities (such as Caesarea Maratima).

■ In September 2007, Israeli archaeologists announced the discovery of a quarry within a Jerusalem suburb that had provided Herod with the stones used in his building projects.

The Sons of God and the Daughters of Men

ONE OF THE MORE enigmatic episodes in the Bible is when "the sons of God went in to the daughters of humans, who bore children to them" (Genesis 6:4) in the time immediately prior to the great Flood, which destroyed the world. On the surface, this appears to tell of a mixing of divine and human races, with semidivine beings as the offspring, triggering God's displeasure and his near-destruction of the human race in the Flood.

Three explanations have been advanced to explain this story. A first approach argues that this is indeed what happened: Divine beings (possibly angels) mated with humans, resulting in giant offspring who were called the "Nephilim." The Bible states, however, that the Nephilim were "warriors of renown," and that they lived during the time in which this story unfolds—not that they were the offspring of a divine-human union. In addition, Jesus stated that angels in heaven do not marry, making this explanation less likely (see Matthew 22:30).

A second approach sees the "sons of God" as ancient dynastic rulers who took wives from among commoners. Some support for this is found elsewhere in Scripture, where the Davidic kings are seen as "sons of God" with God as their "father." The choosing of wives, however, is a weak catalyst for the great punishment that was to follow in the Flood.

A third approach is perhaps the most logical, since it best explains the immediate consequence of the Flood. This approach notes that, immediately preceding the story of these sons of God and daughters of humans, we find two genealogies: The first lists an "ungodly" line descending from Cain (who killed his brother Abel) down to Lamech (who insisted that he be avenged 70-fold for perceived slights), while the second shows a "godly" line descending from Seth (the son born to Adam and Eve after Abel was killed) down to the righteous Noah. In this understanding, then, the problem was the intermingling of the godly line of Seth (the "sons of God") and the ungodly line of Cain (the "daughters of humans").

Regardless of the specific explanation of who these "sons of God" were, it is clear that humans had greatly displeased God by this time. God's patience had run thin, for he saw that "the wickedness of humankind was great in the earth, and that every inclination of the thoughts of their hearts was only evil continually" (Genesis 6:5). Because human depravity deeply grieved God, he resolved to destroy the human race, except for Noah and his family.

Lot

ABRAHAM'S NEPHEW Lot was a foolish and self-centered man. He migrated with his grandfather Terah, his uncle Abraham, and others from Ur of the Chaldeans in Mesopotamia to the land of Canaan, where he encountered many troubles, some of his own making.

The initial story involving Lot shows Abraham offering him first choice of land in Canaan. Lot chose a fertile plain in the Jordan Valley near the Dead Sea. He and his family and livestock settled in Sodom, one of the cities there. This was a foolish choice; as the Bible says, "The people of Sodom were wicked, great sinners against the Lord" (Genesis 13:13).

Next, Lot managed to get captured by a Mesopotamian coalition of kings, but Abraham came to his rescue. Later, God sent messengers to Abraham to announce that he was going to destroy Sodom. Abraham, knowing that Lot lived there, bargained with God, asking him not to destroy the city if 50 righteous people could be found there. The number dropped down to ten, but as the city held not even that many righteous people, Sodom was doomed.

Before the city's destruction, two men (who were angels) visited Lot. The men of Sodom came to his house and demanded that he surrender these men to them, "so that we may know them" (Genesis 19:5). Lot recognized that the Sodomites' intent was to have sexual relations with his guests, and so, in a stunning gesture, he offered them his two daughters instead. The angelic visitors put an end to this episode by blinding the Sodomites.

When destruction came upon Sodom and its sister "cities of the plain," fire rained down from heaven—but Lot had escaped. Even Abraham from a distance saw "the smoke of the land going up like the smoke of a furnace" (verse 28). As Lot and his family fled the city, Lot's wife turned back to look   something the angels had expressly told them not to do—and she was turned into a pillar of salt.

The last time we hear of Lot, his two daughters get him drunk and have incestuous relations with him, resulting in their pregnancies. One daughter's son was Moab and the other's was Ben-ammi; from these sons came the Moabites and the Ammonites—later fierce enemies of Israel.

POSTSCRIPT

■ The region of the Dead Sea is a forbidding place: The Sea itself is so full of salt and other minerals that it does not support any life forms (hence its name). In the Bible, it is called the "Salt Sea."

The Last Supper

THE DEFINING MOMENT in Israel's history came when God freed the people from slavery in Egypt. A series of plagues struck their Egyptian captors, culminating in the Angel of Death killing their firstborn. Prior to this last plague, Moses had told the Israelites to prepare a dinner of roast lamb. The angel would "pass over" the Israelite houses with the blood of the lamb on their doorposts.

Ever since, pious Jews have celebrated this feast, remembering the plagues, the deliverance, and the miraculous crossing of the Red Sea. When Jesus came to Jerusalem late in his ministry, it was at Passover. As the rabbi of his traveling band, he had to make arrangements for the Passover meal.

He sent two disciples to follow a man with a water jug to his house in order to prepare the Passover meal there. Why the cloak-and-dagger? Jesus' enemies were looking for a quiet time to arrest him. Surely Jesus knew the arrest would happen and that Judas was involved in it. He wanted this meal to happen first.

The Last Supper
by Titian

As his disciples arrived for the celebration, Jesus took the role of servant, kneeling to wash their dusty feet. Characteristically, Peter balked at this humble act, but he gave in. No doubt they continued with the rituals of the Passover meal with its cups of wine and its loaves of bread. To this day, every bit of food in that meal means something about God's deliverance of Israel.

Jesus then announced that one of the disciples would betray him, causing a wave of denial. He narrowed it down to Judas, who quickly left, but the meal continued. In his now familiar words, Jesus took bread and called it his body. He took wine and called it his blood. As he shared these ritual elements, Jesus gave them a new meaning, which he called a new covenant—that is, a new way that God would deliver his people.

As the meal progressed, Jesus taught his disciples about what would happen next. He would send them a Counselor, a Spirit of Truth, to help them. They needed to love one another. After singing a traditional Passover hymn, probably from Psalms 115 to 118, they went to the Garden of Gethsemane for prayer.

Anna, the Prophet

ANNA WAS A PROPHET who encountered the baby Jesus at the Jerusalem temple. Her praise and testimony about the Christ child seconded the prophecy of Simeon.

Jesus was probably a little more than a month old when Mary and Joseph took him to the temple. There was a purification ritual for Mary to go through, and they needed to present their firstborn child to the Lord, offering a sacrifice of turtledoves.

In the temple, they were met by a man named Simeon, who took the child in his arms, prayed, and then spoke a poignant prophecy to Mary. While he was still speaking, an elderly woman named Anna came up to them, praising God. Like Simeon, Anna appears in this story out of nowhere. She's mentioned only in this three-verse section of Luke's gospel (Luke 2:36–38), but we get a rather vivid picture of her.

Anna had been a widow for a long time. Her husband had died after only seven years of marriage, and she never remarried. She was 84 when she saw Jesus in the temple, so we can guess she had lived six decades as a widow. She's identified as "the daughter of Phanuel," which might indicate that she went back to live with her parents once her husband died. It also says she "never left the temple but worshiped there with fasting and prayer night and day" (Luke 2:37), so we might guess that after her parents died she came under the care of the religious establishment. (Offerings of devout Jews went to support religious workers, foreigners, widows, and orphans. See Deuteronomy 26:12.)

We're not told exactly what she said to Mary or Joseph or what the specific content of her praise was. But after seeing the baby Jesus, she began to "speak about the child to all who were looking for the redemption of Jerusalem" (verse 38). In a similar phrase, Simeon is said to be "looking for the consolation of Israel" (verse 25). It seems that there were a number of these hopeful Jews, expecting God to comfort his people. Anna's praise erupted in excited evangelism.

POSTSCRIPT

■ The name *Anna* is a Greek form of a Hebrew word meaning "grace."

■ It's no surprise that Luke tells Anna's story as a complement to Simeon's. More than the other gospel writers, Luke includes the experience and testimony of women.

The Books of 1 and 2 Samuel

TRACING THE HISTORY of Israel in its major political transition from being ruled by judges to being ruled by kings, First and Second Samuel narrate some of the best-known stories in the Old Testament. These two books passed through many hands, reaching final form as part of the national history that runs from Joshua through Kings, to the fall of Jerusalem at the hands of Babylonia in 586 B.C. They describe events occurring over a century (c. 1075–975 B.C.).

The books open with the birth and godly life of Samuel, who even as a lad was open to hearing God's Word (1 Samuel 1—3). He was a prophet and priest who countered not only religious corruption but also Israelite fears of growing military threats. The Israelites demanded that they have a king like the kings of their neighboring nations. After showing reluctance, Samuel followed God's instruction, appointing Saul as king by anointing him with oil. Saul led Israel to military success, but he repeatedly acted inappropriately, finally losing the throne and his life (8—15).

God subsequently directed Samuel to appoint a new king, David, who had shown his power and skill by defeating the Philistine giant Goliath and surviving Saul's attempts on his life (16—31). After Saul's death and a struggle for the rule over all twelve tribes with Saul's son, Ishbaal, David became king, uniting neighboring states through either conquest or alliance (2 Samuel 1—21). Second Samuel closes with several of David's poems (22:1—23:7), which are more fully represented in the Book of Psalms, various stories about David's closest fighting men, and events toward the end of his life (23:8—24:25).

An important theme through these books is that God is ultimately Israel's king. Human rulers need to be mindful that they are his delegates and that God can remove their rule. The use and abuse of power plays a key role in these books.

POSTSCRIPT

■ Anointing with oil was a symbolic action used to dedicate priests and kings. Anointed to faithfully serve God, both Saul and David fell far short of what was expected of a true "anointed one" (in Hebrew, "messiah"). This human anointing anticipated the coming of the true king and priest, who is ultimately identified by the Greek "Christ" (also meaning "anointed").

■ Israelite writers do not whitewash Israel's heroes. They do not paint them only in a good light. Saul was disobedient to God; even David, Israel's greatest king, was an adulterer and murderer (see 2 Samuel 11). God does not wait for perfection but for the willingness to obey.

The Hebrew Language

ONE OF THE FIRST THINGS an English-speaking student of the Hebrew language notices is that it reads backward. (Or maybe English is written backward.) Hebrew reads from right to left, unlike English and other Western languages. Other Middle Eastern languages, such as Arabic, Syriac, and Urdu, share Hebrew's direction, and no one knows why.

Some scholars point out that most people are right-handed, and so it makes sense to start on the side where your dominant hand is. It may also have to do with the way letters were made when the language developed. If you were carving in stone, your left hand would hold the chisel while your right hand wielded the hammer (if you were right-handed), so you'd move right to left to see what you had written. But if you were pressing a wedge into clay, as in ancient cuneiform tablets, you might move left to right so your hand wouldn't continually mess up the marks you had just made (and in fact cuneiform is written left to right).

Hebrew is part of the Semitic family of languages developed early in the Middle East. Specifically it's designated as a northwestern Semitic language and a Canaanite dialect.

Another feature of Hebrew writing is that it comprises only consonants. Vowels are pronounced, of course, but early Hebrew had no markings for them. You would recognize a word by its consonants and just know how to say it. Around the fifth century A.D., Jewish scribes developed a system of "pointing"—tiny marks around the consonants to indicate which vowel sound should follow.

Why no vowels? Because Hebrew is a very old language, not far removed from the pictograms of Egyptian hieroglyphics or the syllabic symbols of cuneiform.

Hebrew is a concrete language. With nouns and simple verbs, the Hebrew language observes more than it analyzes. This makes it highly imagistic and richly poetic.

POSTSCRIPT

In the 1970s, archaeologists discovered thousands of ancient tablets at the site of the old city of Ebla. Dating back to the third millennium B.C., these were written in a language that might have been a Canaanite precursor to Hebrew.

The Dedication of Jesus

IN LUKE 2:21–40, Jesus is circumcised and named. Then after Mary, his mother, goes through a time of purification, she and Joseph, her husband, take Jesus to the temple in Jerusalem to be presented to the Lord. "As it is written in the law of the Lord, 'Every firstborn male shall be designated as holy to the Lord,' and they offered a sacrifice according to what is stated in the law of the Lord: 'a pair of turtledoves or two young pigeons'" (verses 23–24).

Jesus and his parents are presented as faithful Jews—people who recognize the significance of the Torah and the temple. Jesus would have been "redeemed" (through an offering given for the firstborn), and then he would have been dedicated or consecrated to God. Just as Samuel's mother had dedicated him (see 1 Samuel 1:21–28), so Mary is seen in a comparable light. She had recognized Jesus' special calling even before his birth.

What initially seems like a simple, traditional ceremony, however, soon takes on a kind of ominous tone. A devout Jew named Simeon was waiting in the temple courts because it had been revealed to him that he would not die until he saw the Christ. When Joseph and Mary arrive, Simeon holds Jesus, acknowledging him as the fulfillment of the messianic prophecy.

In his prayer to the Lord, Simeon says, "Master, you are dismissing your servant in peace, according to your word; for my eyes have seen your salvation, which you have prepared in the presence of all peoples, a light for revelation to the Gentiles and for glory to your people Israel" (Luke 2:29–32). Jesus' parents marvel at his prophetic statement, but Simeon goes on to say that some of the consequences of the good news will be quite troubling. He warns Mary, "A sword will pierce your own soul too" (verse 35).

An elderly prophet named Anna—a woman who resided in the temple— also spoke words similar to those of Simeon. For all who were hopeful for the redemption of Jerusalem, she spoke to this child.

It was a long day. It was a special day. And no doubt those words—"A sword will pierce your own soul too"—portended a troubling future to Mary.

The Great Flood

GOD BROUGHT ON a great flood to "blot out" humanity because of widespread wickedness. It was a great tragedy that Adam and Eve's rebellion against God had snowballed to the point where the earth was completely corrupted and "filled with violence" (Genesis 6:11). Such wickedness deeply grieved God, and he even regretted having created humankind. Thus he resolved to wipe the slate clean and to put in place a new creation, so to speak, starting over with Noah's family and the animals to be saved in the ark.

We do not know why God specifically chose Noah, other than that he "found favor in the sight of the Lord" and "walked with God" (verses 8, 9). In any case, the ark became a symbol of God's grace in that it preserved both the human race and animals. God's grace is seen at the climax and turning point of the story, when the flood waters reached their highest point: Here we read that "God remembered Noah" (Genesis 8:1) along with all the animals. After this, the flood waters receded.

God had told Noah to take with him two of every kind of animal and bird—male and female—and seven pairs of the clean animals, some of which were for sacrifices.

While the waters receded, Noah first released a raven, and then he sent out a dove three times. At first, the dove returned immediately; next, it brought back an olive branch; the third time, it did not return.

After the Flood, Noah built an altar and sacrificed some of the clean animals and birds to God, who accepted the offering as a "pleasing odor." God then vowed never again to "destroy every living creature as I have done" (verse 21). God designated the rainbow as the sign of this promise.

Noah represented a "new Adam" in being the one (along with his wife, three sons, and their wives) who would repopulate the earth. God repeated to Noah what he had said to Adam: He should "be fruitful and multiply, and fill the earth" (Genesis 9:1).

Hagar

HAGAR WAS AN EGYPTIAN slave who served Sarah. Presumably she became the property of Abraham and Sarah when they were in Egypt. Quite possibly, the pharaoh had given Hagar to Sarah when Sarah became a member of his harem.

When Sarah believed she could not have a child, she gave Hagar to her husband so that he could father an heir through her slave. After Hagar conceived, Hagar regarded her mistress "with contempt" (Genesis 16:4). When Sarah appealed to Abraham to intervene, he gave her free rein to treat Hagar as she wished, and so Sarah "dealt harshly with her," causing Hagar to flee into the desert (verse 6).

In the desert, an angel of the Lord came to her and told her to return to her mistress. The angel promised that her offspring would be so numerous that they could not be counted and that she would bear a son from the seed of Abraham, whom she should call *Ishmael* (which means "God hears"). She obeyed and returned to Abraham's household, and Ishmael was born.

Some years later, Sarah bore her own son, Isaac. On the day that Isaac's weaning was being celebrated with a grand feast, Sarah saw Ishmael and Isaac playing together, which upset her. So she told Abraham to cast Hagar and Ishmael from their camp. After the Lord assured Abraham that he would protect his oldest son, Abraham reluctantly complied with Sarah's demand. He provided Hagar with meager rations—some bread and a skin of water—and sent her away.

Hagar and her son subsequently wandered in the wilderness of Beersheba. When the water was gone, she prepared to die, placing her child under bushes so she wouldn't have to watch him perish. But an angel of the Lord appeared to her again and promised her a great nation through her son. The angel then showed her a nearby well.

Ishmael grew up in the wilderness, and Hagar found a wife for him from her Egyptian homeland. Her son grew up to father a great nation.

POSTSCRIPT

■ In ancient Near Eastern law and custom, a child born to a slave was legally the "son" of the slave's mistress. This explains why Sarah gave her slave, Hagar, to Abraham to bear a child. Ishmael was legally Sarah's son.

Betrayal in the Garden

THE GREEN MOUNT of Olives sits across a narrow valley from the Temple Mount and the walled city of Jerusalem. In Jesus' day, the olive grove known as Gethsemane would have provided a great view of the city. In the evening, during Passover, torchlight probably dotted the vista. This was apparently a favorite prayer spot for Jesus, set between the city and his friends' home in Bethany.

Jesus came to the Garden of Gethsemane with his disciples after the Last Supper. As he often did, Jesus selected his three closest disciples, Peter, James, and John, to accompany him away from the others. He then withdrew even from the three of them to pray privately. This was intense prayer, as he begged his Father to try another plan. Yet he concluded, "Not what I want, but what you want" (Matthew 26:39). He repeated this prayer not once but twice, which indicates the tortured agony he endured, knowing what was soon in store for him.

Judas arrived with a retinue of the Temple Guard. Matthew calls them a "large crowd with clubs and swords" (verse 47). If the disciples had been awake, they might have seen the torches snaking their way up the hillside. Even then, Jesus might have fled upward, over the mountain and into the desert, but that was not God's plan.

A kiss from Judas identified Jesus as the man to be arrested. (It was night, and the soldiers probably hadn't seen Jesus up close before.) Peter swung a sword and sliced off the ear of a servant named Malchus, but Jesus reprimanded Peter, saying, "All who take the sword will perish by the sword" (verse 52). Jesus then healed Malchus (John 18:10). In all the chaos, it seems the soldiers made a halfhearted attempt to arrest the disciples, who scattered. Mark tells of a young man (possibly Mark himself) who was nabbed but ran out of his clothes. The soldiers had their main quarry and apparently let the others go. Even the sword-wielding Peter got away.

Yet Jesus maintained calm. "Have you come out with swords and clubs to arrest me as though I were a bandit? Day after day I was with you in the temple teaching, and you did not arrest me" (Mark 14:48–49). Further bloodshed in the garden was avoided as they took Jesus to his trial.

POSTSCRIPT

■ Jesus had predicted that the disciples would scatter, and Peter had contradicted him: "Even though all become deserters, I will not" (verse 29). That might explain why he followed the arrested Jesus, at least as far as the courtyard.

Peter

Simon Peter was a fisherman who became one of Jesus' closest disciples and a leader of the early Church. His impetuous behavior and unrehearsed comments provided Jesus with many teaching opportunities. We get a stunning picture of divine grace in Peter's denial of the crucified Jesus and his restoration by the resurrected Savior.

St. Peter *by Goya*

Peter had several important encounters with the Master. When Jesus was walking on the water toward the disciples' boat, it was Peter who jumped out and began to walk toward Jesus—then got distracted and sank. When Jesus washed the disciples' feet, it was Peter who refused to let the Lord do such a menial task—and was reprimanded.

Perhaps his most important exchange occurred when Jesus asked the disciples who they thought he was. Peter answered, "You are the Messiah, the Son of the living God" (Matthew 16:16). Jesus enthusiastically affirmed that response, saying that upon this "rock"—either Peter himself or his statement of faith—the Church would be built. Matthew, however, next records how Peter soon after went too far, discouraging Jesus from his plan to travel to Jerusalem and be crucified. "Get behind me, Satan!" (verse 23) was Jesus' sharp retort.

Though he claimed that he would never desert Jesus, even if everyone else did, Peter succumbed to cowardice when Jesus was crucified. He was near Jesus' trial, and when bystanders recognized him as Jesus' disciple, he denied the Lord three times. In spite of Peter's betrayal, Jesus made a point of reinstating Peter after his resurrection. Beside the Sea of Galilee, he commissioned Peter to "feed my sheep."

Peter spoke for the disciples at Pentecost and became a leader of the growing Church. As time went on, other Church leaders emerged, and Peter seemed to assume the role of elder statesman. He ended up in Rome and was martyred in the first major persecution, launched by Emperor Nero.

POSTSCRIPT

- According to church tradition, Peter was crucified upside down, because he considered himself unworthy to die in the same way as Jesus.

- Not only did Peter write two New Testament epistles, but tradition also says he was the main source for Mark's gospel.

The Books of 1 and 2 Kings

THE BOOKS OF KINGS trace Israel's history over four centuries from David's death to Judah's exile in Babylonia (c. 970–560 B.C.). Using material from royal archives and other sources, they were compiled during the exile. The historical narrative focuses on people and events on the national and international stage—important folk such as kings, queens, and prophets, as well as Israel's powerful neighbors in Syria, Mesopotamia, and Egypt. These books present Israel's history as proceeding in waves, with the peaks of a few good kings rising between the more frequent troughs of bad ones. Both are judged by whether or not they followed God.

First Kings opens with the story started in Second Samuel in which King David passes away and Solomon is installed on the throne (1 Kings 1—2). Solomon's wise rule included building activities, one being Israel's temple in Jerusalem. His great gains, however, ended with failure when he married a number of pagan women and increasingly turned away from the Lord (3—11). Upon Solomon's death (730 B.C.), the kingdom of Israel split into two nations: Judah (with its capital, Jerusalem) in the south under the rule of the descendants of David and the larger Israel (with its capital, Samaria) in the north under the rule of others.

The history of the two separate nations flowed side by side until 722 B.C., when Samaria fell to Assyria and Israel came to an end. Judah then was on its own until it fell to Babylonia in 586 B.C. Their stories are important in their own right, but doubly useful since they provide a backdrop for some of Israel's most powerful religious/political leaders—the prophets. One of them, Elijah, was key in preserving worship of Israel's God, Yahweh, when King Ahab and Queen Jezebel tried to get Israel to follow the Canaanite god Baal. Both books of Kings show why Israel deserved exile, since almost every ruler turned against the covenant with God.

POSTSCRIPT

- The books of Kings seem to have a pro-Judah slant, deeming good some kings of Judah but not one good king of Israel.
- Episodes surrounding Elijah have more space in Kings (1 Kings 17:1—2 Kings 2:25) than those of any other person except for Solomon.
- Hezekiah had to destroy the bronze serpent, which was a means of saving Hebrew lives at the time of Moses (see Numbers 21:1–9), since the people had been worshipping it for centuries (see 2 Kings 18:4).
- Of the 20 kings of Judah, six were co-kings for a period with their fathers.

The Septuagint

WHEN ALEXANDER THE GREAT swept through the Middle East in the fourth century B.C., he brought the Greek language with him. Though he himself was a Macedonian, he had a great love for Greek philosophy and culture (possibly instilled by his tutor, Aristotle). The great cities of Persia, Syria, Egypt, and even Israel were remodeled on Greek forms, with Greek entertainment, education, and government. In international business, Greek was the common tongue.

Jerusalem resisted this influence more than most cities but was eventually swept along with the tide. Yet the Hebrew language was preserved in the deeply entrenched religion of the Jews. Meanwhile, more and more Jews were living outside of Israel in cities throughout the Mediterranean world. In the five or six centuries before Christ, invasions and famines had caused a scattering (diaspora) of many Jews to other territories. These emigrants would learn the language of their new home, which after Alexander's time was generally Greek. Many forgot Hebrew.

Recognizing this reality, Jewish scholars launched a project to translate the Hebrew Scriptures into Greek. Tradition says a team of 70 scholars accomplished this in Alexandria, Egypt, calling the translation the Septuagint, which means "seventy." The reality is less compact. Alexandria is the likely site of this endeavor, for it was the historical focal point of the integration of Jewish faith and Greek scholarship. And the work itself is obviously the product of multiple translators with different styles. But, while a team of 70 might have started the effort, it probably took several generations to complete. It is thought that the books of Moses were finished in the third century B.C. and the rest over a long period that followed.

We know the Septuagint was being used by the first century A.D. In fact, it was a major boon to the spread of Christianity. As the Apostle Paul and others moved through the Mediterranean world, they went first to synagogues, where they would preach about Jesus as the fulfillment of Jewish prophecy. Then they would welcome Gentiles into an integrated church. Their text was the Septuagint, accepted by Jews and understood by Gentiles.

POSTSCRIPT

■ Most New Testament quotations of Old Testament passages come from the Septuagint.

■ In scholarly works, the abbreviation for the Septuagint is LXX, the Roman numeral for 70.

Raised in Nazareth

Although the Gospels of Matthew and Luke point to Bethlehem as the city in which Jesus was born, Nazareth—the home of Joseph and Mary—seems to have been the town in which Jesus was raised. Nazareth was in Galilee, about 15 miles west of the Sea of Galilee and about six miles west of Mount Tabor. Several main trade routes passed close enough to Nazareth that the people there would have had contact with the outside world.

There are signs that people during the time of Jesus were familiar with Nazareth. According to the Gospel of John, when Jesus started his ministry, he found a man named Philip and said, "Follow me" (John 1:43). Philip then went to Nathanael and told him, "We have found him about whom Moses in the law and also the prophets wrote—Jesus son of Joseph from Nazareth" (verse 45).

Nathanael's only response was "Can anything good come out of Nazareth?" (verse 46).

So although people were familiar with Nazareth, maybe it was not seen as all that spectacular—at least not in Nathanael's eyes. What he meant, however, is not entirely clear. On the one hand, he may have been referring to its small size. Archaeologists have not been able to find any ancient Jewish sources that mention Nazareth. Because the earliest non-biblical mention of Nazareth is from the third century A.D., some believe Nazareth was a small backwater town when Jesus grew up there.

On the other hand, maybe Nathanael's reference reflects a commentary on the people of Nazareth themselves. According to the gospels, the people in his hometown did not accept Jesus as a rabbi with authority. In fact, they looked at him with animosity. The Gospel of Luke says they saw Jesus as impious, and so they took him to the brow of a hill intending to throw him off the side of a cliff (see Luke 4:29).

Nathanael asked, "Can anything good come out of Nazareth?" Maybe the answer was still up in the air. But Philip replied with a simple invitation: "Come and see" (John 1:46).

POSTSCRIPT

■ Nazareth is not mentioned in the Old Testament, in the Apocrypha, or in early rabbinic writings.

The Tower of Babel

AFTER THE GREAT FLOOD, God blessed Noah and his sons, saying, "Be fruitful and multiply, and fill the earth" (Genesis 9:1). This was a means by which to repopulate the earth and ensure a rich diversity of peoples across its entire face.

The story of the tower of Babel, however, shows humanity resisting God's mandate and seeking to be one people in one place. After migrating westward, people settled in the land of Shinar, the ancient area of Babylonia, roughly corresponding to modern-day Iraq. There, they proposed to erect a city, along with "a tower with its top in the heavens," in order to "make a name" for themselves (Genesis 11:4).

Tower of Babel—Confusion of Languages *by Gilberto Guarnati*

This desire to make a name for themselves contrasted with a time before Noah, when "people began to invoke the name of the Lord" (Genesis 4:26). Human pride asserted itself over and against the worship of God. Ironically, Genesis notes that God had to come down to see this city and tower that was supposed to reach into the heavens. Despite grandiose plans, this city and tower appeared puny in comparison with God and all that he had created.

Previously, when human sin had reached a breaking point, God had destroyed most living things with the Flood. Now, in contrast, he was much gentler. He confounded the humans' plans by confusing their language so that they could not understand each other. As a result, they were scattered across the face of the earth, which, ironically, was what God had wanted in the first place.

A final irony is the Hebrew name given to this city: *Babel.* This name sounds like the Hebrew word for "confused" *(balal),* a marked contrast to the Babylonian name for the city, which was *bab-ilu,* meaning "gate of god." What the humans had so desperately set out to do—make a name for themselves and preserve their unity at all costs—resulted in precisely the opposite: their utter linguistic confusion and dispersal across the face of the earth.

Ishmael

ISHMAEL WAS ABRAHAM's first son, born to his wife Sarah's Egyptian maidservant Hagar. As presented in the Bible, his birth is a symbol of Abraham's and Sarah's lack of faith in God; they doubted God's promise that she would bear him a son. Nevertheless, God was gracious to Ishmael, promising his mother that his descendants would be so great that "they cannot be counted for multitude" (Genesis 16:10).

Because Sarah had been barren, she decided to have a child through her maidservant. When Sarah herself finally bore a son, she demanded that her husband expel Hagar and Ishmael from their camp. Abraham complied even though he loved his son, whom he had circumcised at the age of 13 in obedience to the Lord's command.

Abraham provided Hagar and their son with some bread and a skin of water, but the supplies proved to be inadequate. As the mother and child "wandered about in the wilderness of Beer-sheba" (Genesis 21:14), the water ran out. Hagar left Ishmael under a bush and retreated so that she would not have to see her son die. God did not allow them to die, however. He sent an angel to show them a well of water. Fittingly, Ishmael's name means "God hears," for "God heard the voice of the boy" (verse 17) when he lay dying of thirst.

Ishmael grew up in the wilderness of Paran, married an Egyptian woman, and "became an expert with the bow"—all with God at his side (verse 20). Like his nephew Jacob, he was the father of 12 tribes, and with his brother, Isaac, he buried his father Abraham in the cave of Machpelah (see Genesis 25:9).

The Israelites encounter Ishmael's descendants several times later in Scripture. Joseph's brothers sell him to a traveling group of Ishmaelite traders. The Israelites fight them in the time of the Judges under Gideon. And the Ishmaelites are again mentioned around the time of King David.

POSTSCRIPT

■ It is thought that the Ishmaelites gave rise to the Arab tribes of the Arabian Peninsula. After the rise of Islam (seventh century A.D.), Muslims traced their patronage back to Abraham through Ishmael, called *Ismail* in Arabic.

Peter's Betrayal

PETER, ALSO KNOWN as Simon, often boasted and at times tried to set himself above the other disciples. On several occasions, his rash words earned him reprimands from Jesus—or at least loving corrections. At the Last Supper, Jesus predicted that his disciples would abandon him, but Peter insisted that he would never betray his Lord. Somberly, Jesus told him that before a rooster crowed the next morning, Peter would deny him three times.

Later, when soldiers marched into the Garden of Gethsemane to arrest Jesus, Peter showed his foolishness by swinging a sword. That earned him another reprimand from Jesus, who healed the ear Peter had sliced off from a servant's head. Surprisingly, Peter was not arrested. The other disciples fled, except for John, who had some sort of favor with the high priest.

Jesus' trial took place in the house of Caiaphas, the high priest (see Matthew 26:57). Presumably there was a sizable room where business could be conducted. As in most affluent homes of that era, there was also a courtyard at the entry or center of the home where visitors could wait. John managed to sneak Peter in as far as the courtyard.

Once in the courtyard, Peter was close to the trial, and his sense of danger must have been extreme. When a servant girl recognized him as one of the associates of "Jesus the Galilean," Peter denied it. Later, a second servant girl asked about the connection, and he denied it again. Then someone remarked on his Galilean accent. "I do not know the man!" he said with a curse. Then the rooster crowed. Remembering Jesus' words, Peter went out and "wept bitterly" (see Matthew 26:69–75).

After the Resurrection, when the women found the empty tomb, an angel instructed them to "tell his disciples and Peter" that Jesus would meet them in Galilee (Mark 16:7). There, by the sea Peter knew so well as a fisherman, Jesus had a special conversation with him that seemed to mollify the shame of the denial. Three times Jesus asked Peter to confess his love for him, and each time he commissioned Peter to "feed my sheep" (see John 21). The one who denied Jesus would soon be proclaiming him as "Lord and Messiah" (Acts 2:36). Peter had undergone a miraculous transformation—from a boasting coward to a humble evangelist.

POSTSCRIPT

■ Archaeologists have discovered ruins of a first-century structure that might have been the high priest's home. It has a courtyard directly adjacent to a meeting room.

John, the Beloved

JOHN WAS A CLOSE DISCIPLE of Jesus and a leader of the early Church. He seemed to have a fiery disposition early in life, but later he wrote about Christian love.

John worked in a fishing business with his brother, James, and their father, Zebedee, making a living on the Sea of Galilee. Then Jesus called them to leave their nets and follow him. Later, Jesus called the brothers *Boanerges* (Mark 3:17)—Sons of Thunder—a nickname they apparently earned. Once when a Samaritan village refused to receive Jesus, they asked, "Lord, do you want us to command fire to come down from heaven and consume them?"(Luke 9:54). Jesus said no.

Still, John and his brother soon became part of Jesus' inner circle, along with Peter. Jesus often invited the three of them to join him for crucial moments during his earthly ministry—the raising of Jairus's daughter, the Transfiguration, and the prayer in Gethsemane. Perhaps it was because of this special treatment that James and John dared to ask for places of honor in Jesus' coming kingdom. Jesus explained that the kingdom involved commitment to suffering, not a position of fame.

It seems that John had a lot to learn about Jesus' love. Writing his gospel decades later, John never names himself. Instead, he refers to himself as "the disciple Jesus loved." At first, that might sound like another claim to a special position, but instead he probably is saying that his only claim to fame is the love of Jesus. On one momentous occasion, he saw that love close-up when he stood at the foot of the cross. From the cross, Jesus asked him to care for his mother, Mary, which he faithfully did.

After the risen Jesus ascended to heaven, John teamed with Peter to provide leadership for the growing Church. But then we lose his trail as the Book of Acts veers off into the exploits of Paul. Tradition puts John in Ephesus years later, as a senior elder. While other apostles were martyred during Roman persecutions, John was exiled to the isle of Patmos, where he saw the vision that became the Book of Revelation.

In First John, we see the transformation of this "Son of Thunder" to a disciple of love, whose clear and brilliant theme is presented in his books. "We love," he said, "because he first loved us" (1 John 4:19).

The Books of 1 and 2 Chronicles

T HOUGH THESE BOOKS may be a retelling of the history of Israel, they are told from a different perspective to a different audience—people who needed to be reassured of God's relationship to them. Chronicles presents a condensed version of the history of Israel (starting at Creation and ending at the end of the Babylonian Exile in 539 B.C.) that is also found in Genesis through Second Kings. It runs quickly through this period, beginning with a genealogical list (1 Chronicles 1—9), and then retracing the progress of the period from Israel's first king, Saul (1 Chronicles 10—2 Chronicles 36). This larger section is in narrative form. The work is anonymous but was probably compiled from royal annals and other sources in the fifth and fourth centuries B.C.

The audience of Kings was in exile, wondering what was holding back God's saving hand. If God had promised a perpetual ruler of David's line on the throne in Jerusalem (2 Samuel 7), had he forgotten the promises or were his promises false? The writer shows the Israelites deserved the punishment of exile since they all, even their greatest king, David, had broken God's laws and covenant. But the audience of Chronicles was different. They had been allowed back from exile by the Persians and were facing different problems. How could they, a small remnant, rebuild their ravaged country with so many threatening enemies?

These people did not need to hear words of sin and judgment; they needed blessing and hope. They did not need to hear of David's adultery and murderous behavior, of rebellion by his own son, and of his sin of taking a census (as recorded in 2 Samuel), because they were despondent enough. These events are ignored in Chronicles, which does not deny they happened, but rather the writer chooses to highlight the special relationship that David (one truly after God's "own heart"; 1 Samuel 13:14) and his people had with the Lord. The message was that the God who helped their ancestors take control of the land would help them rebuild it.

POSTSCRIPT

■ When David's men brought water from Bethlehem, his hometown, at great risk to themselves (the town was in enemy hands), he poured the water out (see 1 Chronicles 11:18–19), not because he despised the gift, but because it was so valuable that he could not drink it himself, instead pouring it out as an offering to God.

The Dead Sea Scrolls

IN 1947, ANCIENT SCROLLS were discovered in caves at a place called Qumran near the Dead Sea. Over the next decade, hundreds of manuscripts were found in these caves, dating back to the time of Jesus and earlier. Previously the oldest known manuscripts of the Hebrew Scriptures were dated to A.D. 900, but these scrolls apparently were part of the library of a first-century religious community known as the Essenes. It is thought that they intentionally hid these works before the Romans swept through the area in A.D. 70.

Qumran

The entire text of Isaiah is included in this collection, as well as much of Psalms (and some extra nonbiblical psalms), plus portions of every Old Testament book except Esther. Some of the manuscripts date back to 250 B.C. There are also guidebooks on the rules of the Essene community.

This was an enormous gift to biblical studies. Primarily, it allowed experts to assemble a more accurate Hebrew text of Scripture, far closer to the original writings than the medieval Hebrew (Masoretic) text. While there are minor discrepancies, the Masoretic text is amazingly similar to the Dead Sea Scrolls, though as much as a millennium passed between them. (For instance, in the entire text of Isaiah, only 13 substantial changes were found.) In many cases, the Dead Sea Scrolls shed new light on confusing phrases or references.

The information on the Essene community at Qumran helped with New Testament studies as well. Though it is not explicitly mentioned in the New Testament, many scholars think that John the Baptist was connected with this strict sect. Most interesting are the references in the Dead Sea Scrolls to the community's messianic expectations. They were looking for a prophet like Elijah, a king like David, and a priest like Aaron. Of course, the New Testament describes Jesus in all those ways.

POSTSCRIPT

■ The finding of the Dead Sea Scrolls is something of an adventure story. Bedouin herdsmen were throwing rocks at an opening in a cliff. They heard a jar break and went into the cave to explore, discovering ten earthenware vessels with several ancient manuscripts inside. They sold these scrolls to an antique dealer in Bethlehem. The texts eventually found their way to a monastery and a scholar, who determined their breathtaking value.

Jesus, the Carpenter

WHAT JESUS DID AS a carpenter is not entirely clear, but such vagueness has not curtailed speculation, not just in modern novels and movies, but also in some ancient gospels that never became a part of the New Testament canon. The Infancy Gospel of James, for example, describes Joseph at work on an out-of-town building project when Mary first hears that she will be delivering a baby. Joseph is seen as the kind of carpenter who is working on a construction project. Conversely, the Infancy Gospel of Thomas presents Jesus, between the ages of five and twelve, as working with his earthly father in a carpentry shop. In fantasy-filled stories, Jesus is pictured as miraculously stretching wooden boards and planks that were too short for Joseph's projects.

Beyond all the speculation, what we do know is that the earliest gospel, Mark, presents people in Jesus' hometown referring to him as a carpenter (Mark 6:3). What is interesting is that Matthew 13:55—written probably a decade after Mark—seems to be familiar with Mark, but does not speak of Jesus as a carpenter. Matthew notes, rather, that Jesus' earthly father, Joseph, was a carpenter (see 13:55).

Some biblical commentators have explained this difference between the gospels by saying that Matthew might have been reluctant to present Jesus in a position that would have been seen as menial. At the same time, it is not at all unreasonable that Jesus' earthly father would have had strong influence on him and that Jesus would have made a humble living with a profession familiar to him.

Ancient sources note that carpenters and woodworkers did not earn a great amount of money, nor did they have steady employment. Maybe Jesus repaired boats by the Sea of Galilee. Maybe he was involved with building projects. Maybe he built gates, yokes, or "a house upon the rock." Maybe he made repairs. Maybe he built from scratch. At this point, such conjectures remain speculation.

POSTSCRIPT

- Carpenters during Jesus' day also worked with stone and metal.
- Carpenters' tools such as adzes (an all-purpose tool), ax heads, and chisels from this time and region have been recovered.

The Destruction of Sodom

SODOM AND GOMORRAH were the two most prominent cities of a five-city coalition near the Dead Sea in the time of Abraham. The five cities were located in a fertile area of the Jordan Valley, and Abraham's nephew Lot chose to settle in Sodom, despite its established reputation as a wicked city of "great sinners against the Lord" (Genesis 13:13).

The sins of Sodom, and its sister city Gomorrah, were so great that God purposed to destroy them altogether. Abraham, in an impressively large-hearted gesture, bargained with God to spare the cities if there were as few as ten righteous people living there, but not even ten could be found. Only Lot and his wife and two daughters counted as righteous residents of these cities.

The most sordid of Sodom's sins were revealed when the men of Sodom demanded to have sexual relations with two men who were visiting Lot. Their intention was to gang-rape both guests. The two men were in fact angels who had taken human form, and they struck the depraved men of Sodom with blindness in order to frustrate their evil purposes.

Subsequently, God followed through on his intentions and destroyed the five cities in a spectacular display of sulfur and fire coming down from the heavens. The rising smoke was like the black smoke of a furnace. Lot and his family were delivered when the two angels warned them of the impending doom and sent them out of the city with a stern warning not to look back or to stop their flight. Lot's wife, however, did look back, and she "became a pillar of salt," an ironic end for her at a place near the Dead Sea, which in Hebrew is called the "Salt Sea."

Many years later the prophet Ezekiel listed arrogant pride and haughtiness among the sins of Sodom and Gomorrah, as well as their living in ostentatious luxury while ignoring the poor and the needy. Other biblical writers used these cities as symbols of the worse sorts of wickedness. And the desolation of these cities was so spectacular and complete that their destruction was frequently mentioned as a sign of God's wrath and judgment, and God often threatened Israel or other nations with a similar devastation.

POSTSCRIPT

■ Bitumen deposits are still present in the region of this former city.

Isaac

ISAAC WAS THE ONLY son of Abraham and Sarah. His significance lies not so much in what he said or did but in his status as the fulfillment of God's promises to Abraham and as the link between his father, Abraham, and his son Jacob.

God promised Abraham that he would have a son, and that his descendants would be more numerous than the stars of the heavens. His wife Sarah remained childless, however, and so Abraham fathered Ishmael with Hagar, Sarah's maidservant. But God made it clear that Ishmael was not the fulfillment of his promise; rather, his intent was to bless Sarah with a son and through him bring forth a great multitude, who would become God's people.

Isaac was finally born as the fulfillment of that promise. By that time, Sarah was more than 90 years old, so his birth brought special delight to the couple. His name means "laughter," and Sarah said, "God has brought laughter for me; everyone who hears will laugh with me" (Genesis 21:6).

When Isaac had grown into a young man, the Lord tested Abraham by telling him to sacrifice his son Isaac as a burnt offering. Despite the enormity of the demand, Abraham prepared to follow through until an angel from God stopped him and provided a ram to sacrifice instead. Then Abraham sent back to his ancestral homeland in Mesopotamia to find a wife for Isaac; Rebekah was found and brought back to him. The Bible says, "He took Rebekah, and she became his wife; and he loved her" (Genesis 24:67).

Although Isaac was not as actively involved in the Bible's story line as his father, Abraham, or his son Jacob, he nevertheless was one of the three patriarchs referred to in later years, when God identified himself as "the God of your fathers, the God of Abraham, the God of Isaac, and the God of Jacob" (e.g., Exodus 3:6). God worked through all three to bring blessings on his people of Israel and, beyond that, on all nations.

POSTSCRIPT

■ Isaac died at the age of 180, and his sons, Esau and Jacob, buried him. Isaac's death is estimated to have been around 1881 B.C.

Jesus on Trial

DUE TO THE COMPLEX political system in place at the time, Jesus actually had three or four trials, and he was brought up on two completely different charges: blasphemy (Jews) and insurrection (Romans).

It started with his arrest in the Garden of Gethsemane by a contingent of the Temple Guard answering to the high priest. They took Jesus to the high priest's home. It was probably not unusual for a trial to be held there: High officials frequently used their palatial residences for business purposes. The timing of Jesus' trial, however, was suspect. In a crowded city, a midday trial of a popular rabbi might have started a riot, which the Roman army would swiftly put down by force. So Jesus' trial occurred in the early hours of the morning.

John's gospel mentions a private audience with Annas, a former high priest who was the father-in-law of Caiaphas, the current high priest. Apparently Annas still held considerable power. He asked about Jesus' teaching, but Jesus avoided incriminating himself. "Ask those who heard what I said to them" (John 18:21).

Then came the trial before the Jewish council. The charge was blasphemy. False witnesses were found, but they couldn't get their stories straight. Finally, the high priest asked Jesus, "Are you the Messiah, the Son of the Blessed One?" (Mark 14:61). Jesus answered, "I am." To the high priest, it was proof of blasphemy. The council then pronounced the verdict: death.

While the Romans allowed the Jewish council to rule on matters of civic life, capital punishment was excluded. So the council had to send Jesus to the Roman prefect, Pontius Pilate, with their recommendation for punishment. Pilate wouldn't care about a charge of blasphemy against a God he didn't worship, so they altered the charge to something he'd have to act on—insurrection. By claiming to be the Messiah, they said, Jesus was setting himself up as a king, a rival to Roman authority.

Pilate seemed to be trying to wriggle out of a difficult situation. When he heard that Jesus was Galilean, he sent him to King Herod Antipas, who was in Jerusalem for Passover. (Herod was responsible for the region of Galilee.) Herod wanted to see some miracle performed, but Jesus didn't cooperate, so Herod sent Jesus back to Pilate.

Because the subsequent interview failed to convince Pilate of Jesus' guilt, he was ready to release him with merely a flogging, but the Caiaphas-led crowd called for crucifixion. Washing his hands, Pilate gave in, sending Jesus to the cross.

James, the Son of Zebedee

JAMES WAS ONE OF JESUS' closest disciples and the brother of John. It's possible that James and John were first cousins of Jesus, which might explain why they left their livelihoods so quickly to follow him.

James and John were fishermen, working with their father, Zebedee, on the Sea of Galilee. They were also partners with the brothers Peter and Andrew in this trade (Luke 5:10). When Jesus came by and said, "Follow me," James and John immediately "left the boat and their father, and followed him" (Matthew 4:22).

James was most likely the older of the Zebedee boys, since he's always named first. They were known as "the Sons of Thunder," so it can be assumed they were hotheaded. There were also contentions among Jesus' disciples, heated arguments about who was most important, and we have good reason

Apostle St. James the Greater
by El Greco

to think that James and John were in the thick of those disputes. Once their mother (who might have been Jesus' aunt) brought them to Jesus with a request: "Declare that these two sons of mine will sit, one at your right hand and one at your left, in your kingdom" (Matthew 20:21). These places were, of course, positions of prominence.

In response, Jesus asked if they were willing to drink the cup of suffering he would have to drink. Both brothers assured him that they were. It's interesting how that turned out for James. A few years later, as the Church grew, it faced opposition from the authorities. James was arrested and killed "with the sword" at the command of Herod (Acts 12:2), becoming the first of the apostles to be martyred.

POSTSCRIPT

■ James, the son of Zebedee, is known as James the Greater and is distinguished from another apostle—James, the son of Alphaeus, known as James the Lesser. He is also not to be confused with James, the brother of Jesus, who wrote the Epistle of James.

The Book of Ezra

T HE BOOKS OF EZRA and Nehemiah are the most important historical sources for understanding the period following the Babylonian
Exile, approximately 539 to 430 B.C. They were probably compiled by an
unnamed author or editor at the end of the fifth century B.C. Consisting
mainly of historical narrative, Ezra also contains a decree (6:3–12), a letter
(7:11–26), lists (1:9–11; 2; 8:1–20, 25–27; 10:18–44), and a prayer (9:6–15).

The book begins with Cyrus, the Persian king who had overthrown the
Babylonian Empire, establishing a new policy toward captive nations
(1:1–4). While the Assyrians and Babylonians had exiled captive leaders,
shipping them to places far from their homes so they would not rebel
against their conquerors, the Persians allowed them to go to their
homelands to rebuild houses and temples. Some of the people living
in Judah took advantage of this and returned under the leadership of
Zerubbabel to rebuild the temple (1:5   2:70). They rebuilt the foundation, but opposition from the neighboring nations slowed the project.
Following the goading of two prophets, Haggai and Zechariah, they
renewed the rebuilding as decreed by the new Persian king, Darius, and
finished the job (3:1—6:22). At the instigation of a subsequent Persian
king, Artaxerxes, Ezra (a scribe and law teacher) was sent from Persia to
lead others to Jerusalem, taking with him gifts for the temple. He was also
to appoint civic leaders and teach and administer God's law to reestablish
Israel as a nation ruled by God's laws. These laws were the ones given to
Moses at Mount Sinai and recorded in the Pentateuch.

A practice Ezra strongly condemned was intermarriage between the
Israelites and pagans. In response, many of the Israelites divorced their
unbelieving foreign spouses.

POSTSCRIPT

■ In order to show the superiority of his gods, the Babylonian king had plundered
Yahweh's temple and taken the booty to his gods' temple. Cyrus acknowledges
Yahweh's legitimacy at the beginning of Ezra by returning the plunder.

■ The 49,897 Israelites who returned to Jerusalem under Zerubbabel were only
a small fraction of those in exile. Many stayed in Babylonia because they had
gained position and wealth there and did not relish the hard life of rebuilding
a land, even if it was theirs by God's promise.

■ Mixed marriages were not condemned across the board (see Genesis 16:3; Ruth
1:4), but there was always a fear that pagan spouses would sponsor pagan worship. Therefore, intermarriage with Canaanites was forbidden (Exodus 34:11–16;
Deuteronomy 7:1–4; 20:10–18).

Papyrus

PAPYRUS, SOMETIMES KNOWN as bulrush, is a plant that grows in marshes, typically growing 8 to 20 feet tall. In ancient times it was used as food, fuel, medicine, a sweetener, rope, and even chewing gum, but its main use was as a writing surface. The smooth, three-sided stems became the raw material for paper as early as the third millennium B.C.

Since papyrus is plentiful in the swamps along the Nile River, Egyptians were the first to make and use papyrus paper. They would peel the stems, cut them into strips, then flatten, moisten, and press them, creating a single sheet. Sheets would be layered to increase the strength, pressed again, dried, and cut to size.

As a writing surface, papyrus was functional but not very durable. Sheets could be glued together to form a scroll or piled together as a book (known as a *codex* in the ancient world). Thus the most important documents were written on vellum or parchment (treated animal skins) or carved into stone, clay, or wood. Papyrus generally survived in only the driest climates, which is why most modern archaeological finds of ancient papyrus have occurred in Egypt.

Yet there have been hundreds of thousands of ancient documents found on papyrus, many of these just scraps, including many bills and personal notes, which help us understand everyday life in Bible times. But there are also some major portions of Scripture collected in *codices*. For instance, there's a collection of ten epistles of Paul and a copy of the Gospel of John, both dating to about A.D. 200. These finds have helped scholars refine the Greek text of the New Testament, ensuring that it's as close as possible to the original.

POSTSCRIPT

◼ The Egyptians also used papyrus to make light riverboats. Thus it is no surprise that the baby Moses was floated on the Nile in a papyrus basket (Exodus 2:3).

◼ You've already figured out that our word *paper* comes from *papyrus,* but did you know that the inner pith of the papyrus plant was called *byblos*? From this the Greeks got their word for book, *biblion,* from which we got our word *Bible.*

◼ The Roman historian Pliny the Elder said, "Civilization—or at the very least, human history—depends on the use of papyrus."

The Baptism of Jesus

JESUS' MINISTRY DID not begin in the temple or synagogue or within the capital city of his day. He, like many others, traveled beyond Jerusalem and the major cities, through the wilderness, all the way out to the Jordan River, where he was baptized by his cousin John. In the first century, John may have looked like other prophets and revolutionaries who also gathered followers by inviting them to the wilderness. John ate locusts and honey, he wore clothes made of camel hair, and his political and religious claims were better known to the ancient historian Josephus than were even those of Jesus. Today archaeological sites in Jordan commemorate where John and those who followed him once lived.

Why did John baptize Jesus? That is not simply a modern concern; the first evangelists knew that it was necessary to answer that question. Why would God incarnate need to be baptized?

The Gospel of John, for instance, never describes the actual baptism, but rather John the Baptist's recollection of it. Even then, the gospel never specifically says that John baptized Jesus. The Gospel of Matthew presents John as seeing his baptism of Jesus as inappropriate: "I need to be baptized by you, and do you come to me?" (Matthew 3:14). Jesus responds by saying, "'Let it be so now; it is proper for us to do this to fulfill all righteousness.' Then he consented" (verse 15). The Gospel of Luke downplays the specific baptism of Jesus but presents him as being part of a large group that was baptized (see Luke 3:21).

All four canonical gospels do agree (in general) that after Jesus was baptized in the Jordan, the Spirit—like a dove—descended upon him, and a voice said, "You are my Son, the Beloved; with you I am well pleased" (Mark 1:11).

What may stand out the most about Jesus' baptism is not who was involved (John), where it was done (the Jordan), or what rite of passage it started within the Church (the inclusive practice of baptism in place of circumcision). What stands out the most is a clear sense of call and appointment of Jesus of Nazareth.

POSTSCRIPT

- In poetry, literature, and tradition, the Jordan River frequently is used to represent freedom or newness of life.
- In the year 2000, the country of Jordan opened public access to many sites, including where John reputedly engaged in baptism.

The Sacrifice of Isaac

ABRAHAM'S "SACRIFICE" of Isaac is the last major event in Abraham's life recorded in detail. By this time, Abraham had proven to be obedient to God's call on his life, even if at times he had exhibited less than full trust in God's abilities to fulfill his promises. Abraham had left his home in Mesopotamia and settled in Canaan, just as God had commanded. Thus God promised great things for him and his descendants and even changed his name from *Abram* (meaning "exalted father") to *Abraham* (meaning "father of a multitude") to underscore his promises to make Abraham the father of many nations.

God now wanted to test Abraham one final time. God commanded Abraham to take Isaac and sacrifice him in the land of Moriah (later known as Jerusalem). This was an astonishing test, since the Bible is very clear that God's people are never to engage in human sacrifice. Furthermore, this was the long-awaited son God had promised Abraham, and now God was requiring Abraham to kill him.

The Sacrifice of Isaac *by Caravaggio*

Nevertheless, Abraham obeyed, with Isaac as a mostly passive bystander. The story's climax comes when the angel of the Lord intervenes and stops Abraham. Abraham's faith was now evident, and he was not required to follow through. Rather, the angel provided a nearby ram, which he sacrificed instead. This idea of an animal sacrifice substituting for a human one—known as "substitutionary atonement"—is developed later in Israel's sacrificial system. The New Testament develops the idea further, with Christ standing in a sinner's place and absorbing God's wrath on his or her behalf.

POSTSCRIPT

▨ This story took on great significance in Judaism, where it is known as the *Akedah* (which means "binding," since Isaac was bound on the altar), and many details were added over the centuries. Whereas in the biblical account Isaac is primarily a passive observer, in subsequent Jewish writings Isaac is described as a mature, active volunteer, willingly, even joyfully, engaged with Abraham in the entire process.

▨ Jewish tradition holds that Abraham prepared Isaac for sacrifice on the great rock in Jerusalem covered over today by the Dome of the Rock mosque.

Rebekah

REBEKAH WAS ISAAC'S wife, Laban's sister, and Esau and Jacob's mother. She figures in two major stories in Genesis: the search for a wife for Isaac, in which she is a very sympathetic character; and Jacob's deception of his father in order take the birthright from his brother, in which she is portrayed as an unsympathetic manipulator.

When Abraham grew old, he sent his servant back to his ancestral homeland in Mesopotamia to find a wife for his son Isaac. The servant was led to the city and household of Nahor, Abraham's brother, where Rebekah and her brother Laban lived. The servant asked God to show him the right woman for Isaac, and Rebekah, by her generosity to the servant, was revealed to be that woman. The servant presented himself to Laban and his household, and they consented to her marriage to Isaac, sending her off with a blessing.

Shortly after she arrived at Abraham's household, she married Isaac. They had twin sons, Esau (the older) and Jacob (the younger). The Bible says Rebekah suffered through an exceedingly difficult pregnancy, even causing her to want to die. But finally she gave birth to the twins. When the two boys grew up, "Esau was a skillful hunter, a man of the field, while Jacob was a quiet man, living in tents" (Genesis 25:27). Isaac loved Esau, while Rebekah loved Jacob, which no doubt contributed to the subsequent rivalry between the brothers.

When Isaac grew quite old, Rebekah's favor played itself out in an elaborate scheme that she concocted in order that Jacob might receive the blessing that Isaac, by right, was to give to his oldest son, Esau. She prepared a meal of Isaac's favorite food and sent Jacob in with it, wearing animal skins to disguise himself as his brother Esau (Esau was hairy and Jacob was not). His father's eyesight being dim, he felt Jacob and, feeling the skins, thought it was Esau. He blessed Jacob, and when Esau returned from a hunt with his own meal for his father, he naturally was so enraged that he vowed to kill Jacob. Rebekah again stepped in and warned Jacob, who fled to Mesopotamia. Thus the sad consequence of her deception was that she was deprived of the son she loved for the rest of her life.

Many years later, Rebekah died and was buried along with her husband, Isaac, in the family plot in Hebron, where Abraham and Sarah were also buried.

The Crucifixion of Jesus

CRUCIFIXION WAS A BRUTAL, gruesome, and highly public form of capital punishment employed by various ancient societies as a deterrent. Sometimes rulers ordered that members of rebel groups be crucified dozens at a time, with crosses lining the roads. When the Romans took control of the Mediterranean world, they perfected the science of crucifixion.

The gospels' description of Jesus' crucifixion fits with other accounts and with archaeological findings. Prisoners were flogged and then forced to carry the heavy crossbeam to the site of the execution. In Jesus' case, the site was outside the city limits of Jerusalem at a place known as "the Skull." There, the victim would have his hands nailed to the crossbeam, and the beam would be raised atop some sort of post or tree. Often the feet or ankles would be affixed to the post with another spike.

The method was designed to be extremely painful, prolonging death as the victim struggled to raise himself up to breathe. For that purpose, a small seat was sometimes attached to the vertical beam. It might take days for a person to die, with the body left on the cross for scavengers. But Jesus' crucifixion occurred in Judaea on the day before the sabbath, so an effort was made to hasten his death and remove his body before sundown. When the bones of the two bandits crucified alongside Jesus were broken, a soldier pierced Jesus' side with a spear, and blood and water flowed out—an indication that he had expired.

There were several supporters of Jesus around his cross, mostly women, plus some soldiers and jeering bystanders. Two outlaws were crucified with him, one on either side, and one of them joined in jeering at Jesus—but the other expressed faith in him. At one point Jesus was offered a drugged vinegar sponge to dull the pain, but he refused it. Meanwhile, a strange darkness befell the land from noon to three.

From the cross, Jesus asked God to forgive his killers. He also said he was thirsty, and he charged his disciple John with the care of his mother, Mary. When one of the bandits beside him asked to be remembered in the coming kingdom, Jesus promised the man that he would be with him in Paradise. And in a crucial, climactic moment, Jesus cried out in the words of a psalm, "My God, my God, why have you forsaken me?" (Matthew 27:46; Mark 15:34).

Christians now understand the Crucifixion as a victory, not a defeat. Despite the suffering and humiliation, that was where Jesus secured our redemption.

Andrew

ANDREW WAS A DISCIPLE of Jesus and the brother of Simon Peter. It was he who brought Peter to Jesus.

Like several other disciples, Andrew was a fisherman who plied his trade with his brother on the Sea of Galilee. They also lived together, with other relatives, in or near Capernaum. Their home may have become a kind of headquarters for Jesus when he was in the area.

Apparently Andrew was first attracted to the ministry of John the Baptist, who preached repentance and spoke of a soon-to-arrive messiah. In fact, Andrew was with John the Baptist one day when John pointed to Jesus and said, "Look, here is the Lamb of God" (John 1:36). On the spot, Andrew and another man (some think it was John, the brother of James) began to follow Jesus. They spent the day learning from him. Then Andrew went to find his brother and brought him to meet Jesus.

The four gospels record several "callings" of these fishermen, who became Jesus' most faithful disciples. According to Luke, Jesus worked a miracle, allowing Peter to bring in a record catch of fish. Matthew and Mark have Jesus merely walking by the sea and asking Peter and Andrew, James and John, to follow him. Putting the stories together, we might imagine a situation where Jesus was no stranger in this community. These fishermen would have had several interactions with him, culminating in a moment when they left their fishing business to follow him full-time.

Possibly Andrew had a gift for connecting people with other people. He plays the middleman in a couple of other gospel stories as well. It was he who brought the boy with five loaves and two fish to Jesus, and he watched as that snack became a feast for thousands. Later, some Greek tourists wanted to meet Jesus. They talked to Philip, who talked to Andrew, who brought them to Jesus. We might guess then that he was on the edge of Jesus' inner circle. His fishing buddies—Peter, James, and John—accompanied Jesus on many special occasions, but only once do we find Andrew in that select group: when Jesus sat on the Mount of Olives and provided insight about the future (Mark 13:3).

POSTSCRIPT

■ According to tradition, Andrew traveled north to preach the gospel in what is now Russia. It is said he was crucified in Greece.

The Book of Nehemiah

NEHEMIAH CONTINUES the story begun in Ezra, with several of the same characters, the same fifth century B.C. time frame, and some of the same challenges for the Israelites, who had returned from Babylonian exile. The historical narrative includes a prayer (1:5–11) and various lists (3; 7:5–73; 10:1–27; 11:3—12:43).

The Babylonians had destroyed the walls of Israel's capital, Jerusalem, and her central religious shrine, the temple, when they captured it in 586 B.C. The temple was rebuilt under the leadership of Ezra, but the city itself was still in bad shape. Most distressing to Nehemiah was that the city walls were still in ruins. Nehemiah served a Persian king and lived in Susa (capital of what is now Iran); he probably had never been to Jerusalem, but he still viewed it and its people as his own. No self-respecting city could survive without walls, since marauders came and looted at will. After praying, Nehemiah approached the king and received permission to go to Jerusalem to rebuild the walls. The king even provided supplies and a safe-conduct pass. Nehemiah's rebuilding was a success, despite the opposition from neighbors who preferred the vulnerability of the city. People from all walks of life—rich and poor, men and women, skilled and novices—joined the effort. They each built the section nearest their own homes since they had a vested interest in making sure they were secure.

Ezra, the teacher, then taught the people Moses' law, which had not been heard for a long time. The people responded positively, confessing they had broken it and agreeing to uphold it. With Jerusalem protected, its population swelled. Nehemiah led the people in reforms learned from the law, including the observation of the sabbath and a ban on intermarriage with non-Israelites. God's people were again home.

POSTSCRIPT

■ Nehemiah heard the bad news of the day about the destroyed city and did not see it as "their" problem but as "our" problem (1:7), and he became involved.

■ Among those rebuilding the wall were artisans who did fine handwork, including goldsmiths and perfumers (3:8). The rough construction work could well have ruined their hands, preventing them from returning to their livelihoods after the wall was completed.

■ When the law was read, it was interpreted for the people who couldn't understand it (8:8). This probably involved translation from the language of Israel in which it was written, Hebrew, to Aramaic, the language the Israelites spoke while in exile.

The Languages of Jesus

IT'S LIKELY THAT Jesus spoke three, possibly four, languages: Hebrew, Aramaic, Greek, and perhaps Latin.

Latin was the language of the Roman governors and soldiers who oversaw Jesus' homeland. Some official documents were written in Latin, but Greek was the actual "universal" language of the Roman Empire, especially east of Rome. Alexander the Great had spread the Greek language through the territories he conquered in the fourth century B.C., and it stuck. From Capernaum to Corinth, a merchant could do business using the Greek language (known as *koine*—common—or Hellenistic Greek; this dialect was somewhat simplified from the classical Greek of Plato).

The Jews, however, were unusually provincial. Hebrew law limited contact with Gentiles, and so it might have been possible to live and do business in first-century Palestine without the knowledge of Greek. While Hebrew was the language of the Scriptures, it seems that Aramaic was a more common language among first-century Jews. Most scholars think that Jesus originally taught in Aramaic. This language originated in Syria (ancient Aram) and became the "universal" tongue of the sprawling Assyrian Empire in the eighth and seventh centuries B.C. The Jews seem to have adopted it during the Babylonian Exile in the sixth century B.C.

Earlier, however, we find an interesting exchange during the Assyrian siege of Jerusalem. Envoys from the attacking Assyrians approached the city walls and began spouting demoralizing rhetoric *in Hebrew.* The Jewish diplomats said, "Please speak . . . in the Aramaic language, for we understand it; do not speak to your servants in the language of Judah within the hearing of the people who are on the wall" (2 Kings 18:26). So at that time (c. 720 B.C.), Aramaic was the Assyrian language of diplomacy, while the common folk knew only Hebrew. A few centuries later, the commoners would be speaking Aramaic, with Hebrew reserved for religious studies.

As a Semitic dialect, Aramaic is very close to Hebrew, but with a larger vocabulary and a more precise array of tenses. In fact, portions of the Old Testament were originally written in Aramaic. During the time of the exile, classical Hebrew borrowed the block letters of Aramaic to replace its cursive script.

Jesus often began a saying with "Very truly, I tell you." The original reads "*Amen, Amen,* I tell you." It's a common Aramaic phrase.

The Temptation of Jesus

IN 1988, MARTIN SCORSESE directed a movie called *The Last Temptation of Christ*. The film was picketed and protested by people who were not opposed to the film's title but to how it depicted the temptations. Specifically, temptations that went beyond any description in the Bible. Most of us are familiar with the Bible's account of the temptations of Christ. Immediately after he was baptized, "Jesus, full of the Holy Spirit, returned from the Jordan and was led by the Spirit in the wilderness" (Luke 4:1).

During this time in history, many reform movements in Palestine began in the wilderness or desert. It was a place where people focused on their life calling and where they sought to be closer to God. The Jewish community known as the Essenes, who are believed to have written the Dead Sea Scrolls, lived in a community in the desert. So did John the Baptist. The wilderness was a place to find discipline and discern truth, but it was also a place to struggle with meaning. Just as the people of Israel wandered in the desert for 40 years, just as Christians today sometimes wrestle with meaning during the 40 days of Lent, so Jesus fasted for 40 days, and then when he was at his weakest, he faced the Devil.

Playing off of Jesus' hunger, the Devil first tempted him to turn a stone into a loaf of bread (Luke 4:3). Jesus responded by quoting Deuteronomy 8:3: "One does not live by bread alone." In the second temptation, the Devil showed Jesus all the kingdoms of the world and offered them to him if he would only worship him (verses 5–7). Jesus responded again by quoting the Book of Deuteronomy: "Worship the Lord your God and serve Him only" (Deuteronomy 6:13). In the third temptation, the Devil took Jesus to the top of the temple and said, "If you are the Son of God, throw yourself down from here" (Luke 4:9). But then, before Jesus answered, the Devil quoted Psalm 91:11–12, emphasizing that surely the angels would watch over him. Jesus, however, replied by quoting the Book of Deuteronomy a third time: "Do not put the Lord your God to the test" (Deuteronomy 6:16).

The Devil tempted Jesus with food, with worldly power, and with divine status, and all three times Jesus rebuked the Devil by quoting Scripture. Of course, the spiritual battle was not over. Luke 4:13 reads: "When the devil had finished every test, he departed from Jesus until an opportune time."

The Devil is described as patient, recognizing that anyone can have a good day. The Devil is described as one who can whisper doubts, quote Scripture, and wait until people are tired, weak, lonely, confused, or hungry for something other than bread. But in every instance, Jesus rebuked his evil adversary. He never succumbed.

Isaac Repeats His Father's Sin

WHEN GOD CALLED Abraham out of Mesopotamia to journey to the land of Canaan, it was to leave all that he had: "your country and your kindred and your father's house" (Genesis 12:1). He settled in Canaan. But when the time came to find a wife for his son, Isaac, Abraham refused to search among the Canaanites because they worshipped other gods. Instead, he sent his chief servant back "to my country and my kindred" (Genesis 24:4) in order to get a wife for his son.

Isaac and Rebecca *by Simeon Solomon*

The woman who became Isaac's wife was Rebekah. Isaac and Rebekah's marriage was lovingly consummated when Isaac took her into his late mother's tent "and she became his wife; and he loved her" (Genesis 24:67). Their marriage began quite happily.

After Abraham's death, Isaac settled among the Philistines at Gerar. Here, his wife's beauty attracted notice, and he tried to pass her off as his sister, but the local Philistine king, Abimelech, noticed him "fondling his wife" (Genesis 26:8) and confronted him with his deception. Ironically, this was a tactic that Isaac's father, Abraham, had tried twice before with his wife Sarah, once with the Egyptian pharaoh and once with the Philistine king Abimelech. In Abraham's case, his claim was technically true, since he and Sarah had the same father (Terah), though different mothers. Isaac, however, could not make a similar claim. In all three cases, the patriarchs' duplicity was a sign of their lack of faith in God's protection.

POSTSCRIPT

◼ Many have wondered at the hapless "Abimelech," the Philistine king who seems to have fallen for the same deception by both father and son—that is, Abraham and Isaac. The name, however, means "my father is king," and it may simply have been a throne name for any Philistine ruler in the same way that "Pharaoh" was among the Egyptians. If so, then there were probably two different Abimelechs.

Esau

ESAU WAS THE OLDER twin brother born to Isaac and Rebekah. He had conflicts with his brother Jacob from the womb. The Bible says "the children struggled together" even during their mother's difficult pregnancy (Genesis 25:22). Esau came out from the womb "red, all his body like a hairy mantle" (verse 25). Because he became a skilled hunter and spent his time out in the fields, he was his father's favorite. Evidently, Isaac was a man of the outdoors.

Esau was not only outgoing, but he was also impetuous, as illustrated when he gave away his birthright to his brother. One day, upon returning from a hunt tired and hungry, he smelled a rich red stew that his brother was cooking and agreed to sell his birthright in exchange for a bowl of it. This was a very weighty decision to make, since the birthright for the firstborn included inheritance of all of the father's wealth and possessions.

Another example of his foolish decision-making was his marriage to two Hittite women. The Bible says his wives "made life bitter for Isaac and Rebekah" (Genesis 26:35). No doubt Esau was not quite so happy as well. He even married his cousin Mahalath to try to please his father. Although the Bible says his Hittite wives made his mother "weary of [her] life" (Genesis 27:46), it was his father about whom he was concerned (see Genesis 28:8). Apparently Esau not only was angry with Jacob but also harbored a grudge against his mother.

Esau's resentment toward his mother is understandable, since she had always favored his brother. And more importantly, she was instrumental in stealing his father's blessing from him. Because he was very close to his father, that blessing naturally meant a great deal to him.

Nevertheless, over time Esau came to forgive his brother, and the two of them reconciled after 20 years of separation.

POSTSCRIPT

■ Esau also acquired the name *Edom,* which means "red," after he sold his birth-right for a bowl of red stew. He is the ancestor of the Edomites, with whom the Israelites had conflicts for many centuries, sadly perpetuating the hostility that once existed between the two brothers.

The Death of Jesus

A HYMN OF THE early Church describes how Jesus did not cling to his divine prerogatives, but "emptied himself" by becoming human. (That verb is very vivid, like pouring water out from a pitcher.) Then, as a man, "he humbled himself and became obedient to the point of death—even death on a cross" (Philippians 2:8). Becoming a human being was one step in the humbling process; dying as a criminal was another; being crucified was going further still.

People in Jesus' world would shudder if they saw people wearing crosses as jewelry. The cross was a grotesque form of capital punishment, known for immense pain and complete humiliation. Even the bloodthirsty Romans generally reserved this punishment for the worst of criminals, enemies of the state, and foreigners.

Modern preachers, however, almost glorify Jesus' death on the cross, often going to great lengths to describe the intense pain of the crucifixion process. New Testament writers, on the other hand, didn't get into such torturous portrayal. That's not only because people of that time would know all about crucifixion, but also because there was another aspect to Jesus' suffering. His sacrifice involved not only physical pain but spiritual separation from his heavenly Father. "He himself bore our sins in his body on the cross," writes Peter (1 Peter 2:24). Jesus, indeed, felt "forsaken" by his Father (Matthew 27:46).

Putting together the crucifixion accounts in the four gospels, we can collect seven statements that Jesus uttered from the cross. The next to last of these is "It is finished" (John 19:30). We can certainly understand that cry of completion from a man who had been losing blood for three hours and struggling for each breath. But we can also imagine that he was talking about something more. He had fulfilled his mission. He had closed out one era in the history of human interaction with God while opening another.

Then, breathing his last, Jesus said, "Father, into your hands I commend my spirit" (Luke 23:46). Once again, he was the obedient Son, even to the point of death. At that moment, we're told, the earth shook. The curtain in the temple's Holy Place was torn. Symbolically, this was the barrier between God and humanity. At Golgotha, a Roman centurion remarked: "Truly this man was God's Son!" (Mark 15:39). As sundown approached, two secret disciples of Jesus went public, asking the Roman governor for permission to bury the body, which was then placed in the tomb that one of these men, Joseph of Arimathea, had prepared for himself.

Matthew

MATTHEW WAS ONE of the 12 apostles. Once a tax collector, he wrote one of the four gospels, detailing Jesus' earthly ministry. His gospel became the first book of the New Testament.

Tax collectors were despised in Jesus' day. They're not all that popular now, but in first-century Israel there was a political issue involved. Tax collectors were sellouts. They used the power of Rome to collect taxes from their own countrymen for the coffers of already-rich rulers. And they were notorious cheats. They regularly marked up the tax bills and pocketed the profits. This meant that the religious elite considered tax collectors the lowest of the low—not only dishonest but also colluding with impure Gentiles.

Based in Capernaum, near the Sea of Galilee, Matthew collected taxes on merchandise that passed on the *Via Maris,* the road that connected Damascus to the Mediterranean Sea. It was a major trade route, and it is likely that King Herod Antipas wanted his cut of the commerce.

So there was Matthew, sitting at his "tollbooth" by the road when Jesus walked up and said, "Follow me" (Matthew 9:9). And Matthew did. In fact, he invited Jesus to a dinner party at his home. As a tax collector, he probably had an expensive, spacious home, but since the religious folk scorned tax collectors, his dinner guests prior to this would have been other social outcasts like himself. When word of this dinner party spread, the Pharisees asked why such a famous rabbi would dine with such "sinners." That set the scene for one of Jesus' great one-liners: "Healthy people don't need a doctor—sick people do" (Matthew 9:12 NLT).

Outside of this story and various lists of disciples, there is no further mention of Matthew in the New Testament—except that he is credited with writing one of the early gospels. This makes sense, since Matthew's profession would have required education, as well as facility with various languages. Ironically, even though most Jews would have despised Matthew because of his secular profession, his gospel shows a deep knowledge of the Hebrew Scriptures and a great desire to win his people over to Jesus. He seems to be writing for Jewish Christians in the early Church in particular, showing how Jesus fulfilled Old Testament prophecies as the promised Messiah.

POSTSCRIPT

■ Mark and Luke both include the story of Matthew's calling, but they refer to him as Levi. This was probably a family surname.

The Book of Esther

ESTHER WAS A young Jewish girl who lived in exile in Persia during the reign of the Persian king Ahasuerus (Xerxes I in Greek), who ruled from 486 to 465 B.C. No author is identified, but the book probably came from Persia some time between the fifth and third centuries B.C. It is a single historical story tracing the salvation of God's people through an old man's wisdom and a beautiful girl's willingness to stand up for God.

The Persian queen Vashti displeased her husband, so she was banished. Her replacement was found through a beauty contest, which was won by a beautiful Jewish girl, Esther (chapter 2). Her uncle, Mordecai, suggested she not disclose her ethnic background, since there was strong anti-Semitism among some in the nation. Mordecai also helped the king by uncovering a plot against him (verses 19–23).

Haman, a high official, came to hate Mordecai and his people, since Mordecai would not bow down to him. He plotted to hang Mordecai and kill his people

Esther Before Ahasuerus by Gregorio Pagani

(3; 5:9–14), but Esther agreed to intercede for him and the Jews (4). The king remembered Mordecai's help in the past, and when he heard of Haman's plot, he hung him on the scaffold intended for Mordecai (6—7).

The king had written an unchangeable decree that the Jews could be killed, but his new friend Mordecai convinced him to do what had not been done before and write another. This new edict said that the Jews could defend themselves with force. When their enemies came against them, the Jews destroyed them and survived (8—9:17). In celebration, they established the feast of Purim to commemorate their deliverance (9:18–19). Mordecai was raised to a position of great authority in the land.

In the whole book, God is not mentioned once, but he is mightily at work throughout it protecting his people. Events did not happen by chance, but Mordecai's acts paved the way for future salvation, and Esther became queen "for such a time as this" (4:14).

Talmud

JUDAISM IS UNDENIABLY a "religion of the book," but it's also a faith based in teaching. The Scriptures are revered as God's Word, but this instruction from God needs to be interpreted and applied. Jews have long understood the need for oral instruction that would help them understand God's written law. Jewish students of Scripture memorize not only the Torah but also the explanations of their rabbis. Over time, these also had to be written down. That's what the *Talmud* is—an early collection of oral teaching about the written Torah.

The teachings included in the Talmud span nearly a millennium, from four centuries before Christ to five centuries after. Rabbi Akiba ben Joseph and his student Rabbi Meir began collecting this work early in the second century A.D. They sorted through the scriptural law and codified it, according to the oral tradition of the previous centuries. This project became the *Mishnah,* completed about A.D. 200 by Judah ha-Nasi. It makes up half of the Talmud. The other half is further commentary on the Mishnah by rabbis over the next three centuries. This is known as the *Gemara* (which means "completion"). An additional distinction is made between two types of teaching in the Talmud. Legal matters are known as *Halakah,* while illustrative stories and sayings are *Haggadah.*

There are actually two Talmuds: one from Jerusalem, the other from Babylon. They share the same Mishnah but differ in their Gemara, each using commentary from rabbis in their particular region. The Jerusalem Talmud (also known as the Palestinian Talmud) was completed about a century earlier, but the Babylonian Talmud is generally considered the authoritative work.

All in all, the Talmud is a masterwork of religious heritage, capturing the details of Jewish faith and devotion over a great span of time. Life changes, and so do the fine points of behavior that conforms (or doesn't conform) to God's law. The Talmud gives modern Jews a model for living God's way in a rapidly changing society.

POSTSCRIPT

- The word *Talmud* means "study" or "learn."
- The Mishnah portion of the Talmud and quotes from it in the Gemara are written in Hebrew. The rest is in Aramaic.

The Miracle at Cana

THE GOSPEL OF JOHN describes Jesus' first miracle, which occurred in Cana, where Jesus attended a wedding (John 2:1–12). Midway through the reception, the host ran out of wine. Jesus' mother asked Jesus to fix this embarrassment. Hesitant at first, Jesus turned water into wine.

Taken out of context, the miracle seems beneath him. Much more, however, seems to be happening here. The first readers of this gospel would have been familiar with at least one other ancient figure who is said to have turned water into wine. Dionysus, the Greek god of wine, may have been mythical, but a similar act allegedly had been attributed to him. During one visit among the Tyrians, for instance, he came upon a hospitable shepherd, who served him a wonderful meal, but offered only milk and water to drink. Dionysus is said to have transformed the water into wine. Perhaps John's readers would have known this story. If so, they also might have known that Dionysus referred to himself as "the vine." And if they knew that, they would have recognized yet another deeper meaning when Jesus said of himself, "I am the true vine" (John 15:1).

What that means becomes clearer through the words of John 2:1–12. After Jesus' mother informs him that the party has run out of wine, Jesus answers in an unusual manner. He says to her, "Woman, what concern is that to you and to me? My hour has not yet come" (John 2:4). Those words signal that something is happening beyond the supplying of beverages.

The focus of the story then shifts to six stone water jars, the kind the Jews used for ceremonial washing; each would hold from 20 to 30 gallons. Jesus tells the servants to fill those containers with water. They do so. He then instructs them to draw out the contents and take that wine to the banquet.

When they do so, the master tastes the wine—unaware of where it has come from—and says to the bridegroom, "Everyone serves the good wine first, and then the inferior wine after the guests have become drunk. But you have kept the good wine until now" (verse 10). His meaning is clear, but his words also have a deeper meaning within John's gospel. Jesus is seen as the fulfillment of salvation history. He is the new wine, as well as the true vine.

Although Jesus said to his mother, "My hour has not yet come," this first miracle still serves as a reminder that "good wine" also comes with a cost, and that soon Jesus' time would come.

The Birthright and the Blessing

ESAU AND JACOB, twin brothers born to Isaac and Rebekah, were in conflict with each other during their youth. Even in their mother's womb, the Bible says, "The children struggled together within her" (Genesis 25:22). Esau was the older of the two, a hunter, and his father's favorite; Jacob was a quiet man who stayed close to home and was his mother's favorite.

Isaac Blesses Jacob *by Domenico Fetti*

As the oldest son, Esau stood to inherit the greatest portion of their father's belongings in a custom common throughout the ancient Near East. But one day he foolishly bargained his birthright away to Jacob for a pot of red stew because he was famished.

When Isaac grew old, he made arrangements to bless his oldest son, Esau. In preparation, he asked Esau to hunt and prepare his favorite food for him. Rebekah overheard her husband and orchestrated a plot; she prepared her husband's favorite food and had Jacob pass himself off as Esau before Esau returned from the hunt. She had Jacob dress in Esau's clothes and clad his arms and neck with goat skins, since Esau was hairy and Jacob was not. When the feeble-eyed Isaac smelled and felt him, he thought it was Esau, and thus he was fooled into pronouncing his blessing on Jacob instead of Esau.

Not surprisingly, Esau was furious at being tricked out of the blessing. He pressed his father for at least one small blessing, which Isaac granted, but it merely foretold more conflict between the brothers. Esau then plotted to kill Jacob, who fled, with his mother's assistance, back to her ancestral homeland in Mesopotamia.

After many years, Jacob returned with his wives, children, servants, and many possessions. He feared Esau and sent him many gifts to appease him. When they met, Esau forgave him, and they were reconciled. Esau journeyed east of the Jordan River and settled in what became known as Edom, southeast of the Dead Sea, while Jacob settled in Shechem.

Laban

LABAN WAS THE GRANDSON of Nahor, who was Abraham's brother. It was to his household in the city of Nahor in Mesopotamia that Abraham sent his servant to find a wife for Isaac; Isaac sent his son Jacob back to do the same thing years later.

Laban welcomed Abraham's servant into his household. The servant told how God had directed him to Rebekah, Laban's sister, who should be Isaac's wife. Laban acknowledged that God had indeed done this, and he gave his permission and his blessing.

Many years later, when Jacob was ready to take a wife, his parents sent him back to his uncle Laban's household. Jacob met Laban's daughter Rachel at the well there and identified himself as a relative. She brought him to her father, who welcomed him into the household.

Jacob agreed to work for Laban for seven years in exchange for his daughter's hand. When the time for the wedding came, however, Laban tricked Jacob by giving him his older daughter Leah instead, explaining that the custom in their land was for the oldest daughter to be married first. So, after a week-long "honeymoon" with Leah, Laban gave Rachel to Jacob, and he then worked seven more years for her. After 14 years, Jacob prepared to return home with his wives, children, and servants, but Laban prevailed on him to stay longer, saying that Jacob's presence had meant blessings and prosperity for his household.

Laban and Jacob had a precarious relationship during those years; Jacob would say to his wives, Rachel and Leah, that Laban "has cheated me and changed my wages ten times" (Genesis 31:7). Yet, during those years, Jacob worked hard at enriching himself at his father-in-law's expense, breeding his flocks to maximize his own holdings. This displeased Laban, and so Jacob secretly prepared to return home to Canaan.

When they left, Rachel stole her father's household gods. Laban apparently worshipped the Lord, but not exclusively, and he possessed pagan idols. Laban pursued the group bound for Canaan in order to retrieve his idols, but Rachel had hidden them under her saddle and he could not find them. Laban and Jacob sealed their strained relationship by erecting stones as a boundary marker that neither would pass, thus guaranteeing that they would never see each other again.

The Empty Tomb

THE DAY AFTER JESUS' crucifixion was the sabbath, and it was a time of deep mourning for many people. Jesus' body had been placed in the tomb of an affluent civic leader, Joseph of Arimathea, who had secretly supported Jesus even though he belonged to the ruling council of the Jews that had condemned him. The tomb was carved out of rock, with a large stone rolled before its opening.

The next morning, Sunday, a few of Jesus' female disciples made their way to the tomb to make sure his body was properly anointed for burial. There they made a startling discovery! The tomb was open and empty, and angels announced that Jesus had risen from the dead.

It should be noted that the four gospels differ in some details of this story, but it is possible to correlate their accounts. With an event of this magnitude, you can imagine that everyone involved would have a unique perspective. The gospel writers themselves might have found harmonizing the various personal stories to be a challenging task. In any case, it's difficult to reconstruct a precise timeline.

From Matthew's account, the moment of resurrection occurred with a burst of power that felt like an earthquake, knocking out the soldiers who were guarding the tomb. Subsequently, there might have been different groups of women who came to the tomb that morning. In the various listings are Joanna, Salome, and a couple of Marys. Two angels were present, appearing as men in bright white apparel. (Mark mentions only one angel; it's possible that some women saw only one angel and missed the second.) These women went to find the disciples.

Once they heard about the empty tomb, Peter and John ran to investigate. They found "linen wrappings lying there, and the cloth that had been on Jesus' head, not lying with the linen wrappings but rolled up in a place by itself" (John 20:6–7).

Jesus had often spoken of his impending death, but he usually added that he would rise on the third day after his death. The disciples never seemed to fully comprehend what Jesus meant, until now. But later they would preach the Resurrection as an essential part of the Jesus story. "God raised him up," Peter declared in his Pentecost sermon, "having freed him from death, because it was impossible for him to be held in its power" (Acts 2:24). Later, Paul wrote, "If Christ has not been raised, your faith is futile" (1 Corinthians 15:17). The resurrection of Jesus establishes God's ultimate power over death and paves the way for our own resurrection. Because Jesus' tomb is empty, we know we can live forever with him.

Philip, the Apostle

PHILIP WAS A DEVOTED disciple of Jesus from Bethsaida, near the hometown of Peter and Andrew. He seems to have been the fifth disciple called, after the fishing quartet of Peter, Andrew, James, and John.

His calling is recorded in John 1:43–44. Jesus simply found Philip and said to him, "Follow me," and Philip followed. While it's possible that Jesus had a spiritual magnetism that inspired strangers to join him, the Bethsaida connection suggests that Philip was part of a close-knit community that already knew about Jesus.

It is at this point in John's narrative that Philip says to his friend Nathanael (who is also called Bartholomew), "We have found him about whom Moses in the law and also the prophets wrote, Jesus son of Joseph from Nazareth" (verse 45). Nathanael's famous reply, "Can anything good come out of Nazareth?" (verse 46) elicits a response from Philip that evangelists have declared ever since: "Come and see" (verse 46).

We know little else about Philip except for three brief exchanges with Jesus. Before the feeding of the 5,000, Jesus asked Philip for advice: "Where are we to buy bread for these people to eat?" (John 6:5). Philip did the math and determined that the cost would be enormous, but the gospel writer comments that Jesus was just testing Philip—he already knew what he was going to do. Andrew then found a boy with loaves and fish, which Jesus multiplied to feed the crowd.

Martyrdom of Saint Philip *by Pietro Uberti*

Later some Greeks were visiting Jerusalem and wanted to see Jesus. They came to Philip, which suggests that Philip had connections with Gentiles, something that wouldn't be true of many Jews. Philip, with Andrew, went to Jesus to tell him that these Greeks wanted to see him.

Then at the Last Supper, it was Philip who said, "Lord, show us the Father, and we will be satisfied." In response, Jesus showed some disappointment. "Have I been with you all this time, Philip, and you still do not know me? Whoever has seen me has seen the Father" (John 14:8–9).

According to tradition, Philip went to North Africa, where he found great response to the gospel in Carthage. Later, he was martyred in Asia Minor after converting the wife of a Roman official.

The Book of Job

JOB MAY BE ONE of the most heartbreaking books of the Bible. It is part of Israel's wisdom literature, presenting an innocent man challenged by tragedy. No author is named, and suggested composition dates run from the time of Moses to the third century B.C., but there is no compelling evidence for either suggestion. Job's structure is a prose "envelope" (1—2; 42:7–17); the poetic center of speeches by Job and four others is enclosed by narrative.

Job *by Jusepe de Ribera*

The plot is laid out in the prose introduction, where Satan questions God about the loyalty of the wealthy Job. Satan is then allowed to test him. Suffering many natural disasters, Job laments the day he was born (chapter 3), leading to a perennial question: Why do good people suffer? Three friends try to help him understand in three different rounds of speeches (4—14;15—21; 22—26). They base their arguments on their theology that God punishes those who do wrong and blesses those who do right: Since he is suffering, Job must have sinned. Furthermore, they tell Job that God knows everything, so no one should challenge him. Job strongly disagrees, since he is convinced that any bad he has done does not merit his suffering and that something is wrong with traditional theology. He calls on God to curse him if he is wrong (31).

A new character, Elihu, then delivers four speeches (32—37), repeating many previous arguments. He reminds Job of God's power in creation and the need to fear and worship him (36:24—37:24). God finally speaks, saying that he is beyond Job's comprehension (38—40:2; 40:6—41:34). It is not wrong to question, but humans cannot comprehend an answer. Job acknowledges that he is unable to reply adequately (40:3–5; 42:1–6).

God scolds Job's friends in the prose epilogue. They didn't understand God's ways after all. Job prays for them, receives from God even more than he lost, and dies at a ripe old age.

Suffering, as shown in the life of Job, can educate us. While it is natural to try to avoid it, we can learn from it. In this book, we also find that it is appropriate to question God, who welcomes sincere, heartfelt questions. Job does not question whether God exists, but he is puzzled by how he behaves. Doubt, not disbelief, meets God's open ear.

The Scripture Canon

PEOPLE OFTEN ASK, "Who decided what books belong in the Bible, and how did they decide?"

It is thought that the scribe Ezra did considerable work in reclaiming and presenting the books of Moses and possibly some prophetic books as well. But there remained a difference of opinion on some of the Writings. The Books of Esther, Ecclesiastes, and Song of Songs were disputed, and other works were included in the Septuagint (the Greek Old Testament) only to be separated out later (in A.D. 90) as apocryphal or "deutero-canonical" (not to be fully accepted as Scripture).

As for the New Testament, it seems that the four gospels were collected quite early, along with some of the letters of Paul. (Paul told the Colossians to share their epistle with the church in the next town. No doubt that practice of making and sharing copies was common.) We have documents from A.D. 95 to 140 in which Church leaders quote passages from the gospels and epistles, citing them as authoritative.

Meanwhile, the Church finally canonized specific books and letters in order to distinguish them from heretical works. Around 140, the Gnostic teacher Marcion put out a shortened version of the Scriptures, including only part of Luke and some of Paul's letters. Christian writers such as Justin Martyr and Irenaeus responded by reclaiming the Old Testament (which Marcion rejected) and putting it on par with all four gospels and the apostolic epistles. There is, in fact, a papyrus fragment from about A.D. 170 that lists the books accepted by a particular church. It includes 22 or 23 of the 27 books of our modern New Testament.

Over the next two centuries there were minor disagreements over the last nine books of the current New Testament—Hebrews to Revelation. A few other works (the Didache, The Shepherd of Hermas) were considered for inclusion. Churches were looking for authenticity, an apostolic connection, and conformity to the rest of Christian teaching. In 367, Bishop Athanasius of Alexandria published a letter identifying 27 books as the New Testament canon, and the Council of Carthage in 397 ratified that collection.

POSTSCRIPT

▪ The word *canon* comes from the Greek word for a builder's measuring line.

The Miracle of the Fish

AT THE BEGINNING of his gospel, Luke claims that his research about Jesus is exhaustive, indeed, that he has investigated "everything carefully from the very first." This, he notes, allows him to write an "orderly account" (Luke 1:3). The structure of Luke's gospel follows many of the patterns found among ancient historical writings. For those readers who appreciate issues of motivation or who wonder why the disciples would have dropped everything to follow Jesus, Luke's details might help clarify the point more than the accounts of Matthew and Mark.

According to Luke's gospel, Jesus was responsible for Peter's miraculous catch of a number of fish (5:1–11). So when Jesus then called Peter, he already knew that there was something truly distinctive about Jesus of Nazareth.

Luke begins this episode with Jesus standing by the Lake of Gennesaret and teaching a large number of people. As they crowded him, Jesus stepped into a boat belonging to Peter, sat there, and continued to instruct the people. After Jesus taught, he told Peter to go into the deep water and let the nets down. Peter was perplexed since he, along with James and John, had been fishing all night and had caught nothing. Nevertheless, he followed Jesus' instructions.

What resulted was that they caught so many fish that their nets began to break and Peter's boat began to sink.

Peter's response was a recognition that something was happening that was greater than a successful fishing expedition: "He fell down at Jesus' knees, saying, 'Go away from me, Lord, for I am a sinful man!'" (Luke 5:8). For Peter, the miracle was so great that it prompted both awe and a personal recognition of his own weaknesses.

Jesus then called him to a new life. He called on him to catch "people" (verse 10). From then on, Peter became a devoted follower of Jesus. He would lure a countless number of men and women to Jesus, the same way Jesus had shown him how to catch an abundance of fish.

POSTSCRIPT

■ During a 1986 drought in Galilee, two residents found a boat buried in the mud. That boat—now known as "the Galilee boat"—was an ancient fishing vessel similar to the one Peter would have used sometime between 100 B.C. and A.D. 100.

Jacob's Ladder

ONE OF THE MOST visually compelling images in the Bible is Jacob's ladder, which Jacob saw in a dream. The top of the ladder or stairway reached into heaven, while angels were going up and down it. He saw the Lord standing beside him—or perhaps at the top of the stairway. At that point in the dream, God reassured him with promises of his blessing and presence.

Jacob's Ladder *by the Painting School of Avignon*

This dream occurred shortly after Jacob had tricked his twin brother, Esau, out of his rightful inheritance. Esau, as the older brother, was supposed to receive their father Isaac's full blessing, but Jacob deceived Isaac into thinking he was Esau, and Isaac pronounced the full blessing on Jacob. Esau was understandably angry with his brother, and Jacob had to flee for his life. On the way to Haran where his uncle Laban lived, Jacob stopped for the night, set up a stone for his pillow, and slept. While asleep, he had this dream.

God had promised Abraham the land of Canaan, countless descendants, blessings on himself and on others through him, and a special relationship with the Lord. These promises were not solely for Abraham but also for all his descendants. God had reiterated these promises to Abraham's son Isaac, and now, in this dream, God repeated these promises to Jacob.

When Jacob awoke from his dream, he said, "Surely the Lord is in this place—and I did not know it!" (Genesis 28:16). So he set up the stone he'd used as a pillow as a memorial pillar and poured oil on it. He then called the place *Beth-El* (or *Bethel*), which means "house of God."

POSTSCRIPT

◾ The Negro spiritual "We Are Climbing Jacob's Ladder" used the imagery in Jacob's dream to transport people's thoughts to heaven, a far better place away from the miserable conditions endured by slaves in pre-Civil War America. The song has been recorded by artists as diverse as Paul Robeson, the Staple Singers, Pete Seeger, and Bruce Springsteen.

Judah

JUDAH WAS THE FOURTH son of Jacob and Leah. After he was born, his mother declared, "This time I will praise the Lord" (Genesis 29:35). His birth evidently assured Leah that the Lord cared for her, even though her husband seemingly did not. It would not be surprising, therefore, if Judah had a special place in her heart. As time would show, Judah certainly had a special place in God's plans.

Judah was a complex character, having involved himself with Canaanite women and fathering a son by his daughter-in-law, but he also emerged as an advocate for his brothers in Egypt. Although he is not named in the slaughter of Hamor and the people who dwelled in Hamor's city, he probably was one of the plunderers since it was his sister Dinah who was raped. And although he is not named as one of the brothers who sold Joseph into slavery, he probably was also jealous of his father's singular affection for Rachel's firstborn.

Nevertheless, Judah later redeemed himself. When Joseph became a high official in Egypt, ranking second only to Pharaoh, Judah persuaded Jacob to allow Benjamin to go to Egypt with his brothers, which Joseph had set as a condition for them to purchase food during a severe famine, if they came back for more supplies. In Egypt, Judah pleaded with Joseph not to harm Benjamin, as that would kill their father. Judah offered himself in place of Benjamin; this sacrifice caused Joseph to break down in tears and reveal his true identity to his brothers. A joyful reunion followed.

When Jacob was on his deathbed, he blessed each of his 12 sons, and Judah's blessing surpassed them all. Jacob said, "Judah, your brothers shall praise you;... your father's sons shall bow down before you.... The scepter shall not depart from Judah, nor the ruler's staff from between his feet, until tribute comes to him" (Genesis 49:8, 10). Israel's greatest king, David, fulfilled this promise of royal authority by coming from Judah's line. Of course, this was ultimately fulfilled through the divine king who also came from that line: that is, Jesus, "the Lion of the tribe of Judah" (Revelation 5:5).

POSTSCRIPT

■ When the Israelites were numbered in the first census in the Sinai wilderness, the tribe of Judah was first in population. In the wilderness, the tribe of Judah marched on the east side of the tabernacle, and their standard was green with the symbol of a lion.

Jesus Appears to His Disciples

IN THE DAYS and weeks after his resurrection, Jesus appeared many times to his followers. That first morning, Mary Magdalene was lingering at the tomb when she saw someone she thought was the gardener. She asked him for information on the whereabouts of Jesus' body. When he called her by name, she recognized him as the risen Jesus.

He appeared briefly to a group of women (Matthew 28:9), and apparently to Peter (Luke 24:34). It was still Resurrection Sunday when Jesus joined two disciples on their way to Emmaus (Luke 24:13–33). Then a group of disciples saw him as they met in a closed room in Jerusalem (Luke 24:33–48; John 20:19–23).

Supper at Emmaus *by Caravaggio*

Thomas was absent from that meeting. When told about it, he doubted whether it really was Jesus. Eight days later Thomas was with the others when Jesus appeared again. He showed Thomas the nail prints in his hands and the wound in his side. "My Lord and my God!" Thomas exclaimed in faith (John 20:28).

During the month that followed, Jesus made other appearances to his disciples. Paul mentions that he appeared to 500 of his followers at one time, and also to James, Jesus' brother (1 Corinthians 15:5–7). It's possible that this meeting turned James from a skeptic to a believer and a future leader of the Church. John tells of a meeting by the Sea of Galilee with several of the disciples. These fishermen came in from their boats to enjoy a fish breakfast cooked by Jesus (John 21).

Taken together, these stories raise some fascinating questions about the kind of body the risen Jesus had. In some ways, it seemed to be unbound by time and space. Jesus entered a locked room, for instance. He also vanished from the home in Emmaus. And yet this body had some kind of physicality to it. Thomas put his hand into the wound in Jesus' side. Jesus ate with his disciples (Luke 24:42).

In First Corinthians 15:35–55, Paul discusses the "imperishable" heavenly body we will have in the hereafter. Yes, the biblical concept of resurrection is not just spiritual. Strange as it may seem, we are promised a new kind of body in God's coming kingdom. And it seems that Jesus was demonstrating the prototype.

Nathanael Bartholomew

T HE NAME BARTHOLOMEW is mentioned only when the gospel writers list the 12 apostles (Matthew 10:3; Mark 3:18; Luke 6:14; see also Acts 1:13). Many scholars, however, think he is the same man as Nathanael, a friend of Philip's who had a personal encounter with Jesus. This makes sense because Bartholomew is really a surname, "son of Tolmai." And Nathanael had such a significant interaction with Jesus that we would expect him to become one of the Twelve. While we don't find the name Nathanael in any lists that include Bartholomew, he is mentioned with a partial group of disciples who meet with Jesus after his resurrection (John 21:2). The whole problem is solved if we're dealing with a man named Nathanael Bartholomew.

The last part of the first chapter of John's gospel conveys the excitement of people who find Jesus. John the Baptist points to Jesus as the Lamb of God, the one he has been preparing for, and immediately Andrew and another disciple go after Jesus. Then Jesus meets Philip, who is probably a boyhood chum of Andrew and Peter, and invites Philip to follow him. In his excitement, Philip finds his friend, Nathanael Bartholomew, and says, "We have found him about whom Moses in the law and also the prophets wrote, Jesus son of Joseph from Nazareth" (John 1:45).

Nathanael's response is downright deflating: "Can anything good come out of Nazareth?" (verse 46).

What did he mean by that? There are several possibilities. He might have looked down on Nazareth as a small, insignificant village. Yet he himself was from Cana, not a booming metropolis. He might have been judging Nazareth for its interaction with Gentile travelers who came through the area, but again Cana was in the region of Galilee, and the whole region had the same reputation of being tainted by Gentile contact. Most likely, he was aware of the prophecies of the Messiah coming from Bethlehem. The problem with Nazareth was that it wasn't Bethlehem.

But Philip dragged Nathanael to Jesus anyway, and a most interesting exchange occurred. Jesus hailed Nathanael as "truly an Israelite in whom there is no deceit" (verse 47). When Nathanael wondered how Jesus knew anything about him, Jesus said he saw him "under the fig tree" (verse 48).

This is another mystery. We have no clue what Nathanael was doing under the fig tree, but Jesus' knowledge served as convincing proof for this skeptic. He replied, "Rabbi, you are the Son of God! You are the King of Israel!" (verse 49).

The Book of Psalms

PSALMS, THE HYMNBOOK of ancient Israel, contains some of the most famous verses in the Bible. It comes from many hands over a long span of time. Authors range from the famous (David wrote 73 psalms; Moses wrote Psalm 90; Solomon wrote Psalms 72 and 127) to the obscure (Heman, Psalm 88; Ethan, 89; Jeduthun, 39, 62, 77). The psalms vary in their subject matter, with some written for individuals and others written for the community. Among them are laments focusing on present distress (approximately 40 percent of the psalms); thanksgivings to God for deliverance (30, 34); historical reviews of events used to teach the congregation (78, 105, 106); praise hymns responding to God's blessings (8, 19, 29); psalms magnifying God as king (47, 93, 95) and others speaking of human kings (2, 18, 20); liturgical psalms for special religious occasions (15, 24); and others dealing with life questions (32, 37).

Psalms are poetic literature; they look at theology and life through song rather than through logical analysis. In poetry, structural elements are very important. In some psalms (111, 112), each half line—or in the case of Psalm 119, every eighth line—begins with each letter of the alphabet in order. This is lost, of course, when translated into English. But this is not just a literary gimmick; this sort of repetition helps memorization.

The Book of Psalms is divided by four doxologies, or hymns of praise, into five "books" (1—41; 42- -72; 73—89; 90—106; 107—150). Psalms 1 and 2 seem to be an opening to the entire book, and the doxology in Psalm 150 is a powerful conclusion. This indicates that there is an intentional ordering for the book.

The book serves as the theological center of the Hebrew Scriptures, addressing the presence, rule, and worship of God, blessings for obedience and curses (and forgiveness) for disobedience, along with many other themes. It is also important for the New Testament, which quotes it more than any other Old Testament book. For centuries, readers have resonated with this book, which speaks not only to the mind but also to the heart and will, echoing the emotions of so many common life experiences.

POSTSCRIPT

■ Descriptions of religious ceremonies throughout the Old Testament generally describe how things are acted out; one might equate that with the "video" of Old Testament life. The psalms then provide the "audio," the words and music that would have accompanied these occasions.

The Rosetta Stone

IN ONE OF THE MOST fascinating stories of archaeology, French troops under Napoleon's command made a world-changing discovery in Lower Egypt. The year was 1799, and Napoleon had wrested control of Egypt from the Ottoman Empire. As one version of the legend goes, an old wall was slated for demolition to make way for a French fort, but a French officer named Bouchard saw some writing on the wall. Three types of writing, to be precise: Egyptian hieroglyphics at the top, Greek letters at the bottom, and a strange cursive script in between. Bouchard correctly surmised that this might be three versions of the same message, and thus the stone might help unlock the mysteries of the ancient Egyptian language.

Fortunately Napoleon was a fan of ancient history, and he had copies of the Rosetta Stone sent back to Europe for analysis. There scholars identified the middle writing as a cursive "demotic" script— common Egyptian, as opposed to the picture-based hieroglyphs used by the priests. The Greek translation indicated it was a decree praising Ptolemy V, an Egyptian king, and this would set the date at about 196 B.C. Over the following decades, a host of scholars set about the task of deciphering the Egyptian letters. Could they figure out which symbols stood for which words?

British physicist Thomas Young, already known for his research into the nature of light, came up with a crucial theory about the stone: The Egyptian markings were not just a picture-language but also phonetic signs. The French Egyptologist Jean-François Champollion picked up on this theory, noticing a particular mark that accompanied proper names. By identifying names such as Ptolemy and Cleopatra, he began to discover the syllables represented by the hieroglyphic pictures. He eventually unlocked the code and produced a grammar of the ancient Egyptian language.

The value of the Rosetta Stone to biblical studies is considerable. It opened up the ancient world of Egypt to modern scholars, where significant portions of biblical history occurred—particularly the Exodus. The more we understand about the world of the pharaohs, the more we know about Moses, who grew up in Pharaoh's court, or Joseph, who ruled under another pharaoh.

Jesus and the Apostles

W HEN MOSES WAS called to a mission, his brother Aaron was the first to join him. Within Islam, Muhammad was joined by his wife and by a servant. For Jesus, however, there is no sense that any of his relatives followed him when he was alive. After his death, his brothers James and Jude (Judas) clearly came to see him in a different light. Their letters, included in the New Testament, testify to that.

Jesus' primary companions were 12 men. Luke 6:14–16 lists the 12 as "Simon, whom he named Peter, and his brother Andrew, and James, and John, and Philip, and Bartholomew, and Matthew, and Thomas, and James son of Alphaeus, and Simon, who was called the Zealot, and Judas son of James, and Judas Iscariot." (Instead of Judas, son of James, Matthew 10:3 refers to Thaddaeus.)

A number of these men had nicknames. Judas son of James was nicknamed Thomas. In Aramaic, "Thomas" means "the twin." The Apocryphal Acts of Thomas—a writing that was not included in the New Testament—hints that Thomas may have looked so much like Jesus that the nickname could have been a joke about the resemblance between the two. The name Peter, that of the most famous apostle, also was a nickname. His real name was Simon, one of the most common names in the ancient Hebrew world. "Peter" (in Greek) and "Cephas" (in Aramaic) both mean "rock." Perhaps Peter was solid as a rock, perhaps he saw himself that way, or maybe he vacillated a great deal and so was given the nickname ironically. James and John were called "the Sons of Thunder," quite possibly because of their tempers.

The apostles came from varying backgrounds. One was a tax collector. At least one was a Zealot and may have been attracted to Jesus because of the possibility that his kingdom was to be a worldly one. The apostles who stood out the most all had worked as fishermen. Three of them—Simon (Peter), James, and John—witnessed the Transfiguration, were near to Jesus in the Garden of Gethsemane, and were at times mentioned apart from the other apostles.

What did the apostles have in common? The Gospel of Mark indicates that what they had most in common was that they all missed the point of who Jesus really was. They all abandoned Jesus when he was arrested. Mark, however, communicates in his account that God works through the fragility of all sorts of people. The one who was born in a stable does not call nobles, kings, rabbis, the educated, or lawyers. Rather he calls those who are fragile and yet who seek to be faithful, even when they fail.

Leah Is Loved

AFTER JACOB FLED from his home because he feared his brother, Esau, he found refuge with his uncle Laban, who welcomed him warmly as "my bone and my flesh!" (Genesis 29:14). While Jacob lived with Laban and his family, he fell increasingly in love with Laban's younger daughter Rachel. He offered to serve Laban for seven years in return for Rachel's hand. But after he completed his contract with his uncle, Laban tricked Jacob by giving him his older daughter Leah, saying that this was their custom; that is, the firstborn daughter must be married first.

Rachel and Leah *by Dante Gabriel Rossetti*

Thus, in a fateful ironic twist, Jacob, who had tricked and deceived his own father and brother, now was tricked himself. He agreed to serve another seven years if he could marry Rachel after the traditional marriage week with Leah. Laban agreed.

The contrast between how God responded to these two women should be noted. "When the Lord saw that Leah was unloved, he opened her womb; but Rachel was barren" (verse 31; Rachel would later give birth to two sons). Nevertheless, even after giving Jacob several sons, Leah remained "hated" (verse 33). The names of her first three sons express her marital unhappiness and her desperate hope for Jacob's love. Finally, despite her estrangement with her husband after the birth of their fourth son, she declared, "This time I will praise the Lord" (verse 35), naming him Judah. Her faith in God became her abiding strength.

In contrast to Leah is the writer's curious portrait of her sister. In Genesis chapter 31, in still another account of deception, Rachel steals her father's household gods and hides them from him. It is clear how attached she was to pagan idols.

Thus it is a fitting irony: The descendants of two of Leah's sons—Levi and Judah—became the tribes of the priests and the kings, respectively. Moses and Aaron were Levites, who inaugurated the Jewish priesthood. David, the greatest of the Jewish kings, and of course Jesus, the promised Messiah, were descendants of Judah. Certainly the Lord not only blessed Leah but loved her as well. It is also interesting that Jacob specifically asked to be buried with her at the end of his life (see Genesis 49:31). By then, perhaps, he had come to love her as she did him.

Tamar

JUDAH, THE SON OF JACOB and Leah, took a Canaanite woman as his wife, and they had three sons. When the first son, Er, died, leaving a widow named Tamar, Judah urged his second son, Onan, to marry her so that Er would have heirs. But Onan refused to consummate his marriage with Tamar, knowing that any sons born would not be his. As a result of his actions, God took his life, and Tamar became a widow once again.

By custom, Tamar should have become the wife of Judah's third son, Shelah, but Judah, evidently being superstitious, was afraid that Shelah would also die, so he told Tamar to wait until Shelah grew up. In fact, he did not want her to marry his son at all. After some time, Tamar realized that Judah would not honor his promise. Thus she took matters into her own hands after Judah's wife died. She dressed up as a temple prostitute and went out to meet Judah along the roadside. Not recognizing his daughter-in-law, Judah propositioned her, and, when he could not pay her price—a young goat—she took three of his most personal possessions in pledge: his signet ring, his cord, and his staff. She would use these items later to expose him. When Judah returned with a young goat to pay her and get his possessions back, she was gone.

Three months later, Judah was informed that his daughter-in-law was pregnant, and he angrily ordered her to be burned to death. Tamar then brought out the three items she had taken from him. Thus Judah was exposed. To his credit, he confessed, "She is more in the right than I" (Genesis 38:26).

Tamar gave birth to two sons, Perez and Zerah. Remarkably, Tamar and Perez are noted later as ancestors of the great King David, and Tamar is one of only five women mentioned in the genealogies of Jesus in the New Testament (see Matthew 1:3). Her inclusion in Jesus' lineage makes the point that even an outcast such as she was worthy—by God's grace—of being in the line of the Messiah.

POSTSCRIPT

■ There are two terms for "prostitute" in Hebrew. The first, *zonah,* was the type known around the world in every era. Rahab, the woman from Jericho who helped the Israelites take the city, was a *zonah.* The second word is *qedeshah,* meaning "sacred prostitute" or "temple prostitute"; they were attached to Canaanite shrines as part of the debased Canaanite religion. Tamar dressed up as a *qedeshah.* (The word is related to the Hebrew word *qadosh,* meaning "holy.")

Jesus' Ascension

T HERE'S SOMETHING anticlimactic about Jesus' ascension. It seems like a footnote in the gospel story. Only Luke describes it; the other gospel writers end the Jesus story earlier. And yet this must have been a stunning event, as Jesus rose from the earth into glory.

Perhaps the Ascension is overlooked because it's *in between.* In a way, we can see it as a continuation of the Resurrection and also as a prelude to the Holy Spirit's arrival. In fact, that may be why Luke records it twice, both following fast on the Resurrection in his gospel account and again to begin the story of the Church in Acts.

Luke tells us that Jesus spent 40 days with his disciples after the Resurrection, proving that he was truly alive and continuing his teaching about the kingdom of God. At the end of this time, he gathered them once again for his last instructions. Among these

The Ascension *by Otto Ludwig*

instructions was something we call the Great Commission, recorded in various forms in Matthew, Luke, and Acts. The best known wording is Matthew's: "Go therefore and make disciples of all nations, baptizing them in the name of the Father and of the Son and of the Holy Spirit, and teaching them to obey everything that I have commanded you. And remember, I am with you always, to the end of the age" (Matthew 28:19–20).

After his final farewell, Jesus was "lifted up" (Acts 1:9), and eventually a cloud obscured him. You can imagine the disciples' amazement—except they had seen many amazing things since getting to know Jesus. In these last 40 days, Jesus seemed to show up without warning and vanish just as quickly. Did they know this was the last they would see of him?

Well, yes and no. They were still watching the sky when two angels joined them. Literally, they were "two men in white robes" (verse 10), but that's the usual description of angels. These messengers announced that Jesus would return "in the same way as you saw him go into heaven" (verse 11). Yes, there was a note of finality to the whole event, but there was also the promise that Jesus would return. But when? The next day? The next year? Two thousand years later? They didn't know.

Thomas

Thomas was one of the 12 apostles. It is from him that we get the phrase "Doubting Thomas," because Thomas demanded proof of Jesus' resurrection.

We don't know where Thomas came from. We don't have a story of his calling to discipleship. We do know that his name means "the twin" in Hebrew, and the Greek translation of that word, *Didymus,* is sometimes used for him. That leads some to wonder who his twin brother was, but Scripture provides no clues. And yet this unknown disciple plays a crucial role in John's gospel. The other three gospels virtually ignore Thomas, merely listing him with the others, but John includes him at several key points in the story.

When Lazarus fell sick, Jesus delayed at first, but then decided to go and see him. This meant a trip from Galilee to Bethany, which was a suburb of Jerusalem, and that was dangerous. Opposition to Jesus' ministry was headquartered in Jerusalem. For some time, Jesus had been talking about going back to Jerusalem, where he would die and rise again. So this wasn't just a social call. It was the beginning of the end. Thomas understood that. When Jesus decided to make the trip, Thomas said to the other disciples, "Let us also go, that we may die with him" (John 11:16).

In Jerusalem, they enjoyed their final Passover meal with the Lord. Jesus was talking in highly spiritual terms about going away from them: "You know the way to the place where I am going" (John 14:4). It was Thomas who voiced what the others were thinking: "Lord, we do not know where you are going. How can we know the way?" (verse 5). Jesus answered with one of his most important teachings: "I am the way, and the truth, and the life. No one comes to the Father except through me" (verse 6).

Thomas uttered his most-remembered words after Jesus' resurrection. The Lord had appeared to the other disciples when Thomas was absent. They told him about it, but he expressed skepticism: "Unless I see the mark of the nails in his hands, and put my finger in the mark of the nails and my hand in his side, I will not believe" (John 20:25).

A week later, Jesus appeared to the disciples again, when Thomas was in the room. Jesus invited him to touch his wounds, and Thomas responded in faith: "My Lord and my God!" (verse 28).

He is known forever as a doubter, but his skepticism provided an opportunity for Jesus to quell the doubts of many.

The Book of Proverbs

Proverbs, like Psalms, includes material from many hands over a long period. Solomon is given major credit as writer (1:1; 10:1; 25:1), but there are also proverbs from unnamed "wise" authors (22:17; 24:23), the unknown Agur (30:1), and an unheard-of King Lemuel, who was taught by his mother (31:1).

The book is written entirely in poetry, which aids in memorization. Poetry is also a powerful tool in persuading people to choose the right path and avoid the wrong one, and these are the goals the book sets for itself (1:2–7).

Two main sections form the book. The first (1—9) is a collection of discourses or essays, mainly in the form of a father instructing a son on aspects of life. A woman's teaching is also important in the book, since wisdom itself is personified as a woman (8:1—9:12), while folly is pictured as a foolish (9:13–18) or an adulterous woman (7). The second section (10—31) is mainly individual proverbs, which take several different forms. They are short and valuable insights gained by observing the way the world works.

The instructions of the first half contain commands or motives (3:1–23), while statements of wisdom in the second half are closer to the proverbs of today (16:18). There is debate about whether there is an overarching structure to Proverbs, but many themes arise regularly in the book. These themes include wealth/poverty, work/laziness, the importance of words, and ungodly people such as flatterers, gossips, scoffers, whisperers, and liars.

It is interesting to note that sometimes individual proverbs are contradictory, with opposite statements even occurring side by side (26:4–5). Part of wisdom, however, is not only to know the right words to say but also the right time to say them (15:23). As one experiences more of life, of victory and failure, wisdom grows and correct responses become more apparent. One learns to read the times.

Mention of God is not as common in Proverbs as one might expect ("God" is mentioned five times, and "the Lord" appears about 75 times), though God underlies what wisdom is. The "fear of the Lord" is where knowledge starts (1:7). Israel knew God as the creator of the universe, the one who set natural laws in motion. Seeking wisdom is seeking to live in the best way possible in the world God created.

The Apocrypha

THE APOCRYPHA IS A collection of writings from the period between the Old and New Testaments (fifth century B.C. to first century A.D.), running the range from history to fantasy to philosophy to ethical instruction. Some Christians regard these writings as scriptural on a par with the Old and New Testaments. Others honor them as ethical but not doctrinal guides. Still others have no regard for them. Jews do not include them with their holy writings.

The confusion began around 200 B.C. with the Septuagint, the Greek translation of the Hebrew Scriptures (Old Testament). While the five books of Moses and the prophetic writings were not in question, there was a third group of Scriptures that were still in flux—the Writings (Kethubim). The Psalms and Proverbs were readily accepted, but there was some disagreement about Ecclesiastes and Song of Songs. There were also other similar works, more recently penned, that celebrated the history and culture of the Jewish people, and a number of these writings were included in the Septuagint.

A rabbinical council in Jamnia in A.D. 90 settled the matter for the Jews, defining what was and wasn't Scripture. The extra books that were added to the Septuagint were decisively rejected.

Jerome, who translated the Scriptures into Latin in the early 400s, coined the term *Apocrypha* (meaning "hidden") for those extra writings. While they could be beneficial for study, he said, the Church should follow the lead of the rabbinical council and exclude them from authoritative Scripture. Shortly after this, Augustine disagreed.

This ambiguity remained until the Protestant Reformation brought the issue to the surface. The reformers opposed certain teachings that found support in the Apocrypha. Some, like the Lutherans and Anglicans, put the Apocrypha in a clearly secondary position, as Jerome had done. Other Protestants excluded the Apocrypha entirely.

With the Council of Trent, the Roman Catholics took the Augustinian line, declaring most of the books of the Apocrypha fully canonical. (Three were declared "deuterocanonical," a secondary regard.)

Whether or not they are Holy Writ, the Apocryphal books give insight into the development of Judaism during a challenging time. The outside world had encroached upon Israel not only militarily but also culturally and philosophically. How would God's people maintain their identity? The Apocrypha examines this issue in various ways.

Calming a Storm

ACCORDING TO MARK 4:35–41, Jesus and the disciples were in a boat, traveling across a lake, when a powerful storm enveloped them. Waves came crashing over the sides of the boat, filling it with water. Meanwhile, Jesus slept soundly. The disciples, concerned that the boat would sink, woke him with the words: "Teacher, do you not care that we are perishing?" (verse 38).

Jesus rose, rebuked the wind, and said to the sea, "Peace! Be still!" The wind and the sea immediately became calm. Jesus then asked the disciples why they were afraid, demonstrating a lack of faith. They responded by asking each other, "Who then is this, that even the wind and the sea obey him?" (verse 41).

Matthew 8:23–27 shares the same story with Mark, and both show how clueless the disciples were in recognizing the significance of who Jesus was. Their last statement in this episode reveals their amazement at Jesus' astonishing power over nature. That indicates to us that when the disciples interrupted Jesus' sleep, their intention was not for him to use his supernatural powers but more likely to help them bail the water out of the boat. In other words, how could Jesus sleep through this life-threatening storm while they were frantically trying to save themselves from drowning? All hands were needed in this effort, and it would not be surprising if some of the disciples were annoyed with Jesus' lack of concern and even more with his lack of participation. Their reactions were very much like what ours might have been—both before and after the calming of the storm.

This story tells readers that Jesus has the power to calm nature's mighty storms. With power like this, is it difficult to imagine his ability to calm the storms that rage in people's hearts?

POSTSCRIPT

■ Throughout the Old Testament, the sea is seen as a frightening place; it represents the potential for chaos and trouble. Babylonian myths, like the *Enuma Elish,* described violent gods and goddesses as bodies of water; it is not surprising, therefore, that the Hebrew worldview might ascribe similar harsh qualities to the sea.

■ The calming of the waves also hearkens back to the miracle of the Exodus: "Was it not you who dried up the sea, the waters of the great deep, who made the depths of the sea a way for the redeemed to cross over?" (Isaiah 51:10).

Jacob Wrestles with God

As JACOB RETURNED to his homeland after 20 years away, during which time he had married and fathered many children, he was apprehensive about meeting his brother, Esau, whom he had defrauded of his birthright and blessing. Before he met Esau, however, he had an experience that transformed him and changed history for all of his descendants.

Jacob Wrestles with an Angel *by Edward von Steinle*

Jacob had sent everyone and everything with him ahead, and he found himself alone next to the River Jabbok. That night, a man wrestled with him all night, and Jacob more than held his own. At daybreak, the man, seeing that he was not prevailing, touched Jacob's hip socket, putting it out of joint, and yet still Jacob would not relent. He asked the man for a blessing before he would let go.

Jacob must have realized that this was no ordinary mortal with whom he strived; perhaps it was the supernatural "touch" that tipped him off. In any case, the "man" showed his superior position to Jacob by asking his name and then bestowing on him a new name: *Israel,* which means "one who strives with God" or "God strives." This was a far better name than *Jacob,* which means "one who takes by the heel" or "supplanter" (he got this when he was born because he had come out clutching the heel of his brother Esau) or "he deceives" (a fitting name for one who practiced so much deceit earlier in his life).

Then the "man" blessed him, and Jacob realized fully that he had indeed seen God. He called the place *Peniel,* which means "face of God," because, he said, "I have seen God face to face, and yet my life is preserved" (Genesis 32:30). He realized that his mere human strength, impressive though it had been, could never have prevailed, and that he had survived solely by God's grace.

Israel became the name of the nation that sprang from his line, and it serves as a constant reminder of this people's close relationship with their God.

Joseph, the Favored

JOSEPH WAS ONE OF THE 12 SONS of Jacob. His grandparents were Isaac and Rebekah, and his great-grandparents were Abraham and Sarah. His mother was Rachel, Jacob's second wife, the one whom Jacob loved from the day he first set his eyes on her. Rachel died in childbirth when she gave birth to Joseph's brother, Benjamin. Therefore, Joseph not only lacked maternal care from his early youth, but he also had to look after his younger brother—all made more difficult because of the intense jealousy from other members of his family.

The Bible says, "Joseph was handsome and good-looking" (Genesis 39:6); more importantly, he retained a high ethical standard despite being unjustly treated by his brothers, Potiphar and his wife, and the chief cupbearer. But after each reversal, his honesty and God-given talent to interpret dreams brought him closer and closer to the Egyptian throne until only the pharaoh exercised more authority than he. During

Joseph Reveals His Dream to His Brethren *by James Tissot*

his service to Pharaoh, Joseph married an Egyptian maiden who bore him two sons, Manasseh and Ephraim, from whom came two of the 12 tribes of the nation of Israel.

After Joseph was reconciled with his brothers and reunited with his father following many years of separation, Joseph came to realize that God's hand was behind each major occurrence in his life. He even told his brothers, "Though you intended to do harm to me, God intended it for good, in order to preserve a numerous people, as he is doing today" (Genesis 50:20).

Joseph died peacefully at the age of 110, and his bones were eventually returned to Canaan and buried there.

POSTSCRIPT

■ Potiphera (not to be confused with Potiphar, Pharaoh's captain of the body-guard) was a priest of On (Heliopolis). He became Joseph's father-in-law when Pharaoh gave Potiphera's daughter Asenath to Joseph as his wife. *Potiphera* in Egyptian was *pa-di-pa-Ra,* meaning "he whom Ra [the sun god] has given."

The Coming of the Holy Spirit

PENTECOST WAS A JEWISH harvest festival 50 days after Passover. As on the other holidays in the Jewish calendar, many pilgrims would visit the temple in Jerusalem at this time. For several centuries, Jews had been emigrating to other cities throughout the Mediterranean world, so the holidays brought people back to Jerusalem.

Jesus died at Passover time, rising on the third day and appearing to his disciples over a period of 40 days before ascending into heaven. He had told them to wait in Jerusalem for "the promise of the Father" (Acts 1:4), which he had previously explained to them. He was talking about the arrival of the Holy Spirit. At the Last Supper he had talked at length about this Comforter/Counselor who would come to them once he was gone (see John 15—16). Now it was about to happen.

There were about 120 followers of Jesus at this point. They were gathered "in one place" (Acts 2:1), sitting in a "house." We don't know where this was, but it would make sense if it was close to the temple or perhaps part of the temple itself. (That would give the disciples quick access to thousands of people.)

When the Spirit arrived, there were three manifestations. First there was a sound like a violent wind. Then "tongues, as of fire" (verse 3) descended from heaven upon the heads of the disciples. And then they began to speak in other languages, which were understood by people in the international crowd visiting Jerusalem at the time.

There is some disagreement as to whether they were speaking specific languages or some heavenly language that was miraculously translated by the Spirit into the languages of multiple nations. In any case, listeners were amazed that they understood the message in their own language.

Of course, there are always scoffers. Some onlookers thought the disciples had to be drunk. So Peter began the most important sermon in Church history by saying, "Indeed, these are not drunk, as you suppose, for it is only nine o'clock in the morning" (verse 15).

POSTSCRIPT

■ Throughout Scripture, God often signals his presence with a fiery cloud. He led the Israelites through the wilderness with such a cloud after their release from Egypt. At the dedications of the tabernacle and temple, a cloud of fire dropped into the Holy of Holies. Even at Jesus' baptism, the Spirit descended like a dove— that is, a vivid, flying brightness. Was the fire that settled on the disciples at Pentecost pieces of the fiery cloud that had always indicated the Lord's presence?

Simon, the Zealot

Simon, the Zealot, was a disciple of Jesus, one of the 12 apostles. As a Zealot, he would have been involved (at least at one time) in a rebel movement against the Romans.

Israel was a land under occupation. The Romans conquered the territory in 63 B.C., when General Pompey marched his legions into Jerusalem. Soon they installed Herod the Great as king of the Jews, even though the Jews did not consider him one of their own. He began turning the holy city of Jerusalem into a Gentile city, where you could go to an obscene play at a theater or watch violent games in a stadium. Many of the Jews chafed under the yoke of these pagan rulers.

Different groups had different ways of dealing with the Roman occupation. Some opportunists tried to get in good with the Romans, even adopting Gentile ways. The Sadducees and Herodians were in this camp. The Pharisees, on the other hand, sought to keep the nation pure from the corruption of the Romans by promoting strict observance of God's laws (and their own agenda) throughout society.

And then there were the Zealots. Driven by zeal for Jewish independence, they were freedom fighters. Through the first century B.C. and the first century A.D., there were various groups of bandits and rebels; most of these groups were badly organized, and the Romans responded brutally against them and any who supported them (see Acts 5:33–37). The Zealot movement may have begun around the time of Jesus, but it came to fruition some 30 years later with a full-fledged revolt, when they took control of Jerusalem. It took the Roman army several years to quash the uprising, but finally they destroyed Jerusalem in A.D. 70 and then besieged the last pocket of resistance at Masada in 73.

Was Simon a member of this rebel movement? The word *Zealot* could refer to someone who was zealous for any cause, but by the time the gospels were written, this political group was well known. So it's likely that he was involved with this group at some time. Still, Jesus' ministry was pointedly nonpolitical and nonviolent. "My kingdom is not from this world," he told Pilate (John 18:36).

At some point in Simon's life, he had to choose between fighting for Israel's independence and serving Jesus' earthly ministry. That he is listed among the 11 apostles after Jesus' ascension shows what decision he made (Acts 1:13).

The Book of Ecclesiastes

A BOOK FROM the wisdom writings in the Old Testament, Ecclesiastes is a reflection on the meaning of life. It is credited to a king, a "son of David" (1:1). He is traditionally understood to be Solomon, who lived in the tenth century B.C. While Solomon might be the speaker (the "I" in the book), he is not the writer, who speaks of the speaker as if he were another person. The speaker is only identified as *Qohelet,* "the Teacher" (1:1). If Solomon had written the book, he probably would have given his actual name.

The book uses both poetry and prose. It contains short proverbs (7:1–12; 10:1–20), advice urging an action or attitude (5:2, 4), morality stories drawing a lesson from what the author has done or seen (1:12—2:26; 4:13–16, 9:13 16), and an allegory of old age (12:1–7).

The most common theme running through the book is the author's consideration that every aspect of life is "vanity." This term, used 38 times in the book, is described like the morning mist that quickly disappears in the wind, leaving no lasting evidence of its existence. All of life, as the book states at the beginning (1:2) and at the end (12:8), is vanity. The author has tried specific things that have all turned out to be vain and fruitless: gaining wisdom (1:14–18; 2:12–16), pleasure (2:1), work (2:11, 18–23; 4:4–8), justice or wickedness (3:16–21; 7:15; 8:10), status or position (4:13–16), wealth (5:10; 6:2), descendants (6:3–4), and skill in speaking (6:10–11). None provided the meaning he was looking for.

The writer contradicts the established, traditional wisdom that says there is hope in life. Instead, the Teacher points out that life is much more complex than this; everything isn't always rosy and black days do come. He tries to present a more realistic picture of life rather than just an idealistic one.

The author is not completely without hope, however. If life, in all its parts, is all there is, then it should be enjoyed (3:22). Although he cannot exactly explain the "why" of it, he maintains that turning to God, enjoying his gifts, worshipping, and obeying him can give meaning and counter vanity (2:24–26; 3:12–14, 22; 5:18–20; 7:18; 8:12; 9:7–10; 11:9–10). Even though the things the author did to find ultimate meaning did not provide it, these things were not in and of themselves bad and without meaning. Friendship is better than being alone, and while wisdom can come and go, it is better than being a fool (4:9–15).

The Vulgate Bible

IN A.D. 405, CHRISTIAN scholar Jerome completed a Latin translation of the Bible that has served the Church ever since. Known as the Vulgate, from the Latin *vulgus* ("common"), it was intended to bring Christianity together with a common Scripture.

The Roman Empire was falling apart at the time, and the Church was in danger of fragmenting with it. Greek was still the common tongue in the Eastern churches, and they had the Septuagint and the New Testament in its original language. But the Latin-speaking churches in Rome and westward needed a good translation of those Scriptures. There were several Latin Bible versions before Jerome, but they weren't very good.

Damasus, Bishop of Rome from 366 to 384, had worked to centralize the power of the church in Rome. One way to do this: Establish a high-quality Latin translation that would become the new standard for all the churches. He appointed his secretary, Jerome, to the task.

Jerome had a unique combination of secular scholarship and Christian devotion. At one point he felt convicted that he was more devoted to Cicero than to Christ, so in penitence he withdrew to an ascetic life in the Syrian desert, where he studied Hebrew and copied Bible manuscripts. He began his service with Pope Damasus in 382 and jumped into the translation project. "I am not so stupid as to think that any

St. Jerome *by Fra Angelico*

of the Lord's words . . . need correcting," he wrote in a letter. "My aim has been to restore them to the form of the Greek original."

After the death of Damasus, Jerome lived a secluded life in Bethlehem, where he continued his work. He became convinced that his Old Testament translation needed to return to the original Hebrew, not just the Greek of the Septuagint. He even consulted Jewish scholars in order to "give my Latin readers the hidden treasures of Hebrew erudition," he wrote. Influenced by his Jewish sources, he recommended that the Apocrypha be separated as writings beneficial to the Church but not part of canonical Scripture. Nevertheless, he included the Apocrypha in his translation.

Completed in 405, the Vulgate rapidly became the standard it was intended to be—to the point that Latin continued to be the language of the Church long after it stopped being spoken anywhere else.

Light of the World

IN 1630, John Winthrop said, "For we must consider that we shall be as a city upon a hill. The eyes of all people are upon us." He delivered that line in his sermon entitled "A Model of Christian Charity." In that famous sermon, he called upon New England colonists to recognize that the eyes of the world were upon them: The Puritans would be a city on a hill, and if they did not glorify God, others would draw attention to that.

Winthrop's simile, drawn from the Sermon on the Mount, would have been familiar to his congregants. In Matthew 5:14–16, Jesus says, "You are the light of the world. A city built on a hill cannot be hid. No one after lighting a lamp puts it under the bushel basket, but on the lampstand, and it gives light to all in the house. In the same way, let your light shine before others, so that they may see your good works and give glory to your Father in heaven."

Jesus was not simply telling his followers that they needed to have a public presence and message. Like Winthrop some 1,600 years later, Jesus emphasized that people's eyes are on his followers. Those eyes are not looking at the light per se. They are not staring into the sun. Rather, they are looking at what the light illuminates, what good works come through the light, and who—in the process—is glorified.

Today, there is a popular song that many children innocently sing. "This little light of mine, I'm going to let it shine . . ." is often sung during joyous occasions. Originally, however, this song was a black spiritual, emphasizing the importance of working through struggles and having faith in God during severe hardships. This song later became a popular civil rights anthem during the 1950s and 1960s. People living during dark times have sung this song to remind themselves to radiate the light that Jesus emanates through them.

In good times and in bad times, the light that shines through Christians dispels the darkness in the world so that people can see the one who proclaimed, "I am the light of the world" (John 8:12).

POSTSCRIPT

■ The first biblical mention of light is in Genesis 1:3–4: "Then God said, 'Let there be light'; and there was light. And God saw that the light was good; and God separated the light from the darkness." In symbolic terms, God will do the same in the end times.

The Dream Interpreter

DREAMS HAD A SIGNIFICANT impact on Joseph's life. He had two dreams of his own, and he interpreted several dreams of Egyptians whom he met. They all proved to be prophetic.

Joseph was his father's favorite son, and his father gave him a many-colored coat to show his special affection for the son of his beloved Rachel, and this naturally incited his brothers' jealousy. Then he had a dream in which he and his 11 brothers were out binding sheaves of grain; his sheaf stood up by itself and his brothers' sheaves bowed down to it. In his second dream, the sun, moon, and 11 stars bowed down to him. Not surprisingly, these dreams infuriated his brothers even more.

The brothers subsequently plotted to kill Joseph but instead sold him into slavery to a passing caravan. Joseph ended up in Egypt, serving as chief overseer in the household of Potiphar, a high Egyptian official. When Potiphar's wife tried to seduce him, he demonstrated his high integrity by refusing: "How then could I do this great wickedness, and sin against God?" (Genesis 39:9). Potiphar's wife then told her husband that Joseph had attacked her, and Joseph was thrown into prison.

While in prison, he befriended the pharaoh's chief cupbearer and his baker, who were also imprisoned and who both had dreams that he interpreted. In the cupbearer's case, the dream foretold his release and restoration to his former position; in the baker's case, the dream foretold his execution. Both dreams came true.

Two years later, the pharaoh had two dreams: One was about seven fat cows being devoured by seven thin cows and another, similar dream was about seven fat and seven thin ears of grain. Joseph was fetched from prison to interpret these dreams, which he did, predicting seven years of plentiful harvests followed by seven years of devastating famine. He then suggested a plan for storing up food for the years of famine. The pharaoh was so impressed that he promoted Joseph to oversee this national project and made him the second-ranking official in the kingdom.

Ironically, when the famine came, Joseph's brothers came to Egypt to purchase food, where they met Joseph—though they did not recognize him—and bowed down to him, fulfilling the two dreams of his youth. God gave Joseph a special gift, which brought about God's plan to preserve his special people.

Moses

MOSES WAS A TOWERING figure whose legacy as leader and lawgiver was felt throughout Israel's history. He was a reluctant hero, initially resisting God's call on his life, but he grew into the role and became God's instrument for delivering his people out of Egyptian bondage and for revealing his law. At the end of the Torah (the first five books of the Bible), it says, "Never since has there arisen a prophet in Israel like Moses, whom the Lord knew face to face. He was unequaled for all the signs and wonders that the Lord sent him to perform . . . in the sight of all Israel" (Deuteronomy 34:10–12).

Moses barely escaped death at birth, since the pharaoh had ordered that all newborn Hebrew boys be killed. Moses was saved when his mother hid him in a basket, which she floated on the Nile River. Pharaoh's daughter subsequently discovered and adopted him, and he lived in affluence in Pharaoh's court.

His first 40 years were spent in Egypt until he killed an Egyptian who was beating a Hebrew. He then fled for his life and spent another 40 years in Midian, where Jethro, a Midianite priest, befriended him. Eventually he married Jethro's daughter, Zipporah, who bore him a son, Gershom. Moses remained in Midian, living as a shepherd.

The Lord, however, had far greater plans for Moses, who met God in a dramatic encounter at a burning bush, where God told Moses to return to Egypt to deliver his people. Reluctantly, Moses obeyed. After he returned to Egypt, he confronted a different pharaoh from the one he knew when he left. He told Pharaoh to let the Israelites go, but the king refused. Through a series of ten plagues, climaxing with the killing of all the firstborn in the land (save those of the Hebrews), God displayed his power against the Egyptian gods and convinced Pharaoh to let his people go.

Moses led the people to Mount Sinai, where God gave Moses the Ten Commandments and the rest of the law. At this point, the Hebrews had to decide to follow the Lord and his servant Moses or go forward on their own. Those who rebelled were destroyed, and Moses remained the leader of those who remained.

Sadly for Moses, he forfeited his right to enter the Promised Land when he became angry one too many times and disobeyed God by striking a rock to produce water, instead of speaking to it as God had commanded. But God graciously allowed him to see the land from a high mountain before he died. God himself buried Moses at a ripe old age of 120 years. The location of his grave is not known.

Peter's Speech at Pentecost

THE APOSTLE PETER had never been shy about speaking up, but his challenge was to say things that made sense. Peter often said things he regretted later. He became famous for the "wrong answer"—that is, for the misguided statement of bravado that was obviously well intentioned. Yet he had emerged as one of the leaders among the apostles, so it's no surprise that he delivered the keynote address at Pentecost.

The risen Jesus had just ascended into heaven. The disciples were on their own. Suddenly the Holy Spirit came upon them with wind and fire and a miracle that enabled them to speak in languages that visitors from many different countries understood. Onlookers were wondering what was going on, so Peter explained.

Prophecy is being fulfilled, Peter said, citing the prophet Joel, who had predicted the outpouring of God's Spirit. He went on to provide the basic truths about Jesus:

- He performed miracles that showed God's power.
- He was crucified, according to God's purposes.
- He rose from the dead.
- He is now exalted at God's right hand.
- He is Lord and Messiah.
- You need to repent and be baptized in his name.

Peter would follow the same basic outline in sermons recorded in Acts 3 and 5. Scholars have come to call this the *kerygma,* or germ, of the gospel. When people wanted to know about Jesus, this is what the Christians told them.

The results on that day of Pentecost were breathtaking. About 3,000 responded to Peter's call to "repent, and be baptized" (Acts 2:38). In one day the Church grew by a factor of 25. Certainly this caused logistical problems, but a brilliant energy of joy and sharing immediately characterized the Church. Christians met in homes and in the temple, selling their goods to care for the poor while praising God.

POSTSCRIPT

- One of the shocking assertions (for that time) in Joel's prophecy is that the Spirit would be poured out on men and women alike. "Your sons and your daughters shall prophesy" (Joel 2:28). This suggests that the outpouring at Pentecost happened to the whole group of Jesus-followers (both men and women), not just the 12 apostles.

Judas Iscariot

ONE OF THE 12 apostles of Jesus, Judas Iscariot served as treasurer of the group. He betrayed Jesus by leading soldiers to the place where Jesus prayed. Stricken with guilt over the betrayal, he committed suicide. We have no record of Judas's background, except that he was the son of a man named Simon and his nickname (or family name) was Iscariot.

Outside of the betrayal, the only insight we have about Judas is in John's gospel in which he is called a "thief" (John 12:6). Interestingly, he held the common purse for Jesus' band of disciples. After a woman poured expensive perfume on Jesus' feet, it was Judas who commented that it could

have been sold and the proceeds given to the poor. John makes it clear that Judas was not really concerned about relieving poverty, but instead he wanted to pocket the proceeds for himself.

Quite possibly simple greed was the motive behind the betrayal. As soon as Jesus entered Jerusalem in that final Passover week, Judas met secretly with the chief priests, arranging the betrayal. The priests wanted to arrest Jesus, but they feared that accosting him in public would cause a riot—and the Romans would then punish everybody. The city was crowded for Passover, so it was difficult to find him alone. That's why Judas was uniquely valuable to them. They paid him 30 pieces of silver to lead their officers to the hillside grove where Jesus prayed with his disciples.

Judas *by James Tissot*

Jesus knew what was afoot. In fact, at the Last Supper he essentially dismissed Judas to do what he had to do. A short time later, Judas led a band of the Temple Guard to the Garden of Gethsemane, where he kissed Jesus in a common greeting. This was the signal for the arrest, identifying Jesus to the soldiers. (They might not have seen Jesus before, though they would have heard about him.)

After Jesus was tried and sent to the cross, Judas had second thoughts and tried to return the blood money, which was refused. After throwing the coins away, he hanged himself.

POSTSCRIPT

■ The "pieces of silver" paid to Judas were probably Roman denarii or their equivalent. Each piece amounted to a day's wages for a common laborer.

Song of Solomon

THE SONG OF SOLOMON, like Ecclesiastes, is credited to Solomon, who is named in it (1:1; 3:7, 9). The first verse could also read as being "for" Solomon, rather than "by" him. With his 700 wives and 300 mistresses (1 Kings 11:3), Solomon is the exact opposite of the committed and passionate lover portrayed in this book. The book is a collection of love poems about a male and female lover.

The sexuality of the Song of Solomon has led to allegorical interpretations by both Jewish and Christian writers. If one understands human sexuality as distasteful, then the book is better interpreted as referring to the relationship between God and his people, either Israel or the Church. But many believe that there is no good reason why the book should not be taken literally. God's creation is good in its entirety, including the sexual relationship between husband and wife. Poems in praise of these relationships—which are discussed elsewhere in the Bible—should not be interpreted away. Poetry is a suitable means of expressing this erotic desire since it draws on all of the bodily sensations: sight, sound, smell, touch, and taste.

Some see the book as a dramatic piece, showing the growth and consummation of a relationship of passionate love. There does seem to be a progression in the book, which moves between three main characters or groups: the male lover, the female lover, and her friends. The first part of the book builds, increasing in intensity and intimacy until it reaches a literary and physical climax when the lovers come together for the first time (4:16—5:1). Their married relationship grows and deepens through the rest of the book. The erotic descriptions are always restrained and veiled, avoiding any blatant, overly graphic details. Even the sexual intercourse is alluded to rather than explicitly described (5:1; 7:9; 8:14). Sexual love is real, vital, and exciting, but it is also private.

POSTSCRIPT

■ The Song of Solomon is read every year as part of the Jewish Passover celebration because of the reference to spring.

■ While some descriptions of beauty in the book match what we would appreciate today (1:10–11; 4:3), most women would not appreciate references to their horselike strength (1:9) or the fact that they do not have missing teeth (4:2). Each culture has its own criteria with which to examine beauty and sexuality.

The King James Bible

PUBLISHED IN 1611, the King James Version of the Bible is the most popular English translation of the Bible of all time. Until a spate of new versions arose in the 20th century, the KJV was *the* Bible in the English-speaking world. Still today, many enjoy its stately cadences and quaint poetry.

Other English versions were in use before 1611, but King James I of England wasn't happy with them. He set up a team of 54 scholars to create a new translation. His purposes were largely political.

During the 1500s, the Protestant Reformation had torn Europe apart. England had its own Reformation struggles, but Queen Elizabeth I managed to keep the nation poised between the extremes. The Church of England was not quite Catholic, but it wasn't entirely Lutheran or Calvinist, either. Although a populist spirit was brewing, the power of the monarchy continued. When Elizabeth died childless, the throne passed to King James VI of Scotland, who became James I of England in 1603. Presbyterians thought his Scottish background would aid their cause. Puritans pressed for further reform in the Church of England. James managed to alienate everyone.

One thing James believed in was the divine right of kings. The most popular Scripture version at the time was the Geneva Bible of 1560, which bothered James. It contained marginal notes with a decidedly Calvinist bent. In Exodus 1:17, for instance, it applauded the Hebrew midwives for disobeying the king's order. James saw that as a bad precedent. So when the Puritans asked for a new Bible translation, James surprised them by agreeing to it. (He had roundly rejected their other demands.) Appointing a team of scholars, he authorized them to translate "the whole Bible, as consonant as can be to the original Hebrew and Greek, and this to be set out and printed without any marginal notes."

They did amazing work. Beginning in 1607, and working in groups of seven or eight, the translators pored over the accepted Greek and Hebrew texts, making excellent use of previous English versions, but finding their own voice as well. They especially followed the renderings of William Tyndale, who had produced an English New Testament in 1525, when it was illegal to do so.

This Authorized Version, later known as the King James Version, found immediate acceptance in England and later throughout the British Empire. It would have no serious competition for three and a half centuries.

The Lord's Prayer

THE LORD'S PRAYER is one of the most well known prayers. Millions of Christian believers say this prayer every day. Not surprisingly, most English-speaking people are familiar with the words "Our Father who art in heaven, hallowed be thy name," as well as other lines in Jesus' prayer. What many people do not realize is that there are two versions of this prayer in the Bible.

One version is found in Matthew 6:9–13, where Jesus offers the Lord's Prayer as an example of how Christians should pray. Matthew includes this version as part of Jesus' famous Sermon on the Mount, in which he instructs his disciples on the importance of expressing one's faith through prayer, almsgiving, and fasting.

The other version appears in Luke 11:2–4, where Jesus presents the Lord's Prayer as an example of an appropriate manner in which to pray. Here, Jesus' disciples had approached him and asked, "Lord, teach us to pray, as John taught his disciples" (verse 1). Jesus instructs, "When you pray, say: Father, hallowed be your name. Your kingdom come. Give us each day our daily bread. And forgive us our sins, for we ourselves forgive everyone indebted to us. And do not bring us to the time of trial."

The version in Luke may seem abbreviated to those familiar with the prayer as it is spoken within most churches. Some elements are absent in Luke's version. Omitted are "your will be done, on earth as it is in heaven" (Matthew 6:10), "rescue us from the evil one" (verse 13), and "for the kingdom and the power and the glory are yours forever. Amen" (verse 13 KJV).

Apparently Luke wanted his readers to pay close attention to Jesus' focus on the importance of the sincerity of prayer. This is not only apparent in the prayer itself but also in the stories that follow (verses 5–13). We should be less concerned with the outcome of prayer than with the relationship it creates. Indeed, true prayer pulls God and people together; that is, it pulls us up to God and not God down to us.

Just as the Ten Commandments begin by focusing on God and then on humans, so the Lord's Prayer focuses on God first and only then on human needs.

A Baby in a Basket

JOSEPH'S RISE TO THE SECOND-highest position in Egypt represented the high point for the descendants of Abraham in a foreign land. But centuries passed, and memories of Joseph faded. The Bible says, "A new king arose over Egypt, who did not know Joseph" (Exodus 1:8). Quite possibly, a different dynasty had come to rule Egypt—one that lacked any affection for the ancient Hebrews. And so, the current pharaoh subjected the Israelites to forced labor under harsh taskmasters. In spite of this treatment, the Israelites multiplied in number, causing the Egyptians to bear down harder on the Israelites, who had now become their slaves.

To decrease the growing Israelite population, Pharaoh ordered the Hebrew midwives to kill all baby boys, but the midwives, being God-fearing, did not obey Pharaoh. As a result, the Israelites continued to grow in numbers. Pharaoh then issued an edict that all Hebrew baby boys should be thrown into the Nile and drowned.

When Moses was born, his mother concealed him for three months, but then she could no longer hide him at home. She prepared a basket, coated it with tar, and floated it in the Nile to hide him. Moses' sister watched it from a distance to see what would happen to him.

Pharaoh's daughter discovered Moses in the river when she went down to bathe there, and she took pity on him. She adopted him as her own son, and the Bible says, "Moses was instructed in all the wisdom of the Egyptians and was powerful in his words and deeds" (Acts 7:22).

Moses' 40 years in Pharaoh's household quite possibly prepared him in many ways for leading the Israelites and for writing down the great laws and stories that became the first five books of the Bible, also known as "the books of Moses."

POSTSCRIPT

■ The Israelites were also known as *Hebrews,* mostly early in their history. The origins of this name are disputed, but perhaps the most plausible explanation is that *Hebrews* were descendants of Eber, grandson of Shem, Noah's son—that is, *Eberites*. The name *Jew* was used in late Old Testament times and in the New Testament but not in the early eras of Israel's history.

Miriam

MIRIAM WAS MOSES' older sister, and the Bible on several occasions focuses on her relationship with Moses and her importance to her people. She saved his life as a baby but opposed his leadership many years later. She was also recognized as a leader among the Israelite women.

At the time of Moses' birth, an edict from Pharaoh was in effect demanding that every newborn Hebrew boy be killed. In order to save her son, Moses' mother prepared a papyrus basket to hide him in the reeds along the riverbank. She instructed Miriam to stand watch at a distance. Eventually one of Pharaoh's daughters discovered the basket. Miriam then stepped forward and volunteered to find someone to nurse the baby. After Pharaoh's daughter agreed, she brought Moses to his mother to be nursed.

Many years later, when God had dramatically brought the Israelites out of Egypt and through the Red Sea, drowning Pharaoh's army in the process, Miriam led the women in celebrating this miraculous event with song and dance. The Bible says

The Songs of Joy *by James Tissot*

she "took a tambourine in her hand; and all the women went out after her with tambourines and with dancing. And Miriam sang to them, 'Sing to the Lord, for he has triumphed gloriously; horse and rider he has thrown into the sea'" (Exodus 15:20–21).

Some years after that, Miriam and her brother Aaron challenged Moses' authority. The immediate pretext was Moses' marriage to a Cushite woman—that is, a woman from Ethiopia. But an underlying objection was that God had favored Moses over them. "Has the Lord spoken only through Moses?" they complained. "Has he not spoken through us also?" (Numbers 12:2).

In response to their complaint, God told Miriam and Aaron in no uncertain terms that Moses was his chosen leader over the nation and that their jealousy was wrong. Miriam had taken the lead in challenging Moses' authority, and so God afflicted her with leprosy. Aaron and Moses interceded for her, Moses begging God to let her be quarantined for seven days but to restore her after this time, and God agreed to this request. Even in this matter, Moses' authority was affirmed. Miriam died and was buried some time later, before the Israelites entered the Promised Land.

The Lame Beggar

JESUS HAD PROMISED his disciples that they would do even greater works than he had done. After seeing his miraculous healings, that promise must have been difficult for them to imagine. And yet shortly after the Holy Spirit arrived at Pentecost, the Apostles Peter and John had the opportunity to work a miracle themselves. These two disciples were emerging as leaders of the young Church, which was growing rapidly, with groups of Jesus-followers meeting in alcoves of the Jerusalem temple and in private homes.

At three o'clock one afternoon, according to the Acts of the Apostles, Peter and John went to the temple for prayers. This was one of three daily prayer times for Jews, so we see that these disciples were continuing to observe their Jewish faith. It's also quite possible that a group of Christians was meeting in a corner of the temple courtyard immediately after the prayers.

Peter and John were entering the temple at the Beautiful Gate when they encountered a lame beggar. His presence was not unusual, since giving alms was an important part of religious devotion in that culture. But on this occasion the apostles had no money to give, and they said so. Yet they offered the beggar something much more valuable: "In the name of Jesus Christ of Nazareth," Peter said, "stand up and walk" (Acts 3:6).

Peter then grabbed him by the right hand and pulled him to his feet. The man's feet and ankles suddenly acquired strength, and he began walking, even leaping, as he entered the temple with them. This caused quite a stir. People had seen this lame beggar day in and day out for months or years, and now he was jumping around like a child. They crowded around Peter and John to find out about this miracle.

The apostles gave credit where credit was due. "Why do you stare at us," Peter asked, "as though by our own power or piety we had made him walk?" (verse 12). It was the name of Jesus that had given this man his health.

POSTSCRIPT

■ Scholars aren't certain where the Beautiful Gate was. It might have been the main entry from the Court of the Gentiles to the Court of Women. The Beautiful Gate was a magnificently crafted portal, reportedly 75 feet high and 60 feet wide—this is according to the historian Josephus, who called it the Corinthian Gate because it was made out of Corinthian bronze.

Herod Antipas

A SON OF HEROD THE GREAT, Antipas ruled Galilee for more than 40 years, including during the time of Jesus. He was the Herod who ordered the gruesome execution of John the Baptist.

Forty years before Jesus' birth, the Romans installed Herod the Great as king over the Jews, and he built a dynasty by marrying several wives and raising several of his sons to positions of power. Upon his death, shortly after Jesus' birth, his kingdom was divided among several of Herod's relatives. Archelaus, Herod's son, was given Judaea, but he mangled the job so badly that within a decade the Romans dumped him and set up Pontius Pilate as their own governor. Herod Antipas, another of Herod's sons, was given Galilee to the north and Perea to the east. His half brother Philip ruled over some lesser-known areas.

Antipas was in charge of the region where John the Baptist preached and where Jesus established his ministry. In a scandal worthy of the tabloids, Antipas dumped his current wife (the daughter of an Arabian king) to marry Herodias, who was already married to his half brother Philip. John the Baptist publicly condemned this action. We're told that Antipas respected John as a holy man (Mark 6:20), but Herodias wanted revenge, so Antipas had John arrested and imprisoned.

Then the daughter of Herodias danced at a birthday party for Antipas, and he was so smitten that he promised her anything she wanted. At her mother's prompting, the girl requested John's head on a silver platter. With some regret, Antipas had John beheaded.

The king seemed to be spooked by the memory of John. When Jesus came to prominence, at first Antipas thought he might be the resurrected John. Later he threatened Jesus' life (Luke 13:31).

But Luke records an interesting scene in the midst of Jesus' trial before Pontius Pilate: Learning that Jesus is from Galilee, the Roman governor decides that is the jurisdiction of Herod Antipas, who happens to be visiting Jerusalem for the Passover holiday. Antipas is glad to see Jesus for curiosity's sake (he hopes to see some miracle performed), but Jesus remains silent, so Herod and his entourage mock him and send him back to Pilate.

Antipas was ultimately deposed from power in A.D. 39, a victim of the manipulations of his nephew Herod Agrippa I, who gained favor with the Roman ruler, Caius Caligula, and who accused Antipas of secret plots against Rome.

The Book of Isaiah

ISAIAH, WHOSE NAME MEANS "Yahweh saves," was a prophet who delivered God's words to the people of the southern kingdom of Judah in the late eighth century B.C. The book bearing his name could have been written by him or some of his followers, though some suggest several authors from different periods of time wrote the book.

Isaiah *by James Tissot*

Through chapter 39, Isaiah consists of poetic sermons and prose historical narrative mainly relating to Isaiah's time. Using poetic oracles, chapters 40 to 55 anticipate the end of Judah's exile in Babylon (586–539 B.C.), while chapters 56 to 66 are concerned with rebuilding the land of Israel after the exile is finished (539–400 B.C.). Two or more unnamed authors could have supplemented the original work of Isaiah, or he could have written it himself through the inspiration of God.

Isaiah prophesied during a period when Israel was under the domination of Assyria. But a larger threat to the people's well-being was their own willful and continued sinning against God. Warnings against this sin and pleas to return to God in obedience form a large part of the first section of the book. Various literary forms are used for the purpose of calling Israel back, including language of the law court (1), allegory (5), and oracles of judgment (2:5—4:1). Even in the midst of judgment, however, rays of hope still shine through. The book looks beyond short-term punishment to a longer-term restoration (2:1–4).

The second part of Isaiah prepares the people for return from exile after they have suffered due to their sin. A key motif is the servant who serves the Lord God, either as the nation of Israel as a whole (41:8; 54:17) or as a righteous person within the nation (42:1; 52:13). The New Testament picks up this motif by applying it to Jesus as the representative of the people who suffers for the people (Luke 22:37; John 12:38). Isaiah closes with the restoration of God's people to the land.

The anointed Messiah who will restore Israel as their ideal king is another important motif. One of the two times "messiah" is used in the book it refers to the Persian king Cyrus (45:1), who, while not acknowledging Israel's God, was used as his unwitting servant. The other time is when it refers to the Messiah who lies behind the future establishment of God's peaceable kingdom (9:6–7; 11:1–10).

Teaching with Parables

JESUS DIDN'T INVENT parables, but you could say he perfected the art form. He used these stories intentionally, effectively, and often in his teaching.

The word *parable* doesn't change much from Greek *(parabole)* to English. It literally means "thrown alongside." Thus a parable is a story "thrown alongside" some idea to help us understand it. It is a story with a double meaning. In some cases, individual parts of the story stand for parts of the parallel idea, but usually a parable makes a single point.

Prophets made good use of parables in the Old Testament. Nathan confronted the adulterous King David with a story of a rich man who had stolen a prize lamb from his poor neighbor. When the king demanded to know who the culprit was, the

The Good Samaritan *by Vincent van Gogh*

prophet said, "You are the man!" (2 Samuel 12:7). Isaiah 5 has a "song" of a well-tended vineyard that yields no fruit. It's a parable calling God's vineyard, Israel, to greater faithfulness.

Jesus told about 30 parables—some merely a sentence or two, others much longer. When he told the parable of the soils (Matthew 13), he also offered an interpretation. Different soils accepted seeds or rejected them, just as different hearts receive God's message or dismiss it. This in itself is a metaphor for teaching in parables. As we see with Nathan and Isaiah, "innocent" stories can deliver tough truths. Perhaps they till the soil a bit so the true message can take root.

"Why do you speak to them in parables?" Jesus' disciples once asked him point-blank. He responded with a quote from Isaiah: "Seeing they do not perceive, and hearing they do not listen" (Matthew 13:10, 13; see Isaiah 6:9–10). His answer raises more questions, but it seems that he's saying the indirect approach gets through people's defenses. It's also possible that he spoke in parables to veil his controversial message from the religious authorities, who were already mobilizing against him. Perhaps Jesus felt that the common people would "get" these simple stories and the elite leaders wouldn't.

Jesus Teaches Simon a Lesson

IN THE FIRST CENTURY, hospitality was seen as such an important Christian virtue that Hebrews 13 presents it as an example of "brotherly love." First Peter 4:9 qualifies the act by saying, "Be hospitable to one another without complaining."

In an incident recorded in Luke 7, however, there was much grumbling. When a Pharisee named Simon invited Jesus to dinner, we are told that a woman in the city, who was a sinner, brought an alabaster jar of ointment and approached Jesus. She wept, bathed Jesus' feet with her tears, dried his feet with her loose hair, and then continued kissing his feet. It is easy to imagine onlookers either being scandalized or feeling very uncomfortable by such a public display of affection. But Jesus neither condemned the woman nor drew away from her actions.

And that was what bothered Simon. He grumbled to himself, "If this man were a prophet, he would have known who and what kind of woman this is who is touching him   that she is a sinner" (Luke 7:39).

Jesus responded to Simon's snickering by telling him a parable about forgiveness in the hope that Simon would see the sincerity of the woman's actions. Jesus said to Simon, "Do you see this woman? I entered your house; you gave me no water for my feet, but she has bathed my feet with her tears and dried them with her hair. You gave me no kiss, but from the time I came in she has not stopped kissing my feet. You did not anoint my head with oil, but she has anointed my feet with ointment. Therefore, I tell you, her sins, which were many, have been forgiven; hence she has shown great love. But the one to whom little is forgiven, loves little." Jesus then went on to tell the woman her sins were forgiven (verses 44–48).

Simon was so focused on what was wrong with this woman's actions that he failed to do what he should have done. The story about Simon the Pharisee is a story about how petty we can be, how our lives can focus far too much on the faults of others. But it is also a story about how we are called to a life of gratitude. The woman's response to Jesus stands above that of Simon, who was so focused on the sins of others that he failed to recognize both his own sin and the love that is born out of gratitude for forgiveness and healing.

The Burning Bush

AT THE AGE OF 40, Moses fled from Egypt until he found himself in the wilderness of Midian, where he met a Midianite priest, Jethro (see Acts 7:23–32). Eventually, Moses married Jethro's daughter Zipporah. And so, away from the land where he was raised and away from his people, Moses settled in a foreign land to raise a family.

One day, however, an unexpected and startling occurrence interrupted his quiet and uneventful life. While watching his father-in-law's flocks, "the angel of the Lord appeared to him in a flame of fire" in a bush

(Exodus 3:2). The flame did not consume the bush, a sight that attracted Moses' curiosity. From this burning bush, God told Moses to take off his sandals because the spot upon which he was standing was holy ground.

In this encounter, God assured Moses that he had seen the misery of his people, the Israelites, and that he would deliver them from Egyptian bondage and take them to Canaan, a land "flowing with milk and honey" (verse 8). The catch was that he intended to use Moses as his instrument for accomplishing their deliverance.

Moses Before a Burning Bush *by Domenico Fetti*

Moses was clearly reluctant, raising several objections to God's plan. The Lord patiently answered all of Moses' objections and questions, even to the point of promising to speak for him when Moses said he could not speak very well ("I am slow of speech and slow of tongue," Exodus 4:10). Finally, Moses was reduced to plaintively pleading, "O my Lord, please send someone else" (verse 13). This plea naturally angered God, and he appointed Aaron, Moses' brother, as Moses' spokesman. But he didn't let Moses off the hook. Moses still had to return to Egypt to lead the Israelites out of Egypt. To his credit, Moses obeyed despite his fears, and God molded him into a great and eloquent leader.

As proof that he was indeed God, he promised Moses that he would speak with him again at Mount Sinai (see Exodus 3:12). After the Israelites escaped from Egypt, Moses did again meet the Lord there, and it was at this place that God gave him the Ten Commandments and the rest of the law.

Jethro

JETHRO WAS A GENEROUS, wise, and discerning Midianite priest who became Moses' father-in-law and embraced Israel's God as his own. Without him, Moses' life would have been far more difficult.

When Moses fled for his life from Egypt, he went to the land of Midian in the northern Arabian Peninsula. Jethro invited him into his home and extended his gracious hospitality. Moses settled down there, marrying Jethro's daughter Zipporah and tending Jethro's flocks. But when God called Moses to free his people, Jethro readily gave him his blessing to leave, saying, "Go in peace" (Exodus 4:18). He did this even though it meant his daughter and grandsons would be traveling to a hostile country.

Later Moses led the Israelites out of Egypt and brought them to Mount Sinai. He had sent his wife and two sons, Gershom and Eliezer, back to Jethro, probably because he feared for their lives. So when Jethro heard of their arrival, he brought Zipporah and Moses' two sons back to Moses at the mountain, where they were joyfully reunited. Moses then told Jethro about all that God had done, and Jethro blessed God, saying, "Blessed be the Lord . . . Now I know that the Lord is greater than all gods, because he delivered the people from the Egyptians" (Exodus 18:10–11). Jethro also brought offerings and sacrifices to God. In essence, he became an Israelite by these expressions of loyalty to Israel's God.

The Israelites had just come out of 400 years under Egyptian rule as slaves, and they had never governed themselves. Consequently, while they were in the wilderness, Moses began to hear people's disputes. The burden, however, quickly overwhelmed Moses, as people lined up from morning till night to seek his guidance in settling their arguments.

Jethro wisely saw the foolishness of this system, with Moses exhausting himself by doing it alone. He advised Moses to delegate his duties to others who would settle most disputes, with only the most difficult cases coming to Moses for adjudication. "You should," Jethro said, "look for able men among all the people, men who fear God, are trustworthy, and hate dishonest gain" (verse 21). He instructed Moses to set them up "as officers over thousands, hundreds, fifties, and tens" (verse 21).

Moses followed Jethro's advice, and his burdens were greatly reduced. With that, Jethro returned to his own country with a deeper faith in the Lord God and a son-in-law well situated to lead the Israelites.

Ananias and Sapphira

IT WAS A THRILLING TIME of growth and giving for the early Church. Filled with the Spirit of God, the believers felt empowered by the Lord. The apostles were preaching with authority and performing amazing miracles, just as Jesus had done in the preceding years. What's more, Jesus' followers were fulfilling his command to love one another. They were sharing their possessions freely. Many of the Christians sold property and brought the proceeds to the apostles for charitable work and the common good.

Ananias and Sapphira sold a plot of land and decided to donate a portion of the money from the sale to the common fund. It seems donations were made at a public gathering, perhaps at a worship or teaching service where at a certain point gifts were brought forward. In any case, the husband, Ananias, appeared first. He brought a sum of money before Peter, claiming it was the entire amount of the sale. He lied.

Death of Sapphira, Wife of Ananias
by Sebastian Le Clerc

With spiritual discernment, Peter recognized the lie and berated Ananias for it. Lying to the Holy Spirit was a major offense. It would not be tolerated in the Church. Peter acknowledged that Ananias had every right to do whatever he wanted with his money. He could give any portion of the proceeds or none at all, but this was not about money. It was about the deceptive spirit in this man's heart. "You did not lie to us, but to God," Peter charged (Acts 5:4). With that, Ananias fell over and died. A group of young men took his body out and buried it.

A few hours later, Ananias's wife, Sapphira, came in, and Peter asked about the sale price of the land. Since she was complicit in the deception, she also lied about the amount. She, too, was struck dead, and the young men, having completed one burial, now had another to do.

"Great fear seized the whole church" (verse 11). The harsh judgment upon Ananias and Sapphira made it clear that this was God's Church. Everyone ultimately answered to God, and they needed to answer honestly.

Nicodemus

NICODEMUS WAS A JEWISH LEADER who met privately with Jesus. He later went public as a disciple of Christ.

The Gospel of John specializes in the stories of Jesus' personal encounters. In an early account, Nicodemus probably visited Jesus in secret. Jesus' miracles fascinated him, and he wanted to learn more about him, but he was a member of the Pharisees, a religious party that held considerable power in Judaea. The Pharisees sought to follow God's law to the letter, while urging other Jews to do the same, and many of them opposed Jesus.

For the most part, the Pharisees felt threatened by the ministry of John the Baptist, and that antagonism carried over against Jesus, who also preached repentance and who dared to forgive sins as well (see Mark 2:5–6). That's why Nicodemus used such stealth in approaching Jesus, coming by night. It's not clear whether he was coming on his own or on a fact finding mission for a minority group of Pharisees, but Jesus took the opportunity to connect with him personally. "Are you a teacher of Israel," Jesus teased him, "and yet you do not understand these things?" (John 3:10).

Jesus spoke of himself as the Son, sent by God into the world to save those who would trust in him. It appears that Nicodemus began a journey of faith with that conversation. We catch a glimpse of him a bit later at a council meeting as the Pharisees and chief priests debate their policy on Jesus. After berating the Temple Guards for not arresting Jesus when they had the chance, one Pharisee leader asked rhetorically, "Has any one of the ... Pharisees believed in him?" (John 7:48). Nicodemus spoke up, not exactly answering the question, but affirming the need for due process. They needed to give Jesus a "hearing" (just as Nicodemus had done personally).

Obviously this man was in the minority, and the Jesus story proceeds to a nighttime arrest, a speedy trial in which no one seems interested in hearing Jesus, and a brutal crucifixion. Then Nicodemus appears again, along with Joseph of Arimathea, who is described as "a disciple of Jesus, though a secret one" (John 19:38). That description might also apply to Nicodemus, who brought expensive spices for Jesus' burial. The two men claimed Jesus' body and buried it in Joseph's tomb.

Did this act of devotion finally signal Nicodemus's commitment as a follower of Jesus? Probably. The very fact that John records his story indicates that he became known within the Christian community.

The Books of Jeremiah and Lamentations

JEREMIAH AND LAMENTATIONS are books of judgment and tears. Jeremiah prophesied for about 40 years, from the seventh century B.C. until at least the start of the Babylonian Exile (586 B.C.) under King Josiah and three of his sons. Jeremiah contains both prose—sermons (7:1—8:3), a salvation speech (31:31–34), narratives (13:1–11; 39:1–10), and autobiographies (20:7–18)—and poetry, including judgment (46—51) and comfort speeches (30—31).

Jeremiah's message of judgment against his own people and family was difficult to preach and caused much personal sorrow. Attacked by his audience, he faced death on several occasions. Claiming that God forced him to prophesy, he was unable to stop doing so (20:7–9). Jeremiah urged God's people to trust God and not the superpowers, Egypt and Babylonia, that were fighting each other with Judah in the middle. When Judah turned to a weak Egypt for help, powerful Babylonia finally put a stop to Judah's fickle foreign policy by destroying the capital and exiling its leaders. Jeremiah showed Judah they would return from exile by buying land, a poor short-term but good long-term investment. Ironically, the anti-Egyptian Jeremiah ended his days in Egypt when he was spirited away by a group of anti-Babylonian fugitives (42—44).

Lamentations reflects the tears of God's people when the Babylonians destroyed Jerusalem and the temple in 586 B.C. Judah's exile lasted until 539 B.C., so this collection of poetic laments, or dirges, and complaints of both individuals and the community would have been written during the intermediate years. Since the people believed David's kingdom and the temple were permanent and untouchable, national destruction and exile led to a crisis of faith and a questioning of God. But hope accompanies anguish, causing the people to call on the Lord to forgive and restore those he has punished. For Jeremiah, because God is just, he punishes sin—but he also forgives those who truly repent.

POSTSCRIPT

■ The Hebrew text of Jeremiah, upon which English translations are based, is some 2,700 words shorter than the earlier Greek text, and there are significant differences in the order of sections of the book. The Greek was probably based on a superior, older Hebrew text that we no longer have.

The Hebrews

THEY HAVE BEEN CALLED Hebrews, Israelites, and Jews. They have been fought against and feared, persecuted and prayed for. More than once, they have faced attempted genocide. They have gone through numerous forced relocations. Still they have maintained their identity as a unique people—the people of God—carrying on the traditions God gave them.

They are children of Abraham but not the only children of Abraham. Arabs rightly call Abraham their ancestor, too. Abraham had two sons, Ishmael (ancestor of the Arabs) and Isaac, and Isaac also had two sons, Esau and Jacob, who was renamed *Israel* (which means "he struggles with God"). Jacob had 12 sons, and these sons became the patriarchs of the tribes of Israel. Thus the nation became known as the "children of Israel."

Abraham followed God's lead to a promised land, the land of Canaan. That began an on-again, off-again relationship between this people and their territory. At one point in their early history, Jacob's family migrated to Egypt during a terrible famine, where their descendants became slaves. It took ten plagues, one miraculous sea-parting, and 40 years of wandering before the Israelites returned to the Promised Land. Then they had to fight to settle and keep it.

There were glorious years of military and economic power under kings David and Solomon, but then the nation split, ten tribes to the north and two tribes to the south. The southern kingdom became known as Judah for its dominant tribe (and that's where the term *Jew* comes from). In 722 B.C., the Assyrians conquered the northern kingdom of Israel, the Israelites were forcibly relocated, and the bloodlines of the Israelites were intentionally mixed with other ethnic groups. These "ten lost tribes" disappeared from history.

Judah had its own relocation a century and a half later, when the Babylonians devastated the southern kingdom and destroyed Solomon's Temple—but the Jews returned and rebuilt it. The Babylonian Exile, however, taught the Jews an important lesson: Their identity had more to do with their commitment to Yahweh and less to do with their land or even their temple. In the following centuries, many Jews scattered throughout the world for survival's sake, but they took their faith with them, observing the law given to Moses and meeting in synagogues to pray together and read the Scriptures. This firm sense of identity was often misunderstood and sometimes vilified, but it stood up against frequent and fierce trials.

"In Remembrance of Her"

IN THE NONCANONICAL COLLECTION of sayings that has come to be known as the Gospel of Thomas, Peter is recorded as saying to the other disciples, "Make Mary leave us, for females don't deserve life" (verse 114). Jesus responds by saying, "Look, I will guide her to make her male, so that she too may become a living spirit resembling you males. For every female who makes herself male will enter the kingdom of Heaven."

Most scholars believe the text of the Gospel of Thomas was written far later than the New Testament gospels, and they do not believe Jesus' words in this work are genuine. In the broader philosophical world, Aristotle had seen women as primarily emotional and men as rational. Some view the words attributed to Jesus in Thomas as exalting the importance of rationality in men while lowering the significance of women.

A very different picture of women, however, pervades the four gospels in the New Testament. Women are accepted, they are conversation partners, and they even travel with Jesus and the disciples. In fact, according to Luke 8:2–3, the disciples traveled with Jesus, "as well as some women who had been cured of evil spirits and infirmities: Mary, called Magdalene, from whom seven demons had gone out, and Joanna, the wife of Herod's steward Chuza, and Susanna, and many others, who provided for them out of their resources." Apparently out of gratitude to Jesus, these women responded with hospitality and financial support.

In the patriarchal world in which Jesus lived and in which the New Testament was written, the ways in which the gospel writers portray women toward the end of Jesus' life stand out. They have more faith than the men, they are present at his crucifixion, they go at sunrise on Easter Sunday to his tomb, and according to John, Mary Magdalene was the first of Jesus' disciples to see him after the Resurrection. Because she then shared the good news with the others, some have referred to her as "the apostle to the apostles."

In Mark 14:3–9, after an unnamed woman breaks an alabaster jar of ointment and pours the ointment on Jesus' head, the disciples scold her. In contrast to the words that the Gospel of Thomas places in Jesus' mouth, Jesus responds to the disciples by noting that this woman truly recognizes who he is and that he will have to die. Jesus goes on to tell the disciples that whenever the good news is proclaimed, what this woman did will be told "in remembrance of her" (verse 9).

Ten Plagues Against Egypt

GOD SENT MOSES and Aaron to Pharaoh to demand that he let the Israelites go. Initially, they sought Pharaoh's permission to let them go "a three days' journey into the wilderness to sacrifice to the Lord our God" (Exodus 5:3). Pharaoh refused and ordered his taskmasters to bear down harder on the Israelites by not providing them with the straw needed for brick-making but requiring the same output of bricks.

God then launched a series of "signs and wonders," or plagues, against the Egyptians: (1) water turned to blood; (2) frogs; (3) gnats; (4) flies; (5) diseased livestock; (6) boils; (7) thunder and hail; (8) locusts; (9) darkness; and (10) death of the firstborn.

The Water of the Nile Turned Blood Red
by John Martin

Pharaoh's magicians were able to imitate the first two, but they could not replicate the third, and they were not heard from again. The plagues affected the Egyptians and their lands, but not the land of Goshen, where the Israelites lived.

God's purpose in all this was twofold: (1) to deliver the Israelites from Egyptian oppression so they could return to Canaan—the land promised centuries earlier to Abraham—and (2) to make a statement about the power of Israel's God versus the gods of the Egyptians. Every one of the plagues struck at an area of life governed—at least, in the Egyptians' minds—by one or more of their gods. The climactic tenth plague struck at the heart of the Egyptian religious system, which considered Pharaoh himself to be divine. When the Lord's angel killed Pharaoh's own first-born son, he was exposed as weak at best, and at worst as a fraud.

God continually spared his own people from the effects of the plagues. The Bible says this was "that you may know that the Lord makes a distinction between Egypt and Israel" (Exodus 11:7). Before the final, climactic plague, God instructed the Hebrews to sacrifice an animal and spread some of its blood on the two doorposts and the lintel of the doorways of their homes. When the Lord's angel passed through the land killing the firstborn of the Egyptians and their servants, he would see this blood and "pass over" those houses. This was the origin of the "Passover" festival that has been celebrated as a memorial among Jews ever since.

Aaron

AARON WAS MOSES' older brother. His importance initially stemmed from his relationship with Moses and his ability to speak eloquently. He later became the high priest of Israel, and all high priests after him were his descendants. But he was a flawed person, at one point leading the people into egregious idolatry and at another point rebelling against his brother's authority.

When God called Moses to lead his people, speaking to him from a burning bush at Mount Sinai, one of Moses' objections was that "I am slow of speech and slow of tongue" (Exodus 4:10). God was displeased with Moses, but he noted that Aaron could speak for him. Interestingly, God either knew that Aaron was "coming out to meet" Moses (verse 14) or already knew that Moses would need a spokesman and had led Aaron to his brother.

Subsequently, in several encounters with Pharaoh, Aaron performed the task of demanding Israel's freedom and announcing the plagues that would befall Egypt. Moreover, Aaron triggered several of the early plagues by stretching out his staff at God's command, including turning the Nile waters to blood and bringing forth frogs and gnats.

When the Israelites left Egypt and arrived at Mount Sinai, God established Aaron and his sons as priests, saying to Moses, "bring near to you your brother Aaron, and his sons with him . . . to serve me as priests" (Exodus 28:1). Elaborate priestly vestments were made, including a breastpiece, an ephod, a robe, a tunic, a turban, and a sash, made of "gold, blue, purple, and crimson yarns, and fine linen" (verse 5).

Yet, at a critical moment, Aaron failed. When Moses was on Mount Sinai receiving the law from God, he was gone a long time. The people, thinking that Moses would not return, asked Aaron to make gods for them, which he did by taking their gold jewelry and molding a golden calf, which they fell before and worshipped. When Moses confronted his brother, Aaron disingenuously protested that he had simply taken the people's gold and thrown it into the fire "and out came this calf!" (Exodus 32:24).

Years later while at Hazeroth, Aaron joined with his sister, Miriam, in challenging Moses' authority. They said, "Has the Lord spoken only through Moses?" (Numbers 12:2). God, however, rebuked them and affirmed Moses. Seeing how the Lord afflicted his sister with leprosy, Aaron said to Moses, "Oh, my Lord, do not punish us for a sin that we have so foolishly committed" (verse 11). Although God spared Aaron, he did not allow Aaron into the Promised Land.

The Church on the Move

THE EARLY CHRISTIANS displayed their Spirit-given communication skills by proclaiming Jesus to everyone who would listen. The apostles especially showed their courage—preaching despite official warnings to desist. People demonstrated radical love by sharing their possessions with those in need. The Church was bursting with power and marvelous love.

The strange deaths of Ananias and Sapphira had also shown that this Christian movement was nothing to toy with. On a more positive note, the healing ministry of the Church increased as numbers grew. The apostles held court in the colonnade of the temple, and sick people were brought before them—much as the sick had been brought before Jesus. Some sick people were even brought out to the streets leading to the temple, "in order that Peter's shadow might fall on some of them as he came by" (Acts 5:15). We're not told that his shadow actually healed anybody, but we're not told otherwise. And why couldn't it? God's power was working through the apostles as a testimony to the truth of their message.

The authorities took notice. They had arrested Peter and John once before but had failed to take them seriously. They had released them with a warning. Now matters had gotten out of hand. The Temple Guard was dispatched to arrest and imprison the two apostles.

When the leaders arrived the next morning to conduct the trial, there were no defendants to be found. The prison was locked and guarded, but the apostles were absent. Then somebody arrived, saying, "The men whom you put in prison are standing in the temple and teaching the people!" (verse 25). An angel had arrived in the middle of the night, released Peter and John, and told them to return to the temple to preach.

Rearrested and ordered to defend his actions, Peter explained, "We must obey God rather than any human authority" (verse 29). The council finally realized what it was up against. Gamaliel, a respected member of the council, said that if this was a human-based movement, it would fade away, but if it came from God, they shouldn't dare oppose it. So they released the apostles with a flogging.

POSTSCRIPT

▪ Gamaliel had mentored Saul of Tarsus (later known as the Apostle Paul).

▪ A similar jailbreak occurs in Acts 12, where Peter is mysteriously set free by an angel.

Zacchaeus

A VERY WEALTHY TAX COLLECTOR in Jericho, Zacchaeus climbed a tree to catch a glimpse of Jesus. The Lord saw Zacchaeus, singled him out, invited himself to his home for dinner, and changed his life.

It was not unusual for tax collectors to be rich. They had a lucrative racket going. Collecting revenue for the Romans, they could tack on a surcharge. If anyone resisted, there were Roman soldiers to assist in the shakedown. Zacchaeus is described as a "chief tax collector," suggesting he had regional authority and might have had a piece of the action from other collectors further down the pyramid. Think mob boss.

And Jericho was something of an ancient Las Vegas. Surrounded by desert, this city was perched on the Jordan River, a verdant oasis in an arid world. Herod had a winter palace nearby.

But Jesus the wonder-worker was coming to town, and Jericho was abuzz. Crowds thronged to see him as he walked by. Zacchaeus was short of stature but resourceful, so he ran ahead and climbed a sycamore tree to get an upper-deck view of the action. To his surprise (and probably everyone else's), Jesus looked up at the tax collector and called him by name. "Zacchaeus, hurry and come down," he said, "for I must stay at your house today" (Luke 19:5).

Hospitality was a virtue prized in that society. It would have been difficult for Zacchaeus to say no even if he wanted to. But for a respected rabbi to dine with a lowlife like this tax collector was shocking. The onlookers grumbled about it.

We're not sure what happened at that meeting. Was it a private dinner or did Zacchaeus invite his friends? What did they talk about? Chances are, Jesus spoke on his favorite subject, the kingdom of God. It's likely that he invited Zacchaeus to repent of his sin and to enter a relationship with God, enjoying forgiveness for past sins and grace for the future.

In any case, Zacchaeus emerged from the encounter with a new resolve. "Half of my possessions, Lord, I will give to the poor; and if I have defrauded anyone of anything, I will pay back four times as much" (verse 8). Jesus then proclaimed Zacchaeus's salvation.

POSTSCRIPT

■ This was not the first criticism Jesus endured for dining with tax collectors and sinners. This also happened when he called Matthew to be his disciple (Matthew 9:10–13).

The Book of Ezekiel

EZEKIEL, WITH ITS USE of symbolic language and allegory, is an interesting book but difficult to interpret. Ezekiel, a prophet, was among the Judaeans who were exiled to Babylonia in 597 B.C. with King Jehoiachin. Ezekiel's prophecies took place starting in 593 B.C. (1:1–3) and ending some 20 years later (40:1). Using prose and poetry, the prophet describes visions of God (1; 8—11) and oracles of judgment against Judah (12—24) and the nations (25—32), as well as visions of restoration and hope (33—48). Ezekiel's use of highly symbolic language (1:4–28) and a number of allegories (16; 23—24) makes the message difficult to interpret.

The Whirlwind: Ezekiel's Vision *by William Blake*

Ezekiel used symbolic language to explain in concrete terms a God who is not concrete but is spiritual. As he appeared to Ezekiel, God was invisible, with only elements of his glory shining through (1:28). God's glory is often spoken of in the Book of Ezekiel. The departure of God's glory from within the temple in Jerusalem (9:3; 10:18–19) and its movement toward the east (11:22–23) showed that God's people, and not the temple building, were a symbol of God's glory, even in exile. This was not to be their eternal destiny, however, since the glory of God would come back to the temple, as would God's people return from their exile. They would have a temple rebuilt by God when they returned to their land (40—48).

The best-known section of Ezekiel is his vision of the valley of dry bones (37:1–14). The exiled nation of Israel, which had been divided into northern Israel (exiled in 722 B.C.) and southern Judah (exiled 586 B.C.), was spiritually dead because of their sinful disobedience (verse 11). Some day they will receive new life from God, but this event has not yet taken place. In 539 B.C., Judah was allowed to return from exile, but Israel was assimilated with the nations among whom they were exiled and have never returned as a group. In this book, the reunification awaits its fulfillment.

POSTSCRIPT

■ A belief held by Israel's neighbors, at times by Israel itself, was that each nation's gods could act only in that nation's land. Israel's God broke this understanding when Judah found God's glory and his prophet Ezekiel prophesying in Babylonia.

Israel's Neighbors

STRICTLY SPEAKING, the term "Arab" applies to people of the Arabian Peninsula, but today it's also commonly used for people throughout North Africa and the Middle East united by the Arabic language and culture. Many are Muslim. Yet it would be a mistake to equate Arabs with the Islamic religion. Many Muslims are not Arabic, and many Arabs are not Muslim. Historically, Islam arose in the seventh century A.D., but significant Arabic civilizations existed long before that.

It's hard to pin down a specific line of descent for Arabic people. There has always been migration between Arabia and Mesopotamia, Canaan, and Egypt, so connections can be made with ancient nations in all those regions.

Linguistically, Arabic belongs to a family of languages called "Semitic," and the people who speak these languages have come to be called "Semites." The name derives from Shem, one of the sons of Noah. And while the genealogies of Genesis still create questions, they remind us of a basic point: The various races of the Middle East are related to one another.

We see this in Abraham's family. The Israelites trace their lineage through his son Isaac, but he had another son, Ishmael, from the Egyptian girl Hagar. Ishmael became the patriarch of a nation that inhabited central and northern Arabia. The Israelite line comes through Isaac's son Jacob, while Jacob's twin brother, Esau, became the father of the Edomite nation that settled at the western edge of Arabia. These people-groups were cousins of the Israelites—as were the Moabites (descendants of Abraham's nephew Lot) and the Midianites (descendants of a later son of Abraham). These people settled south and east of the land of Israel on the Arabian Peninsula.

In biblical times, the Israelites struggled with these and other nations. The Moabites detained the Israelites on their way to the Promised Land, Gideon led a small army against the Midianites, and King Saul fought Edom. But relations weren't always so violent. Moses' father-in-law is described as a "priest of Midian," a nomadic Arabian group. Ruth was a Moabite and the great-grandmother of King David. And the Queen of Sheba, who visited King Solomon, was probably from Arabia.

POSTSCRIPT

■ Islamic tradition holds Ishmael in high esteem, claiming that it was he and not Isaac who was nearly sacrificed by Abraham on Mount Moriah.

Faith of a Centurion

A T ONE POINT IN JESUS' earthly ministry, he sent out his disciples, commissioning them to "Go nowhere among the Gentiles, and enter no town of the Samaritans, but go rather to the lost sheep of the house of Israel" (Matthew 10:5–6). It is evident from this instruction, as well as from others, that Jesus' mission was primarily to his people— the Jews. Nevertheless, in the closing lines of Matthew's gospel, Jesus instructs his disciples to "make disciples of all nations" (28:19). Why this difference?

Given Jesus' singular focus on the children of Israel prior to his arrest, trial, crucifixion, and resurrection, it should not be surprising that the centurion described in Luke 7 did not approach Jesus directly. He wanted Jesus to heal his servant, but as a Gentile, the centurion sent Jewish elders to intercede on his behalf.

Jesus had a reputation for being a healer. Even his opponents acknowledged that many believed Jesus was an effective healer. So it's not surprising that the centurion not only had heard stories of Jesus' miraculous healings but also believed those stories to be true.

The centurion was evidently God-fearing, a person who was supportive of Judaism and who was active in some aspects of the Jewish community but who was not Jewish by birth, not circumcised, and not a full participant in Jewish community life. Because of his respect for Jewish tradition, he did not expect Jesus to enter his home (and become ceremonially unclean). And because he himself had authority, he also recognized Jesus' authority, saying to him, "But only speak the word, and let my servant be healed" (Luke 7:7). The centurion's words amazed Jesus, who turned to the surrounding crowd and said, "I tell you, not even in Israel have I found such faith" (verse 9).

After Jesus healed the centurion's slave, he focused on the centurion's faith. As a God-fearing man, he and his faith had grown out of Judaism. The Jewish elders even had interceded on his behalf, so he could have the opportunity to express his faith to Jesus. Thus the story not only speaks of a healing in Capernaum, but it also anticipates a change in how the Jewish covenant would be understood—through the faith and with the inclusion of Gentiles who would recognize the need for their own healing. Jesus would commend this revolutionary idea to his disciples before his ascension into heaven.

The Exodus

AFTER THE CLIMACTIC tenth plague when all the firstborn in Egypt were killed, Pharaoh and the Egyptians frantically urged the Israelites to leave immediately. The Israelites left and headed toward the Red Sea. The Israelites had been slaves for more than 400 years. Now God provided them with navigation aids through the wilderness: a pillar of cloud during the daytime and a pillar of fire by night. When these pillars moved, the people followed, and when they stopped, the people stopped as well.

Even at this point, however, God intended to further drive home the point that he possessed far greater power than Pharaoh and his gods— so he hardened Pharaoh's heart. Pharaoh then changed his mind and pursued the Israelites with all his chariots. The Egyptians overtook the Israelites by the Red Sea, which threw the Israelites into a great panic. But an angel moved the pillar of cloud so it stood between them and the Egyptians, obscuring the Egyptians' view.

God also ordered Moses to stretch out his staff over the sea, which caused a great east wind to blow so that the sea was divided. The Israelites were able to cross over on dry ground between two walls of water. When the Egyptians pursued them across the same path through the sea, the Lord, using the pillars of cloud and fire, confused them so that they turned around to retreat, but their chariots

Moses Divides the Waters of the Red Sea
by Christoffer W. Eckersberg

got stuck. God then ordered Moses to stretch out his staff again, and the waters rushed back over the Egyptians, killing them all.

The significance of this event cannot be overstated. Immediately following it, Moses and his sister, Miriam, composed a song of victory celebrating the event, which all the people sang and the women danced to with tambourines. In later Israelite history, the Exodus from Egypt stood out as the signal event: Over and over again, Israel was reminded that God had delivered them from Egyptian bondage in this way. The Exodus stood as a perpetual reminder that God had decisively acted on his people's behalf at the beginning of their history as a nation, and that he would continually do so.

Balaam

BALAAM WAS AN ENIGMATIC FIGURE. He was a Mesopotamian seer and soothsayer who was summoned by Balak, an enemy of Israel, to curse the Israelites. Instead, he came and uttered blessings, which enraged his patron. They then parted ways. In the end, however, Balaam subverted his own words by his actions.

The Israelites' successes against Sihon and Og, their enemies in the wilderness, caused Balak, king of Moab, to fear them (see Numbers 21). He sent for Balaam from far-off Mesopotamia, offering him handsome rewards for cursing Israel. At first, Balaam refused, since God forbade him to perform this deed. Balak persisted, however, offering greater rewards. Finally, God gave Balaam permission to go (see Numbers 22:20).

As he traveled, an angel from God blocked his way; the angel was invisible to Balaam but not to his donkey, which stopped. Three times the donkey stopped, and three times Balaam beat his donkey until the Lord opened the mouth of the animal, which rebuked Balaam, saying,

Balaam and the Ass *by James Tissot*

"What have I done to you, that you have struck me these three times?" (Numbers 22:28). The donkey then asserted its past good behavior. When Balaam could not attest to any past misbehavior on the part of the donkey, the Lord opened his eyes. Balaam saw the angel, bowed down, and confessed his sin in entertaining Balak's offer.

Nevertheless, he still met Balak, and he uttered a series of three oracles toward Israel, each delivered from a different mountaintop. In each case, the words that Balaam spoke were blessings on Israel, and so Balak had him move to another location, hoping for a better result. In the end, Balaam would not curse Israel, and Balak angrily sent him away.

In a strange epilogue to the story, after Balaam left, the Moabite women seduced the Israelite men, and the Israelites worshipped the Moabite gods because of the Moabite women, angering the Lord and causing a plague to break out. Later, the Israelites discovered that Balaam had been behind this incident, instructing and encouraging the Moabite women's actions against the Israelites, and they killed Balaam.

The Bible says *God* opened the donkey's mouth, and it spoke. The incident was a clear act of God.

Seven Men of Good Standing

Aculture war was occurring in Israel during Jesus' day. When Alexander the Great conquered the area some three centuries earlier, he had promoted Greek language, Greek philosophy, and Greek arts. Just one century before Jesus, the Romans had taken over, imposing their own ways. In the time of Jesus, some Jews struggled to maintain the purity of their Hebrew way of life, free from all these competing Gentile influences. Others had no problem adapting to the Greek and Roman cultures—in language, dress, entertainment, and so on.

As Christianity grew in Jerusalem, Jews of both types—those who tried to maintain Jewish purity and those who adopted Greek and Roman customs—joined the Church. But soon there were complaints about discrimination. The Church had established a food distribution program for widows and orphans using pooled resources, but the widows who had adopted Greek culture complained that they weren't receiving their fair share, compared to the widows who maintained their Hebrew practices.

To their credit, the apostles took the matter seriously. Rather than sorting out the logistics themselves, they decided to appoint seven "deacons" to take over this program. "It is not right," the apostles announced, "that we should neglect the word of God in order to wait on tables" (Acts 6:2).

The requirements for this new position were substantial. Deacons would need to be "men of good standing, full of the Spirit and of wisdom" (verse 3). The seven who were chosen all seem to have Greek names, which suggests that the Greek-speaking widows who had complained would accept their decisions.

Foremost among these seven was Stephen, who turned out to be not just an effective administrator but also a powerful preacher, becoming the first Christian martyr. Another deacon was Philip the Evangelist (not to be confused with the apostle of the same name), who led a revival in Samaria and then introduced an Ethiopian official to the Christian faith. The other five deacons—Prochorus, Nicanor, Timon, Parmenas, and Nicolaus—are unknown outside this list. But we can guess they served the Lord with distinction, because there is no further mention in Scripture of this dispute.

In some ways, this was the first of a series of steps that opened the Church to new groups of people. Here Greek-speaking Jews were treated on an equal plane with Hebrew-speaking Jews. In a short time the Church would also welcome Samaritans, who had some Jewish blood but also a long history of rivalry with the Jews. Eventually, Gentiles would be invited as well.

Jairus

A SYNAGOGUE LEADER, Jairus begged Jesus to heal his daughter, who was gravely ill, but she died before Jesus could arrive at his home. Nevertheless, Jesus brought her back to life.

Though the temple existed in Jerusalem, Jews had been gathering in local synagogues for centuries. These were places of prayer, Scripture reading, discussion, instruction, and sometimes community business. Jairus is described as a "leader" of the synagogue (Mark 5:22), which probably means he was a layperson elected to oversee the various synagogue activities.

Jesus had been on the northeastern side of the Sea of Galilee and had "crossed again in the boat to the other side" (verse 21). We're not told exactly to what town he had returned, but Capernaum had been his base of operations. It's likely then that Jairus was attached to the synagogue at Capernaum.

The man's only daughter, age 12, was extremely sick. Jairus made his way through the crowd, knelt before Jesus, and pleaded for him to save his daughter. Obviously Jesus had needy people all around him, but this man had some status in the community, so no one would have been surprised when Jesus began to go with him. What may have been surprising to some in the crowd, however, was that a leader in a synagogue would humble himself before someone who was not popular among the scribes, the Pharisees, the Sadducees, and other Jewish rulers.

Jesus and Jairus were met on their way to Jairus's home by someone who told them that his daughter had already died: There was no need for the healer anymore. Freeze this moment, and imagine how Jairus must have felt. They had lost valuable time when Jesus had stopped to heal a woman who must have been a social outcast, since her bleeding would have made her ritually unclean. How could Jesus make that *nobody* a priority over this community leader? We don't know if Jairus felt this way, but he might have.

Yet Jesus went to the home of Jairus, urging him not to fear, "only believe" (verse 36). The mourners were already gathering in the house, but Jesus sent them away after explaining that the girl was only asleep, which caused them to laugh at him. He entered the daughter's room with his three closest disciples and told her to get up. Miraculously, she did.

There is no other mention of Jairus in Scripture outside of this story, but we can imagine how this event must have affected him. Jesus had many enemies among the religious leaders, but here he certainly made a friend.

The Book of Daniel

DANIEL IS AN APOCALYPTIC BOOK that tells a story. It also contains revelation that looks forward to salvation. An apocalyptic book explains present-day suffering in an end-time way in order to make today's suffering tolerable by showing the benefits to come. Daniel is the story of a young Judaean man (Daniel) who was exiled to Babylon around 597 or 596 B.C. and lived until after its conquest by the Medes and Persians in 539 B.C. The book is traditionally dated close to this period. It is made up of stories (1—6) and visions (7—12).

In the book, Daniel comes to the favorable notice of a Babylonian king because of his ability to interpret dreams (one being of a statue made of four different materials). The king is said to have faith in Daniel's God because of Daniel's character and extraordinary ability (2:47). Denounced by those who do not like the Jews, however, Daniel is sentenced to death and thrown into a lions' den, but God saves him (6).

During this period, Daniel also has visions of weird, symbolic creatures and angels, another characteristic of apocalyptic literature (7—12). These visions are of beasts that come from the sea and creatures with multiple horns. The dreams and visions of both parts of the book are difficult to understand, but they anticipate upcoming world events. Four different empires come and go over the course of these visions, each falling to its successor. (The Babylonians, Medes and Persians, Greeks, and Romans are currently thought to be those empires.) A mighty stone crushes the last empire (the Romans); the stone probably represents the Maccabeans. Throughout the book, the main emphasis is clear, in spite of symbols that are difficult to interpret: The sovereign God is in control.

POSTSCRIPT

■ In the Jewish Bible, Daniel is not placed among the other prophets but is instead part of the Writings. This could be because of a suggested later date, but more likely it is due to its apocalyptic nature being very different from most other prophetic books.

■ Unlike most of the Old Testament, which was written in Hebrew, a large part of Daniel was written in a related language, Aramaic (2:4—7:28). This was the common language during the period of the exile, and people in New Testament times also spoke it daily.

Passover

EVERY SPRING JEWS celebrate a feast that goes back three millennia. Passover is a time when families gather to reflect, give thanks, and honor the Lord. It began in Egypt at a crucial time in Jewish history.

The Israelites were slaves in Egypt, and Moses challenged Pharaoh to "Let my people go" (Exodus 5:1). Each time Pharaoh refused, God sent an increasingly worse plague upon Egypt—frogs, flies, hail, and so on. Ten plagues in all were unleashed on the nation of this stubborn ruler. The last plague was the most deadly: The Lord "struck down" the firstborn of every household in Egypt (Exodus 12:29). Israelites were spared if they painted the blood of a lamb on their doorposts. Seeing that blood, the Lord would "pass over" Hebrew homes.

The sacrificed lamb was to be roasted and eaten. The Israelites ate this meal in their traveling clothes, because they were about to leave Egypt. And sure enough, Pharaoh buckled under this final plague and released the Israelites. As we know, he again changed his mind, setting up the Red Sea crisis, but that first Passover night remains a key moment in God's miraculous deliverance of his people.

"This day shall be a day of remembrance for you" (verse 14), the Israelites were told. Thus each Hebrew family held an annual feast to commemorate Passover. They swept their homes for traces of yeast, according to God's command. Each household selected a perfect lamb. The family followed a kind of script, with children asking about the meaning of the meal and the parents retelling the story. All of this is explained in the Book of Exodus.

Over time, details were added to the Passover meal. Different foods came to represent different parts of the story: bitter herbs for the bitterness of slavery; a fruit-nut mixture *(haroset)* for the mortar used by Israelite slaves; a vegetable *(karpas)* for renewed hope, dipped in salt water to represent tears; and unleavened bread *(matzo)* because they had no time for bread to rise. Eventually four cups of wine were drunk during the meal, becoming known as the Cups of Sanctification, Deliverance, Redemption, and Acceptance, harking back to the promises God made in Exodus 6:6–7. A fifth cup, the Cup of Elijah, was poured but not drunk, looking forward to a future messiah. A liturgy for the celebration also developed with songs, prayers, and questions.

Parable of the Sower

RELENTLESS QUESTIONING characterizes the teaching style of Socrates, and proverbial wisdom characterizes the teaching of Confucius, but parables seem to most characterize the teachings of Jesus. Through parables, abstract thoughts could be communicated in very concrete and understandable ways.

The English word *parable* is built from two Greek roots. One is the preposition *para,* which—in this context—means "alongside of." The other is related to the Greek word *ballein,* which means "to throw" (as in the English word *ballistics*). Thus a parable means "to throw alongside." Generally a parable is a story that evokes a variety of responses. Such is the case in the parable told in Matthew 13:1–23.

The Sower *by Vincent van Gogh*

Here Jesus tells a parable about a sower. (The story is also found in Mark 4:1–20 and Luke 8:1–15.) In Matthew, Jesus says some of the sower's seeds fell on the path (where birds ate them). Others fell on rocks (where they grew quickly, but then the sun killed them). Still other seeds fell among thorns (where the thorns choked them). And then some seeds fell on good soil (where they yielded 30-, 60-, and 100-fold). As an agricultural description, the parable makes sense. It is a metaphor whose literal meaning would not have been lost on those hearing it.

Generally, Jesus shared a parable and then left the interpretation up to those who were listening. In this case, however, Jesus interpreted the parable for his disciples. He noted that if people do not understand the Word of God, it is as if the devil snatched it away (much like birds would eat seed on a path). Furthermore, some people hear the Word of God and immediately become enthusiastic, but their faith has no strong grounding (their faith has no roots, like seeds that fall on rocks). Other people hear the Word of God, but they end up ignoring it because that message gets choked out by all of the cares and attractions of the world (like seed within thorn bushes). Whoever hears the Word of God and abides by it, however, they are like seeds that bear fruit upon fruit.

Why did Jesus interpret this parable verse by verse? Immediately after this passage, still in Matthew 13, six other parables—all of which focus on the kingdom of heaven—are brought together. Undoubtedly, Jesus did not want to cast his seed on a path, upon rocks, or among thorns.

Moses Receives the Ten Commandments

IN THE THIRD MONTH after the Israelites had escaped from Egypt, they arrived at Mount Sinai in the southern Sinai Peninsula and encamped there. Here, Moses went up the mountain to meet God, and God gave him two stone tablets on which were written the Ten Commandments. During his time on the mountain, God also gave him much of the rest of what came to be known as the "Law of Moses," found in the books of Exodus, Leviticus, and Numbers.

The Ten Commandments, however, have pride of place: They were given first; they were written on the two stone tablets; they were reiterated almost verbatim 40 years later to the next generation of Israelites; and they are referred to several times in the Bible as the "Ten Words," distinguishing them from the rest of the law.

Moses with the Tablets of the Law *by Rembrandt van Rijn*

The most common numbering of the Ten Commandments is as follows:

1. You shall have no other gods before me.
2. You shall not make for yourself an idol.
3. You shall not make wrongful use of the name of the Lord your God.
4. Remember the sabbath day, and keep it holy.
5. Honor your father and mother.
6. You shall not murder.
7. You shall not commit adultery.
8. You shall not steal.
9. You shall not bear false witness against your neighbor.
10. You shall not covet.

These short imperatives have universal application. The form in which they were given—"You shall . . . You shall not . . ."—differs from the "If . . . then . . ." form of most of the rest of the laws, which are much more specific to precise situations. Indeed, the rest of the law can be seen as an expansion or elaboration of the Ten Commandments. A modern-day analogy might be the relationship between the U.S. Constitution, which was written on four (large) pages, and the U.S. Federal Law Code, which issues specific laws based on the Constitution and which runs to thousands upon thousands of pages.

Joshua

JOSHUA WAS MOSES' successor and Israel's leader when the Israelites entered and took the land of Canaan. His original name was *Hoshea,* meaning "salvation" or "deliverance," but Moses changed it to *Joshua,* meaning "the Lord saves."

When the Israelites left Egypt, Joshua was the military commander who defeated the Amalekites in the wilderness. He was Moses' aide from his youth, and he accompanied Moses partway up Mount Sinai when Moses received the law. Later, he was one of 12 spies sent into Canaan, and he and Caleb were the only ones who brought back a positive report. As a result, they were the only ones of that generation allowed to enter the Promised Land.

In the wilderness, God's Spirit was in him, and he was designated as Moses' successor in a solemn commissioning service through the laying-on of Moses' hands. Then, when Moses was about to die, Joshua went with him to the tent of meeting to meet God, and God encouraged him to be strong and courageous, assuring him of his continuing presence. After Moses died, the Israelites listened to Joshua, for a spirit of wisdom was upon him because Moses had laid hands on him.

Joshua was a worthy successor to Moses. When the Israelites crossed the Jordan River into Canaan under his leadership, the Bible says, "The Lord exalted Joshua in the sight of all Israel; and they stood in awe of him, as they had stood in awe of Moses, all the days of his life" (Joshua 4:14). Thereafter he stands out for his faithfulness in seeking God's will and following God's instructions. He led the Israelites in successive military campaigns in central, southern, and northern Canaan, and he subdued much of the land and its people. Probably the most famous battles were at Jericho, where the walls crumbled after the Israelites marched around them for seven days, and at Gibeon, where the sun and the moon "stood still" and "stopped" (see Joshua 10:13).

At the end of his life, Joshua bid farewell to the tribes in a series of speeches in which he urged them to put away the gods of the Canaanites and to never abandon their relationship with the one true God. Before he led them in a covenant-renewal ceremony, he uttered these memorable words of commitment to the Lord: "As for me and my household, we will serve the Lord" (Joshua 24:15).

Joshua died at the ripe old age of 110, and he was buried "in his own inheritance" (verse 30). During his lifetime, the people served the Lord, and this speaks highly of his leadership.

Simon Is Dazzled

JESUS SAID that his disciples would be "witnesses" for him in Jerusalem, Judaea, Samaria, and to the ends of the earth (see Acts 1:8). The Lord's words serve as a precise outline for the Acts of the Apostles, because that's exactly what occurred. The first seven chapters of that book take place in Jerusalem. When Caiaphas and his council stepped up their opposition to the Church (as we see with the stoning of Stephen), Christian activity was forced outward to the outlying towns of Judaea and the neighboring area of Samaria. And then, as we read in Luke's telling of the missionary journeys of Paul, the gospel began its spread throughout the Mediterranean world.

Most Jews regarded the Samaritans as ethnic half-breeds and religious heretics. Jesus, however, had broken cultural barriers when he spoke with a Samaritan woman (John 4) and portrayed a Samaritan in a positive light in one of his most famous parables (Luke 10:30–37), so it should be no surprise to learn that Philip the Evangelist, a follower of Christ, began to preach in Samaria. And because healing and exorcism accompanied his evangelism, the Samaritans "listened eagerly to what was said" (Acts 8:6).

Previously the main attraction in Samaria was a sorcerer named Simon, who had dazzled the people with powerful displays of magic. You might expect some professional jealousy, but Simon also responded to Philip's message. As a wonder-worker himself, Simon was especially impressed with the spiritual power of Philip's miracles. He seemed even more impressed when Peter and John showed up and laid their hands on the believers. As a result, many received the Holy Spirit.

Simon wanted to buy the power the apostles displayed, so he offered money to Peter and John, but they refused it with a stern rebuke: "You have no part or share in this, for your heart is not right before God" (verse 21). Peter urged the sorcerer to repent, and it appears that Simon did.

This magician, known as Simon Magus, became a favorite character of fanciful writers in the following centuries. Some depicted elaborate competitions of spiritual power between him and the Apostle Peter.

POSTSCRIPT

■ The term *Magus*, Simon's title, is the singular form of *Magi*. It could refer to scholars in ancient Persian wisdom—like the wise men who visited the baby Jesus—or to practitioners of sorcery.

Mary Magdalene

A FAITHFUL FOLLOWER OF JESUS, Mary Magdalene was apparently the first to see Jesus after his bodily resurrection from the dead.

Although authors and filmmakers have said much about Mary Magdalene, the gospels actually say very little about her. She is grouped with several other women who joined Jesus' disciples on some occasions; she witnessed his crucifixion; and she came to the tomb the morning he arose. She is mentioned alongside other women who supported Jesus' ministry financially, so she probably did so as well.

Penitent Magdalene
by Titian

Luke tells us that Jesus had cast seven demons out of her (see Luke 8:1–2). That's all we know about that incident. We aren't given the story of that exorcism. Legend has tagged her as a former prostitute, but Scripture says nothing about that. Recent fiction has suggested that she and Jesus had a love affair or were even married. Again, Scripture says nothing on that score.

John has the story of her post-resurrection encounter with Jesus. Mary had come (with other women) to the tomb that Sunday morning and had found it empty, the stone rolled away. She ran to tell Peter and John, who ran to investigate for themselves and then left. Mary stayed near the tomb, crying. First she saw angels. Then she saw a figure she thought was the gardener, and she asked where the body had been taken (see John 20:1–18).

Of course, it was Jesus. He simply spoke her name, and at that point she recognized and worshipped him. It was a tender moment, but soon Jesus sent her off to tell others about his resurrection, which she did. But amazingly, there is no further mention of her in the Acts of the Apostles. We would expect her to participate in the Church as it grew, but it looks as though she may have done so anonymously.

POSTSCRIPT

■ Mary probably came from Magdala Nunayya, on the western shore of Galilee, south of Capernaum.

■ Speculation about Mary Magdalene is nothing new. She's mentioned in various fake gospels and fantasies from the third century and beyond and is sometimes called an apostle or a rival of the apostles. It would be a mistake to treat these as reliable historical documents.

The Book of Hosea

HOSEA WAS FROM NORTHERN ISRAEL, where he prophesied in the late eighth century B.C., about the same time as Isaiah, Amos, and Micah. Despite the constant threat from Assyria, it was still a time of economic prosperity—but religious laxity. The opening biographical narrative explains the driving pulse of Hosea's life and prophecy: his marriage to a prostitute—not once, but twice (1; 3)—and the birth of her children. The rest of the book is mainly poetic expressions of hope (2; 6:1–3; 11) and judgment (4—5; 6:4—10:15; 11—13), with a closing plea for repentance (14).

Hosea's marriage to a prostitute was an effective tool to catch people's attention. Their disgust at this action was turned back on them when Hosea pointed out the marriage's symbolism: Hosea represented God, the prostitute was Israel. Israel was worshipping the Canaanite god Baal (2:8–23), and their faithlessness to God was disgusting. In spite of her unfaithfulness, Hosea did not divorce or even kill his wife, though he could do both under the Law of Moses (Deuteronomy 22). Just as God's great love for Israel would not allow him to disown his chosen nation (Hosea 11), Hosea decided to take back his wife.

There was also powerful symbolism in their children's names. Hosea's son Jezreel, named after a fertile plain in Israel, reminded the people of a bloody battle where the current king's grandfather killed the previous king's entire family (see 2 Kings 9—10). The names of the other two children also had bad overtones. *Lo-ruhamah* means "no compassion" and *Lo-ammi* means "not my people." Both of these are saying no to earlier promises of God. He had promised loving mercy (Exodus 34:6; Deuteronomy 4:31) to his people (Exodus 6:7). Since they had turned away from their covenant relationship of faithfulness to him, God was turning his back on them for a time. This was not forever, since he yearned for restoration and to remove the "no" and "not" from their names (Hosea 2:21–23).

Baal worship was attractive to Israel. The people gained most of their livelihoods from agriculture, and Baal was the storm god. His rain could bring fertility, producing abundance of grain, wine, and olive oil. Israel had forgotten that the true and only source of all provision is God (2:8). Thus God told Israel to stop using Baal's name because it was replacing his name (2:17). Unlike Amos, who condemned the wrong worship of the right God, Hosea condemned the people for the right worship of the wrong god.

Egypt

E GYPT IS THE LAND of the Nile, the land of the pharaohs, the land of the pyramids, and home to an ancient civilization. About 200 miles southwest of Palestine, Egypt also figures prominently in biblical history as the backdrop for important scenes in the lives of Joseph, Moses, Jeremiah, and Jesus.

The starting line for Egyptian history is about 3100 B.C., with the merging of the kingdoms of Lower Egypt (the delta region in the north) and Upper Egypt (the Nile Valley extending southward). Massive building projects began around 2700 B.C., with the well-known pyramids at Giza constructed between 2600 and 2500 B.C. Overall, the period of the Old Kingdom (2700–2200 B.C.) saw substantial development of art and science. This political system fell apart, but unity was restored by rulers from the southern territory of Thebes, who established another period of growth, now known as the Middle Kingdom (2050–1780 B.C.).

Invaders from Asia (the Hyksos) took control for a time (c. 1780–1550 B.C.), but they were eventually beaten back, clearing the way for a third great period of advance, the New Kingdom (c. 1550–1090 B.C.).

The ups and downs of Egyptian history give us insight into a key biblical situation. Joseph was carried to Egypt as a slave, but he rose to become the right-hand man of a pharaoh. His family soon joined him, but centuries later these "children of Israel" were slaves. Why? Because "a new king arose over Egypt, who did not know Joseph" (Exodus 1:8). One of those seams in Egyptian history was crossed, and a new regime was in place. Scholars disagree about the exact dates, but they all place the Israelites' exodus from Egypt somewhere in the New Kingdom era.

From Egyptian history, we know that slavery was part of the Egyptian economy and social structure. We know the Egyptians became experts in construction, developing new methods of stonecutting, and that they loved to build massive structures (the Israelite slaves contributed to at least one of these efforts). The Egyptians worshipped gods of nature, including the Nile River itself, and so the ten plagues were not just an ecological disaster but also a significant theological statement.

After the Israelites settled in Canaan, there were occasional skirmishes with Egypt, but there were times of alliance, too. When the Babylonians invaded Judah between 606 and 586 B.C., many Jews fled to Egypt, including Jeremiah. Six centuries later, another Joseph would take his wife, Mary, and her son, Jesus, to Egypt, fleeing the jealous wrath of King Herod.

Born Again

TOWARD THE BEGINNING of the Gospel of John, the writer relates an incident that occurred during the night. It was, of course, dark. Jesus was apparently alone. A lone figure approached him in the darkness. The man was a ruler of the Jews. His name was Nicodemus.

Because Nicodemus was a respected leader among the Jews, he was probably wiser than most. And because he was respectful to Jesus, he was evidently a humble, religious person. Nevertheless, he had great difficulty in comprehending the words of Jesus, who began by telling him, "Very truly, I tell you, no one can see the kingdom of God without being born from above" (John 3:3). These words stunned and puzzled Nicodemus.

Interview Between Jesus and Nicodemus *by James Tissot*

Like so many others, Nicodemus mistakenly took Jesus' words literally. What Jesus said seemed absolutely incredible, perhaps even ridiculous, and so he asked, "How can a man be born when he is old? Can he enter a second time into his mother's womb and be born?" (verse 4).

Jesus could have used many other analogies to describe what it means to be right with God, but birth is an intense process and an effective illustration. There is pain, disorientation, and dislocation. Birth involves leaving the familiar and the safe, and so it also involves a kind of death to a former way of life. As the Apostle Paul notes in Romans 6, baptism into a new life first involves death and burial in the water. Only through death is rebirth possible.

But Nicodemus thought about his own mother's womb and missed the point entirely. He came at night, and his mind remained enveloped in darkness. After Jesus' resurrection, his teaching about being reborn became abundantly clear. Since Nicodemus later demonstrated his love for Jesus after he was crucified by helping with his burial, it is almost certain that Nicodemus finally came to a full understanding.

The Golden Calf

W HEN MOSES REMAINED up on Mount Sinai for a long period of
time, the people grew impatient and restless. They told Moses'
brother, Aaron, the high priest, to "make gods for us, who shall go before
us" (Exodus 32:1). Aaron complied, directing them to bring him their
gold earrings, from which he cast a golden calf.

Aaron then presented the calf to the people, saying, "These are your gods,
O Israel, who brought you out of the land of Egypt!" (verse 4). This was a
startling statement, since God had stated that *he* was "the Lord your God,
who brought you out of the land of Egypt" (Exodus 20:2). Rather than
asserting that this calf had brought them out of Egypt, Aaron probably
meant for the calf to be a visual representation of God himself, and it
was probably God *and this representation of him* that were "your gods" to
which he referred.

Whatever Aaron's intent, what he did in crafting this object of worship
was a violation of the second commandment, which stated that "You shall
not make for yourself an idol . . . You shall not bow down to them or worship them" (verses 4–5). This commandment may not have been officially
given to the people at this time, but it certainly was understood from what
had recently transpired since God's deliverance of the Hebrew people.

When God saw their idolatry, his anger burned, and he threatened to
destroy Israel on the spot and start over with Moses. Moses, however,
intervened, and God relented. Yet, when Moses actually descended from
the mountain and saw what was happening, he too became incensed.
He shattered the two tablets of the Ten Commandments, and he burned
the calf, ground up the remains into a powder, scattered it on the water,
and made the Israelites drink it. In addition, he enlisted the help of the
Levites and killed about 3,000 of the idolaters. Then God sent a plague
on the people.

God's anger finally abated. Moses then made a second set of tablets of the
Ten Commandments, and the people finished building the tabernacle
according to God's instructions.

POSTSCRIPT

■ Many years later, King Jeroboam I erected two golden calves at Dan and Bethel
in a conscious echo of this incident. His words were almost identical: "Here are
your gods, O Israel, who brought you up out of the land of Egypt" (1 Kings 12:28).

Caleb

CALEB WAS ONE OF 12 SPIES whom Moses sent out to reconnoiter the promised land of Canaan before the Israelites entered it. The Israelites had journeyed from Mount Sinai and were now poised to take the land.

What the spies found was impressive. They reported that it was a land flowing with milk and honey. They brought back grapes, figs, and pomegranates to show the plentiful fruit of this land to their fellow Israelites. To people who had been subsisting on manna for many months, this was an incredible bounty.

But the spies also reported dangers. They said the land was filled with fierce peoples and strong, fortified cities. They found giants there as well. They reported that "to ourselves we seemed like grasshoppers, and so we seemed to them" (Numbers 13:33). They said that this was "a land that devours its inhabitants" (verse 32). Thus ten of the spies counseled against entering Canaan.

Meanwhile, Caleb had declared, "Let us go up at once and occupy it, for we are well able to overcome it" (verse 30). Joshua, another one of the spies, then joined him, and together they said, "The Lord is with us; do not fear them" (Numbers 14:9). Their faith in God to deliver them was based on their previous experiences with God. He had delivered the nation with a mighty display of power through the plagues and the parting of the Red Sea, and he had already defeated some of Israel's enemies in the wilderness. But the people listened to the despairing counsel of the ten spies and threatened to stone Caleb and Joshua.

Because of this rebellion, God sentenced the entire nation to 40 years of wandering in the wilderness until the unfaithful generation passed away. No one over the age of 20 would be allowed to enter the Promised Land, *except* for Caleb and Joshua, who were allowed to enter as a reward for their faith.

When the time came many decades later, Caleb asked Joshua for his inheritance at Hebron, which was also known as Kiriath-Arba (meaning "city of Arba"). He was making a statement by this request, because he had to drive out the Anakim in order to take this city—Arba being the greatest of them. Ironically, the Anakim were the very giants who threw Caleb's fellow spies into such a terror many years earlier, but Caleb was fearless before them and took the city.

On the Road to Damascus

THE HIGH PRIEST'S OFFICE was determined to crush the emerging Church. Old Annas led a corrupt dynasty, which included his son-in-law, Caiaphas. For decades Annas and his family held the powerful high priest position and controlled the Sanhedrin, the Jewish ruling council. They had convicted Jesus of blasphemy, arrested Peter and John, and stoned Stephen. That stoning launched a new offensive. As the apostles scattered from Jerusalem, the high priest expanded his search for believers in neighboring cities.

A man named Saul was present at Stephen's stoning. We're not sure if he was leading it, helping out, or just observing, but he approved. He became an active opponent of the Church, arresting and imprisoning those who followed Jesus.

The Jewish response to the Christians was not universally negative. It appears that, in Damascus, as in some other places, followers of Jesus were often welcomed in synagogues. So when Saul carried "letters to the synagogues of Damascus" (Acts 9:2) from the high priest, these messages were probably alerting them to the dangers of Christianity and asking for help in rounding up heretics.

Saul, however, experienced a life-changing encounter. On the road, Saul was knocked to the ground by a dazzling light. He heard the voice of Jesus saying, "Saul, Saul, why do you persecute me?" (verse 4). Jesus then told Saul to go to a certain house in Damascus. Temporarily blinded, Saul followed the instructions, and Ananias was sent to restore his sight.

Saul's conversion was a private moment—his companions on the road heard no voice. Some have conjectured that it was some sort of epileptic seizure. Yet it is described three times in Acts (chapters 9, 22, 26) and always treated as an objective reality. Besides, its impact was enormous. Saul did a complete turnaround, from persecutor to proclaimer. He became the Church's greatest missionary, carrying the good news of Jesus into the Gentile world using his Roman name, Paul.

POSTSCRIPT

Many biblical characters have multiple names, usually a Hebrew name as well as a Gentile name, depending on what culture they are dealing with. Daniel was known as Belteshazzar in Babylon. Esther was the Persian name for Hadassah. In the New Testament, we find Tabitha/Dorcas and Cephas/Peter. Saul/Paul probably had both names from childhood, but he began to use the Roman name *Paulus* when he journeyed throughout the Gentile world.

Lazarus

Lazarus was a good friend of Jesus'. He was the brother of Martha and Mary, who were also Jesus' friends. After Lazarus died and was placed in his tomb, Jesus brought him back to life.

The Raising of Lazarus from the Dead

Jesus once commented that foxes and birds had homes to stay in, but he didn't. As he conducted his itinerant ministry, he relied on the kindness of others, and we're told about several followers who funded his ministry and housed him. Lazarus was one of these supporters, along with his sisters Martha and Mary. They lived in Bethany, just around the bend from Jerusalem, so when Jesus visited the temple for the high holy days, he generally stayed with them. Because he traveled with an entourage of at least 12 and possibly 20, we can assume that Lazarus had a sizable home.

On one occasion, Lazarus desperately needed Jesus' help. He had fallen ill, and his sisters sent word to Jesus, who was in Galilee at the time, generally a four-day walk from the Jerusalem area. Jesus didn't set out right away, but purposefully waited. By the time he reached Bethany, his friend Lazarus had been dead four days.

Martha went out to meet Jesus and began to scold him. "Lord, if you had been here, my brother would not have died" (John 11:21). But she also expressed faith in his power "even now" (see verse 22). Jesus then promised a resurrection for all in terms that could apply to one's current life or a future kingdom.

Jesus approached Lazarus's tomb and asked that the stone be rolled away. Martha protested, saying that the smell of decomposition would be horrible, but Jesus insisted. He called out to Lazarus, and the once-dead man walked out of his grave with the wrappings still on him.

This resurrection testified even further to Jesus' divinity, and it galvanized the opposition against him. People flocked to see not only Jesus but also Lazarus, the former corpse. This was such a powerful testimony that the religious leaders began to plot the murder of Lazarus as well. This could be the reason why such a significant miracle is omitted in the three earlier gospels—to protect Lazarus during his lifetime.

The Books of Joel and Amos

APART FROM HIS FATHER'S name, Joel's ancestry is largely unknown. The dates of both his ministry and the composition of the book bearing his name are unknown, but since he refers to Solomon's Temple, which was destroyed in 586 B.C., his book was probably written earlier.

The trigger event for Joel's prophecy was a locust plague, a disaster to people who depended on agriculture for their livelihoods. If locusts devoured their crops, they would not have anything either to eat or plant. The arrival of the locusts in Joel is compared to a violent army approaching on the Day of the Lord (2:4–11)—a final day of judgment on those who do not follow God. When the people turn back to God (2:17), God responds and gives them victory (2:18—3:21). Part of the coming blessing is equipping everyone for God's service by his Spirit (2:28–29), an event that comes to pass in the New Testament at Pentecost (Acts 2:17–21).

Amos prophesied in the mid-eighth century B.C., at the same time as Isaiah, Hosea, and Micah. The prophecies in his book come in many forms: oracles against neighboring nations (1:3—2:5), judgment speeches (3—4), laments (5:1–17), oracles of woe (5:18—6:14), visions (7:1—9:10), and promises of salvation (9:11–15). He uses these powerful and varied rhetorical devices to catch the attention of his audience, the people of the northern kingdom of Israel. Amos makes a series of accusations against Israel's neighbors that the Israelites can loudly agree with, but Amos also ends with a condemnation of the real culprit—Israel itself! Amos condemns Israel for their worship: They worship the right God, but they do it the wrong way. Israel worships in words and outward religious actions but not with their hearts, as demonstrated in their lack of care of the poor and the needy.

All is not lost for Israel, however. God will bring back his dispersed people, rebuilding and replanting what has been destroyed (9:11–15).

POSTSCRIPT

■ Israel anticipated the coming of the Day of the Lord, when God would bless those who have obeyed him and punish those who have not. Amos had to remind them that the Day of the Lord might be a bad day for them if they did not start acting in the ways that God had instructed them.

■ Amos 5:1–2 is in the form of a funeral dirge. When Israel gathers to ask who has died, it finds that the funeral is for the nation itself.

The Sinai

A WEDGE OF RUGGED DESERT at the intersection of Asia and Africa, the Sinai Peninsula was an unwanted home to the Israelites for 40 years after they escaped Egypt. Nevertheless, it was the site of the giving of the law, which identified and invigorated this young nation.

The biblical story of the Sinai begins with Moses, not as a leader, but as a shepherd. After he had fled from Egypt because he had killed an Egyptian officer, he labored for a nomadic herdsman, Jethro. He even married Jethro's daughter. But while tending sheep on Mount Horeb (also known as Mount Sinai), he encountered a mysterious burning bush, where God asked him to return to Egypt for a special mission: *Lead my people to freedom from Egyptian bondage.*

When the Israelites marched out of Egypt, the Lord parted the Red Sea to let the Israelites out of Egypt and into the Sinai desert. Almost immediately there were questions and complaints about food and water, with some wanting to return to Egypt, where at least they wouldn't starve. The Lord then provided manna from heaven, water from a rock, and coveys of quail for their sustenance. In three months, Moses led them to Mount Sinai, which he climbed alone to meet with God. There the Lord gave him the Ten Commandments. The Israelites camped at the mountain for more than a year before packing up and heading for the Promised Land—that is, Canaan. Unfortunately, the Israelites were disobedient and had to turn back from the Promised Land and wander in the desert for 40 years, until almost the whole generation that had left Egypt died in the wilderness.

The exact location of Mount Sinai is disputed. The traditional site is Jebel Musa (Arabic for "Mount Moses"), toward the southern tip of the Sinai triangle, but a few other peaks have been suggested.

POSTSCRIPT

- More than a thousand years before the Israelites arrived at Sinai, the Egyptians had turquoise mines there.

- Long after the time of Moses, the prophet Elijah would flee the wrath of Queen Jezebel and end up at Mount Horeb (Sinai). There, in a bout of depression, he would hear God's gentle whisper (see 1 Kings 19:12).

- Sinai is probably named for "Sin," a local moon god.

The Demoniac

I**N AN INCIDENT DESCRIBED** in Matthew 9:32–34, Jesus exorcised a mute demoniac who had been brought to him. After the exorcism, the mute man spoke, and the surrounding crowds were amazed, saying, "Never has anything like this been seen in Israel" (verse 33). Within Israel, Jews were familiar with the miracles of prophets such as Elijah and Elisha, but nowhere else in the Bible can we find the sort of healings that Jesus performed.

In a society without specialized hospitals, Jesus' healings and exorcisms brought large crowds of people seeking him. As people sought to be healed, the crowds grew so large that Jesus frequently needed to withdraw and be alone with his heavenly Father.

Immediately preceding this passage, Jesus had healed two blind men (see verses 27–31), but then he had told them, "See that no one knows of this" (verse 30). Perhaps he said this because the crowds had become over-whelming. Perhaps he said this because he recognized that the miracles might detract attention from his actual mission. Perhaps he said this because too much attention could be unhealthy for him. Others might look upon him with suspicion. The authorities might see his power and charisma as a threat.

Indeed, that was the case in this particular story of the demoniac. After Jesus' exorcism and the man's speech amazed the people, the religious authorities—that is, the Pharisees—declared, "By the ruler of the demons he casts out the demons" (verse 34).

Some Bible scholars note the Pharisees' words were little more than jealous slurs or prejudiced attacks against one whose power was note-worthy. Perhaps, however, Jesus' power and control over demons was so strong that the Pharisees could not come up with any other logical explanation that made sense to them. They clearly believed that Jesus had exorcized a demon out of the man. Therefore, it is not surprising that later Jesus' enemies would accuse him of being in alliance with Beelzebul (see Matthew 12:24). Such charges would continue until Jesus was crucified.

Meanwhile, the former demoniac was delivered from his affliction, and God's mercy was once again shown through his Son.

The Fall of Jericho

Y EARS BEFORE THE ISRAELITES crossed the Jordan River into the promised land of Canaan, Joshua had been commissioned as Moses' successor in a solemn ceremony with the entire congregation of Israel attending and Eleazar, the high priest, presiding. Joshua had large shoes to fill, for the Bible says of Moses that "Never since has there arisen a prophet in Israel like Moses" (Deuteronomy 34:10). Nevertheless, God repeatedly exalted Joshua among the people.

The Seven Trumpets of Jericho *by James Tissot*

Joshua's first test in Canaan was the gateway city of Jericho; it was large and well fortified. Joshua sent two spies into Jericho, and a prostitute named Rahab befriended and protected them. In fact, Rahab cast her lot with Israel's God, saying, "I know that the Lord has given you the land . . . The Lord your God is indeed God in heaven above and on earth below" (Joshua 2:9, 11). Rahab voiced the words that Moses himself had uttered, speaking of the exclusivity of Israel's God: "The Lord is God in heaven above and on the earth beneath; there is no other" (Deuteronomy 4:39). With these words, Rahab was stepping apart from the polytheistic religious system she had grown up with in Canaan and affirming her loyalty to Israel's God. Because of this remarkable confession, Joshua directed that she and her family be spared. Rahab, in essence, became an Israelite—not by birth, but by her faith in Israel's God. She was assimilated into Israel and became an ancestor of Jesus, the promised Messiah.

God's way of putting Jericho into the Israelites' hands was curious: The Israelites were to march around the city once a day for six days, while the priests blew rams' horns. On the seventh day they circled the city seven times. Then, at Joshua's signal, the people raised a great shout and the priests blew on the horns, and the city wall "fell down flat" (Joshua 6:20).

Joshua pronounced a curse on the city that it should never be rebuilt. Years later, a man named Hiel tried to rebuild it, but he lost his two sons in the process, fulfilling the words of the Lord spoken by Joshua.

Deborah

AFTER ISRAEL TOOK possession of the promised land of Canaan, the nation settled into a long period in which there was no centralized authority, and as a result, "all the people did what was right in their own eyes" (Judges 17:6). It was a time of increasing apostasy; that is, the Israelites increasingly turned to the Canaanite gods and away from the true God. For punishment, God subjected the Israelites to oppression by one foreign neighbor and then another. Each time God would hear the cries of his people during their days of oppression, he would relent and send a "judge" to deliver them.

The judges were both military deliverers and "judges" in the modern sense. Although the Bible stories primarily focus on the judges' battles and military victories, many judges are recorded afterward as judging Israel for many years, during which time they kept social order and made certain that the Israelites served the Lord. But for the most part, the judges were part of the problem and did not turn peoples' hearts to God. The most notable exception to this pattern was Deborah. First, she was not only a judge but also a prophet. Second, she was the only woman judge of whom we are aware. Third, in contrast to many of the other judges, she was *not* part of the problem; her life was exemplary in every way.

The Bible says Deborah "used to sit under the palm of Deborah . . . and the Israelites came up to her for judgment" (Judges 4:5). Clearly she exercised wise judicial authority, as well as military leadership. God gave her a prophetic word for Barak, an Israelite general, that he should muster a coalition to fight against Jabin, king of Hazor, and his general, Sisera. Fearful, Barak declined to go unless Deborah went with him. She did so, but she told him that he would not be covered in glory because "the Lord will sell Sisera into the hand of a woman" (verse 9). That woman was not Deborah, but Jael, in whose tent Sisera had entered to sleep. She killed him with a tent peg through the temple.

After God gave Jabin and his army into the Israelites' hands, Deborah and Barak sang a victory song praising God for his mighty hand against Jabin. This long song has come to be known as the "Song of Deborah." It mentions Deborah as "a mother in Israel," an acknowledgment of her special leadership (Judges 5:7). And, after this, things were quiet for a time: The Bible says, "the land had rest forty years" (verse 31).

Ananias Restores Saul's Sight

SAUL TRAVELED TO DAMASCUS on a deadly mission. His job was to round up the followers of Jesus the Nazarene and transport them back to Jerusalem for trial. Before he arrived, however, he had an otherworldly experience that changed his life. Frankly, it changed history. He saw a light from heaven and heard the voice of Jesus. Blinded by that light, he was led into the city to an address Jesus had given him.

Meanwhile, the Lord spoke to a Christian in Damascus named Ananias (obviously not the Ananias who was struck dead in Acts 5), sending him to that same address to look for a man named Saul of Tarsus and to restore his sight. *Um, Saul of Tarsus? The persecutor?* Ananias knew all about Saul's violent mission. Everyone might be better off if Saul just stayed blind.

But Ananias was a man of virtue, who was well respected by his fellow Jews and Christians alike. Despite his qualms, Ananias obeyed the Lord's instructions. Finding the house, he entered and said, "Brother Saul, the Lord Jesus...has sent me so that you may regain your sight and be filled with the Holy Spirit" (Acts 9:17). The Bible reports that "something like scales" fell from Saul's eyes (verse 18), and he could see again.

This was not just a physical healing but part of a spiritual transformation. Saul was able to see Jesus, the Church, the world, and himself in a new light after Ananias imparted the Spirit to him. As he testified later before King Agrippa, Saul (then known as Paul) said, "I was not disobedient to the heavenly vision" (Acts 26:19). The same could be said of the otherwise unknown Ananias, who obeyed the Lord and changed the history of the Church.

POSTSCRIPT

- When the blinded Saul arrived in Damascus, he waited for three days without eating or drinking before Ananias arrived.

- Answering an objection, the Lord told Ananias that Saul was his chosen "instrument" (Acts 9:15). The Greek word can refer to any utensil or vessel. Later, Paul used the word to refer to himself and other ministers as clay vessels or jars (2 Corinthians 4:7).

Martha of Bethany

MARTHA WAS THE SISTER of Lazarus and Mary, and they lived together in Bethany not far from Jerusalem. Martha was a woman of faith who supported Jesus' ministry.

Two Bible stories speak to Martha's character. In one, Jesus shows up with his ministry team, and Martha scurries to provide hospitality for them. Lazarus, Mary, and Martha lived in what must have been a sizable house in Bethany, a suburb of Jerusalem. Luke speaks of it as "her" home, suggesting that Martha was the oldest sibling or that she was the sole owner. In any case, during this time she finds a lot of work to do, preparing food and lodging for Jesus and his 12 disciples, plus whatever other followers they might have attracted. Understandably, she is "distracted by her many tasks" (Luke 10:40).

Meanwhile her sister, Mary, is sitting at Jesus' feet, listening attentively. Since Jesus often told amusing stories, we can imagine her laughing along with the disciples, and we can also imagine that sound wafting over to the kitchen, where Martha is slaving away. Martha complains to Jesus, asking him to send Mary to help her. Jesus takes this as a teaching moment.

"Martha, Martha," he says, "you are worried and distracted by many things; there is need of only one thing. Mary has chosen the better part, which will not be taken away from her" (verse 41). You can almost hear Jesus' attempt to calm this busy woman, but his message is clear: Be calm, and rest in the Lord.

On another occasion, Lazarus fell ill, and the sisters sent for Jesus. By the time he arrived, Lazarus was already dead. After Jesus identified himself as "the resurrection and the life" (John 11:25), he asked Martha if she believed that. "Yes, Lord," she responded, "I believe that you are the Messiah, the Son of God, the one coming into the world" (verse 27). This is almost identical to Peter's confession in Matthew 16, which Jesus hails as God-given truth (see verses 16–19). Clearly Martha had not only learned from Jesus but also intuitively knew who he was.

POSTSCRIPT

■ The name *Martha* means "lady" or "mistress."

The Books of Obadiah and Micah

OBADIAH, WHOSE NAME means "servant of God," prophesied in the mid-sixth century B.C. His prophecy, which is the shortest book in the Old Testament, is a long poem consisting of a summons to battle and judgment (1, 18) and concluding with a promise of salvation (19–21). The first half of the book brings judgment against Edom, Israel's neighbor across the Jordan River to the west. Edom took advantage of Judah's capture by Babylon in 586 B.C., joining in the looting and even turning in escapees (10–14). The second half of the book has warnings of the coming Day of the Lord, with judgment upon all nations (15–18) and the restoration of Israel (19–21). Yahweh, Israel's God (1, 21), is king over all the earth.

Micah, an eighth century B.C. prophet of the same period as Amos, Hosea, and Isaiah, caught the ear of the righteous Judaean king Hezekiah, whose positive response to God saved Judah from destruction for a time (Jeremiah 26:17–19). Micah's prophecy consists of three poetic sections, each started by a call to hear and/or listen (Micah 1:2; 3:1; 6:1). Each section also contains messages of both judgment (1:2—2:11; 3; 4:9—5:6; 5:10–14; 6:1—7:13) and hope (2:12–13; 4:1–8; 5:7–9; 7:14–20).

Assyria had taken the northern nation of Israel into captivity in 722 B.C., and Judah had been warned it would suffer the same fate if it did not leave behind its corrupt ways. The rich stole from the poor because they had the power to do so (2:1–3, 8–9; 3:1–3, 9–10), and even Judah's leaders were corrupt, including the prophets (2:6, 11; 3:5–7), priests (3:11), and judges (7:1–4). God challenged his people to live righteously (6:1–8). Even though God himself was plaintiff, prosecuting attorney, judge, and executioner, the people's response was to offer to do increasingly more outrageous things, even going as far as human sacrifice. All God called for was "to do justice, and to love kindness, and to walk humbly with your God" (6:8).

POSTSCRIPT

- Edom's capital, Petra, was impregnable from the ground, being carved out of rock at the end of a steep, narrow canyon. It is best known today as the place filmed as the resting place of the Holy Grail in the movie *Indiana Jones and the Last Crusade*.

- Ahab, who is condemned by Micah (see Micah 6:16), was married to the infamous Jezebel. She is still remembered as an evil and malicious woman (see 1 Kings 16:31; 21).

The High Priest

BOTH MOSES AND AARON belonged to the tribe of Levi. While Moses was the first political leader of the ancient Israelites, his brother, Aaron, had a separate leadership role. As the first high priest, Aaron oversaw the early religious activities of the people. His sons assisted him in the work of the tabernacle, sacrificing the animals people brought as sin offerings, presenting the grain offerings before the Lord, burning incense, lighting the lamps, and baking the holy bread.

Over time, the high priesthood passed on to Aaron's descendants. All men of the tribe of Levi could help out in the tabernacle (and later, the temple), but only descendants of Aaron could serve as priests. Of these, one was designated as the high priest.

The high priest was in charge of the whole religious operation, but he also had a unique duty. He alone could enter the Holy of Holies, and he could do that only on the Day of Atonement, when he sprinkled blood on the lid of the ark of the covenant.

The Book of Hebrews describes the role of the high priest succinctly: "Every high priest chosen from among mortals is put in charge of things pertaining to God on their behalf, to offer gifts and sacrifices for sins" (Hebrews 5:1).

All the priests wore fine linen garments, but the high priest had a special, intricately embroidered outfit. This included the ephod (sort of a sacred apron), a turban, and an ornate breastplate, bearing a gem for each of the 12 tribes of Israel. That way, the law said, the priest would bring the people with him as he went before the Lord.

Among the other named high priests in Scripture are Hilkiah, who rediscovered the Torah during the reign of King Josiah, and a man named Joshua in the prophecies of Zechariah, who restored worship in Jerusalem. In Jesus' time, the high priest was Caiaphas, son-in-law of Annas, who had also served in that role. Without an indigenous political leader in place, the high priesthood had become a position of great power, influencing Jews not only in Judaea but also throughout the Mediterranean world. Annas was the patriarch of a corrupt dynasty that occupied the high priesthood in Jerusalem from A.D. 6 to 42.

Meanwhile, the New Testament makes a case for Jesus as a high priest of a different order. While a mortal priest must offer sacrifices for his own sins, Jesus, "having been made perfect, . . . became the source of eternal salvation for all who obey him" (Hebrews 5:9).

Feeding of the Five Thousand

ACCORDING TO MATTHEW 14, after Jesus disembarked from a boat, he saw a great crowd, had compassion for them, and healed the sick. Afterward, his disciples urged him to send the crowds away because it was late and no one had had anything to eat. Jesus told the disciples that there was no need to send the crowds away, but rather they should feed them. The disciples replied, "We have noth-

ing here but five loaves and two fish" (Matthew 14:17). Jesus had the crowds sit down, and then he took the food. Then, looking to heaven, he blessed and broke the loaves. He gave the loaves to the disciples, who gave the loaves and fish to the crowds, and everyone ate until they were full. When the disciples gathered the broken pieces and leftovers, they realized that 12 full baskets remained.

Only after the story is the most amazing element revealed: "And those who ate were about five thousand men, besides women and children" (verse 21).

The Feeding of the Five Thousand *by Gian Cavagna*

Although most readers might react to this miracle with astonishment, it is interesting to note that there is no description that those in the crowd were astounded. Matthew seemingly was not concerned with those reactions. Rather, Matthew evidently wrote this story knowing his readers would have been familiar with this kind of miracle. In Second Kings 4:42–44, Elisha, for instance, took bread and then ordered that it be given to many. Although he was asked how such an act would be possible (considering the numbers), everyone ate, and food was leftover. Matthew in this sense presents Jesus as a miracle-worker like Elisha.

More significantly, however, this story anticipates the Last Supper, described in Matthew 26:20–29. Although there are a number of parallels between the Last Supper story and this miracle feeding story, what stands out the most is Jesus' blessing and breaking of the loaves in front of the crowd. When Jesus stood in the desert in front of more than 5,000 people, he offered them food because he felt compassion for them. Although we are not told what Jesus said, his compassion speaks loudly in ways that anticipate words that we find in the Gospel of John: "I am the bread of life. Whoever comes to me will never be hungry, and whoever believes in me will never be thirsty" (John 6:35).

Samson Triumphant

SAMSON IS RENOWNED for his great strength and his long hair. Even before he was born, an angel announced to his parents that he would be God's special man for his turbulent times. In his day, the Philistines were Israel's greatest threat. Throughout Samson's life, he performed great feats of strength, from killing a lion with his bare hands, to killing 30 Philistine men for their garments to pay back a pledge, to killing 1,000 Philistines with the jawbone of a donkey, and more.

Samson, however, was not a godly man. He had been dedicated to God before birth: He was to consume no wine or strong drink; he was to avoid

contact with the dead and anything unclean; and he was never to cut his hair or his great strength would vanish. By the end, however, he had violated all three of these conditions: He had taken part in a drinking feast at his wedding; he had had plenty of contact with the dead, killing thousands himself; and in the end, he allowed his hair to be cut short. Furthermore, he entangled himself repeatedly with Philistine women: He married one; he later consorted with a Philistine prostitute; and finally, he took up with Delilah, yet another Philistine woman.

Despite his personal failings, God used him to abate the Philistine threat, and his greatest failure was inextricably entangled with his greatest and final success. After Delilah had a man cut Samson's hair while he was asleep, the Philistines were able to subdue and capture him. They then put out his eyes and imprisoned him. His final act came after his hair had grown back, and he was taken to the Philistine temple as a public spectacle. While standing between two pillars, he asked the Lord for strength one last time, and God granted his request. Samson used his God-given strength to pull down the pillars supporting the temple, destroying 3,000 Philistines as well as himself.

POSTSCRIPT

■ The Philistines were worshipping their national god, Dagon, when Samson killed them. Dagon was an ancient Mesopotamian deity with a body of a fish and a human head and human hands. He was the symbol of water. The Philistines built temples in his honor at Ashdad, Gaza, and other towns.

Gideon

GIDEON WAS A JUDGE perhaps best known for the test he devised in which he asked God to perform miracles with a fleece. Yet his life encompassed more than that: He was a conflicted character who did great things for God but also undermined them with his lack of faith.

When Gideon first met an angel of the Lord, he asked for and received a sign to confirm that God was sending him to fight against the Midianites, who were oppressing Israel. The angel raised a fire from a rock and that fire consumed the meal that Gideon had prepared for the angel. Despite this, Gideon remained fearful of the Midianites, as well as his fellow Israelites, who were worshipping Baal. So he gathered a group of men and knocked down the altar of Baal and the wooden Asherah pole next to it—but he performed this deed at night when no one could identify him as the leader of the group.

Later, Gideon asked God to prove himself again, devising a two-part test that revealed his continued fear and lack of faith (he had already received one clear sign from God). He laid out a woolen fleece and asked God to wet it overnight but to keep the ground around it dry. God did so. Gideon then asked God to perform the sign in reverse: Keep the fleece dry overnight and make the ground wet. Gideon knew he was pushing his luck, begging God, "Do not let your anger burn against me" (Judges 6:39). But God again complied with Gideon's request.

When Gideon issued a call to arms, 32,000 men responded. God told him that this was too many, since the victory, when it came, was to be clearly from God. So Gideon dismissed all who wanted to leave, and 22,000 departed. Because the 10,000 remaining were still too many, the number was whittled down to 300. At night, God had Gideon ambush the Midianites, who ended up slaughtering each other. After the battle, the Israelites asked Gideon to be their king, "for you have delivered us" (Judges 8:22). To his credit, Gideon refused, saying just the right thing by noting that God was their king and would fight their battles.

Nevertheless, Gideon began acting like a king. He directed the people to bring him their valuables, and he made an ephod, which became an object of illegitimate worship and a snare to Gideon and his family.

POSTSCRIPT

■ A further sign of Gideon's insincerity in refusing the offer of kingship is that he named his son *Abimelech*, which means "my father is king."

Peter Awakens Tabitha

JESUS HAD COMMISSIONED his disciples to "Cure the sick, raise the dead, cleanse the lepers, cast out demons" (Matthew 10:8). A few years after his resurrection, they were obedient to his command. And they knew very well that it was not their own power but the name of Jesus that was accomplishing these miracles (see Acts 3:12, 16).

The spiritual explosion that had occurred in Jerusalem at Pentecost was rippling outward. As Jesus had predicted (see Acts 1:8), his disciples were his witnesses in Judaea, Samaria, and beyond. Peter visited the thriving ministry of deacon Philip (the Evangelist) in Samaria and then went to Lydda, a town on the coastal plain of Judaea, where he healed a paralyzed man named Aeneas.

Meanwhile, ten miles up the coast in Joppa, a beloved Christian woman had become sick and died. Her name was Tabitha, though some knew her by the Greek name *Dorcas*. She had carried on a charitable ministry for poor widows, which had involved making them clothing, as well as performing other kind deeds. She would be greatly missed.

Someone decided to send for Peter, and he came immediately. When he arrived, the keening was already in full swing, with widows weeping and showing the clothing that Tabitha had made for them. Peter sent everyone out of the upstairs room where Tabitha's body rested. Then he knelt and prayed.

Peter had seen Jesus raise a young girl from death, but he was not Jesus, and he knew it. Yet he had been working miracles in the name of Jesus. Could he raise this woman? Could he restore her to the community that sorely needed her? No wonder he took time out to pray, summoning divine power for the deed he was about to attempt.

"Tabitha, get up," he commanded (Acts 9:40). The woman opened her eyes and sat up. Peter helped her to her feet and invited the mourners to come and see the one they'd been mourning for.

POSTSCRIPT

■ When the text says the widows were "showing" the clothing Tabitha had made, it uses a rare middle voice. The best translation is that they were "modeling" the clothes. In her honor, they were wearing the outfits she had given them to her funeral.

■ Joppa served as a seaport for Jerusalem, which was 35 miles to the southeast.

Mary of Bethany

MARY WAS THE SISTER of Martha and Lazarus. She supported, loved, and learned from Jesus. Her extravagant act of worship, pouring expensive perfume on Jesus' feet, prepared Jesus for his death and burial.

She is one of many Marys in the New Testament, and her story creates questions that open up rampant speculation. Let's start with what we know.

These three siblings—Mary, Martha, and Lazarus—lived in a sizable house in Bethany, a town just a few miles from Jerusalem. It seems that Martha was the oldest and might have owned the house. They were all friends of Jesus, and he often stayed there when he visited the big city.

On one such visit, Martha complained that she was doing all the work while Mary sat at Jesus' feet and listened. Martha wanted Jesus to tell Mary to help her, but Jesus refused, saying that Mary had chosen a better activity (see Luke 10:38–42).

When Lazarus died, both Martha and Mary separately expressed their disappointment to Jesus for him not being there earlier to heal their brother. Somehow Mary's tears disturbed Jesus, and he also wept, but then he raised Lazarus from the dead (see John 10).

Not long after that, and not long before the Crucifixion, there was a dinner in Bethany in honor of Jesus. Martha served, Lazarus was present, and Mary came in with a container of expensive perfume, which she poured on Jesus' feet. She wiped his feet with her hair. Judas Iscariot complained that the perfume should have been sold, the proceeds used to help the poor, but Jesus praised Mary's act as an anointing for his burial (see John 12:1–11).

Now here's where it gets tricky. The gospels have two other stories of women anointing Jesus' feet with perfume. Mark and Matthew have it happening in Bethany at the home of Simon the Leper (see Matthew 26:6–13; Mark 14:1–11), while Luke puts it in the home of Simon the Pharisee, identifying the woman as a "sinner," which is probably a nice way to say "prostitute" (see Luke 7:36–48).

Were these three incidents separate anointings, or two, or the same one? If we merge the three, the anointing occurred in the home of Simon the Pharisee, who used to have leprosy and who was probably a neighbor of Martha's because she served the meal. But it would also identify Mary of Bethany as a former prostitute (or adulteress), possibly a "prodigal sister" who had returned to live with her siblings after Jesus changed her life.

The Book of Jonah

JONAH MAY BE ONE of the best-known characters in the Bible, but his story is more than the tale of being swallowed by a giant fish. Jonah prophesied during the eighth century B.C., and he is mentioned in connection with Israelite territorial expansions (2 Kings 14:25). The prophecy bearing his name differs somewhat from other prophetic books. It consists almost entirely of stories about his life, as well as a prayer (Jonah 2) and a royal decree (3:7–9). It also contains a prophecy, not directed toward God's people, Israel, but rather against a foreign power, Assyria (who controlled Israel until the late seventh century B.C.), and its capital, Nineveh (3:4).

Jonah was a reluctant prophet, refusing God's call to travel east and speak against Nineveh, instead sailing west toward Tarshish. God sent a violent storm, however, and the pagan sailors with Jonah recognized his foolish actions even if he did not. Thrown overboard by them to save the ship, Jonah's life was spared when he was swal-

Jonah and the Whale *by Pieter Lastman*

lowed by a large fish, in whose belly he lived for three days (1:17). Praying for deliverance (2:1–9), he was vomited out and finally went to Nineveh to deliver the message of pending destruction. Nineveh's people repented, and God had mercy on them (3). But Jonah was angry at God's decision and sulked, so God rebuked him (4).

Why did Jonah refuse to go to Nineveh, and why was he angry? Knowing that God would forgive Nineveh if the Assyrians repented, Jonah did not want to preach of its judgment and destruction only to have his prophecy not come to pass (4:2). Also, Jonah did not want Nineveh, and the Assyrian nation as a whole, to be spared. They were the hated occupiers of Israel and her neighbors, demanding heavy tribute payments, cruelly exercising their power against those who opposed them. Preaching for their repentance and salvation was treason, as was offering aid and comfort to the enemy, and Jonah wanted no part of it.

Jonah could be a historical narrative, though there is no known record of Nineveh converting to worship Israel's God. Some suggest it is a parable, a short story using known figures but teaching a spiritual truth. Whichever interpretation one takes, the point of the story remains the same: Israel's God is the God of everyone, even the enemies of his people.

Urim and Thummim

WHEN IT CAME TIME for Joshua to succeed Moses as the leader of the Hebrews, the high priest performed a curious ceremony before the people. Eleazar, a son of Aaron, was now the high priest, and he consulted the Urim stone to confirm that Joshua was God's choice (see Numbers 27:21).

What was this strange Urim stone, and how could it decide anything?

Actually there were two stones, Urim and Thummim, which were carried in the breastplate of the high priest. Only a few passages in Scripture mention them, but the context of each makes it clear that they were used to discover what God desired in certain situations.

King Saul used the stones on one occasion when he felt somebody's sin was preventing the army's success, but he wasn't sure who the culprit was. "If this guilt is in me or in my son Jonathan, O Lord God of Israel, give Urim," he said, "but if the guilt is in your people Israel, give Thummim" (see 1 Samuel 14:41 in the Septuagint). This gives us a slight clue as to how the stones were used. In an either-or situation, it was like flipping a coin. Perhaps the high priest merely reached into his breastplate pouch and blindly pulled out one stone or the other. In this case, Urim came out, indicating that the problem was with either Saul or Jonathan. So the king tried it again to narrow down the guilt. It was Jonathan.

The Bible does not refer to Urim and Thummim again until 500 years later in the time of Ezra and Nehemiah, when people were applying to be priests in a rebuilt Jerusalem. For those who could not prove they belonged to a priestly family (a job requirement), only the sacred stones could confirm their heritage.

It might seem odd that God's will would be determined by something akin to rolling dice or flipping a coin, but the practice was rooted in the idea that God can direct the outcome of these situations. We see other biblical cases where issues are decided by the casting of lots. For example, Jesus' disciples did this in order to choose a replacement for Judas Iscariot. When God is involved in all of life, the disciples believed there is no such thing as pure chance.

And yet it might be significant that Urim and Thummim disappeared between Saul and Ezra. That was a period when God spoke through prophets, such as Nathan, Elijah, Isaiah, and Jeremiah. His messages were more complex than a simple roll of a stone.

The Tax Collector of Short Stature

WHEN JESUS WENT THROUGH Jericho, a wealthy chief tax collector by the name of Zacchaeus wanted to get a view of him (see Luke 19:1–10). Because Zacchaeus was short and because the crowds were large, he climbed a sycamore tree in order to get a glimpse. When Jesus saw him, he said, "Zacchaeus, hurry and come down; for I must stay at your house today" (verse 5). No doubt, the crowd who heard Jesus grumbled and was upset.

Presumably Jesus was going not only to eat with a sinner but also to stay with him. Jesus had taken the initiative in doing so; Zacchaeus had not even asked him. And by chance that we as readers might miss the inappropriateness of this act, Zacchaeus is described not only as a rich tax collector but as a "chief" tax collector. What did a "chief tax collector" do? We do not know. The expression is found only here in the New Testament. What we do know is that Zacchaeus is not presented in a positive light at all.

This encounter, however, clearly touched Zacchaeus profoundly. Perhaps he experienced grace that he had not expected, for he responded with such gratitude that he promised, "Look, half of my possessions, Lord, I will give to the poor; and if I have defrauded anyone of anything, I will pay back four times as much" (verse 8).

Jesus' words to Zacchaeus confirmed the tax collector's change of heart: "Today salvation has come to this house, because he too is a son of Abraham" (verse 9). When Zacchaeus heard the Lord's words, he undoubtedly stood tall.

POSTSCRIPT

■ The name *Zacchaeus* literally means "pure" or "untainted."

■ Because of a children's song, many people know that Zacchaeus was a "wee little man" who "climbed up in a sycamore tree." A sycamore tree often serves as a shade tree with its short trunk and wide branches. Ironically, the city of Jericho, in which Jesus met Zacchaeus, was known and characterized by another kind of tree. Frequently Jericho was called the "City of Palms."

■ Zacchaeus was a "publican." Tax gatherers received this name because they placed money into the treasury *(in publicum)*.

God Calls Samuel

SAMUEL WAS THE FINAL JUDGE in Israel before the first king was installed. Indeed, his role was to help in Israel's transition to kingship.

Samuel was a "miracle baby" of sorts, for his mother Hannah had not been able to bear children. She prayed earnestly to God at the sanctuary where Eli the priest served, and she vowed to dedicate her son to God if he answered her prayers. When Samuel was born, Hannah followed through on her vow and took him to the sanctuary, where she brought offerings to God and left Samuel in Eli's care. "As long as he lives," she said, "he is given to the Lord" (1 Samuel 1:28).

Young Samuel prays to the Lord.

One night while Samuel was still a boy and lying down in the temple of the Lord, he heard the Lord calling his name. Thinking it was Eli, he ran to him, but Eli told Samuel that he had not called him. After Samuel went back to his bed, the Lord called Samuel a second time, and again he thought it was Eli—but again Eli said he had not called.

The third time this happened, Eli realized the voice was from God, and he instructed Samuel to respond, "Speak, Lord, for your servant is listening" (1 Samuel 3:9). Samuel obeyed, and God gave him a message of doom for Eli, for Eli's sons had blasphemed God and Eli had not restrained them. When Samuel conveyed the Lord's message to Eli, the priest declared, "It is the Lord; let him do what seems good to him" (verse 18).

This event signaled to Eli that Samuel, and not his sons, would become God's servant to Israel. And for the rest of his days, Eli saw that Samuel grew in stature in the eyes of the Lord and Israel. "As Samuel grew up, the Lord was with him and let none of his words fall to the ground. And all Israel from Dan to Beer-sheba knew that Samuel was a trustworthy prophet of the Lord" (verses 19–20).

Samson

SAMSON WAS THE SON of Manoah from the tribe of Dan. He was the last of a succession of about 12 judges mentioned in the Book of Judges. The Lord raised judges up to deal with specific crises that plagued the Israelites before they had a king.

During this time, Israel's political organization was tribal, decentralized, and minimal. Meanwhile, the Israelites repeatedly succumbed to the temptations of Canaanite worship, which, among other things, was highly sexualized with "sacred prostitutes" associated with their shrines. As punishment, God repeatedly gave the Israelites up into the hands of their pagan enemies.

The Philistines posed the greatest threat to Israel at this point, and God used Samson to break their power over his people. An angel announced to Samson's parents even before his birth that their son would begin to deliver his people from this threat. The angel said their son should be a "Nazirite," someone separated for or consecrated to God. A "Nazirite vow" involved abstaining from drinking any alcoholic beverages, touching the dead, or cutting one's hair. It was through his hair that the Lord endowed Samson with extraordinary strength. In addition, Samson was not to eat any unclean food.

Despite his God-given strength, Samson was no great paragon of virtue. He ended up violating all of the conditions of the Nazirite vow. Yet, despite his personal failings, God used him to abate the Philistine threat against Israel.

When Samson was about 20, he encountered a Philistine girl, whom he married. At the wedding feast, he offered a riddle to his guests, who persuaded his bride to reveal the answer. Although Samson fulfilled his promise of rewarding those who could solve the puzzle, he killed 30 Philistine guests. His father-in-law then gave his wife to his companion. This story reveals much about Samson's character—both his violent nature and his weakness for calculating women. Both traits would continually mark his life until they led to his eventual fatal downfall at the hands of Delilah, his lover, and at his own hands.

POSTSCRIPT

■ The name *Samson* means "little sun."

Peter's Vision

IF YOU HAD TO PICK three or four of the most important events in the Acts of the Apostles, Peter's vision would probably be one of them. It brought about what modern writers call a "paradigm shift." It forever changed the identity of the Christian Church.

There was something inevitable about it. Old Testament prophets hinted at a time when the whole world would get in on God's promises. Jesus came and was hailed as "a light for revelation to the Gentiles" (Luke 2:32). And since Pentecost the Church had moved steadily outward from Jerusalem through Judaea and Samaria, challenging social and cultural boundaries. Even an Ethiopian proselyte was baptized.

But when Peter climbed to the roof for his noontime prayers on this day, the Church was still Jewish. Jesus was preached as the fulfillment of promises God had made to Israel. It was unthinkable that Gentiles could be part of this promise unless they became Jews first (presumably the case with the Ethiopian official). But God was about to change the Church's view.

As lunch was being prepared, Peter entered a trance and saw a sheet lowered from heaven bearing all sorts of unclean animals. A voice said, "Kill and eat" (Acts 10:13). As hungry as Peter was, he refused to indulge in such a nonkosher feast. The voice replied, "What God has made clean, you must not call profane" (verse 15). The vision occurred twice more.

The previous day, up the coast in Caesarea, a Roman centurion named Cornelius had seen a separate vision in which he was told to send for Peter. Though a Gentile, Cornelius was known as a God-fearer, one who avidly worshipped the God of Israel. His messengers arrived at Peter's lodgings just as the sheet trance was concluding. Normally Peter would refuse to visit the home of a Gentile for religious reasons, but the Spirit directed him to make this trip.

When he arrived in Caesarea, Peter preached the Jesus story to Cornelius's whole household. "I truly understand that God shows no partiality," he began (Acts 10:34). Before he finished, the Holy Spirit came upon his listeners. They spoke in tongues and were baptized with water in the name of Jesus.

This event sent shock waves through the Church, and some Jewish believers criticized Peter, but he explained his vision and won them over. "Then God has given even to the Gentiles the repentance that leads to life," they agreed (Acts 11:18).

Caiaphas

DURING THE EARTHLY ministry of Jesus, Joseph Caiaphas served as the Jewish high priest from A.D. 18 until a Roman proconsul deposed him by A.D. 36. As head of the Sanhedrin, he played a crucial role in the arrest and execution of Jesus.

Judaea was a hotbed of anti-Roman sentiment in these years. There had been revolts from time to time, and the Romans crushed any uprisings without mercy. Jesus was gaining fame as a healer, and the people were talking about making him king. With the resurrection of Lazarus, Jesus mania reached a new peak, and Caiaphas was quite worried (see John 11). As high priest, he was the most powerful Jew in Judaea. At the helm of the ruling council, he answered only to the procurator, Pontius Pilate. He would have had no special fondness for Pilate or Rome, but as long as things remained calm, the Romans tended to leave things well enough alone. If there was disorder, however, heads would roll—and perhaps his.

In a council meeting shortly before Jesus' Triumphal Entry into Jerusalem, Caiaphas argued, "It is better... to have one man die for the people than to have the whole nation destroyed" (John 11:50). This turned out to be an unwitting prophecy about the atoning nature of Jesus' death. He did, in fact, die "for the people."

The plot to arrest Jesus was hatched in the high priest's residence, and when Jesus was brought in, Caiaphas presided at the trial. After various witnesses delivered trumped-up charges, Caiaphas demanded a response from Jesus, but Jesus remained silent. Finally, Caiaphas put it point-blank to Jesus: "I put you under oath before the living God, tell us if you are the Messiah, the Son of God" (Matthew 26:63).

"You have said so," Jesus replied. "But I tell you, 'From now on you will see the Son of Man seated at the right hand of Power and coming on the clouds of heaven'" (verse 64).

It was a clever reply, quoting from the Book of Daniel about a "Son of Man" who appears in glory, sharing God's authority (Daniel 7:13). On the face of it, he was merely citing Scripture, but the high priest tore his clothes in righteous indignation, calling this blasphemy. The council quickly handed down a guilty verdict and a death sentence.

The Books of Nahum and Habakkuk

NAHUM PROPHESIED in the mid-sixth century B.C. His prophetic oracle (1:1) starts with a praise hymn (1:2–8), includes descriptions of siege and battle (2:1, 3–10; 3:2–3), and concludes with a lament for Nineveh, the capital city of Assyria (3).

God's righteous anger sets the stage for condemning powerful yet doomed Assyria. With an attack on its enemy (1:14; 2:1), Judah will be blessed (1:12–13, 15; 2:2). A very detailed battle (2:3–10; 3:2–3) results in Assyria's defeat and disgrace (2:11–13; 3:4–7). Ironically, Assyria, who felt herself invincible, is vanquished (3:8–19).

Habakkuk probably prophesied during the reign of the Judaean king Jehoiakim (609–598 B.C.), before Babylon's invasion in 586 B.C. (Habakkuk 1:6). His book is described as an oracle (1:1), and it consists of Habakkuk's poetic complaints (1:2–4, 12–17) and God's responses (1:5–11; 2:2–20). It ends with a psalm (3).

Habakkuk's first problem is that people in Judah are disobeying the covenant made with God but are not suffering any consequences. God responds that he will punish them through the Babylonians, who will soon fall upon Judah. Habakkuk is upset at this response, since the Babylonians are notorious for their cruelty, often committing atrocities upon those they capture. God finally responds that Babylon will also be held responsible. They are God's instrument of judgment, but their excesses will lead to their own defeat as well. Habakkuk then sings a song of faith and reverence to the creator and sustainer of the universe.

POSTSCRIPT

■ Nahum's opening hymn is different from most hymns because it pictures a wrathful God rather than one who blesses. God shows this side of his character against his enemies, but he still blesses his followers.

■ Habakkuk did what few dare to do: argue directly with God. Habakkuk asks the question that many of us wonder: Why do good things happen to bad people?

■ Habakkuk sounds almost like a spoiled child. He demands an answer from God and waits impatiently for the answer to come (see 2:1). God does not punish him, however. Instead, he graciously answers the real question that he brings.

■ Part of Habakkuk's message ("the righteous live by their faith"; see 2:4) is quoted three times in the New Testament (Romans 1:17; Galatians 3:11; Hebrews 10:38).

The Sabbath

THE CREATION ACCOUNT in Genesis sets the sabbath pattern for God's people. God spent six days crafting the universe, and then he rested on day seven. As we read in Genesis: "And on the seventh day God finished the work that he had done, and he rested on the seventh day from all the work that he had done. So God blessed the seventh day and hallowed it" (Genesis 2:2–3).

That story gets revisited in the Ten Commandments, as God's people are called to follow the same pattern: "Remember the sabbath day, and keep it holy. Six days you shall labor and do all your work. But the seventh day is a sabbath to the Lord your God; . . . For in six days the Lord made heaven and earth, the sea, and all that is in them, but rested the seventh day; therefore the Lord blessed the sabbath day and consecrated it" (Exodus 20:8–11).

The sabbath became an important element in the rhythm of life for the Israelites. The seventh day of each week became Israel's resting day. Once they settled in the Promised Land, the rhythm even extended to the soil. Every seventh year, their land was supposed to lie fallow. This demonstrates a rather contemporary approach to labor and agriculture, acknowledging the inherent need for workers and soil to have times of restoration.

The question arose among students of God's law: *What constitutes work?* Plowing and harvesting were obviously forbidden (Exodus 34:21), and merchants couldn't transport merchandise (Jeremiah 17:27), but home-makers weren't even allowed to light a fire on that day (Exodus 35:3). This became a matter of hair-splitting debate among rabbis, as they sought to protect people from violating God's commandment.

Jesus faced this issue head-on. The Pharisees, who took a strict view of the sabbath law, often criticized him for flouting their rules. On one occasion, as Jesus and his disciples walked through a field on the sabbath, they plucked heads of grain to snack on. When the Pharisees questioned their actions, Jesus replied, "The sabbath was made for humankind, and not humankind for the sabbath" (Mark 2:27).

In modern Jewish observance, the sabbath begins on Friday at sundown. It usually involves a sabbath meal with the family and synagogue services on Friday night and/or Saturday morning. Sabbath then ends on Saturday at nightfall.

Parable of the Unmerciful Servant

P ETER CAME TO JESUS and asked him, "Lord…how often should I forgive?" (Matthew 18:21).

Did someone injure Peter, and was Peter looking for some way not to forgive? We do not know. We only know that Jesus did not give him any room not to forgive. "As many as seven times?" Peter first suggested to Jesus, but Jesus then quickly answered Peter's query: "Not seven times, but, I tell you, seventy times seven" (verse 22).

Jesus did not intend for Peter—and all who follow his teachings for that matter—to take what he said literally. Rather, he emphasized that forgiveness needs to be ready and willing to go far beyond what most humans would see as "fair."

Lest the point be lost, he then presented a parable comparing the kingdom of heaven to a king who wanted to settle accounts with his slaves. One slave owed him 10,000 talents—an amount that also should not be understood literally. Simply stated, it was a huge, vast amount, far beyond any person's ability to set the account straight.

The king decided to sell the slave as well as his family, but the slave begged for mercy. The king had compassion on him and forgave the debt. Later the slave saw a fellow slave who owed him a small amount of money. The slave grabbed the other slave's throat and demanded, "Pay what you owe." The fellow slave pleaded for patience, but instead the first slave threw him into prison.

When other slaves let the king know what had happened, the king summoned the slave whose debt he had forgiven. Incredulous that the man did not extend forgiveness to his fellow slave, the king called him wicked, asked for an explanation, and "handed him over to be tortured until he would pay his entire debt" (verse 34).

Jesus' conclusion to the parable puts the burden squarely on those who hear or read his words. Jesus' last words to Peter were: "So my heavenly Father will also do to every one of you, if you do not forgive your brother or sister from your heart" (verse 35). Although Jesus' words may seem particularly harsh, millions of people seek God's mercy in this way when they pray the Lord's Prayer: "And forgive us our debts, as we also have forgiven our debtors" (Matthew 6:12).

For people who find forgiveness difficult, Jesus calls them to recognize the grace and forgiveness that they daily experience from God.

Israel Demands a King

SAMUEL WAS A PROPHET and the last of the judges. He prepared the way for the transition from a loose, decentralized way of life in Israel under the judges to one where a godly king could govern. The Bible says, "Samuel judged Israel all the days of his life. . . . He administered justice there to Israel" (1 Samuel 7:15, 17). Meanwhile, as God's representative, he anointed both Saul and David as Israel's first two kings.

In Samuel's day, the Philistines posed a terrifying threat to Israel. So the Israelites came to Samuel and demanded that he appoint a king "to judge us like all the nations" (1 Samuel 8:5 KJV). In other words, what they wanted was a king to do what the judges had done, which was to "go out before us and fight our battles" (verse 20). The difference was that God had raised up the judges in an *ad hoc* fashion, as the need arose. A warrior-king, on the other hand, would require a standing army with all its trappings. With this request, the Israelites were asking God for a king just like their neighboring nations: one who would lead them in glorious battle. God's model for a king, however, was radically countercultural: A godly king was to be centered in a study of God's Word and leave the fighting to God.

So, with their request for a king "like all the nations," the Israelites were "deposing" God as their warrior, and God gave them what they asked for (and what they deserved). Saul cut a splendid figure, standing head and shoulders over everyone else, and God directed Samuel to anoint him as king, which he did.

Saul had some initial successes against the Ammonites and the Philistines, but he became arrogant and twice disobeyed God in dramatic fashion, once offering a sacrifice that only a priest should have offered and once sparing the Ammonite king's life when he should have killed him. As a result, he forfeited the kingship, and God turned to David as the next king—one who would come to represent the true, godly model that God had intended.

POSTSCRIPT

■ At times in the Bible, the term "king" is loosely used to refer to local rulers, such as the kings listed in Genesis 14.

Delilah

DELILAH, WHOSE NAME has become synonymous with "betrayal," is one of the most famous characters in the Bible, and yet she appears in only one chapter in the Book of Judges, where she is Samson's lover and betrayer. Presumably she was a Philistine, since she was from the valley of Sorek, a Philistine territory. Nothing else is known of her background.

The Bible says Samson loved her, and this was the point of entry for the Philistine lords who wanted to kill him. They offered Delilah a thousand pieces of silver to discover the source of his strength. Three times she asked him, and three times he deceived her. In succession, he said that he would lose his strength if they

- tied him up with seven fresh bowstrings that had not dried out;

- bound him with new ropes that had not been used;

- and weaved his hair into seven locks in a loom, fastened with a pin.

Delilah tried out each of these options on Samson, and in each case, when the Philistines tried to surprise him, he burst his bonds and avoided capture. It is interesting that the Philistines would continue to pursue Samson's capture through Delilah, but they did—and finally, she succeeded in finding the information they wanted.

The Bible says she "nagged [Samson] with her words day after day, and pestered him" until "he was tired to death" (Judges 16:16). Eventually, he told her the true secret: If his head were shaved, he would lose his strength. After Delilah informed the Philistines of his secret, they cut his hair while he was asleep and then were able to capture him.

POSTSCRIPT

- As a symbol of treachery and/or seduction, Delilah is one of the Bible's most well known characters. From as far back as Roman times, she has figured in prominent works of literature, art, and music.

Barnabas Sent to Antioch

AS THE CHRISTIAN movement grew, pioneers appeared. That's what we see occurring in the middle chapters of the Acts of the Apostles.

Jerusalem was the mother church at this point, born at Pentecost and enduring the brunt of the high priest's persecution. A number of the apostles were probably still based there, and James, the brother of Jesus, emerged as the leader of the Jerusalem church with a style steeped in Judaism.

In the wake of Peter's groundbreaking ministry to Cornelius and the Gentiles at Caesarea, there were reports of mission work among Greeks in Antioch. It was one thing for the great Simon Peter to challenge tradition, but the apostles didn't know who these preachers in Antioch were. They dispatched Barnabas to check it out.

Located on the Mediterranean coast, north of Caesarea, Antioch had become one of the major cities of the Roman Empire. Roads and seaways put it in touch with the whole world. It had a large Jewish population, but many more Gentiles. Apparently, as Christians fanned out after Stephen's martyrdom, they brought the good news of Jesus to Jewish communities along the Phoenician coast and the island of Cyprus. But when they got to Antioch, they encountered a large group of God-fearing Gentiles eager to hear their message.

Loved and respected by the apostles, Barnabas was known as an encourager. He had made a large donation early in the Church's life, and he brought the former persecutor Saul (Paul) into the Church as an ally. He carried his positive spirit to Antioch and saw that the activity there was God's doing. With Barnabas's official sanction on behalf of the apostles in Jerusalem, the ministry in Antioch mushroomed.

Antioch's location also made it a perfect launching pad for a more extensive mission to the Gentiles. Barnabas realized that they had the ideal missionary to the Gentiles sitting on the bench back home in Tarsus. He found his old friend Paul and brought him into the leadership of the Antioch church.

POSTSCRIPT

■ In New Testament times, Antioch had an estimated population of 500,000. About 25,000 of these were Jewish.

Annas

ANNAS, WHO CAME FROM a wealthy, influential family, was the high priest of the Jews during Jesus' adolescence. He continued to be honored as the former high priest even after his son-in-law, Caiaphas, officially gained the position. Annas played a central role in the trial of Jesus and later in the trial of Peter and John.

The high priest was a position of great power among the Jews, since he was also head of the Jewish council. With the Romans occupying Judaea, only the procurator held more authority in the region. Annas became high priest in A.D. 6 when Quirinius, proconsul of Syria, appointed him to the position. About nine years later, however, he must have done something to offend the presiding Roman authority, because he was officially stripped of that title. Several others briefly held the post before Joseph Caiaphas secured it in A.D. 18. He held it for nearly two decades.

Caiaphas was a son-in-law to Annas, and it appears Annas never completely gave up his power. It's possible that the Jewish leaders were fed up with the Roman manipulation of their religious matters and that they decided to honor Annas as their high priest no matter who officially held the position. And with a relative such as Caiaphas in place, Annas would still be able to pull the strings. Besides Caiaphas, Annas placed five sons and a grandson in the role of high priest.

This may explain a certain ambiguity in the gospel accounts. Luke's gospel starts the story of John the Baptist's ministry "during the priesthood of Annas and Caiaphas" (Luke 3:2). According to John's gospel, when Jesus was arrested, he was brought first before Annas and then to a council meeting chaired by Caiaphas (see John 18:13, 24). When Peter and John stood trial for preaching about Jesus in the temple, Annas is called the high priest, though Caiaphas was in attendance (see Acts 4:6).

POSTSCRIPT

■ The family of Annas was known for its wealth and greed. The Jewish Talmud contains the curse, "Woe to the family of Annas!"

■ Annas (and Caiaphas) most likely belonged to the Sadducees, a group that opposed the Pharisees on many key points. Sadducees doubted the existence of angels, spirits, and the resurrection of the dead. They tended to adopt Greek customs. The party was popular among affluent aristocrats of the priestly class—such as the family of Annas.

The Books of Zephaniah and Haggai

ZEPHANIAH WAS A CONTEMPORARY of Nahum, Habakkuk, and Jeremiah. He preached to the southern nation of Judah in the late sixth century B.C. His name ("God has protected") could reflect his parents' gratitude for surviving the bloody reign of the evil king Manasseh (see 2 Kings 21:16; 24:3–4). His book opens with a judgment oracle (1:2–6) and concludes with a lengthy description of the coming Day of the Lord (1:7—3:20).

Zephaniah pronounced judgment against humanity and Judah, in particular. For Judah, the problem was that they were following pagan religious practices and neglecting God (1:4–6). This judgment also can be seen as God's final judgment against all humankind. It is a concept that did not originate from Zephaniah, but it is one he explored in great depth. This judgment would be two-sided. For God's followers it would be a time of blessing and hope (3:9–20), but for those opposing him, whether Judah's pagan neighbors or Judah itself, it would be a time of judgment (1:8–18; 2:4—3:8). The fact that Judah had a covenant with God would not help unless they followed it; a good family tree going back to Abraham was insufficient. They needed to "seek the Lord" and obey him (2:1–3).

Haggai, who was among the Jews who returned to Jerusalem after Judah's exile in Babylon, prophesied during the reign of the Persian king Darius. His book is made up of four oracles concerning the rebuilding of the Jerusalem temple, which had been destroyed in 586 B.C. (see Ezra 5:1–2; 6:14).

Both leaders and the people neglected the rebuilding of the temple, blaming it on economic difficulties. Haggai rebuked them, saying these problems resulted from their not having finished the temple (Haggai 1:1–11). Another message by Haggai encouraged the builders even though the new temple was disappointing when compared to the original temple (2:1–9). He called the people to repentance (2:10–19) and then encouraged their leader, Zerubbabel (2:20–23). Israel needed to get its priorities straight—that is, correctly worshipping the Lord before looking after itself.

POSTSCRIPT

■ Zephaniah presents the longest personal genealogy of any prophet, a total of five generations. In case anyone thought he might not be an Israelite (since his father's name, *Cushi*, can mean "Ethiopian"), he traces his line back to Hezekiah, Judah's 14th king.

The Tabernacle

W HEN THE ISRAELITES first received God's law, they were a migrant people en route from Egypt to Canaan. That journey would last 40 years, and it would take even longer to claim and possess their own land as a single nation. Yet the Lord wanted to establish a holy place where the people could worship him. How do you build a temple for a nation on the move?

With tents.

The Book of Exodus includes elaborate instructions regarding the building of a portable sanctuary, made mostly of poles and fabric, that could be set up *anywhere* as the Israelites traveled through the desert. Despite its mobility, there was nothing cheap about this structure. The fabric was fine linen, used along with coverings of animal skin and goat hair. The poles were acacia wood overlaid with gold or bronze. Nearly a ton of gold was used in the tabernacle and its furnishings, along with several tons of bronze and silver.

The tabernacle was set up in the middle of the Israelite camp, with fabric walls marking out a courtyard of 150 by 75 feet. Sitting in that open courtyard were a bronze washbasin and a large bronze altar, where the priests would offer sacrifices brought by the people. Also within that courtyard was a covered structure that was 45 by 15 feet. This was the Holy Place, where only the priests were permitted. Here the golden lampstand burned continually beside an incense altar and a bread stand. Within the Holy Place, set off by elaborately embroidered curtains, was the Holy of Holies, where the ark of the covenant was kept. Only the high priest could enter the Holy of Holies.

A craftsman named Bezalel was in charge of the construction of the tabernacle and its furnishings. We're told that the Spirit of God "filled" him for this task (Exodus 35:31), a phrase usually reserved for prophets.

When the Israelites entered Canaan, the tabernacle took up a somewhat permanent home in Shiloh, about 20 miles north of Jerusalem, centrally located within the country. (It was moved once, when Shiloh was threatened in battle.) When Solomon built the temple in Jerusalem, the temple took the place of the tabernacle.

POSTSCRIPT

It was exactly one year after the Israelites left Egypt that the tabernacle was first put up.

The Woman at the Well

WHEN JESUS LEFT JUDAEA to return to Galilee, he had to travel through Samaria. At one point, Jesus, tired from his travels, sat by a well alone while his disciples went to the city to purchase food. John's gospel adds that it was around noon when an extraordinary event occurred. A Samaritan woman went to get water at the well, and Jesus spoke to her, saying, "Give me a drink" (John 4:7).

Christ and the Samaritan Woman at the Well *by Christian Schleisner*

The woman was naturally caught off guard. Jews considered Samaritans unclean because they were ethnically mixed. Thus Jews refused to share bowls, jugs, or vessels with them. Moreover, rabbis (and many considered Jesus a rabbi) ordinarily would have had stronger boundaries with women. They would not have spoken to a woman, particularly a female stranger, in such a familiar manner.

Although the gospel says Jesus was tired, his words were no ethical lapse or religious error. In fact, his words, which were addressed to a Samaritan woman, intentionally broke down boundaries of both ethnicity and gender.

When Jesus asked the woman for a drink, the conversation immediately became spiritual. Jesus said to her, "If you knew the gift of God, and who it is that is saying to you, 'Give me a drink,' you would have asked him, and he would have given you living water" (verse 10). Soon she realized that Jesus was offering her something far greater than whatever she might draw out of the well.

Jesus' other words to her eventually led her to acknowledge that Jesus was a prophet (see verse 19). She was so struck by him that she made two faith statements, apparently to get his perspective. In her first faith statement, she noted that the Samaritans worshipped on Mount Gerizim, but the Jews worshipped in Jerusalem. Her statement was an implied question, and Jesus responded by saying that the hour was coming when those differences would be inconsequential.

In her second faith statement, the Samaritan woman said, "I know that Messiah is coming... When he comes, he will proclaim all things to us" (verse 25). Jesus responded: "I am he, the one who is speaking to you" (verse 26). Jesus' declaration revealed not only his divine identity but also his life-changing ministry.

David Slays Goliath

THE PHILISTINES WERE the major threat to Israel during Saul's reign as king. At one point, the armies of these two nations gathered for battle at Socoh in Judah. For 40 days, morning and evening, the Philistines sent out their champion, the giant Goliath, to challenge Israel to send someone out to fight one-on-one. For 40 days, the Israelite soldiers cowered and did nothing.

Meanwhile, back in Bethlehem, David tended his family's sheep. He was the youngest of eight brothers, and his father would send him back and forth from their home to the battlefield with provisions for his three oldest brothers, who were part of Saul's army. On one of his visits, David heard the taunts coming from Goliath, and he asked, "Who is this uncircumcised Philistine that he should defy the armies of the living God?" (1 Samuel 17:26).

After David quarreled with his eldest brother, Eliab, over his talking with the soldiers, King Saul sent for him. It was then that he volunteered to go up against Goliath. Saul tried to dissuade him, but he would not listen. So Saul outfitted him with his own royal armor—but David found it too cumbersome. He took it off and armed himself only with a sling and five smooth stones from the brook nearby.

When David approached Goliath, who was heavily armed with a coat of mail, a bronze helmet, bronze leggings, a javelin, a heavy spear, and a shield-bearer who went before him, the giant mocked him: "Am I a dog, that you come to me with sticks?" (verse 43). He then cursed David, saying, "Come to me, and I will give your flesh to the birds of the air and to the wild animals of the field" (verse 44).

The young lad, however, showed no fear. Instead, David answered Goliath's taunts with confident boldness, declaring, "This very day the Lord will deliver you into my hands, and I will strike you down and cut off your head" (verse 46). The giant must have laughed at his words or become incensed. In either case, David needed only one shot with his sling to bring down the Philistine champion. He then took Goliath's own sword and cut off his head. At this, the Philistines fled before the pursuing Israelites.

The legacy of this encounter was that David was seen as Israel's deliverer. Yet the Bible carefully notes that it was God who gave David the victory. Indeed, for all his military prowess during his lifetime, after his death the Bible remembers David not for his victories in battle but for being a man after God's own heart.

Naomi

T HE STORY OF NAOMI and Ruth is one of the most beautiful stories of love and loyalty in all of literature. The story forms a shining contrast to the mostly sordid history of Israel in the period of the judges, during whose time it takes place.

Naomi and her husband were Israelites from Bethlehem, in Judah, who were forced by a famine to travel to the land of Moab in search of food. While there, their two sons married Moabite women, Ruth and Orpah. Sadly, Naomi's husband died, and then her two sons also perished. Thus the three women were left alone without any man to support them.

Naomi decided to return to Israel, where relatives might care for her. Since her daughters-in-law were not Hebrew, she saw no reason for them to go to Bethlehem with her, so she told them to go back to their families. Both women loved Naomi and were distressed at the thought of separating from their mother-in-law. Naomi must have been a loving mother to them, for they both wept at this news—but only Orpah obeyed. Meanwhile, Ruth refused to part with Naomi.

Naomi allowed Ruth to return with her, but she was still full of grief, even bitterness, when they arrived in Bethlehem. She told the townspeople no longer to call her *Naomi,* which means "pleasant,"

Ruth and Naomi *by Lucien Levy-Dhurmer*

but to call her *Mara,* which means "bitterness." Nevertheless, Naomi put aside her bitterness and became a supportive mother-in-law to Ruth.

In time, Ruth married Boaz, a relative of Naomi's, and gave birth to a son, Obed. The townspeople rejoiced with Naomi, saying, "Blessed be the Lord, who has not left you this day without next-of-kin; . . . [Obed] shall be to you a restorer of life and a nourisher of your old age; for your daughter-in-law who loves you . . . has borne him" (Ruth 4:14–15). Then Naomi embraced the child and became his nurse. The women rejoiced, saying, "A son has been born to Naomi" (verse 17). Obed became the grandfather of the great King David.

Naomi's life, which had been "bitter," was now "pleasant" once again.

James Martyred

T HE REPORT TAKES about a dozen words: King Herod "had James, the brother of John killed with the sword" (Acts 12:2). Yet we can read between the lines to understand the impact of this event.

Herod Agrippa I, part of the Herod dynasty that had ruled parts of Palestine for eight decades, executed James. This Herod was the grandson of Herod the Great, nephew of Herod Antipas (who had John the Baptist beheaded and interviewed Jesus), and father of Herod Agrippa II (who would later interview Paul toward the end of Acts). The Herod family was a high-living Roman-style dynasty stuck in a conservative backwater. They hobnobbed with Roman nobles, or tried to, but they had to rule over an extremely religious people. Some ruled effectively; others didn't. From a political standpoint, Herod Agrippa I was doing fairly well.

Meanwhile, the Roman overlords used the Herods like pieces in a chess game. When one Herod failed miserably in Judaea, they installed a number of Roman prefects to govern that land, which explains why Pontius Pilate conducted Jesus' trial. But a few years later, the Romans were impressed enough with Herod Agrippa I that they gave him Judaea to rule.

But ruling Judaea meant dealing with the Jewish leadership—that is, the high priest and the Jewish high council. Herod wanted to keep them happy, so he supported their efforts to eliminate the Christian movement. Luke tells us that he "laid violent hands upon some who belonged to the church" (Acts 12:1), suggesting that other believers were killed or at least beaten. But the most notable victim was James.

James, son of Zebedee, was one of the first disciples Jesus had called, and he remained part of Jesus' inner circle, along with his brother John and Peter. But James had never done much to distinguish himself, either before or after the Crucifixion. John became a leader of the Church, along with Peter, but we stopped hearing about James—until now. (Don't confuse him with another James—the brother of Jesus—who emerged as a Church leader.)

Yet James and John were known at one time as "Sons of Thunder," which makes us think they had fiery tempers. Is it possible that James spoke out too passionately about Herod's pride or immorality? Whatever the reason, he was arrested and "killed with the sword," which generally means beheading. Because this execution pleased the Jewish rulers, Herod went ahead and arrested Peter as well.

Pontius Pilate

PILATE WAS THE ROMAN procurator of Judaea during Jesus' earthly ministry. Before he ordered the crucifixion of Jesus, Pilate had a remarkable exchange with this prisoner.

In A.D. 26, Emperor Tiberius had appointed Pilate to be the fifth prefect (sometimes known as procurator or even governor) of Judaea. (The Romans had taken leadership of the province away from King Herod Archelaus back in A.D. 6.) Pilate was relieved of his duties ten years later in A.D. 36. His tenure was tumultuous. He incited the Jewish faithful with insensitive actions, and he often responded to unrest with inappropriate force. Still, it was his job to keep the peace, and it was with such an appeal that Caiaphas and the Jewish leaders brought Jesus before him.

The Jewish council had tried Jesus for blasphemy and found him guilty. This was a capital offense within the Jewish religion, but they had no authority to exact capital punishment. Only the Romans could do that, but what did Pilate care about blasphemy? Thus the charge brought to Pilate was treason. It was claimed that Jesus had set himself up as king of the Jews, which would be insurrection against Caesar.

Jesus had been generally silent during his questionings thus far, but John records some pithy responses to Pilate. Jesus says at one point that his kingdom is "not from this world" (John 18:36); pouncing on that, Pilate asks, "So you are a king?" (verse 37). Jesus answers that he was born to "testify to the truth" (verse 37). The philosopher-prefect sighs, "What is truth?" (verse 38).

Pilate was convinced that Jesus had committed no crime. In addition, his wife warned him of a dream she had concerning Jesus' innocence. Nevertheless, the Jewish leaders pressed him hard for Jesus' execution. Then Pilate remembered a custom in which a popular prisoner was released during Passover as a Roman sign of goodwill to the Jews. He set up a choice between Jesus and an insurrectionist named Barabbas. Spurred on by their leaders, the crowd called for Barabbas's release. Literally washing his hands of the whole mess, Pilate ordered Jesus to be crucified.

Scripture does not tell us what happened to Pilate after Jesus' crucifixion, but other historians do mention him in their accounts. According to the Jewish historian Josephus, Pilate was so embroiled in political crises that he was called to Rome to defend himself before Caesar. And according to another eminent historian, Eusebius, he committed suicide.

The Books of Zechariah and Malachi

ZECHARIAH PROPHESIED at the same time as Haggai (October 520 to December 518 B.C.) His book is divided into two parts. The first part (1—8) begins with a call to repentance (1:2–6), followed by eight visions intermixed with oracles (1:7–6:15), and closing with four more oracles concerning justice and promise (7:1–8:23). A number of the visions have apocalyptic elements, just as those described in Daniel.

The Prophet Zechariah *by Michelangelo*

The second section is divided into two subsections, each beginning with "An Oracle" (9:1; 12:1).

Zechariah supported the temple rebuilding project (see Ezra 5:1–2; 6:14; Zechariah 1:16; 6:12–15). His book also has a special interest in seeking God's kingdom through correct worship while showing concern for the poor. It speaks of both a human and a divine king, even in a period when Israel had no king.

Malachi, whose name aptly means "my messenger," prophesied after the temple had been rebuilt in 515 B.C. His prophecy, called an "oracle," consists of six disputes or arguments in which God makes a statement only to have the people rebut it, indicating that they don't believe God. God then gives evidence for the claims he has made, attempting to teach rather than discipline, as would be his right. This questioning of God by the people is not serious questioning. Instead, the people sound almost like a petulant teenager who agrees with nothing a parent says.

A key returning concept throughout the book is that of the covenant, which the people are accused of breaking. As an example, Malachi points to the covenant of marriage, which the people have been treating too lightly (2:10–16).

The prophecy closes with two small additions. The first urges these unruly people to keep Moses' law (4:4), while the second speaks of Elijah returning to usher in the Day of the Lord (4:5–5). Malachi calls for reconciliation between God and his people. Much later, the New Testament relates Elijah to John the Baptist, who points to Jesus, the bringer of true reconciliation between God and humanity (see Matthew 11:12–14; 17:9–13; Mark 6:14–15; Luke 1:17).

Cities of Refuge

T HE LAW OF MOSES assumed that the nearest relative of a murder victim would seek vengeance against the murderer. It was viewed as an obligation (see Numbers 35:19). Since there was no police force, the law of reciprocity applied. An eye for an eye, a tooth for a tooth, and if you kill my brother, I will kill you.

But what if someone was accidentally killed? It would be difficult for a relative of the victim to make that distinction. If you were guilty of manslaughter but not murder, would you have any hope of a fair trial?

Six Israelite cities were designated Cities of Refuge for just that purpose. These cities were situated at intervals throughout the land, west and east of the Jordan River. Hebron and Shechem are the best known of these cities. If a person caused an accidental death, he or she could flee to one of these cities and be temporarily safe from the avenging relative, and then a trial would be held. The elders of the city would determine whether the crime was murder or manslaughter. Was the killing done with hatred? Were weapons used? Was there previous feuding? These and other questions would be considered.

If it was murder after all, the killer would be returned to his hometown for execution. But if it was deemed an accident, the person could stay safely in the city of refuge. Safety was not guaranteed outside the city, however. If the accidental killer left the city, the avenging relative still had the right to kill that person. But in the city, he or she was officially the responsibility of the high priest; that is, the obligation to avenge the wrongful death (or not to) rested with the spiritual leader of Israel and not with the victim's relative. When the high priest died, that obligation vanished, and the accidental killer could return home, safe from further vengeance.

This system created considerable hardship for one who committed manslaughter. Moving to a new city and separation from loved ones was the price for taking life, accidentally or not. Still, the remarkable feature of this refuge program is its mercy—unusual during ancient times.

POSTSCRIPT

■ Scripture gives an example of an accidental death: Two people are chopping trees down, but "when one of them swings the ax...the head slips from the handle and strikes the other person who then dies" (Deuteronomy 19:5).

■ When the land of Canaan was divided among the tribes of Israel, the tribe of Levi didn't receive a territory because they were the priestly tribe. Instead, they were allotted 48 cities throughout the land. Six of these became Cities of Refuge.

The Healing at Bethesda

IT HAD BEEN A BUSY DAY for Jesus and his band of itinerant disciples. As a faithful Jew, Jesus had traveled to Jerusalem for a Jewish festival. A few hours after he arrived, he healed a sick man on the sabbath, which caused many of the religious rulers to continue their persecution of him, with some even plotting his death.

At this point, John describes Jesus' encounter with an invalid who was lying near the pool at Bethesda in Jerusalem. The blind, lame, and paralyzed used to lie near this pool, waiting for the water to be stirred, because they believed the stirred water from this pool could heal them. When Jesus saw a man who had been ill for 38 years, Jesus approached him and asked, "Do you want to be made well?" (John 5:6). The man responded by saying he had no one to help put him into the pool.

Jesus then told him, "Stand up, take your mat and walk" (verse 8). The man obeyed, taking up his mat, and walked.

What happened next is painful to read. When a group of religious leaders saw the man carrying his mat, they told him that what he was doing was not permissible on the sabbath. He responded by drawing attention away from himself, saying, "The man who made me well said to me, 'Take up your mat and walk'" (verse 11). He then told them that it had been Jesus who had healed him.

When Jesus' enemies located Jesus, they began to verbally persecute him. In what sounds like an explanation, Jesus said to them, "My Father is still working, and I also am working" (verse 17).

Rather than appease their anger, his statement incensed them further. Not only was Jesus breaking the sabbath, but he also called God his own father, "thereby making himself equal to God" (verse 18). Such blasphemy was seen as deserving death.

By the end of the passage, we are left with a healed man who appears to express no gratitude, only blame, and people who are seeking all the more to kill Jesus. It should also be noted that when Jesus asks the man, "Do you want to be made well?" (verse 6), no answer is given. Jesus, like his Father, is always ready to heal. The sick, however, may not always be ready for healing.

POSTSCRIPT

■ The Mishnah and Talmud codified various restrictions of behavior on the sabbath.

Samuel Anoints David

DESPITE AN AUSPICIOUS BEGINNING, King Saul quickly spent his political capital by dramatically disobeying God on two different occasions. God then vowed to give the kingdom to someone else, "a man after his [God's] own heart" (1 Samuel 13:14).

Subsequently, God sent Samuel the prophet to the house of Jesse, who was from Bethlehem in Judah, to choose Saul's successor from among Jesse's eight sons. The first seven were impressive, but God had someone else in mind. When the oldest brother came before Samuel, God said, "Do not look on his appearance or on the height of his stature, because I have rejected him; for the Lord does not see as mortals see; they look on the outward appearance, but the Lord looks on the heart" (1 Samuel 16:7). Samuel asked if there were any more sons, and David, the youngest, who had been away tending the sheep, was brought before him. God said, "Rise and anoint him; for this is the one" (verse 12), and Samuel did so.

Life, however, did not immediately become easy for David. Saul grew jealous of him, and David spent many years on the run for his life. On two occasions, David could have killed Saul: Both times he found Saul asleep or vulnerable, but he refused to take his life out of respect for the office of God's anointed king. David was even forced to flee to the Philistines for a time.

Eventually, Saul was killed in battle, and David became king. Samuel then anointed David publicly twice more: once before the men of his own tribe, Judah, and later before all Israel.

David was the greatest king in Israel's history. He became the standard of righteousness against which all later kings were measured. In fact, the following laudatory judgment on King Hezekiah expresses a common praise of David: "He did what was right in the sight of the Lord just as his ancestor David had done" (2 Kings 18:3).

David's ascent to the kingship fulfilled a promise given centuries earlier to Judah, Jacob's son. Jacob had blessed Judah by saying, "The scepter shall not depart from Judah, nor the ruler's staff from between his feet, until tribute comes to him, and the obedience of all the peoples is his" (Genesis 49:10 RSV). David was the initial fulfillment of this blessing. Eventually, Jesus, as the greatest descendant of David (and Judah), was the ultimate fulfillment.

Ruth

THE UPLIFTING STORY of Ruth is brief but critical to the history of
Israel. Interestingly, the Book of Ruth follows the Book of Judges,
which describes the downward spiral of the wickedness of the Israelites.
The story of Ruth, however, is the story of a pagan girl whose strong faith
lies in stark contrast to the rebelliousness of the Israelites and is a powerful statement of God's compassion on any who truly trust in him.

Because of a severe famine in Israel, Elimelech journeyed to Moab with
his wife, Naomi, and their two sons, Mahlon and Chilion. Here the sons
married Ruth and Orpah, two Moabite women. In time, Naomi's husband
and her two sons died, leaving the women alone. When Naomi decided
to return to Bethlehem (the famine having ended), her daughters-in-law
chose to go with her, but Naomi urged them to remain in Moab and
find husbands there. She was thinking of what was best for them. Orpah
decided to stay, but Ruth refused to leave her mother-in-law, saying,

> *Where you go, I will go;*
> *where you lodge, I will lodge;*
> *your people shall be my people,*
> *and your God my God* (Ruth 1:16).

Back in Bethlehem, Ruth went out to glean in the field of Boaz, a rich
relative of Naomi's husband. She caught his eye, and when he heard of
her loyalty to Naomi, he blessed her, invited her to eat his food, and
instructed his reapers to purposely drop some extra grain, so she might
glean even more. He said, "All that you have done for your mother-in-law
since the death of your husband has been fully told me, and how you
left your father and mother and your native land and came to a people
that you did not know before. May…you have a full reward from the
Lord, the God of Israel, under whose wings you have come for refuge!"
(Ruth 2:11–12).

Later, Naomi sent Ruth to lie at Boaz's feet while he was sleeping and to
follow his instructions when he awoke. When he did, he promised to care
for her as her near kinsman. There was one man more closely related to
Naomi than Boaz, however, so Boaz asked him if he wanted to buy some
land that belonged to Elimelech. When this man learned that he would
also have to marry Ruth in the bargain, he refused, paving the way for
Boaz and Ruth to marry.

Remaining faithful in a life filled with many hardships and uncertainties,
Ruth stands among the remarkable women of faith in the Bible.

Peter Escapes from Prison

KING HEROD HAD LAUNCHED an all-out assault against the Jerusalem church. He had already snagged one of the apostles, James, and beheaded him. Noting how this execution pleased the Jewish rulers, he had also arrested Peter, the apparent spokesman for the fledgling Jesus cult. He was the big prize, Jesus' right-hand man, the one who had been preaching at the temple and healing folks by just walking past them. Now Peter was locked in prison, guarded around the clock by

four squads of soldiers. In an effort to gain their political support, Herod planned to present Peter to the Jewish leaders after the Passover. Was he imagining a scene like the death of Stephen or of Jesus himself—a stoning or a crucifixion?

Remembering how Peter and John were mysteriously sprung from prison a few years earlier, the guards were taking no chances. Peter was chained with a guard on each side of him and more at the door. But the night before the presentation was to happen, an angel appeared in Peter's prison cell, nudging Peter out of slumber, saying, "Get up quickly" (Acts 12:7). His chains then fell off.

Liberation of Saint Peter by Giovanni Battista Tiepolo

Peter thought he was still sleeping, that this was a dream, but the angel coached him through the process of putting on sandals and a cloak. Led by this emancipating angel, Peter went past the guards and out to the city streets. Then the angel vanished, and Peter "came to himself" (verse 11). Realizing this was not a dream, he found the house where Christians were gathering to pray for him, and he knocked at the outer gate.

The following scene is one of Scripture's great moments of comic relief. A maid named Rhoda answered the knock. Seeing Peter, she was so delighted that she ran in to tell everyone that the man they were praying for was there at their gate. Of course, the others thought she was crazy, but she insisted it was true. While they were debating this, Peter was still outside, knocking at the gate. He could get out of prison, but he could not get into a prayer meeting.

Eventually the Christians found Peter and brought him inside. He told them the whole story and then went into hiding.

Barabbas

BARABBAS WAS A NOTORIOUS criminal in Roman custody when Jesus was tried before Pontius Pilate. Because of the insistence of some Jewish leaders and a mob, Pilate failed in his attempt to free Jesus. Instead, he freed Barabbas.

Different gospels call Barabbas a "notorious prisoner," a "bandit," and "a murderer" because of his involvement in an "insurrection." The fact is, there were many such lawbreakers roaming around Jerusalem and the outlying villages of Judaea and Galilee. In general, Jews resented Roman occupation. The Jewish leaders had found ways to coexist with the Roman authorities, but among the common folk there brewed a spirit of rebellion. Some of these insurrectionists were freedom fighters who targeted Romans.

Apparently Barabbas was involved in some sort of uprising in Jerusalem, and someone was killed—either a Roman soldier or an innocent bystander. Thus Barabbas was branded as a bandit, a rebel, a murderer. We can surmise that he was not a popular hero. On the contrary, he had probably alienated his fellow Jews by causing unrest and bringing the retaliation of Rome upon them all. That's why Pilate chose him.

Pilate, the Roman prefect in charge of Judaea, was looking for a way to release Jesus. The Jewish ruling council had delivered Jesus as a revolutionary, a would-be king committing treason against Caesar. They had assembled an angry mob calling for Jesus' crucifixion. But Pilate's interrogation revealed no capital crime. The Barabbas option must have seemed like a perfect solution. From time to time, Pilate would curry favor with the people by releasing a prisoner during the holidays, so he set up a choice between Jesus and this despicable bandit Barabbas.

He must have been shocked when the crowd, stirred up by the corrupt leaders, called for Barabbas to be released. At that point, Pilate gave up, washing his hands of the matter, releasing Barabbas and sending Jesus to the cross. There is no further mention of Barabbas in the Bible or recorded history.

POSTSCRIPT

■ Christians have long seen themselves in Barabbas: a guilty man set free because an innocent man died in his place. Appropriately, his name has a kind of generic meaning that could apply to anyone: "son of the father."

■ Some scholars think Barabbas was a member of the Zealots, a first-century revolutionary group.

The Gospel of Matthew

THE FOUR GOSPELS are all anonymous writings. The titles "According to Matthew," "According to Mark," and so on, were added by scribes on the basis of Church tradition. That tradition may be correct, but it is well to remember that it represents the memory of the Church, not the autograph of the author. It should also be noted that since Matthew was a tax collector—a profession widely despised—it is probable that his name would not have been attached to this gospel had he not actually authored it.

The first gospel in the New Testament is attributed to Matthew, one of the 12 disciples of Jesus. Matthew's gospel gives Jesus' teachings the most prominent place of all the gospels, organizing them in five large blocks: the Sermon on the Mount (5—7), the Missionary Discourse (10), the Parables of the Kingdom (13), the "Community Rule" (18), and the Apocalyptic Discourse (24—25).

The Gospel of Matthew is thought to have been written in the middle of the first century. Matthew preserves many stories of controversy and tension between Jesus and some Jewish leaders. These stories might have been especially important to remember and reflect upon during those decades after the destruction of Jerusalem and the temple, when Jewish communities seemed to become less tolerant of the diversity of peoples, including Jewish Christians, in their midst.

Of all the four gospel writers, Matthew shows the greatest interest in describing how Jesus' life, from his birth to his resurrection, unfolded "as it is written" in the Old Testament prophets (Matthew 26:24). His gospel presents Jesus as the focus and culmination of the Jewish scriptural hope.

Matthew is also interested in presenting Jesus as a reliable teacher concerning the fulfillment of God's law. He reassures readers that as they follow Jesus' teachings they are living in line with God's higher standards of righteousness. By bringing together so many of Jesus' teachings on ethical topics, Matthew seems very interested in shaping the character of the Christian communities that will read his gospel. These communities are challenged to practice forgiveness and accountability, to engage in acts of charity and kindness to those who are in need, and to reflect on God's generous character as one who gives the blessings of sun and rain both to those who are grateful recipients and to those who are not (5:45).

Sackcloth and Ashes

SACKCLOTH WAS A COARSE, cheap material woven from goat or camel hair. It was used to make bags, often to ship or sell grain. You could easily make a garment from such a sack by cutting holes for your arms and head, but this would be the least flattering thing you could wear. It might also irritate your skin.

But if you wanted to humble yourself, to repent of your sin, or to mourn publicly, it was the perfect attire—poor, ugly, and uncomfortable. To further humiliate yourself, you might sprinkle ashes on your head or smear ashes on your face, arms, or clothing. If you had no ashes, dust would do.

The idea was to match your exterior to your interior. When Jacob was given the bloody coat of his son Joseph, he assumed the worst and went into mourning, dressing himself in sackcloth as he grieved for the boy he thought was dead (see Genesis 37:34). Jeremiah pictures the leaders of a conquered Jerusalem sitting amid the ruins in silence: "They have thrown dust on their heads and put on sackcloth" (Lamentations 2:10). When he learned of a plot to exterminate the Jews, Mordecai "put on sackcloth and ashes, and went through the city, wailing with a loud and bitter cry" (Esther 4:1).

Yet sackcloth was associated with more than mere grief. It was a sign of self-humiliation, mourning for one's own sin. As the Jews returned to Jerusalem after the Babylonian Captivity, they rediscovered God's law and were struck by their own failures. Wearing sackcloth, with dirt on their heads, they "stood and confessed their sins and the iniquities of their ancestors" (Nehemiah 9:2). Jesus once quipped that if foreign towns had seen the miracles he was doing in Galilee, "they would have repented long ago in sackcloth and ashes" (Matthew 11:21).

Sometimes it just seemed right to humble oneself with sackcloth while making a big request of God. Asking God for deliverance from the Assyrian army at their doorstep, King Hezekiah and his cabinet dressed in sackcloth (see Isaiah 37:1–3). They were beggars before God; why not dress the part?

POSTSCRIPT

■ After Jonah preached in Nineveh, the people repented so thoroughly that even their animals wore sackcloth (see Jonah 3:8).

■ The Hebrew word for "sack" is *saq*.

The Transfiguration of Jesus

WHEN JESUS LED PETER, James, and John up a high mountain, it was only the beginning of a truly remarkable experience. First, Jesus was transfigured before them with his clothes becoming dazzling white. Then Elijah and Moses appeared, and the two giants from Jewish history conversed with Jesus. Caught in the middle of this mountaintop experience, Peter, we are told, was terrified and did not know what to say. He ended up suggesting, "Rabbi, it is good for us to be here; let us make three dwellings, one for you, one for Moses, and one for Elijah" (Mark 9:5).

It becomes clear that Peter had missed the point of this special event, for a voice from a cloud responded to Peter's suggestion by saying, "This is my Son, the Beloved; listen to him!" (verse 7). And then Moses and Elijah suddenly vanished. As Jesus and his three disciples walked down the mountain, Jesus commanded them to tell no one what they had seen, "until after the Son of Man had risen from the dead" (verse 9).

Peter, James, and John had participated in an amazing mountaintop experience, which they undoubtedly weren't sure how to process or understand. They had an experience on which Jesus had put something like a time lock. What they saw they could not share until later, perhaps because it was still too difficult to comprehend.

Furthermore, Jesus' transfiguration preceded a conversation we never hear. Why Moses and Elijah, and what did they say? Moses fought for justice, he freed God's people from bondage in Egypt, and he delivered God's law to the people. Elijah fought against false gods and saw them as the underlying cause of the problems of Israel. Moses was seen as the lawgiver par excellence. Elijah was seen as the prophet par excellence.

When Moses and Elijah disappeared, it did not necessarily mean that Jesus was a better teacher or that Jesus fulfilled the law and the prophets. The message is far more significant—Jesus is not just a great teacher or prophet; he is, in fact, God's beloved Son.

Although the disciples would not fully understand that truth until after his death (until they saw the meaning of the Transfiguration through the lens of the Resurrection), God did give a command that they could understand: "This is my Son, the Beloved; listen to him!" (verse 7).

The Medium at Endor

ONE OF THE STRANGEST stories in the Bible concerns Saul's apparent encounter with Samuel, the prophet, whose spirit appears to come back from the grave, aided by a medium.

After Samuel's death, Saul rid the land of all mediums and wizards. Meanwhile, because the Philistines were menacing Israel, Saul tried to consult God for help, but God would not answer in any of the usual ways—by dreams, by the Urim (a special stone sometimes consulted to discern God's will), or by direct prophetic word. So, in a great ironic twist, Saul, who had just rid the land of them, asked his servants to find a medium for him to consult. They replied that there was one such woman at Endor.

Consulting mediums and wizards was expressly forbidden in the law. Mediums consulted spirits using a ritual pit in the ground from which the spirits could rise and be heard. They employed mysterious speech in advising people: The prophet Isaiah spoke of spirits who "chirp and mutter," whose voices come "from the ground like the voice of a ghost," and whose speech would "whisper out of the dust" (Isaiah 8:19; 29:4).

Saul disguised himself and went to the medium, asking her to conjure up Samuel. After she complied, Samuel appeared to her, looking like a god of some sort coming up out of the ground. Apparently Saul did not see Samuel but could hear him. Samuel angrily asked Saul why he had disturbed him in this way, and Saul replied that he was in great distress because God would not answer him. Samuel replied with a stern reminder of what he had told Saul in life: that Saul had forfeited the kingdom because of his disobedience, and, moreover, that Saul would die the very next day.

The episode has perplexed Bible interpreters from the beginning. Many explanations are offered as to what actually happened. Chief among them are the following:

- The medium had true supernatural powers and was able to conjure up a spirit or a demon that represented itself as Samuel.
- The medium used paranormal powers to read Saul's mind and picture Samuel in her own mind.
- God actually allowed the spirit of Samuel to appear to the medium.

Whatever the truth, the apparition delivered a message that came true, for Saul died the next day at the hands of the Philistines.

Hannah

HANNAH WAS MOTHER to Israel's last judge, Samuel, who was a transitional figure between the time of the judges and the institution of the monarchy. He was crucial to that transition, and the stories of his miraculous birth and his mother dedicating him to God are heartwarming.

Hannah's husband, Elkanah, had two wives: Hannah and Peninnah. Peninnah bore many sons and daughters, but Hannah was barren. Year after year, Elkanah would give gifts to his wives and children, always including a double portion for Hannah, because he loved her best. Meanwhile, Peninnah would mock Hannah for her barrenness, causing her to weep and refuse to eat.

Her husband was solicitous of her, saying, "Hannah, why do you weep? Why do you not eat? Why is your heart sad? Am I not more to you than ten sons?" (1 Samuel 1:8). But how could Hannah feel truly of value to Elkanah when she could not bear her husband any children? And so she remained deeply sad.

In the cultures of the ancient Near East, the more children a woman had, the higher her status. In the Bible, forebears of Hannah—such as Sarah, wife of Abraham, and Rachel, wife of Jacob—also could not bear children for a time and suffered for it, but God eventually (and miraculously) gave them children. Hannah could only hope that the Lord would be compassionate toward her, as well.

On one of their annual trips to the house of God at Shiloh, Hannah prayed earnestly to the Lord, vowing that, if he gave her a son, she would dedicate him as a Nazarite—one consecrated to God—all the days of his life. Eli the priest saw her lips moving as she prayed fervently and thought she was drunk, so he scolded her. But she protested that she was petitioning God, and so he sent her away with assurances that God would grant her petition.

In due time, Hannah did have a son, and she named him *Samuel,* which sounds like the Hebrew for "heard of God." She said, "I have asked him of the Lord" (verse 20). She then brought him to the sanctuary when he was weaned, and Samuel served the Lord there under the care of Eli the priest. Hannah would bring him a little robe every year when she and her husband went up to the sanctuary at Shiloh to worship, and God later blessed Hannah with three more sons and two daughters.

Paul and Barnabas Are Set Apart

THE CHURCH AT ANTIOCH was on the cutting edge of evangelism. It dared to reach out in ways the Jerusalem church wouldn't. They were already connecting with Gentiles within their city, and now they were thinking about sending missionaries farther out into Gentile territory.

An interesting group of "prophets and teachers" led the church there and are listed in Acts 13. Barnabas is mentioned first, probably because of his connection to the apostles in Jerusalem. The apostles had sent him to scout out what the Spirit was doing in Antioch; perhaps he had pulled together this leadership team.

The next two names on this list of leaders are Simeon Niger and Lucius of Cyrene. *Niger* means "black," and Cyrene is in northern Africa, so it's likely that these were both dark-skinned men from Africa's Mediterranean coast. Some think "Lucius of Cyrene" was Luke, the doctor who accompanied Paul and wrote the third gospel and Acts, but it was a common Roman name, and why would Luke name himself here and not elsewhere in this book?

The fourth member of the leadership team listed is Manaen, who is identified as a member of Herod's court. (One textual reading says he grew up with Herod.) In any case, he must have been from the elite class. We can only guess how he landed here in Antioch, outside of Herodian territory, as a Christian leader.

The last of this group was Saul, the former persecutor, who had been cooling his heels in Tarsus for the previous decade. Barnabas, who had originally connected him with the apostles a decade earlier, had now brought him into the exciting Antioch church as a preacher/teacher. But even that role would soon change.

The leadership team (and perhaps the whole congregation) fasted and prayed, seeking the Spirit's guidance. The language of Acts 13:2 suggests they specifically asked about a missionary enterprise, and the Lord responded favorably. "Set apart for me Barnabas and Saul for the work to which I have called them," the Spirit said. From the time of his conversion, Saul/Paul was designated as one who would bring light to the Gentiles. Since this ministry would be controversial, it made sense to send the well-respected Barnabas along, too.

After more fasting and praying, the leaders laid their hands on the two missionaries in a commissioning ritual. Then Barnabas and Saul headed for Cyprus.

Simon of Cyrene

Simon was a pilgrim who had traveled to the holy city of Jerusalem. While there, he helped Jesus carry his heavy cross to the site of his crucifixion.

In the preceding centuries, Jews had emigrated to many different parts of the world. Most major cities of the Mediterranean region had substantial Jewish populations, including Cyrene in North Africa. In the first century

Simon of Cyrene Helps Jesus *by Martin Feuerstein*

A.D., with the Roman navy patrolling the seas and the Roman army building roads, travel was easier than ever before. Therefore, many Jews would make occasional pilgrimages to Jerusalem for the high holidays, especially Passover.

That seems to be the case with Simon, a traveler from Cyrene, who happened to cross paths with Jesus one fateful day. Jesus was carrying the heavy beam of the cross on which he would be nailed (the vertical post would most likely be in place at the crucifixion site). Jesus had already been brutally flogged, so it's not surprising that his strength had ebbed. When it became apparent to the Roman soldiers that Jesus was not physically capable of taking the crossbeam to Golgotha, they grabbed a passerby to do the work. That passerby was Simon.

There is no indication that Simon had any previous connection to Jesus or his disciples, but the fact that he is named in the gospels suggests that he connected later. What's more, Mark identifies him as the father of Alexander and Rufus. Apparently these two sons were well known to the Christians to whom Mark was writing. In the last chapter of Romans, Paul sends greeting to a man named Rufus and his dear mother. Perhaps these were Simon's son and wife.

Jesus said, "If any want to become my followers, let them deny themselves and take up their cross and follow me" (Mark 8:34). Simon of Cyrene must have smiled when he heard that, for that is literally what he did.

The Gospel of Mark

TRADITION ASCRIBES this gospel to Mark, who was first a member of Paul's missionary team and later an assistant to Peter in Rome. Mark's gospel preserves sayings of and stories about Jesus of Nazareth that circulated throughout the early Church through Christian preaching and teaching before the gospel was written. The gospel may well have been compiled as early as A.D. 60. Although it is the second gospel found in the New Testament, Mark was probably written first. The similarities among Matthew, Mark, and Luke suggest that Matthew and Luke both used the Gospel of Mark as their basic source, each fleshing out the picture of Jesus with additional traditions about Jesus' acts and, especially, his teachings.

Mark did not just collect and record sayings and stories. He selected and arranged them in order to present the significance of Jesus and following Jesus. There were many expectations for what the Messiah would be and what the Messiah would do, but most involved military conquest, establishing political independence for Israel, or establishing a renewed, purified priesthood. Mark crafted his gospel to stress that Jesus as Messiah takes on a very different shape.

To this end, as he performs miracles and signs in Mark, Jesus tries to silence any attempts to draw attention to himself as the Messiah until he begins to teach that the Messiah will suffer disgrace, abuse, and execution and after that will rise from the dead (see 8:31; 9:31; 10:33–34). The example of the Messiah in Mark is an example of giving up one's life for the sake of others in obedience to God, and therefore the shape of discipleship is also the shape of the cross. The gospel remains "good news" insofar as God promises that such faithful obedience will be rewarded with resurrection.

POSTSCRIPT

■ The ending to Mark currently found in English Bibles (Mark 16:9–20) is not found in the earliest surviving manuscripts. Two endings—a shorter ending and the longer one that readers are more familiar with—begin to show up in manuscripts copied in the fifth century. It is likely that Mark's original ending was lost very early and that scribes used other available and revered traditions of Jesus' postresurrection activity to supply what was missing.

The Jordan River

THE ISRAELITES WANDERED 40 years in the desert, and then they saw the Promised Land in front of them. One problem: The Jordan River lay between them and their future home. No matter. One body of water had already parted for them on their journey from Egypt; now another one would. The priests carried the ark of the covenant forward, and as soon as their feet touched the water, the river stopped. The people walked across on dry ground (see Joshua 3:14–16).

In Hebrew, *Jordan* means "flowing downward," and that's exactly what this river does. Its tributaries begin in the north near Mount Hermon. The Jordan then moves southward and downward to Lake Huleh (230 feet above sea level), to the Sea of Galilee (685 feet below sea level), and ultimately to the Dead Sea (1,274 feet below sea level), the lowest body of water on earth. That's where the river ends, and that's why the Dead Sea is dead. With nothing flowing out of it, the Dead Sea's water evaporates, leaving rich mineral deposits that choke off any marine life.

As the eagle flies, it's 65 miles from the Sea of Galilee to the Dead Sea, but the Jordan River snakes along, taking 200 miles of twists and turns to cover that distance. In some places, the river runs wide and shallow, easily fordable. In other spots it's deep. In this arid climate, the Jordan creates a kind of oasis with lush vegetation springing up along its banks, especially in the southern portion, approaching Jericho.

The Jordan served as a natural boundary for Israel, a moat that warded off attacks from the east. Israel's invaders tended to come in from the north.

The Jordan River figures into several biblical stories. Elijah and Elisha duplicated the crossing of the Jordan on dry ground before Elijah hailed a chariot to heaven. Elisha made an ax head float in this river and told a leprous Syrian general seeking healing to bathe in it.

The Jordan may be most famous as the site of Jesus' baptism. Crowds flocked to the river to see John the Baptist call for repentance. When Jesus showed up, John didn't want to baptize him, but Jesus insisted. As Jesus came up from the water, the Spirit descended on him as a dove, and a voice from heaven confirmed that he was God's Son (Matthew 3).

POSTSCRIPT

■ Among some believers, the Jordan River has become a symbol for entry into heaven. It is the border one must "cross over" in order to reach the Promised Land.

Parable of the Good Samaritan

THE JEWS AND THE SAMARITANS had an adversarial relationship. They worshipped at different locations and focused on different books of the Hebrew Bible. The Jews saw the Samaritans as half-breeds, not real Jews. Even referring to Samaritans in a conversation would have been enough to create uncomfortable feelings among Jews. But Jesus shattered this prejudice.

In a discussion with Jesus, a lawyer said that he knew that he was to "love your neighbor as yourself," but he seemed to be more interested in finding legal loopholes that would limit those the law commanded him to love. He seemed to wonder how one could do as little as possible and still be faithful to the law. His question to Jesus seemed almost defiant: "And who is my neighbor?" (Luke 10:29). Jesus responded with a parable that has since become one of the most famous stories in the world.

He told the story of a man who, when traveling from Jerusalem to Jericho, was mugged, stripped, beaten, and left half dead by a number of robbers. When a Jewish priest came down the road, he crossed over to the other side in order to avoid the victim. A Levite then came down the same road and also saw the victim, but he, too, went to the other side of the road. Finally, a Samaritan who

Parable of the Good Samaritan *by Julius Schnorr von Caroisfeld*

was traveling down the road saw the victim and was moved with pity. He treated the man's wounds and bandaged them, put him on his animal, and brought him to an inn where he nursed him further. The next day he gave money to the innkeeper to take care of the man and noted that if the innkeeper spent anything else on the man, he would pay him the next time he returned.

Jesus asked the lawyer, "Which of these three, do you think, was a neighbor to the man who fell into the hands of the robbers?" (verse 36). The lawyer said, "The one who showed him mercy." Jesus said to him, "Go and do likewise" (verse 37).

Jesus himself went on with his earthly mission, reaching out to the lame, the blind, the sinners, the tax collectors, and even the prostitutes.

God Punishes David

DAVID'S SINS OF ADULTERY with Bathsheba and the murder of her husband Uriah represent a critical turning point in David's life. Prior to these acts of wickedness, David had always seemed to be in God's hands: He had defeated the giant Goliath; the Israelites had acclaimed his heroism because of his many military victories; he had escaped from Saul on many occasions; and the Lord had chosen him to be the next king. But after his grievous sins, nothing seemed to go right: His son Amnon raped his daughter Tamar; another son, Absalom, killed Amnon; Absalom tried to wrestle the kingdom from David; and many other troubles came his way.

The trouble began when David sent his troops out to do battle against the Ammonites, but he remained in Jerusalem instead of leading his army. While strolling on the palace roof, he noticed a beautiful woman bathing nearby. Overcome with lust, he learned that her name was Bathsheba and that she was the wife of one of his most devoted soldiers. Despite the warnings of his conscience, he sent for her and slept with her. Then he sent her home. Unfortunately for David, she became pregnant, and she quickly notified him of her condition.

David then attempted a cover-up. He had Bathsheba's husband, Uriah, brought home from the battlefield, thinking that Uriah would sleep with his wife and thus the baby would be thought to be his. But Uriah, an honorable man, refused the comforts of his home while his comrades in arms suffered the ravages of war on the battlefield, so David's plan was foiled. His new plan was to send Uriah to the battlefront with orders to his commander to place Uriah at the point of the fiercest fighting and then to withdraw, leaving him exposed to the enemy. Uriah was thus killed. David then took Bathsheba as his wife, and their son was born.

David's blatant wickedness greatly displeased God, and he sent Nathan the prophet to confront him. Nathan set a trap for David by informing him of a rich man with many flocks who stole a poor man's only lamb to serve to his guests. David erupted with furious indignation at this injustice. Nathan then sprang the trap by abruptly exclaiming, "You are the man!" (2 Samuel 12:7). Conveying God's message to the king, Nathan told David that he would suffer great travails in his life as a result of his sin. To his credit, David did not deny his sin, but confessed: "I have sinned against the Lord" (verse 13). Nevertheless, the son born to Bathsheba died, and David's family story descended into one tragedy after another.

Samuel

SAMUEL WAS ISRAEL's final judge. He brought an end to a tumultuous period when "all the people did what was right in their own eyes" (Judges 21:25). He was also a prophet, and God was with him, letting "none of his words fall to the ground" (1 Samuel 3:19); that is, his words came true, and none were wasted. He served the Lord in the transition from the earlier, decentralized, tribe-based system to the establishment of a centralized system under one king.

The Israelites revered Samuel as a trustworthy prophet of the Lord and honored him as God's divinely appointed judge, but they became increasingly anxious about what would happen once he passed away. When Samuel became old, his sons succeeded him as judges, but they took bribes and perverted justice. So the people came to Samuel and requested a king "like other nations," one who would "go out before us and fight our battles" (1 Samuel 8:20). This was a direct rejection of God's rule over them and his status as their Divine Warrior, because the model of kingship among the "other nations" was that the king led his people in battle and took all the credit for it. Naturally, Samuel became angry at their petition, but God told him to grant the request, identifying Saul from the tribe of Benjamin as their first king.

After Samuel anointed Saul, he gave a passionate speech urging the Israelites and their king to follow God. He promised to pray for them and to instruct them "in the good and the right way" (see 1 Samuel 12:23). Unfortunately, Saul turned away from God, forfeiting his kingship.

Samuel Anointing David *by Jan Victors*

God then directed Samuel to the house of Jesse, in Bethlehem, where he revealed David as his chosen one to succeed Saul. There Samuel anointed him as king. After this, Samuel's main work was done. When he died, "all Israel assembled and mourned for him. They buried him at his home in Ramah" (1 Samuel 25:1).

We Are Not Gods!

PAUL AND BARNABAS began their first missionary journey in Cyprus, the homeland of Barnabas. Then they traveled to the mainland of Asia Minor, visiting some towns along the inland trade route. Because some of these places had Jewish settlements, they would first preach at the local synagogue. Some Jews would hear about Jesus and trust in him; others would disagree, sometimes so strongly that it led to violence against the two apostles.

The town of Lystra didn't have a synagogue, so Paul and Barnabas probably began their work in the town marketplace. There they encountered a man who was crippled from birth. Paul looked at him "intently" and discerned that the man "had faith to be healed," so he shouted, "Stand upright on your feet" (Acts 14:9–10). The man sprang up and walked.

This event has significant parallels with the story of Peter and John healing a lame man at the temple in Jerusalem (see Acts 3). Peter had looked "intently" at that lame man (verse 4), who sprang up and walked, causing a public commotion. Just as Peter and John had started their Jerusalem ministry with that miracle, Paul and Barnabas were starting their mission to the Gentiles when they healed the crippled man in Lystra.

Unlike most other towns along the way, Lystra had few Jews. What kind of reaction would this miracle get from these pagans? "The gods have come down to us in human form!" the people exclaimed (Acts 14:11). They began worshipping Barnabas as Zeus and Paul as Hermes. In his *Metamorphoses,* the great Roman poet Ovid presented a legend of Jupiter and Mercury (the Roman equivalents of Zeus and Hermes) visiting people in Phrygia, a neighboring district. No doubt the Lystrans thought they were getting their own visitation. Of course, the two missionaries would have none of it. "We are mortals just like you," they protested (verse 15), before they shared their good news about the living God.

"Even with these words," Acts goes on to say, "they scarcely restrained the crowds from offering sacrifice to them" (verse 18). Apparently in the days that followed they continued to preach about Jesus, and some Lystrans responded. But then their enemies from previous stops caught up with them, stirring up the Lystrans against them. Paul was brutally stoned, dragged out of the city, and left for dead. But as the believers attended to him, he got up and went back into the city.

Joseph of Arimathea

FOR A TIME, JOSEPH was a secret disciple of Jesus. After Jesus died on the cross, Joseph asked Pilate for Jesus' body, which Pilate granted. He then took Jesus down from the cross and buried him in his family tomb.

Each of the four gospels mentions Joseph. Matthew calls him a rich man who was a disciple of Jesus (27:57). Mark calls him a "respected member" of the Sanhedrin, the Jewish ruling council, adding that he was "wait-

Joseph of Arimathea *by James Tissot*

ing expectantly for the kingdom of God" (15:43). Luke adds that he was a "good and righteous man" who had not agreed with the council's decision to condemn Jesus (23:51). John confirms that he was a disciple of Jesus, but a "secret one" because he feared the Jewish leaders (19:38).

The four gospels create a clear picture of a man of position and privilege who believed Jesus' teaching about God's kingdom but couldn't quite go public with his commitment to Jesus... until the end. Perhaps the trial of Jesus pushed him over the edge, as he saw the manipulations of the power-mad Annas and Caiaphas, the cowardice of Pilate, or the frenzy of the mob preferring a common criminal to Jesus. Approaching Pilate to ask for Jesus' body was a bold move, but Joseph was uniquely positioned to do this. Not only did he have status that Pilate would respect, but he also had a tomb where the body could rest. Nicodemus, another council member sympathetic to Jesus, joined Joseph in wrapping Jesus' body and burying it. This process was somewhat hasty, since it was already Friday afternoon. With sundown came the sabbath, and they would have to rest.

Joseph's tomb, which he had intended for himself, was new, carved out of rock, in a garden, with a stone that sealed its entrance. The early Christians noted a prophecy from Isaiah about the Messiah having "his tomb with the rich" (Isaiah 53:9).

POSTSCRIPT

■ The location of Arimathea is unclear, but it might be a variation on *Ramathaim*, and thus a later name for Samuel's hometown, Ramathaim-zophim, eight miles northwest of Jerusalem.

The Gospel of Luke

THE OPENING OF THE GOSPEL OF LUKE presents us with the "I" of the author in a way that we do not encounter in Matthew or Mark. While the author does not explicitly name himself, there are several clues as to his identity in the book's sequel, the Acts of the Apostles. In a number of places in the narrative of Paul's travels, the story is told from the viewpoint of "we," suggesting that the author was a traveling companion and coworker of Paul's. Tradition has named Luke as that coworker.

While Matthew and Mark may have been written before A.D. 70, the year in which Roman armies ended the Jewish revolt by besieging Jerusalem and destroying the temple, Luke possibly wrote his gospel after these events. It seems he took certain prophetic sayings of Jesus about the trials to befall Israel and recast them in ways that suggest that Luke understood these prophecies to have been fulfilled in the dire hardships at the end of the Jewish war with Rome.

Luke's particular selection of Jesus' teachings and his shaping of Jesus' larger story reveal a number of purposes. First, Luke wants to confirm for a largely Gentile Christian readership that the promises of God are reliable. The promises God gave to Abraham, David, and Israel have not failed but have been fulfilled in Jesus and among the people gathered around Jesus. Moreover, it was always God's larger intention to bring all people to himself, not just Israel.

Second, Luke, like Matthew, seeks to anchor the events of Jesus' life, death, and resurrection in the prophecies of the Hebrew Scriptures, a process that continues in Acts. Third, Luke places a strong emphasis on God's compassion for the poor, the sinner, and the outsider. Some of the teachings of Jesus found only in Luke's gospel—the parables of the Prodigal Son (15:11–32), of the Good Samaritan (10:30–37), and of the Rich Man and Lazarus (16:19–31)—especially encourage restoring the sinner, reaching across boundaries, and using one's wealth to relieve the needs of one's neighbor.

POSTSCRIPT

■ Matthew and Luke share an impressive number of sayings of Jesus that are not found in Mark or John. Many scholars now believe these shared sayings originally circulated independently, prior to the writing of Matthew or Luke, as a kind of handbook of Jesus' teachings. This hypothetical collection is often referred to as the "Q" document, a name derived from the German *Quelle,* which means "source." To date, no manuscript evidence for Q has ever emerged.

Canaanite Culture

THE PROBLEM WITH PROMISING the Promised Land was that there were already people there. The land we know as Israel, Palestine, or the Holy Land was also known as Canaan, and it was home to a thriving culture in the time of Abraham and long before that. Ancient documents, mostly written on clay tablets, show Canaanite civilization in place throughout much of the second and third millennia B.C.

The term "Canaanite" is geographical more than ethnic. Various peoples settled in Canaan—mostly Amorites but also early Assyrians and Hittites. At times, Egyptians or Mesopotamians overran the area, but the records on ancient tablets also show Canaanite leaders interacting diplomatically and economically with the nations around them.

Politically, the territory was broken into many different city-states ruled by kings and nobles. Sometimes they joined together against an opponent, but they also struggled with one another. Genesis 14 tells of Abraham and Lot getting in the middle of a war that pitted four kings against five kings. Joshua 12 lists 31 different kings conquered by the invading Israelites. No doubt the infighting among those kingdoms weakened them before the Israelites arrived

Most of the common folk were farmers, so it makes sense that their religion would focus on fertility. Baal was the sky god, the one who brought rain to the earth. Crops grew when he mated with the earth goddess. Canaanite mythology was full of sex stories about these gods, and their worship practices were often sexual in nature.

Canaanite worship occurred in "high places," often sacred groves on hilltops. Animal sacrifice was routinely practiced, but there is also evidence of human sacrifice, particularly child sacrifice. In this light, it would not have seemed strange to Abraham when God asked him to sacrifice Isaac on Mount Moriah. According to the rituals of his Canaanite neighbors, that was acceptable worship. (Of course, God stopped Abraham from killing his son and offered a ram as a substitute.)

The Old Testament puts a high priority on separating the Israelites from the Canaanites and their practices. Canaan was already a melting pot of ethnicity, culture, and religion, so it would have been easy for Israel to melt into the local identity. Instead they received repeated commands to wipe out the Canaanite culture from the land "so that they may not teach you to do all the abhorrent things that they do for their gods" (Deuteronomy 20:18).

Lazarus Leaves His Tomb

MARY AND MARTHA sent an urgent message to Jesus about their brother, Lazarus: "Lord, he whom you love is ill" (John 11:3). Some days passed. When Jesus actually arrived at the village of Bethany, the accusations began. Lazarus had died, and so first Martha, then Mary, told Jesus, "Lord, if you had been here, my brother would not have died" (verses 21, 32). The sisters had similar thoughts. They had probably seen Jesus heal the sick. Why couldn't he have hurried to his friend and healed him? But they could not have fathomed what the Lord had planned for both their brother and himself.

As Jesus stepped to Lazarus's tomb, he saw Mary and others weep. He was deeply moved, and then he, too, wept. When he came to the tomb, he commanded the stone in front of the tomb be rolled away, but Martha said, "Lord, already there is a stench because he has been dead four days" (verse 39). Martha, and undoubtedly all who were present—including Jesus' disciples—still did not comprehend what was about to take place.

Jesus responded to Martha by telling her that if she believed, she would experience the glory of God. He then looked heavenward, spoke to God, and then cried out with a loud voice, "Lazarus, come out!" (verse 43). With his hands, feet, and face still bound in burial cloth, Lazarus came out of the tomb. "Unbind him, and let him go" (verse 44), Jesus ordered.

This story is important because it is a dramatic precursor to Jesus' own death and resurrection. When Jesus revealed his intention to go to Lazarus, his disciples warned, "Rabbi, the Jews were just trying to stone you, and are you going there again?" (verses 7–8). Although Jesus faced a threat, he returned to Judaea. His healing of Lazarus sealed his fate with the Jewish leaders of Judaea. After he healed Lazarus, John records, "from that day on they planned to put him to death" (verse 53).

Lazarus's resurrection is also significant because it caused many Jews to believe in Jesus. In addition to the animosity this raised against Jesus, it also raised anger against Lazarus, the one who was living proof of Jesus' power. "So the chief priests planned to put Lazarus to death as well, since it was on account of him that many of the Jews were deserting and were believing in Jesus" (John 12:10–11).

That the three earlier gospels are silent regarding one of the most significant events in the life of Jesus indicates that Lazarus's life was in danger for some years even after Jesus' crucifixion. God, however, did not want this miracle to be omitted from his Word because of what it tells of Jesus' power and compassion.

Solomon and the Two Mothers

KING SOLOMON WAS THE SON of King David and Bathsheba. He was the third king of Israel. His greatest fame was his extraordinary wisdom, which people came from hundreds of miles to hear.

He was a prolific writer and was the primary author of two of the great wisdom books in the Bible: Proverbs, which is full of practical wisdom for living, and Ecclesiastes, which consists of the mature reflections of a man who has "tried it all" and found everything except fearing God to be meaningless. First Kings 4:32 says he composed 3,000 proverbs, several hundred of which have been preserved in the Book of Proverbs, and 1,005 songs, two of which are preserved in the Book of Psalms (72 and 127).

The Wisdom of Solomon *by James Tissot*

The biblical account of Solomon's wisdom begins immediately after he becomes king, when God appears to him in a dream and offers him anything he wants. Instead of asking for a long life, riches, or victory over his enemies, King Solomon asks for wisdom—for "an understanding mind to govern your people, able to discern between good and evil" (1 Kings 3:9). His humble request pleases God, who not only promises him "a wise and discerning mind" like no one before or since but also riches and honor in his lifetime (verse 12).

Solomon's wisdom was soon put to the test when two prostitutes came to him with a dispute. Both had given birth to sons. One woman's son had died at night, but she had surreptitiously switched babies. Now both were claiming the one live baby. It was up to Solomon to decide between the two. So he ordered the live boy to be cut in half, and half given to each woman. The baby's real mother was horrified. She begged the king to give the boy to the other woman, whereas the latter coldly said, "divide it" (verse 26). Solomon rightly discerned who the true mother was and gave her the boy. News of Solomon's wise decision soon spread throughout the land.

David

DAVID WAS ONE of Israel's most important and beloved figures. He was a man of many talents: He was a shepherd, musician, warrior, poet, politician, and administrator, but he is most prominently remembered as Israel's greatest king, setting a high standard for all rulers who came after him.

David came from humble beginnings as a shepherd boy, the youngest of his father's eight sons. At one point, David was called to Saul's court to play soothing music for Saul's troubled mind. He also proved himself in battle by killing Goliath. Popular sentiment swung over to David, which caused Saul to be so jealous of him that he tried on numerous occasions to kill him. Although David spent many years on the run, he refused to kill Saul when he had the opportunity to do so on two occasions because Saul was the Lord's anointed king.

After Saul's death, David was anointed king first over his own tribe, Judah, and then over all Israel. As king, he unified the nation—no small feat, considering that only a few decades earlier the tribes had battled each other in an unseemly civil war, and a few decades after his reign, the kingdom would be divided permanently along north-south lines. He had great successes as Israel's military leader, although the Bible is careful to say that his successes ultimately came from God.

David had many wives. His first wife was Saul's daughter Michal, who "loved him" (1 Samuel 18:28) in her youth and helped him escape from her father. During David's absence, Saul gave her to another man, but when David assumed the throne after Saul's death, he reclaimed her. By this time, David had married other women, including Abigail, who had shown deep reverence toward him.

Meanwhile, Michal's love for David had died, possibly because David's marital affection was divided or because she was forced from a loving and devoted husband. In any case, when David celebrated the return of the Ark of the Covenant in a dance that she thought was unbecoming to a king, she scorned him. As a result, she bore him no children, but his other wives bore him many children. In addition, his later wives, including Bathsheba, bore him several more sons, and the rivalry among these sons brought grief to him time after time.

Despite David's spectacular failings, David was "a man after God's own heart" (1 Samuel 13:14).

The Council at Jerusalem

PAUL AND BARNABAS had stirred things up on their first missionary journey. They came back to the Antioch church that had sent them and reported on the marvelous new activity of God among the Gentiles. But some Jewish believers weren't so sure that was a good thing. They still saw Christianity as an outreach effort for only Judaism. Gentiles could be invited into the fellowship, but only if they became Jews. For men, the conversion process would involve circumcision.

The debate in Antioch came to the attention of the apostles in Jerusalem, who convened a symposium on the matter. Paul and Barnabas gave their report about the Gentile mission, and others made their point about the need for circumcision.

Peter was the first of the Jerusalem apostles to weigh in, reminding everyone that God had sent him to the household of the Italian centurion Cornelius. Since the Holy Spirit had come upon the Gentiles in Cornelius's household in the same way that it had descended upon the apostles at Pentecost, who could make any distinction between Jewish and Gentile believers? "We will be saved through the grace of the Lord Jesus, just as they will," he concluded (Acts 15:11).

Finally, James ruled on the matter. This was the brother of Jesus—not one of the 12 apostles—who had moved quickly into Church leadership. While Peter was respected as an elder statesman, it was James who made the ruling here. With a loose quoting of Amos 9:11–12, he said, "I have reached the decision that we should not trouble those Gentiles who are turning to God" (verse 19). He then proposed a letter to be sent to the Gentile converts, asking them to abstain from four things that would be especially troublesome to devout Jews: eating meat offered to idols; sexual immorality; eating meat from strangled animals (thus having the blood still in it); and consuming blood. Two men, Judas Barsabbas and Silas, were chosen to accompany Paul and Barnabas back to Antioch, taking such a letter with them.

Writing later to the churches, Paul would maintain that Christians are free from the law and that law-keeping is not a requirement for salvation. In fact, he specifically mentions one of James's four rules—eating meat offered to idols—as a matter of personal discretion (see 1 Corinthians 8), though he acknowledges that Christians should sometimes curtail their freedom out of concern for a weaker and more legalistic brother (see Romans 14). Considering all of that, we might guess that Paul was happy with the general permission the council granted to minister to Gentiles.

Matthias

FROM THE BEGINNING of Jesus' ministry, Matthias was a devoted follower of the Lord. After Jesus' ascension, the apostles chose Matthias by lot to take the place of Judas Iscariot among the Twelve.

Judas's betrayal and later suicide must have stunned the other 11 disciples, but many things had happened since then: the crucifixion and resurrection of Jesus, 40 days of further instruction by the risen Jesus, and his ascension to heaven. When they regrouped in Jerusalem, there were about 120 Jesus-followers in the movement. Citing a Scripture that says, "May another seize his position" (Psalm 109:8), Peter suggested that they choose a twelfth apostle to take Judas's place. They selected two candidates, men who had been following Jesus from the start (though not originally called to be part of the Twelve): Matthias and Joseph Barsabbas. Then they prayed and cast lots, selecting Matthias (Acts 1:21–26).

We usually think of Jesus having only 12 disciples, but he had a larger group of men and women who followed him. The Twelve were those who left their livelihoods to travel with him, but there were scores of other Jews who believed his teaching and committed themselves to his cause. At one point, Jesus sent out 72 of these disciples on a mission project (Luke 10). This was probably the group from which Matthias and Joseph Barsabbas were chosen.

As to the selection of Matthias, some have been troubled by the apparent trust in chance to make such an important decision. Yet the casting of lots was a time-honored tradition in Scripture, rooted in the faith that God ultimately controls such matters. "The lot is cast into the lap," says Proverbs 16:33, "but the decision is the Lord's alone."

Installed as the twelfth apostle, Matthias joined the others, and a few days later he was a part of the miracle at Pentecost, when the Spirit came upon them and they spoke in languages understood by those from many nations. He was also likely involved in the early prayer meetings and the selection of deacons to oversee the charitable work of the Church. Matthias probably participated in the council meetings that considered the expansion of Christian ministry to the Gentiles. But we have no record of him after he replaces Judas Iscariot in Acts 1.

POSTSCRIPT

■ The name *Matthias* means "gift of Yahweh."

The Gospel of John

THE "BELOVED DISCIPLE" is traditionally assigned authorship of the fourth gospel. Tradition also affirms that John, the son of Zebedee, was this Beloved Disciple. The Beloved Disciple, moreover, seems to have been quite familiar with Jerusalem's sites and geography and was even known by the high priest. These characteristics would not be beyond a Galilean fisherman, such as the Apostle John.

Interestingly, when Lazarus, who lived just a few miles outside of Jerusalem, fell ill, his sisters sent word to Jesus naming Lazarus only as "he whom you love" (11:3). The name "Beloved Disciple" only appears after that point. Whether written by John, Lazarus, or another disciple, the fourth gospel bears clear marks of firsthand knowledge of Jesus and compelling testimony to his significance. This is probably the last gospel to have been written, perhaps as late as A.D. 90.

One important circumstance that seems to have shaped this telling of the story of Jesus was the conflict between Jesus and the Jewish authorities. The author responds by presenting a Jesus who is the culmination and embodiment of all that was valuable in the audience's Jewish heritage, from which they were increasingly alienated by their Gentile neighbors. Thus Jesus is the embodiment of the divine *Logos*, the wisdom of God known from Proverbs 8. He is the new temple, the light and living water that was formerly experienced though the law, the shepherd that God promised would lead Israel, the bread from heaven that satisfies more than manna, the Lamb of God in the ultimate Passover from death into life, and the hope of the resurrection.

The author also presents lengthy instructions by Jesus aimed at instilling the main values of mutual service, love, unity, and reliance upon the Holy Spirit to the communities gathered around the Beloved Disciple.

POSTSCRIPT

■ In its current form, John includes one of the most beloved stories about Jesus: his protection of the woman about to be stoned for adultery, calling for a sinless person to throw the first stone (see 8:3–11). This story, however, does not appear in the earliest surviving manuscripts and occasionally appears in a different place in other copies of John or Luke. How do we explain this? Authentic stories about Jesus continued to circulate long after the gospels were written down. This particular one was so true to the character of Jesus and his mission that scribes refused to allow it to be lost

Baal

IN THE CANAANITE PANTHEON, El was the grandfather god—the white-bearded supreme who dallied in paradise with his three wives, vaguely overseeing a council of the other gods, who were his children. Baal was his second-in-command, and eventually he took charge.

Statuette of Baal

Baal was the sky god—the sun god with a thunder-bolt in his hand and the bringer of rain. He was responsible for the growth of crops. Every year he went down to the underworld to battle with the death god, Mot. But every autumn, summoned by the rituals and prayers of his worshippers, he came back to bless his people with produce.

This was the religious backdrop of Elijah's famous showdown with the priests of Baal on Mount Carmel. There had been a drought in the land for more than two years. Elijah challenged the Baalists to a duel: Which of them could call fire from heaven to consume a sacrifice? If Baal was truly the storm god, he should have no problem causing it to rain.

We get a glimpse of Baal-worship in this episode. For hours the prophets called out to Baal (as if to summon him from the underworld), "limping" around the altar (probably dancing with bent legs like other cultures' rain dances), ultimately cutting themselves with knives (in case Baal required human blood). Meanwhile, Elijah mocked them, urging them to call louder. Maybe Baal was asleep, he taunted, and must be awakened. When it was his turn, Elijah successfully called a lightning strike from heaven. A rain cloud then appeared, ending the drought (1 Kings 18).

What we don't see here is sexual excess, but that was also part of Baal-worship, as people tried to coax their god into making their land fertile. Baal was worshipped along with the earth goddess Asherah. (The mythology here differs a bit from source to source: Anath, Asherah, and Astarte are all named as Baal's consorts, and their names take different forms.)

As the Israelites moved into Canaan, Baal-worship surrounded them. Though the Israelites took political control over much of the land, the Baal-based culture remained a regular temptation with its fertility myths and sexual license. In the ninth century B.C., Queen Jezebel imported priests of Baal from her homeland in Sidon, and even after Elijah's decisive victory, Baalism remained strong. A century later Hosea complained that the Lord gave his people gifts that they thanked Baal for (Hosea 2:8).

Parable of the Prodigal Son

Jesus' best-known parable focuses on a father who has two sons. The younger son asks for his share of the inheritance and then leaves home. He travels to a distant country, where he rapidly wastes his money on prostitutes and sinful behavior. He eventually finds a job feeding pigs, a task particularly repulsive to Jews. His hunger, however is so great that he even covets the pods that the pigs eat.

He realizes that he has sinned and wonders whether his family would ever welcome him if he went back home. He concludes that even being a hired hand and having something to eat would be better than his present situation. So he returns home, and when his father sees him from a distance, his father runs to him, hugs him, and kisses him. Although the son declares that he is no longer worthy to be called his father's son, the father pays little attention to his words and instead calls for a slave to get his son his best robe, a ring, sandals, and a fatted calf for a banquet.

When the older son returns from his work in the fields, he hears music and dancing. After he learns of the homecoming celebration for his brother, he stews outside with anger and refuses to join the festivities. The father comes out and pleads with him to join the party, but he lectures his father on how he has been obedient his entire life, yet he has never had such a celebration.

The father responds, "Son, you are always with me, and all that is mine is yours. But we had to celebrate and rejoice, because this brother of yours was dead and has come to life; he was lost and has been found" (Luke 15:31–32).

Some readers of the story may relate to the younger son—the way he loses his direction and the way he finds grace despite what he may deserve. Others may relate to the older son, who has always tried to be responsible but who feels slighted by his father's response to his brother's return. In many respects, however, the key character in the story is the father. He sees the mistakes that his son has made; he knows that he himself has been slighted, but he so deeply loves his son that he only wants his son to find life. When he sees his son from a distance, he does not act like a dignified patriarch. Rather, he runs, hugs his son, and kisses him. The story is not really the story of the prodigal son or even the angry older son. It is the story of the loving father. Jesus' parable is a reminder of a divine love far greater than what anyone deserves.

Solomon's Temple

EVEN THOUGH IT'S NOT one of the noted "Seven Wonders of the Ancient World," Solomon's Temple in Jerusalem easily could have been. It was seven years in the making and a wonder to behold.

Solomon's father, David, had originally wanted to build the temple, but God forbade him because he had been a man of too much warfare. So God designated Solomon to be the builder instead. Nevertheless, David marshaled the nation's resources in preparation. He set stonecutters to cutting great stones, offered bronze "in quantities beyond weighing" for the project, and gathered "cedar logs without number" from Lebanon (see 1 Chronicles 22:3–4). He also organized the Levites, priests, musicians, gatekeepers, treasurers, and other officials who would attend to all the temple activities.

Solomon, however, took the work to a whole different level. In addition to 30,000 Israelite workers, he assigned 70,000 foreign men to carry burdens, 80,000 to quarry, and 3,600 as overseers. He hired Hiram, a craftsman skilled in working "gold, silver, bronze, and iron, stone, and in purple, crimson, and blue fabrics" (2 Chronicles 2:7). He provided tens of thousands of bushels of wheat and barley and tens of thousands of gallons of wine and oil to feed these foreign workers.

The temple ended up being approximately 90 feet long, 30 feet high, and 30 feet wide. It was divided into three parts: (1) the outer vestibule, flanked by two massive bronze pillars; (2) the inner nave, containing a golden altar, a golden table for the "bread of the Presence," and ten golden lampstands; and (3) the Holy of Holies, which contained two great cherubs made of wood overlaid with gold, with wings outstretched over the ark of the covenant. Most of the temple interior was overlaid with gold, ivory, or precious stones.

Outside the temple was a large "molten sea," used for ritual cleansings and serviced by ten bronze basins on ten wheeled stands. A large bronze altar also stood in front of the temple.

The temple became central to Israel's worship. The faithful would make regular pilgrimages there to worship and bring sacrifices and offerings. Its destruction by the Babylonians more than 300 years later was a wrenching event for God's people. No longer did they have a central place for worship and sacrifice. They had to cling to their Scriptures, which are the foundation of the Jews, who are known as "people of the Book."

Jonathan

JONATHAN WAS THE OLDEST son of Saul, the first king of Israel. Although he was in line to become the second king in Israel's history, his close friendship with David was more important to him. In fact, his bond with David has become one of the most intriguing examples of selfless loyalty in the Bible.

When Saul first became king, it seemed that he personally led the people in battle against all comers: Moabites, Ammonites, Edomites, Philistines, Amalekites, and the kings of Zobah. But it was actually Jonathan who was instrumental in a critical early battle against the Philistines. They had mustered 30,000 chariots, 6,000 horsemen, and many more troops, thus spreading fear in the Israelite camp. Jonathan then executed a daring raid against a Philistine garrison at a narrow pass at Michmash, aided only by his armor-bearer. They killed 20 Philistines in close-quarters fighting. This spread terror throughout the Philistine army, and the Israelites were able to rout them.

Thus Jonathan was in a good position to succeed his father as king—the Israelites, after all, had asked for a warrior-king to "go out before us and fight our battles" (1 Samuel 8:20). Meanwhile, Saul had disqualified himself as king for having disobeyed the Lord. As a result, God told Samuel to anoint David, who was from a different tribe, as king. This, in effect, eliminated the possibility of Jonathan succeeding his father to the throne.

While Saul became insanely jealous of David, the loss of the crown did not have the same effect on Jonathan. Instead, the Bible says he and David became best friends and that "Jonathan loved him as his own soul" (1 Samuel 18:1). They pledged their loyalty to each other, and Jonathan became David's advocate before his father, urging him not to kill David. Moreover, he warned David of several of his father's plots on his life. Finally, when David had to flee Israel, the two friends parted with great sorrow. After this, they only saw each other one last time, when Jonathan visited David's hideout. Jonathan later perished in the same battle with the Philistines in which his father was killed.

David mourned the deaths of both men, saying, "How the mighty have fallen in the midst of the battle!" (2 Samuel 1:25). He went on to say of his dear friend, "I am distressed for you, my brother Jonathan; greatly beloved were you to me; your love to me was wonderful, passing the love of women" (verse 26).

Paul Confronts Peter

WHO KNEW THAT the seating arrangement at a church dinner could cause such a fuss? But when Peter withdrew from the Gentile table to sit with the Jews, he was making a major theological statement, intentional or not. Paul recognized this error and took him to task for it.

The incident occurred in Antioch in Syria. The church there was active, adventurous, breaking new ground to reach the Gentiles. The mother church in Jerusalem was far more cautious about these matters. Whenever a new people-group began coming to faith in Jesus, they would send a team to investigate or they would hold a symposium.

Peter's faux pas happened while he was visiting Antioch, perhaps on one of those fact-finding missions. At first, he freely enjoyed the company of Gentile Christians, but then a delegation of Jewish Christians arrived from Jerusalem, sent by James (this was Jesus' brother, who was now leading the Jerusalem church). These new guests were part of the group that demanded the keeping of the Jewish law, holding that Gentiles could be accepted as Christians only if they converted to Judaism. Part of this law-keeping involved separation from Gentiles at mealtime, since Gentiles were by nature nonkosher. Apparently these Jewish believers set up a division, withdrawing to one side of the room or going to another room to eat their meal.

That gave Peter a tough decision to make. Would he go along with this division as a law-keeping Jew, or would he make a statement about equality by remaining with the Gentile Christians? No doubt he flashed back to his rooftop vision, where he heard a voice from heaven telling him to eat nonkosher food, because God had cleansed it. That vision had led him to preach the gospel to a Roman centurion and his household (see Acts 11). So Peter was no stranger to these issues. He had already broken barriers, but here he buckled under pressure, withdrawing from the Gentiles and joining the separated Jews.

Paul was livid. He would have thought that Peter, of all people, would be on his side. If those Jerusalem visitors were applying pressure to divide the Church, Paul would fight to unite it. This was a struggle for the very identity of the Christian movement.

There is no record of any immediate reaction from Peter, but if this happened before the Jerusalem Council, it might have motivated Peter's speech of support in Acts 15:7–11.

Stephen

THE APOSTLES SELECTED Stephen to be a deacon because they needed a group of spiritually respected brothers in Christ who would manage the practical work of food distribution. Stephen not only became one of the first deacons in the growing young Church, but he also proved to be a powerful preacher. After he presented the message of Jesus in the face of the Church's enemies, Stephen was stoned to death, becoming the first Christian martyr.

Stephen was one of seven men, "full of the Spirit and of wisdom" (Acts 6:3), appointed by the apostles as deacons to take over the Church's charitable meal plan. Caring for widows and orphans was an important part of Jewish devotion, and the Church embraced it, too. (Some women who became Christians might have been disowned by their husbands, thus joining the ranks of widowhood.)

The Sermon of St. Stephen *by Charles Natoire*

Stephen is described as full of "faith and the Holy Spirit" and "full of grace and power" (verses 5, 8). He even worked miracles. But then he won a debate with the members of a particular synagogue, and they plotted revenge. False witnesses arose, accusing Stephen of blasphemy against God and the temple. He was arrested and brought before the council. When the high priest asked him if the charges were true, Stephen launched into a sermon that takes up most of Acts 7.

He spoke about the history of Israel—Abraham, Joseph, Moses—how they trusted God and he helped them. But throughout time, Stephen went on to say, there were always those who didn't get it, those who opposed what God was trying to do. He accused the council of doing that same thing: "You stiff-necked people, uncircumcised in heart and ears, you are forever opposing the Holy Spirit, just as your ancestors used to do" (Acts 7:51). That was not a way to win the favor of his listeners, but Stephen had his sights set higher.

Enraged, his audience rushed at him, dragged him out of the city, and stoned him to death, as he gazed into heaven and prayed.

Acts of the Apostles

THE ACTS OF THE APOSTLES is the literary sequel to the Gospel of Luke. The same author wrote both and clearly intended them to be read in connection with each other. The prologue of Acts even refers to the earlier work.

The first seven chapters tell of the birth and rapid growth of the early Church in Jerusalem despite the attempts of the temple authorities to silence its leaders. The story widens to include the Church's mission to Samaria and Galilee. This expansion was a result of the persecution of the church in Judaea. The pivotal episode in the book tells of Peter's conversion of a centurion and his household (10:1–48), which leads to the convening of a Church council to decide whether or not converts to Christ must also become converts to the Jewish way of life. It is decided they do not.

After this, the focus of the book shifts to Paul's successful missionary work among the Gentiles throughout Syria, Asia Minor, and Greece, until he is arrested during a relief effort for the Jerusalem church. But Paul's lengthy series of hearings finally brings him to Rome, where he preaches for two years. Acts closes here, having shown the spread of the Church from Jerusalem to Rome.

Why does Luke tell the story in this way? He wishes to present Christianity as a legitimate continuation of the ancient Hebrew faith, not a novel superstition. He repeatedly relates the faith and emerging story of the Church with the Hebrew Scriptures as fulfillment of prophecy. He particularly stresses that the inclusion of Gentiles into the people of God was a fulfillment of scriptural prophecy and a move guided by the very Spirit of God. Luke also tells a story in which Roman authorities consistently find nothing blameworthy in the Christian movement, a feature that should further assure Gentile converts that they have joined a legitimate movement.

POSTSCRIPT

■ Paul does not provide dates in any of his letters. Perhaps the most important anchor for dating Paul's activity comes from the reference in Acts to his activity in Corinth during the proconsulship of Lucius Junius Gallio (Acts 18:12). The chance discovery of an inscription in Delphi establishes that Gallio was proconsul over that region in A.D. 52. Paul's activity in Corinth can therefore be placed between A.D. 51 and 53.

The Philistines

ORIGINALLY FROM the Aegean area, the Philistines were a sea people who migrated to the Middle East around 1200 B.C. They battled Egypt and lost, but Rameses III allowed them to settle on the southern portion of the coast of Canaan. There they prospered, establishing five major cities—Ashdod, Ashkelon, Gaza, Gath, and Ekron. Soon they were moving inland to claim more territory. The problem was, the Israelites lived there.

For more than two centuries, the Philistines were Israel's greatest foes. The Book of Judges records some victories of Shamgar and Samson against the Philistines, but these appear to be guerrilla attacks against a generally dominant force. Samson's story occurs during a 40-year period when "the Lord gave [the Israelites] into the hand of the Philistines" (Judges 13:1). The Philistine landgrab forced the tribe of Dan—to which Samson belonged—to leave their allotted territory and migrate to the very north of the holy land.

When Israel became a monarchy under King Saul, their unified front helped them against the Philistines, but they were still losing the war. The fact that David fought Goliath in the valley of Elah, not far from Bethlehem, shows how far into Israelite territory the battle lines had been drawn. What was the secret of Philistine success? Iron. Their coastal connections provided the latest technology. They had iron chariots, spears, and swords, and the Israelites didn't (see 1 Samuel 13:19).

The famous battle where David felled Goliath with a slung stone seems to have been a turning point, at least in the Israelites' attitude. Despair turned to determination. The war raged on, and David became a mighty warrior, fighting the Philistines under Saul's command. When David became king, he finally put down the Philistine threat. They managed a few uprisings against later kings but they never again dominated the region.

Dagon (probably a fertility/rain/grain god) was the primary deity of the Philistines, but they also worshipped the earth goddess Ashtaroth and Baal-zebub (literally "lord of the flies"). All of these are Semitic names, so it seems that whatever religion they brought from the Aegean was quickly assimilated into Canaanite culture. A temple of Dagon became the temporary home for the ark of the covenant after the Philistines captured it in battle. The next day, the people found the statue of Dagon fallen before the ark. They put it back, and the next day it had fallen again, with its hands and head cut off. They began looking for a way to return the ark to Israel.

The Healing of Ten Lepers

AT THE BEGINNING of his ministry, when Jesus had returned to his home in Nazareth, he read Scripture at a synagogue and then preached. Although the townsfolk initially were impressed with Jesus, they soon became so angry with his teachings that they wanted to kill him. The turning point, in part, was Jesus' use of Naaman as an example. In the Old Testament, the writer of Second Kings 5:1–14 tells the story of Naaman, an army commander of Aram who suffered from leprosy. In his preaching, Jesus said, "There were also many lepers in Israel in the time of the prophet Elisha, and none of them was cleansed except Naaman the Syrian" (Luke 4:27). It was clear to the townsfolk that Jesus was being critical of his fellow Jews. He was using examples of Gentiles who had proven faithful to God in ways that Jews had not.

Jesus' familiarity with the story of Naaman should shape our understanding of Luke 17:11–19. When Jesus was on his way to Jerusalem, he entered a village where ten lepers approached him. It was not unusual to encounter a group of lepers. They tended to live with each other apart from society. At the same time, they needed to live close enough to cities, towns, and roads in order to beg for alms so they could survive.

In this story, Jesus' reputation had preceded him, so the lepers called him by name, saying, "Jesus, Master, have mercy on us!" (verse 13). Jesus responded by telling them that they should go and show themselves to the priests. As they did so, they were made clean. "Then one of them, when he saw that he was healed, turned back, praising God . . . He prostrated himself at Jesus' feet and thanked him. And he was a Samaritan" (verses 15–16).

Jesus drew attention to the fact that ten lepers had been made clean, but none of them returned to praise God except the Samaritan. Jesus' concluding words to the Samaritan were "Get up and go on your way; your faith has made you well" (verse 19). Because the Samaritan already had been healed of leprosy, Jesus' words seem to point to a deeper healing.

What that healing involved is perhaps best understood by looking at the Samaritan's response to his healing. He did not continue on his way as if his life had not changed. He paused and returned to Jesus. What stands out is his praise of God and his willingness to acknowledge Jesus as healer.

His words of thanks to God show a wholeness that others lacked. Their leprosy had been cured, but that was only the first step to true wholeness.

Solomon Succumbs to Idolatry

SOLOMON WAS A WISE and great man in many respects, but he also had his weaknesses, including a love of riches and especially his love of women. In fact, he had 700 wives and 300 concubines.

It would seem his downfall began early in his reign as king of Israel. The Bible says this about the beginning of his reign: "So the kingdom was established in the hand of Solomon. Solomon made a marriage alliance with Pharaoh king of Egypt; he took Pharaoh's daughter" (1 Kings 2:46—3:1). The Israelites were not supposed to marry foreigners unless they had embraced Israel's God as their own. And the Scriptures explicitly said of Israel's king that "he must not acquire many wives for himself, or else his heart will turn away" (Deuteronomy 17:17).

Solomon and His Harem *by James Tissot*

So, when the first thing said about Solomon after he becomes king is that he married a foreign woman, we know there is trouble ahead. This little fact was like a ticking time bomb, which exploded in his face later in his life. At the end of his reign, we read that "King Solomon loved many foreign women along with the daughter of Pharaoh" (1 Kings 11:1) and that "when Solomon was old, his wives turned away his heart after other gods; and his heart was not true to the Lord his God" (verse 4).

Although Solomon's idolatry angered God, who wanted to strip Solomon of his kingdom, God relented for the sake of the promises he had made to King David. He had promised David that there would be peace during his son's reign, and so there was. Nevertheless, the long-term effects of Solomon's apostasy were tragic. Soon after his death, his kingdom was divided, and in time foreign powers destroyed both kingdoms.

POSTSCRIPT

■ According to the first and second commandments of the Ten Commandments, idolatry of every form was strictly forbidden. In fact, the nearest relatives of an offender were obligated to denounce and deliver over the offender (see Deuteronomy 13:6–10), who would be stoned to death with the evidence of at least two witnesses (see 17:2–7).

Bathsheba

BATHSHEBA IS ONE of the more famous women in the Old Testament. Her adulterous act with King David is one of the few blemishes in an otherwise admirable career of a great king. Whether Bathsheba was a willing participant in their love affair or an innocent victim of David's unbridled lust is often debated. But what is little discussed is how important her role was in placing David's successor on the throne of Israel.

Bathsheba was married to Uriah, a Hittite and one of David's elite warriors (see 1 Chronicles 11:41). Unfortunately, she lived so near the king's palace that King David saw her bathing late one afternoon from his terrace. David had many beautiful wives and concubines, and he probably only rarely had to deny his sexual appetite. When he saw the physical charms of this beautiful woman, he lusted after her. Even after he discovered her marital state, he could not deny himself, and so he sent for her.

Meanwhile, Uriah was away with the army, fighting for Israel against the Ammonites. He was unaware that David had sent for his wife, who either willingly submitted or was coerced into an immoral union with the king. In either case, Bathsheba became pregnant, and David tried to cover up his involvement by bringing Uriah home from battle to be with his wife. Uriah, however, refused to enjoy the pleasures of his marriage while his comrades were in danger on the battlefield. Having his plot foiled by this upright soldier, David ordered Uriah killed in battle. As a consequence of David's wicked murder of Uriah, the Lord took the life of David and Bathsheba's baby shortly after birth.

It is difficult to know how Bathsheba felt about the murder of her husband, but certainly the death of her baby must have been deeply painful for her. The Bible, however, is silent about her feelings throughout this episode, focusing only on David's reactions, particularly to the death of their son. Bathsheba's character surfaces more when David is old and feeble and the crown is about to change hands.

At this time, Adonijah, Solomon's older stepbrother, had lined up an impressive list of allies, including Joab the general of David's army and Abiathar the priest. Nathan the prophet, however, was a supporter of Solomon, and he enlisted Bathsheba to speak to David on her son's behalf. She reminded David of his solemn promise to his son Solomon, and she told David that she and Solomon would be killed if Adonijah became king. David reassured her, and Solomon ascended to the throne with his blessing. After this, Bathsheba is not mentioned again in the Bible, except indirectly in Psalm 51, which is David's prayer of confession for his sins involving Bathsheba and Uriah, and in Jesus' genealogy in Matthew 1.

Paul and Barnabas Split

THE APOSTLE PAUL is certainly a hero of the New Testament. We can applaud his courage, his dedication, and his keen mind, but there are strong indications that he wasn't always easy to get along with. He had more than his share of enemies on account of his all-out commitment to a controversial cause, and he probably owed a few more to a somewhat abrasive personal style.

Understanding that, the Antioch church was wise to pair Paul with the congenial Barnabas, whose name means "Son of Encouragement." As those two set off on their first mission trip, Barnabas brought along his young cousin John Mark. Later Paul would show interest in mentoring young associates, so he probably didn't mind including this intern. Mark was well known to the apostles as the son of a Jerusalem Christian named Mary, whose home was sometimes used for Christian gatherings.

Their journey began in Cyprus, the homeland of Barnabas. And since Barnabas was related to Mark, it's likely that Mark had extended family there, too. The island of Cyprus had a substantial Jewish community, and this is where the missionaries focused their efforts, preaching that Jesus was the Messiah. But then they sailed on to the mainland of Asia Minor, and Mark "left them and returned to Jerusalem" (Acts 13:13). Of course, Paul and Barnabas went on with their mission, but Mark's desertion left a sour taste in Paul's mouth.

When it came time to plan a second mission journey, Barnabas wanted to take Mark along again, but Paul said no. "The disagreement became so sharp that they parted company" (Acts 15:39). Barnabas took Mark back to Cyprus, while Paul teamed with Silas to revisit the towns of Asia Minor.

Why did Mark bail out of that first trip? Perhaps he was merely homesick or the trip suddenly became difficult when they left Cyprus. (The fact that Mark's mother had a home big enough to host meetings suggests that Mark might have enjoyed an affluent upbringing.) Or maybe Mark just couldn't take Paul's abrasive personality. Some have suggested that Mark disapproved when Paul began taking leadership of the team or when Paul redirected the mission toward the Gentiles.

In any case, we know that Paul and Mark did reconcile. Toward the end of Paul's ministry, while he was being held in a Roman prison, he told Timothy to "get Mark and bring him with you, for he is useful in my ministry" (2 Timothy 4:11). It is a tribute to both the Lord and Paul that Christ had made him more forgiving and humble.

Philip the Evangelist

PHILIP WAS ONE of the seven deacons chosen to manage food distribution within the early Church in Jerusalem. He also became an effective missionary. The Spirit interrupted a successful ministry in Samaria to put him in the path of an Ethiopian official, whom Philip evangelized and baptized.

Jesus had told his followers they would be witnesses for him "in Jerusalem, in all Judaea and Samaria, and to the ends of the earth" (Acts 1:8). Indeed, it started in Jerusalem, with the explosion of the Spirit at Pentecost, but the apostles got bogged down in a food-distribution controversy until they selected seven deacons (including Philip) to manage that ministry of mercy. The old opponents of Jesus were now moving against his followers. Another deacon, Stephen, was stoned to death, beginning "a severe persecution against the church in Jerusalem" (Acts 8:1). Christians were forced to take the next steps in Jesus' original plan, scattering outward to the villages of Judaea and Samaria.

Philip went to Samaria, preaching and working miracles before a very receptive populace. Simon, a local sorcerer, was predictably fascinated by Philip's miracles and was baptized (though he later tried to buy the gift of the Holy Spirit).

But then an angel of God directed Philip to travel south on the Gaza road to Jerusalem. There he encountered an Ethiopian official who was heading home after worshiping in Jerusalem. In his carriage, the man was reading aloud from Isaiah and puzzling over it. Prompted by the Spirit, Philip explained how Jesus fulfilled Isaiah's prophecy concerning the promised Messiah (see Isaiah 53). The Ethiopian believed and soon found a roadside pool where he could be baptized. As Philip came out of the water, the Spirit whisked him away to another city (see Acts 8:39).

POSTSCRIPT

■ Philip the Evangelist and Philip the Apostle were two different people. This Philip was one of the seven deacons, not one of the original 12 disciples.

■ Philip appears to have settled in the coastal city of Caesarea. The Apostle Paul and his team stayed with Philip once on their way to Jerusalem. It's mentioned that Philip had four unmarried daughters who had the gift of prophecy (see Acts 21:8–9).

■ There is a Christian group in Ethiopia today that traces its history to this Ethiopian official.

The Epistle to the Romans

PAUL APPEARS ON THE SCENE of the Christian story as a committed opponent of the Jesus movement, but he goes on to become one of its most effective and committed missionary teachers. Thirteen of the 27 books of the New Testament are attributed to his hand.

By the time Paul wrote Romans, he had already planted churches from Syria all the way to Greece and Macedonia, making it one of Paul's later letters. At this point, Paul was contemplating further missionary work in Western Europe, with Spain as his eventual goal. He wrote to the churches in Rome, founded independently of his evangelistic endeavors, to enlist them as a base of support for the next phase of his ministry. Three years later, when he would finally go to Rome in A.D. 60, it would be as a prisoner awaiting trial.

Paul was a controversial figure. He claimed that the gospel meant an end to the old ways of defining the people of God, particularly the keeping of those commandments of the Torah that most clearly set apart the Jews from the Gentiles (such as the circumcision of males, avoidance of certain meats as "unclean," and observation of the Jewish sabbath). Because of this, Paul knew that some people slandered him as a lawless renegade who was critical of all Jewish rules and someone who even encouraged sin. He wrote Romans, in part, to clear up these misunderstandings. Faith in Christ does not lead to lawlessness but to a deeper obedience to God. Disciples allow the Spirit of God to empower and teach them to fulfill the moral vision not only of the Law of Moses but also of the prophets and of Jesus himself.

But Paul also knew there were some problems within the churches in Rome, which were divided along Jewish and Gentile lines, so he brings his gospel to bear on that situation. He writes that the Jewish Christian must not look down on the Gentile Christian, since both stand on the same level in God's sight. The Gentile Christian must not look down on the Jewish Christian, for the Gentile is grafted into the tree of life that springs up from Israel (11:11–24). Instead, each is to welcome the other (15:7–13) and accept the other's customs of honoring the one God without passing judgment (14:1–12). A church that is thus unified will be in a far stronger position to support long-range missionary work.

Gehenna

THE OLD TESTAMENT doesn't discuss hell. When people died, they were just gone. They went down into the earth—into "the Pit"—whether they were good or bad. They called that Pit *Sheol*. When he thought he had a fatal illness, good King Hezekiah moaned, "I am consigned to the gates of Sheol for the rest of my years" (Isaiah 38:10). It was not a place of punishment, just the place of the dead.

Not until the period between the Old and New Testaments, a century or two before Christ, did people begin to make a distinction between the eternal fate of good people and that of bad people. In essence they subdivided Sheol (which in Greek was being called *Hades*). Jesus told a story that reflected this idea, where Lazarus, a righteous and poor beggar (not to be confused with Lazarus, the brother of Mary and Martha), was enjoying his afterlife existence at Abraham's side while the rich man who had refused to help him in life was burning in eternal torment. Both were in the place of the dead, but one side was far nicer than the other, and there was a "great chasm" between the two places (Luke 16:19–31).

Jesus used the image of "eternal fire" as punishment for the wicked (Matthew 25:41). He also used a very specific term with an interesting history: *Gehenna*. Literally it means "the Valley of Hinnom," and it was a real place on the south side of Jerusalem. In Jesus' day it was sort of a garbage dump. In fact, fires were probably smoldering there all the time. But historically it had been the site of heathen worship. Children were burned there in the name of Molech (see 2 Chronicles 28:3). It may have been used as a mass grave (see Jeremiah 7:31–34). This became an ideal word picture for the threat of fiery torment in the afterlife.

"Hell" is variously described in Scripture as a place of weeping and teeth-gnashing anguish, as "the second death," and as a lake of fire prepared for the Devil and his angels (Revelation 20:14). The Apostle Paul describes a future scene of Christ returning in flaming fire to wreak vengeance on those who don't obey the gospel: "These will suffer the punishment of eternal destruction, separated from the presence of the Lord and from the glory of his might" (2 Thessalonians 1:9).

It's a harsh picture and difficult to equate with the fact that the same gospel is characterized by love. There have been various attempts made to reconcile divine love with fiery hell. The general explanation is that people choose this separation from God themselves. He freely offers salvation, but some people reject it.

Triumphant and Victorious

ON PALM SUNDAY, Christians annually commemorate Jesus' last entry into Jerusalem. As described in Mark 11, after Jesus had sent his disciples to bring him a colt, they put blankets on the animal, and Jesus sat upon it. While Jesus entered Jerusalem on the colt, people put their cloaks and leafy branches on the path before him. Then they shouted "Hosanna!" and quoted the words from Psalm 118:26: "Blessed is the one who comes in the name of the Lord."

When Jesus entered Jerusalem, he sent a strong message to the religious authorities and to the inhabitants and pilgrims of that city. Like him, they were aware of the prophecy of Zechariah 9:9, which said, "Rejoice greatly, O daughter Zion! Shout aloud, O daughter Jerusalem! Lo, your king comes to you; triumphant and victorious is he, humble and riding on a donkey, on a colt, the foal of a donkey." By choosing to ride on a colt into Jerusalem, Jesus was fulfilling a prophecy, and it was not surprising that people picked up on the imagery. Immediately they started to quote the Book of Psalms, seeing him as King David's representative.

On that day of Jesus' last entry into Jerusalem, people spread their cloaks and leafy branches on the ground. People shouted "Hosanna!" and saw in Jesus the fulfillment of prophecy: he was the one who was coming in the name of David. Within five days, however, the cheers had subsided. His followers had abandoned him, and he was crucified.

Jesus had entered Jerusalem as a king. On the cross on which he was crucified was a sign that proclaimed him as "King of the Jews" (John 19:19). Only later, however, would his kingship be fully understood.

POSTSCRIPT

■ In the pre-Christian Greek and Roman words, the palm leaf was associated with victory. That connotation of the palm leaf can be seen in the motto of the University of Southern California: *Palmam qui meruit ferat* means "Let him bear the palm who has deserved it."

■ In early Christian art and on Christian tombs, images of palms represented martyrs. Those who died for the faith frequently were portrayed as holding palm leaves. Using traditional symbolism, their victory was shown to be one over death and into newness of life.

The Judgment of Rehoboam

AFTER SOLOMON REIGNED over all of Israel for 40 years, he died and was buried in Jerusalem. His son Rehoboam then became king, but he soon made a decision that would tear his kingdom apart.

While Solomon was king, he noted the management skills of a young man named Jeroboam. After the king promoted Jeroboam, the prophet Ahijah told the young man that God would give ten tribes of Israel to him because Solomon had departed from the ways of God. When Solomon heard about this prophecy, he tried to kill Jeroboam, but Jeroboam fled to Egypt. He returned to Israel upon learning that Rehoboam was to be crowned king in Shechem. It was then that Jeroboam and the assembly of Israel came to the new king, asking him to lighten the burden of government that Rehoboam's father, Solomon, had imposed on them, which had been exceedingly harsh. In return for a lighter load, they pledged, "We will serve you" (1 Kings 12:4).

Rehoboam asked for three days to consider their request, during which he consulted with the elders who had counseled his father. They responded with wise advice: Treat them kindly, and they will be your servants forever.

Rehoboam, however, chose to reject their advice. Instead, he asked for the thoughts of some of his friends, with whom he had grown up. They advised a tightening of the screws, so to speak, in order to gain more respect from the people than had been given to his father. They recommended that Rehoboam tell them, "My little finger is thicker than my father's loins. Now, whereas my father laid on you a heavy yoke, I will add to your yoke. My father disciplined you with whips, but I will discipline you with scorpions" (verses 10–11).

Needless to say, this did not go over well. The Israelites under Jeroboam returned home, disavowing their kindred in Judah (the tribe of David, Solomon, and Rehoboam). "What share do we have in David?" they said. "We have no inheritance in the son of Jesse. To your tents, O Israel! Look now to your own house, O David" (verse 16). Thus the tone was set for 300 years of conflict between the two kingdoms (the northern kingdom of Israel comprising ten tribes and the southern kingdom of Judah comprising the tribes of Judah and Benjamin).

Absalom

ABSALOM WAS THE THIRD son of David, born at Hebron before David was anointed king over all Israel at Jerusalem. The Bible says he was handsome: "Now in all Israel there was no one to be praised so much for his beauty as Absalom; from the sole of his foot to the crown of his head there was no blemish in him" (2 Samuel 14:25). Yet he was also proud and vengeful, which ultimately led to his untimely death.

Not long after David's adultery with Bathsheba and his murder of Uriah, David's family spiraled out of control: His oldest son, Amnon, became infatuated with his stepsister Tamar, lured her into his room where he raped her, and then callously spurned her; Absalom, who was Tamar's

brother from the same mother, Maacah, became incensed but bided his time until he killed Amnon two years later. He was then forced to flee to the land of Geshur, where he stayed for three years.

Although David mourned his son Amnon's death, he eventually sent for Absalom, who returned. David, however, refused to see him for a full two years, which probably was a mistake, for it allowed more time for resentment to grow within Absalom's heart. When David finally relented, the two met and seemingly were reconciled.

Absalom Hanging on the Oak Tree *by James Tissot*

The reconciliation did not last long, for Absalom began to spread dissension in the land regarding his father, and after four years, he rallied those loyal to him and had himself crowned king in a public ceremony at Hebron. Word reached David that the people had turned against him, and he fled the capital city. Absalom then entered the city, and adding insult to injury, he publicly went into his father's harem and slept with his concubines.

Absalom left Jerusalem to fight David, but he met his end ignominiously when his horse raced under a great oak tree and his long hair was caught in the branches, leaving him dangling in midair. When Joab, David's general, heard of Absalom's plight, he went and killed the rebel. David's men then threw his body into a pit and covered it with a great heap of stones. Despite Absalom's rebellion, David was greatly saddened by his death, and he mourned, "O my son Absalom, my son, my son Absalom! Would I had died instead of you, O Absalom, my son, my son!" (2 Samuel 18:33)

Lydia Becomes a Believer

A PEBBLE HAD BEEN THROWN into a pond, and the ripples were moving outward. The pond was Jerusalem, and the pebble was Jesus. He had told his disciples they would not only testify for him in the nearby regions of Judaea and Samaria but also "to the ends of the earth" (Acts 1:8), and they were doing exactly that. The Acts of the Apostles chronicles that outward movement. Step by step, group by group, region by region, the Church extended its activity: first, the Samaritans and then Gentile converts; first, the Mediterranean coast and Cyprus and then Asia Minor. What was next? Europe.

It might look like just another place on a map, but to Christian missionaries, Europe was a whole different world. It was Athens, the birthplace of Greek civilization—high philosophy but abhorrent morals. It was Macedonia, the launching pad for Alexander the Great, who spread Greek culture throughout the Middle East. It was Rome, the new magnet for political power. To enter Europe was to step into the dragon's jaws. And that's exactly what had to happen.

On his second mission trip, Paul (now paired with Silas) revisited the churches he had planted in the inland towns of Asia Minor. The intention was to continue north or west to the neighboring regions, but the Spirit "did not allow them" (Acts 16:7). Instead, Paul had a vision of a man calling, "Come over to Macedonia and help us" (verse 9). That meant crossing the Aegean Sea and entering Europe.

Philippi was the leading city of that territory, a colony the Romans had tried to populate with retired army officers. It had a very small Jewish population, apparently lacking the ten men required to form a synagogue. Yet each sabbath, a group of women met by the river for prayer. Among those women was Lydia, a Gentile with a deep respect for the Jewish faith. She was from Asia Minor and worked as a merchant of purple cloth, a pricey commodity in the ancient world.

As Paul talked about Jesus, the Lord "opened her heart" (verse 14). Lydia became a baptized Christian, along with her household (probably she was single but had servants). In gratitude, she urged Paul and his team to stay at her house as they continued to minister in Philippi.

This businesswoman thus became the first recorded person to convert to Christianity in Europe, signaling a new era for Christian ministry.

James, Brother of Jesus

JAMES BECAME A MAJOR leader of the church in Jerusalem. He also wrote a New Testament epistle that bears his name. Nevertheless, we have little record of James before Jesus' crucifixion, and what we have is somewhat negative.

James is listed first among the brothers of Jesus in Matthew 13:55. (It should be noted that Roman Catholics translate the word as "cousins" or "kinsmen," holding that Mary was always a virgin.) On one occasion, Jesus was preaching and healing so steadily that he didn't have time to eat. His family came to "restrain" him, having heard people say, "He has gone out of his mind" (Mark 3:21), but Jesus rebuffed their efforts. John's gospel mentions that Jesus' brothers didn't believe in him (see John 7:5).

That attitude must have changed, because James is identified as a leader—perhaps *the* leader—of the Jerusalem church in the Book of Acts. Is it possible that James was less of a "wanted man" after the Crucifixion because he *wasn't* one of the Twelve? Or did his kinship with Jesus give him a sense of authority? In any case, we find Peter, newly sprung from prison, saying, "Tell this to James and to the believers" (Acts 12:17). When a Church council was held to consider the inclusion of Gentiles, James apparently presided (see Acts 15:13). Later, Paul refers to the heads of the Church as "James, Cephas [Peter], and John" (Galatians 2:9). Note whose name comes first.

The main issue for Christians at that time was the role of the Jewish law. It was generally agreed that non-Jews could follow Jesus if they adopted the Jewish faith, with its various rules and customs. But what if they didn't? Could they continue to be Gentiles and still be Christians? Paul vehemently said yes, and many of his epistles argue this point. James might have taken a more cautious view. As head of the church in Jerusalem, the heart of Judaism, he probably wanted to keep the Christian faith connected to its Jewish roots.

We see this concern in the epistle of James, a practical guide for Christian believers who want to live righteously in a difficult world. While Paul was trumpeting salvation by faith alone, not by doing the works of the law (see Ephesians 2:8–9), James chose a different emphasis. "What good is it ... if you say you have faith but do not have works?" (James 2:14). His letter includes the famous phrase, "So faith by itself, if it has no works, is dead" (verse 17).

The First Epistle to the Corinthians

PAUL PLANTED A CHRISTIAN community in Corinth around A.D. 50, a city that the gifted Christian speaker Apollos, and perhaps Peter as well, would visit shortly after Paul's departure. The "church" in Corinth consisted of a number of smaller groups that met in the homes of the wealthier members and occasionally assembled as a full congregation in the house of Gaius.

A number of these converts had difficulty leaving behind their pre-Christian ways. The cultural bent toward competition persisted as believers tried to outdo one another in displays of spirituality or claimed the prestige of being associated with the more impressive Christian teacher. The Corinthian society's more relaxed attitude toward sexuality continued to show up within the church. The wealthy patrons of the house churches tended to treat the celebration of the Lord's Supper—the rite that was to exhibit Christian unity—like the banquets they threw for one another before their conversion, saving few scraps for the poorer members of the church.

These wealthier members also tried to defend participation in the private parties of non-Christians who remained important business partners and even in the rituals that infused the civic life of Corinth. The problem, of course, was that these events involved some degree of participation in idolatry. But, they argued, if they knew that there was only one God, what possible harm could come from going through such motions?

These and other problems came to Paul's attention through two separate and simultaneous "embassies" from Corinth—a further indication of the divisions in the congregation. In First Corinthians, he seeks to restore unity by stressing that all Christian teachers work toward a common goal, and he calls for consideration of one's fellow believers above oneself. This involves seeking spiritual gifts that encourage others and considering the impact of one's behavior on those who are most vulnerable, such as the poor. Following Jesus, he argues, means not insisting on one's own freedoms and "rights" but rather giving ground where it will serve to nurture harmony and holiness.

POSTSCRIPT

■ "First" Corinthians was not Paul's first letter to these house churches. He makes mention of a previous letter (see 1 Corinthians 5:9) that occasioned some misunderstanding that he clarifies in this letter.

The Assyrian Empire

BEGINNING IN THE eighth century B.C., a series of superpowers dominated the Middle East. The first of these was Assyria.

Living by the Tigris River in what is now Iraq, the Assyrians had a long history, going back to the third millennium B.C. Like other nations in the region, they rose and declined, gaining territory and losing it. In 745 B.C., Tiglath-pileser III (also known as *Ful*) took the throne and moved quickly to dominate the entire region of Mesopotamia. King Ahaz of Judah actually asked for his help against Syria and Israel (a move Isaiah warned against), and the Assyrians gladly obliged. Damascus fell to the Assyrian juggernaut in 732 B.C., and Samaria, capital of the northern kingdom of Israel, fell in 722.

The Assyrians had a brutal policy of deportation and assimilation. Not satisfied with subjugating a nation they transported many of its people to other territories and replaced them with other captured peoples. Thus the ten tribes that made up the northern kingdom of Israel were "lost" to history. Scattered among other Assyrian-controlled lands, they intermarried and lost their ethnic identity. The new residents of northern Palestine were brought in from Babylonia, Elam, Syria, and Arabia. Their descendants became the Samaritans.

After making a move to conquer Babylon to the east, the Assyrians came back to threaten Judah, which was now ruled by the faithful Hezekiah. Through prayer, Judah was miraculously delivered from an Assyrian siege. Later, in the 660s B.C., the Assyrians moved on to conquer Egypt, thus extending their kingdom from the Persian Gulf to the Nile. Yet the reenergized nation of Babylon was soon nipping at their heels, swallowing up some Assyrian territory in the east. The Assyrian capital, Nineveh, fell to the Babylonians and Medes in 612, and Babylon won a decisive battle at Carchemish in 605. Suddenly Babylon was the new superpower.

The Assyrians left a legacy as ruthless warriors, greedy for territory, wealth, and power. But we also have evidence of a rich Assyrian culture from an ancient library excavated at the site of Nineveh, including medical, mathematical, astronomical, and even religious documents.

POSTSCRIPT

◼ In Assyrian annals, King Sargon II boasts: "I besieged and conquered Samaria, led away as booty 27,290 inhabitants... I rebuilt it better than before and put in it people from countries I had conquered."

Parable of the Pharisee and Tax Collector

Arrogance and contemptuousness can easily be disguised in spiritual trappings, and Jesus' parable of the Pharisee and tax collector illustrates that lesson well. Concerned with those who saw themselves as righteous while looking at others contemptuously, Jesus told a story of a Pharisee and tax collector who went to pray.

From the beginning of the story, Jesus used the stereotypes of his society. The Pharisee clearly represented the seemingly righteous, and the tax collector, a collaborator with the Romans, would have been seen as unrighteous. As the two prayed, the Pharisee said, "God, I thank you that I am not like other people: thieves, rogues, adulterers, or even like this tax collector. I fast twice a week; I give a tenth of all my income" (Luke 18:11–12). The tax collector, conversely, would not even presume to look toward heaven, but he cried out, "God, be merciful to me, a sinner!" (verse 13).

Pharisee and the Publican *by James Tissot*

Jesus finished by saying that the latter man went away justified before God, "for all who exalt themselves will be humbled, but all who humble themselves will be exalted" (verse 14). Because sincerity and humility are so integral to this parable, within the Eastern Orthodox Church this parable is read during the time that leads to Lent. There it is seen as portraying the only appropriate way to approach God, and that is through the words of humility: "God, be merciful to me, a sinner!"

POSTSCRIPT

■ The gospels record 30 parables, most of which are found in Matthew and Luke. The Gospel of John has none.

■ The parable of the Pharisee and tax collector appears only in the Gospel of Luke.

Showdown on Mount Carmel

ABOUT A HALF CENTURY after Israel and Judah split from each other, Ahab became king in Israel and established a standard of wickedness previously unknown even by the ungodly standards of that kingdom. The Bible says, "Ahab . . . did evil in the sight of the Lord more than all who were before him" (1 Kings 16:30). He was the first king to establish the worship of the Canaanite god Baal as the official state religion, under the influence of his wife, Jezebel. He set up worship centers to Baal and Baal's consort, Asherah, and supported 450 prophets of Baal and 400 prophets of Asherah.

Into this situation came Elijah, a mighty prophet of the Lord. God had placed on Israel a three-year drought, which was a great hardship in an agrarian society. At the end of this time, God sent Elijah to Ahab. Elijah issued a challenge to Ahab's priests: They would set up identical altars to Baal and Yahweh and prepare them for sacrifice; whichever god would send fire down on his altar would be acknowledged as the true God.

The prophets of Baal tried all day to bring down fire from Baal to his altar on Mount Carmel, but to no avail. As the day progressed, Elijah taunted them, saying, "Cry aloud! Surely he is a god; either he is meditating, or he has wandered away, or he is on a journey, or perhaps he is asleep and must be awakened" (1 Kings 18:27). The prophets grew more frenzied—shouting, dancing, even cutting themselves with knives and spears. Still, nothing happened.

When Elijah's turn came, he had them soak the sacrificial bull and the altar with water in order to make the miracle, when it came, all the more remarkable. He called on God, and God answered dramatically with fire from heaven that consumed the sacrifice, the altar, and even the water that flooded the altar.

When this happened, all the people fell facedown and cried out, "The Lord indeed is God; the Lord indeed is God" (verse 39). Elijah ordered them to seize the prophets of Baal, and he had them all killed.

In a fitting final touch, it soon began to rain; the three-year drought was over. In the climactic showdown between the true God and Baal, Yahweh decisively showed himself to be greater than the god of the Canaanites.

Solomon

Solomon was a complex character. On the one hand, he embodied great wisdom and devotion to God. On the other hand, he allowed his heart to be led astray by his foolish marriages and worship of pagan gods. The tragic consequence of his idolatry was that after his death Israel would be split into two rival kingdoms, Israel (with the ten northern tribes) and Judah (with the two southern tribes).

Solomon Is Made King *by James Tissot*

Solomon was the son of David and Bathsheba. He became the third king of Israel. At the beginning of his reign, he ruled wisely, and so God blessed him with more wisdom, as well as fabulous wealth. He also authored parts of the Bible and built a magnificent temple for the Lord. Yet even early in his political career Solomon made poor choices, such as marrying foreign women who brought idolatry into his kingdom.

Meanwhile, Solomon's fame spread far and wide even beyond Israel. The Bible says his wisdom "surpassed the wisdom of all the people of the east, and all the wisdom of Egypt" (1 Kings 4:30). The Queen of Sheba traveled 1,500 miles from her kingdom in southern Arabia to witness for herself the wisdom of this famous king, and he obviously amazed her, for she declared, "I did not believe the reports until I came and my own eyes had seen it. . . . your wisdom and prosperity far surpass the report that I had heard" (1 Kings 10:7).

Solomon's reign came to a tragic end, however. He took 700 wives and 300 concubines, most from foreign lands, and they turned his heart away from the Lord. What began as a reign of peace and prosperity became a rule in which Solomon was pitted against many enemies from within and without his kingdom. But even more tragic was his own internal strife, bereft of the presence of the Lord.

POSTSCRIPT

■ The name *Solomon* means "peaceable." He ruled Israel from 970 to 930 B.C.

Paul Performs an Exorcism

WITH THE CONVERSION of Lydia and her household, Paul had established a base of operations in Philippi. He continued to meet at the "place of prayer" (Acts 16:16) by the river with the Jewish women who met there every sabbath day. But a demon-possessed slave-girl began to follow Paul and his team, shouting, "These men are slaves of the Most High God, who proclaim to you a way of salvation" (verse 17). This continued on several occasions, and Paul was "very much annoyed" (verse 18).

Why? Wasn't she telling the truth about them? Paul often described himself as God's slave, and his mission was proclamation. Yet Paul was concerned about the public image of Christianity, and having a demonic Sibyl as a barker wouldn't help matters. This is not to mention the annoyance of having this announcement shouted at full volume while trying to engage in conversation. And surely, as he saw this slave-girl used by her owners as a fortune-teller, he would have been distressed by her situation. But what probably annoyed him the most was that she declared that they were preaching *a* way of salvation—that is, one way among many other ways.

Finally, Paul turned and ordered the demon cut of her in the name of Jesus Christ. The demon left her, but that was just the beginning of Paul's troubles in Philippi. The girl's owners had made a good bit of money from her fortune-telling, and now that revenue stream had dried up. They took Paul and Silas to court for "disturbing our city" (verse 20). The missionaries were beaten and imprisoned.

It's interesting to compare this account with other biblical exorcisms. Demons seemed to know quite well who Jesus was, and they feared him. In fact, the "legion" of demons in the country of the Gerasenes used the same term that we hear in Philippi, calling Jesus the Son of the "Most High God" and begging him not to torment them (see Luke 8:26–33). Jesus used his own spiritual authority to exorcise demons, but the apostles invoked Jesus' name. In fact, one group of exorcists tried to cast out a demon in the name of "Jesus whom Paul proclaims," but the demon attacked them, saying, "Jesus I know, and Paul I know; but who are you?" (Acts 19:13, 15).

POSTSCRIPT

■ Literally the slave-girl is described as having a "python" spirit. The Greek and Roman god Apollo was associated with the python and also with fortune-telling.

Barnabas

BARNABAS AROSE as one of the most prominent members of the early Church. He was an associate and mentor of the Apostle Paul. His given name was Joseph, but people knew him as Barnabas, which means "Son of Encouragement." That's a quality that characterizes this man throughout the biblical record.

We first meet Barnabas at the offering plate. The early Christians were giving freely of their possessions to support the poor, and Barnabas was no exception. In fact, he sold a field he owned and brought the proceeds to the apostles (see Acts 4:36).

His next task of encouragement was the most crucial. Saul, later known as Paul, had been a vicious persecutor of Christians, but suddenly he was claiming a miraculous conversion, and he wanted to meet the apostles. Naturally they would suspect a trap, but Barnabas sought out Paul, befriended him, and vouched for him among the brethren, forging a valuable connection between Paul and the original disciples of Jesus.

Barnabas served as an important liaison in the Church's ministry to the Gentiles. The "mother church" in Jerusalem heard that the maverick church at Antioch was sending missionaries to Gentile areas. They sent Barnabas to check it out. Instead of squelching this enterprise as "unauthorized," he encouraged it. Then he went to Tarsus, Paul's hometown, to find Paul and bring him back to Antioch, where they taught in the Antioch church and were eventually sent out as missionaries (see Acts 11:22–26). On their first journey they visited Barnabas's homeland of Cyprus and continued on to several towns in Asia Minor (modern Turkey). They eventually returned to Jerusalem to argue the case for ministry to the Gentiles.

As they prepared for a second journey, a dispute arose. A young cousin of Barnabas, John Mark, had bailed out from their first journey. Barnabas the Encourager wanted to give his cousin a second chance, but Paul adamantly refused. It was a deal breaker. Paul chose another partner, and Barnabas went with John Mark on a separate mission trip to Cyprus (see Acts 15:36–41).

POSTSCRIPT

■ Crowds in the town of Lystra thought Barnabas and Paul were Greek gods (see Acts 14:12). They thought Paul was Hermes, the speaker/messenger. But Barnabas they hailed as Zeus, the chief god, probably because he was older or larger or seemed to be in charge.

The Second Epistle to the Corinthians

IN THE TIME BETWEEN the writing of First and Second Corinthians, certain matters went from bad to worse in Corinth. Some traveling Christian leaders raised questions about Paul's legitimacy as an apostle. These teachers were either better equipped or just more willing to play to the expectations of the cosmopolitan Corinthians, making impressive displays of public speaking and spiritual prowess to win them over. When Paul made an unplanned stop in Corinth, one church member challenged him so harshly that Paul abruptly left Corinth and sent back a strong letter, now lost, calling the congregation to discipline this person. Titus, a coworker of Paul's who carried this letter to Corinth, returned with a positive report that the majority of the congregation was still standing by Paul's side.

Paul wrote Second Corinthians (now the fourth letter to the community) to solidify this reconciliation and to address some root problems. The believers were still measuring their religious leaders' divine gifts and legitimacy by outward appearances—whether they delivered flawless speeches that delighted the ears, projected an impressive image, or visibly "played up" their contact with the divine. Paul argues, on the contrary, that it is the inner transformation of the person into the likeness and character of Christ that is the measure of God's gifts and the legitimacy of a preacher, something that is usually seen in the midst of weakness and hardship. In the face of death, all human strengths are for nothing: The inner working of God is what counts for eternity.

It seems that Paul won back his congregation. He visited them a third time, and they showed their goodwill by participating in Paul's collection of relief funds for the poor among the Christians in Jerusalem.

POSTSCRIPT

▪ Paul's collection for the poor in Jerusalem was an important symbol of the solidarity of Gentile Christians converted by him with the "home church" in Jerusalem, comprised mainly of Jewish Christians. The acceptance of these funds by the Jerusalem church would be, for Paul, an important expression of the unity between Jews and Gentiles for which he strove throughout his ministry.

▪ The problems that the Corinthian churches had with their leaders did not disappear entirely. Around A.D. 95, some junior members of the congregation deposed their duly appointed leaders. Clement, a leader in the church at Rome, wrote a lengthy letter to them in which he referred to the community's earlier revolt against Paul and the letters Paul wrote in response, addressing the problems of divisions in their church.

The Babylonian Empire

THE ORIGINS OF BABYLON go about as far back in the history of the Middle East as you can go. Babylon was possibly the world's first city. The biblical story of the Tower of Babel connects with Babylon. Historians trace the original Babylonian settlement as far back as 3200 B.C. Various people-groups migrated to the southern Euphrates region and took power for a time—the Sumerians, Akkadians, Amorites, Hittites, and later the Chaldeans. These peoples all brought elements of language, culture, and religion to forge the Babylonian identity.

The name *Babylon* refers to the city, the region (the eastern corner of the Fertile Crescent), and the empire that once ruled much of the Middle East. The city of Ur, Abraham's hometown, was in the region of Babylon, and excavations at that site reveal a highly advanced culture in the 21st century B.C.

In the seventh century B.C., the once-proud Babylonians found themselves vassals of the neighboring Assyrians. Yet, just when Assyrian power was at its height—their empire stretching as far as Egypt—the Babylonians rebelled. Allying with the Medes, they conquered the Assyrian capital in 612 B.C. and continued westward to put down the stragglers (and the Egyptians) at Carchemish in 605. In essence, Babylon inherited the Assyrian Empire, and at their helm was King Nebuchadnezzar II, an arrogant, powerful, and effective leader.

His conquest of Judah came in three waves. The first, in 605, made Judah a vassal state, but he kept it mostly intact; some of its best and brightest young people (including Daniel), however, were transported to Babylon. A second invasion, from 599 to 598, involved a siege of Jerusalem and the installation of a new king over Judah, Zedekiah, a puppet of Babylon. But Zedekiah rebelled in the next decade, and the full fury of Babylon was unleashed. Jerusalem was destroyed in 586 B.C., its temple plundered and burned, and its people carried off.

Thus begins the period of the Babylonian Exile, which the Hebrew prophets foretold as God's punishment—but always with the promise that it would end. While the Assyrians tried to erase their captives' identities, the Babylonians merely relocated them. Most of the Jews lived together by the river Chebar in Babylon.

After Nebuchadnezzar's death, the empire weakened with a quick succession of ineffective rulers. For one of these, Belshazzar, Daniel interpreted the "writing on the wall"—a message of doom written by a mysterious hand. The Persians were at the gates and ready to take over.

The Cleansing of the Temple

THE FOUR GOSPELS present Jesus in a wide range of situations: Jesus encouraged those who were persecuted to "turn the other cheek." Jesus shared a loving parable of a lost lamb. Jesus told his disciples to let children come to him.

Meanwhile, a different picture of Jesus, one that might be uncomfortable to some of us, can be found in all four gospels when Jesus enters the temple and recognizes the need for change. John says Jesus entered the temple grounds with a whip made out of cords—a detail that Mark omits (see John 2:15).

"And he entered the temple and began to drive out those who were selling and those who were buying in the temple, and he overturned the tables of the money changers and the seats of those who sold doves; and he would not allow anyone to carry anything through the temple. He was teaching and saying, 'Is it not written, "My house shall be called a house of prayer for all the nations"? But you have made it a den of robbers'" (Mark 11:15–17).

From this point on, according to Mark, Matthew, and Luke, the chief priests and scribes tried to find a way to kill Jesus. He had struck at the heart of their sins—greed. Evidently they could no longer tolerate his disruption of their status among the populace and their financial dealings with the people. Therefore, in their eyes, the best solution was for Jesus to die.

Most Bibles refer to this passage as "the cleansing of the temple." Jesus' actions are seen as a cleansing: He wanted to rid the temple of unfair prices and practices. But to the Jews who had made pilgrimages to this temple three times a year, to those who exchanged money and sold animals to these weary travelers, and to the priests and to the pious, this was no cleansing. It was an assault not just on their traditions but also on the way they viewed God.

Jesus emphasized that the temple had become too much a business ("a den of thieves"; Jeremiah 7:11) and that it had exploited the poor, when it should have been "a house of prayer for all nations" (Isaiah 56:7). Jesus' words and actions questioned the faithfulness of those who profited by the temple.

Quite possibly the same people Jesus angered at the temple became the mob who cried for his crucifixion.

God Whispers to Elijah

THE CONFRONTATION BETWEEN Elijah and the 450 prophets of Baal on Mount Carmel was high drama, climaxing with God sending down a consuming fire from heaven in a decisive defeat of Baal and his prophets and a vindication of Elijah, the prophet of the Lord. The adrenaline must have been pumping overtime for Elijah, because the Bible says he outran King Ahab's chariot as they returned to Jezreel.

The high, however, soon wore off, and Elijah's emotions plunged into the depths of despair. Ahab had informed his wife, Jezebel, of what Elijah had done, including killing the 450 prophets of Baal, and she was furious. She vowed to kill Elijah, and so he fled to Beersheba at the southern tip of Judah. He left his servant there and went on a day's journey into the wilderness. He was exhausted, physically and emotionally, and he cried out to God, "It is enough; now, O Lord, take away my life" (1 Kings 19:4). Then he lay down to sleep and perhaps never expected to wake up.

Elijah Dwelleth in a Cave
by James Tissot

God, however, had plans for Elijah. An angel woke him and fed him and gave him water, and then he fell back asleep. This happened again, and the angel directed him to go further into the wilderness. For 40 days and nights the angel provided for him until he reached Mount Horeb (i.e., Mount Sinai), where God had met Moses and given the Ten Commandments centuries earlier. Elijah entered a cave and slept.

Here, Elijah experienced a whirlwind, an earthquake, and a fire, but God was not in any of these natural phenomena. But after the fire, there was a still, small voice, like a soft whisper. God asked him, "What are you doing here, Elijah?" (verse 13), and Elijah answered that he had been very zealous for God, but that the forces against him were too great and that he alone was left of the faithful. He was demoralized.

God responded with encouraging words, telling him that there were still 7,000 people in Israel who had not bowed their knee to Baal. God instructed him to travel to Damascus and anoint Hazael as king over Aram, Jehu as king over Israel, and Elisha as a prophet and his successor. He promised that, between the three of them, they would destroy the followers of Baal. After hearing God whisper these words of encouragement to him, Elijah was no longer a demoralized prophet welcoming death; instead, he pressed on with his prophetic duties until the end of his life.

Elijah

ELIJAH WAS ONE of the most important prophets in the Bible. God sent him to preach to the Israelites in a time of spiritual crisis and to confront King Ahab and his wife, Jezebel, about their apostasy. Jezebel was a Phoenician princess who brought with her the formal worship of Baal and other Canaanite deities, and this brought about the lowest point in Israel's history up to that time. Through Elijah—and Elisha after him—God performed a series of miracles, the likes of which had not been experienced for centuries.

Elijah began his ministry by announcing a drought—devastating in a land dependent on crops for food. The cause for this drought was the widespread idolatry in Israel. The drought ended when Elijah defeated the priests of Baal on Mount Carmel in an astounding display of the power of Yahweh.

During the drought, Elijah performed an equally amazing miracle in Zarephath, in Sidon. The Lord had told Elijah, who was from Tishbe in Gilead, to go immediately to Zarephath and live there, where a widow would feed him. Although the widow and her son had hardly enough to feed themselves, the widow obeyed Elijah and gave him food. The first miracle in this encounter with the widow was that her jar of meal "was not emptied, neither did the jug of oil fail" (1 Kings 17:16). But a greater miracle was to come. When her son perished from an illness, the widow accused Elijah of being the cause of his death, but Elijah carried the body to his own bed, where he "stretched himself upon the child three times," crying out, "O Lord my God, let this child's life come into him again" (verse 21). The Lord listened to Elijah's plea and restored the child's life. The widow then said to Elijah, "Now I know that you are a man of God, and that the word of the Lord in your mouth is truth" (verse 24).

Elijah performed many more miracles, and more and more people believed that he was God's chosen servant. Through the centuries, others, including other writers of the Bible, have exalted him as one of the great Hebrew prophets. In fact, the prophet Malachi foretold, "Lo, I will send you the prophet Elijah before the great and terrible day of the Lord comes" (Malachi 4:5). And Jesus said of John the Baptist, "For all the prophets and the law prophesied until John came; and if you are willing to accept it, he is Elijah who is to come" (Matthew 11:13–14).

So great was Elijah as God's servant that he actually did not die. Instead, God took him up to heaven in a whirlwind, accompanied by a fiery chariot and horses.

Paul and Silas in Prison

Paul had cast a demon out of a slave-girl, robbing her owners of the profit they made from her fortune-telling. They dragged Paul and his associate, Silas, to the magistrates. As Roman citizens, they had a right to a fair trial, but they were seen as foreigners disturbing the city. The judges had them beaten and thrown into prison.

Don't think of a modern penitentiary. Ancient prisons were literally holes in the ground—dark, dank, with chains cemented to rock walls. Cast into the "innermost" cell (Acts 16:24)—farthest from freedom—Paul and Silas had their feet in stocks. And yet they still sang.

The other prisoners listened as the two Christians prayed to their God and sang hymns. These might have been some favorite psalms, but it's more likely that they used newer Christian lyrics sung in a Greek musical style. (*Hymn* is a Greek word, and elsewhere it's differentiated from *psalm*. Besides, in a non-Jewish city, they would use a medium that would connect with those around them.)

Suddenly there was an earthquake. Chains came loose; doors sprang open; yet none of the prisoners escaped. The jailer rushed in, expecting to find an empty prison—something he would be executed for. And so he drew his sword to kill himself, but Paul shouted, assuring him that all prisoners were accounted for.

What's the greater miracle here: the earthquake or the fact that no one escaped? Or perhaps the fact that Paul and Silas could sing in such a situation? Is it possible that the other prisoners were so awestruck by the spiritual power of these Christians that they would stay in prison when they had a chance to escape?

The jailer was certainly struck by the scene. In fact, he took Paul and Silas out of the prison and into his own home. "Sirs, what must I do to be saved?" he asked them (verse 30). Had he been listening to the fortune-telling slave-girl, who had said that Paul and Silas were proclaiming "a way of salvation"? Somehow their calm demeanor, their honesty and honor, or their sheer joy indicated that they had something he needed. Their response: "Believe on the Lord Jesus, and you will be saved, you and your household" (verse 31). That is precisely what happened.

In the morning, perhaps fearing that the earthquake was a bad omen, the magistrate ordered the release of the two missionaries. But Paul and Silas identified themselves as Roman citizens and demanded that the judges come in person and apologize, which they did.

John Mark

JOHN MARK WAS THE AUTHOR of the second gospel in the New Testament. He was a member of the early Church and was related to Barnabas. He also became a valuable associate of both Paul and Peter.

In Mark's account of Jesus' arrest, chaos breaks out. Judas the betrayer and soldiers following him invade the peaceful Garden of Gethsemane. Peter immediately draws a sword but Jesus forbids violence. So the disciples scatter. Interestingly, Mark's gospel has a detail that the other accounts omit: "A certain young man was following [Jesus], wearing nothing but a linen cloth. They caught hold of him, but he left the linen cloth and ran off naked" (Mark 14:51–52). Some scholars suggest that this is Mark's own signature, in the fashion of ancient writers, identifying himself in the story as this nameless "young man."

Whether this is true or not, his mother, Mary, was a faithful follower of Jesus, and she had a house where Christians often met in Jerusalem. (This leads to some speculation: Could this house have been the site of the Last Supper? Was Mark the water carrier the disciples followed to get there? Did this teenager run to the garden to warn Jesus of Judas's betrayal?)

Regardless, Luke identifies John Mark as a cousin of Barnabas, who took him, along with Paul, on a mission trip to Cyprus and Asia Minor. But Mark apparently abandoned this company soon after they left Cyprus. This put him on the outs with Paul, who refused to take him along on a second journey. Barnabas stood up for his young cousin, which caused an agonizing split with Paul. Mark then continued with Barnabas to Cyprus. (We might guess that this was an easier training ground for Mark, since it was Barnabas's homeland. Mark might have had family there as well.)

Mark stayed active in Christian ministry, and though the New Testament is silent about this matter, there must have been an emotional reconciliation between Mark and Paul, for Paul would later write to Timothy from prison: "Get Mark and bring him with you, for he is useful in my ministry" (2 Timothy 4:11). The relationship between Mark and Paul tells us that even deeply committed Christians can be at odds, but even more importantly that Christ can heal any broken relationship.

In his first epistle, Peter sends greetings from Mark, calling him "my son" (1 Peter 5:13). We know from later Church leaders that Mark worked closely with Peter. In fact, one ancient writer calls Mark's gospel "the memoirs of Peter."

The Epistle to the Galatians

ONE OF THE MOST DIFFICULT questions faced by the early Church was whether or not Gentile converts to Christianity had to follow Jewish law. Would Christians be part of the people of God on the basis of their trust in and obedience to Jesus or on the basis of their taking on the qualities and behaviors that had characterized God's historic people, Israel? The latter would include things such as circumcision, avoiding certain foods as "unclean," and observing the Jewish sabbath. Many Jewish Christians favored this latter position and viewed Paul's mission with deep suspicion, since he did not teach that Jewish law should continue to regulate life among converts.

Some Jewish Christian teachers set out to "clean up" Paul's work. At some point, they arrived among the Christians in the cities of Galatia, where Paul had been active early in his ministry. They taught that circumcision was a necessary mark for those who wished to belong among the children of Abraham, the heirs of God's promises, and they marshaled scriptural support for their argument. They may also have taught that living by the specific rules of Jewish law would provide a disciplined path to attain virtue and rise above the power of sinful desires, cravings, and impulses. They certainly called Paul's authority and understanding of the gospel into question.

Galatians is Paul's spirited, three-pronged response. He first defends the divine source of his commission and his understanding of the gospel and its significance for the ongoing role of the Torah. When Paul himself had been most zealous for the law, he found that he was most opposed to the work of God in Jesus, persecuting the very people of God (1:6—2:10). He argues that Jesus' death was the means by which the promise of God would come to all people, Jew and Gentile alike. Trying to secure that promise through circumcision and other laws only made a mockery of Jesus' death (2:15–21; 5:2–6). Finally, he reminds the believers that trusting Jesus has opened them up to God's gift of the Spirit, and the Spirit will empower and guide them to die to their self-centered impulses and to live lives pleasing to God (5:22–26).

While non-Christian Jews would have been much happier with the rival teachers' version of Christianity, Paul's insistence that the Jewish law had played out its limited role in God's plan opened the way for the Church to become a multiethnic movement in which neither Jew nor Gentile had the position of privilege over the other.

The Persian Empire

EACH CENTURY, it seemed, there was a new superpower dominating the Middle East. First, the Assyrians built an empire from the Persian Gulf to the Nile. Then the Babylonians swallowed them up. In 539 B.C., it was time for the Persians to take over.

The Book of Daniel gives us the story in vivid tones. Belshazzar, crown prince of Babylon, was partying with a thousand of his closest friends when he saw a mysterious hand writing on the wall. Only Daniel could interpret the message it left: "God has numbered the days of your king-dom . . . your kingdom is divided and given to the Medes and Persians" (Daniel 5:26, 28). The story goes on to say that Belshazzar was killed "that very night" (verse 30), and the Persians then took over. And history con-firms that this conquest was amazingly easy. Babylonian troops defected to the Persian side rather than dying to protect their self-serving prince.

Persia was a land just east of the Fertile Crescent, north of the Persian Gulf and south of the Caspian Sea. It is the area of modern Iran. The Persian ruler who launched the empire was Cyrus the Great, skilled at diplomacy, organization, and warfare. He had brought the Medes into the Persian Empire with a style that was much kinder and gentler than that of the Assyrians or Babylonians. Cyrus seemed to appreciate national identity. He wanted people to return to their homelands and prosper there, so they could be loyal subjects of a Persian governor and faithful taxpayers. Almost immediately he set in motion plans to send the Jews back to rebuild Jerusalem.

Sheshbazzar and Zerubbabel led a group of Jews back to Jerusalem in 537 B.C., but they found the rebuilding difficult. At the urging of the prophet Haggai, the temple was finally reconstructed in 515. The scribe Ezra brought back more exiles in 458 B.C., and the bureaucrat Nehemiah did the same in 444 B.C. Many Jews, however, remained in Babylon or Persia, including Daniel and Esther.

Persia had a series of strong rulers following Cyrus. Darius the Great took power in 522 B.C. and extended the empire's territory into India and Asia Minor. A system of local leadership allowed this massive expansion. Dari-us is the one who threw the aged Daniel into the lions' den and regretted it later. Xerxes became king in 486 and tried to extend the empire into Greece but failed. He is probably the king in the Esther story. Coming to power in 465, Artaxerxes was the king whom Nehemiah served.

From 333 to 323 B.C., Alexander the Great defeated the Persians, whose territory was divided among his generals after his death.

The Sheep and Goats

LATE IN JESUS' EARTHLY ministry, when he was teaching on the Mount of Olives, he told his disciples a story about sheep and goats that serves as an explicit reminder that faith needs to shape how people interact with others. The story is eschatological in nature, focusing on the end of the world and the last judgment that Jesus will bring.

"When the Son of Man comes in his glory," Jesus said, "and all the angels with him, then he will sit on the throne of his glory. All the nations will be gathered before him, and he will separate people one from another as a shepherd separates the sheep from the goats, and he will put the sheep at his right hand and the goats at the left. Then the king will say to those at his right hand, 'Come, you that are blessed by my Father, inherit the kingdom prepared for you from the foundation of the world; for I was hungry and you gave me food, I was thirsty and you gave me something to drink, I was a stranger and you welcomed me, I was naked and you gave me clothing, I was sick and you took care of me, I was in prison and you visited me'" (Matthew 25:31–36).

The righteous ask King Jesus when they have served him in these ways. They seem to question whether they are worthy. But the king responds, "Truly I tell you, just as you did it to one of the least of these who are members of my family, you did it to me" (verse 40).

When King Jesus turns to those represented by goats at his left hand, it is clear that they have not served others in the way of the righteous. And the result for them will be eternal punishment, just as the result for the righteous will be entrance into his kingdom.

The story is not a parable or an allegory. Although it begins with a discussion of sheep and goats, those words are dropped after the initial verses because it is obvious that what is being discussed is the final judgment. Jesus points to the importance of kindness and mercy, of simple acts of love and charity, of reaching out to the most vulnerable in society. Jesus also points to the presumptions that humans have; what awaits the "sheep" and "goats" astonishes both of them.

It should no longer surprise Jesus' followers, however, that he places a high premium on helping the sick, the poor, the hungry, the thirsty, and the imprisoned—for this was a major focus of his own life.

Naboth's Vineyard

NABOTH WAS A SMALL landowner who owned a vineyard in Jezreel next to Ahab's palace. King Ahab wanted Naboth's vineyard in order to plant a vegetable garden. Day and night, Ahab thought about Naboth's property. He desired the vineyard so badly that he offered Naboth a better one in another location. The king was even willing to compensate Naboth monetarily. Naboth, however, refused to sell, saying, "The Lord forbid that I should give you my ancestral inheritance" (1 Kings 21:3). Selling such land was expressly prohibited in the Law of Moses, which said, "No inheritance of the Israelites shall be transferred from one tribe to another; for all Israelites shall retain the inheritance of their ancestral tribes" (Numbers 36:7).

When Naboth refused, Ahab petulantly returned to his house and sulked. His wife, Jezebel, asked what the problem was, and he told her his dilemma. Jezebel did not feel as helpless as her husband: She did not hesitate to get the vineyard for him by arranging for two "scoundrels" (some versions say "worthless men") to falsely accuse Naboth of cursing God and the king (1 Kings 21:10). They did so, and Naboth was dragged out of the city and stoned to death. Jezebel then informed Ahab that he was now free to take the vineyard, which he did.

God's response to these actions was to send the prophet Elijah to King Ahab and pronounce a punishment on him and Jezebel. The message was one of doom for Ahab: "In the place where dogs licked up the blood of Naboth, dogs will also lick up your blood"

Jezebel and Ahab Meeting Elijah in Naboth's Vineyard by Frank Dicksee

(verse 19). And there was a similar message concerning Jezebel: "The dogs shall eat Jezebel within the bounds of Jezreel" (verse 23).

Both prophecies came true. Ahab was killed in battle by a random arrow shot by an enemy archer, and we read that "the dogs licked up his blood, and the prostitutes washed themselves in it" (1 Kings 22:38). Several years later, Jehu, who had a commission from God to kill all the household of Ahab, told two eunuchs from Jezebel's household to throw Jezebel out of an upper-story window, which they did. She died with her blood spattered everywhere and horses trampling on her corpse. Within a short time, dogs had eaten all her remains except for her skull, hands, and feet.

Ahab

AHAB AND HIS FATHER, Omri, established standards of wickedness unprecedented among earlier kings. Both made their mark on the international stage, and both are among the few Israelite kings mentioned in extrabiblical texts of the time. The Bible's verdict on each is that they did more evil "than all who were before him" (1 Kings 16:25, 30).

While Asa was king in Judah, Ahab succeeded his father to the throne in Israel. Many times in Israel's history, an assassin would murder the king and seize the throne, unlike the succession of David's heirs in Judah. In Ahab's case, however, the imperial transition was peaceful, and Ahab began a 22-year reign in Samaria (874–853 B.C.).

Ahab married Jezebel, a Phoenician princess who brought Baal-worship to Israel. Ahab then made Baal-worship the official state religion. In

effect, this was the first time that this had ever been done. Ahab erected an altar and built a temple for Baal-Melcarth in Samaria, the capital city of the northern kingdom of Israel. He employed 450 prophets of Baal and 400 prophets of Baal's consort, Asherah, and established shrines to both throughout the land.

Ahab also constructed an ivory house for himself, as well as several cities (see 1 Kings 22:39). Although he kept the capital in Samaria, his royal residence was in Jezreel in the plain of Esdraelon. The highlights of his military campaigns were his three engagements with King Ben-hadad I of Damascus. The first two

Elijah Denounces Ahab

ended favorably for Ahab, but the prophet Micaiah warned him that an expedition against Damascus a third time would fail. In Ramoth-gilead it did fail, when an arrow struck Ahab between his scale armor and his breastplate even though he had disguised himself. And so Ahab died as Elijah had prophesied (see 1 Kings 21:19), and he was buried in Samaria.

POSTSCRIPT

■ Assyrian monuments, including the Monolith Inscription, feature Ahab's military clash with the forces of Shalmaneser III. The Monolith Inscription resides in the British Museum.

Paul Goes Before the Areopagus

BY THE TIME the Apostle Paul arrived in Athens, the Golden Age of Greek civilization had passed four centuries earlier. Yet even though the city had now become a minor player within the vast Roman Empire, the Athenians still treasured their heritage as a center of learning, a birthplace of democracy, and a patron of the arts.

Speaking about Jesus in the local synagogue and in the public market-place, Paul found himself debating with Stoics and Epicureans. Eventually, he was summoned to present his ideas to the Areopagus, the city council. Among other municipal matters, the Areopagus gave or withheld approval regarding the various teachings that came to town. Thus it was not Paul who was on trial but his message.

Paul once wrote that he became "all things to all people" in order to bring them to faith (1 Corinthians 9:22). In Athens, this rabbi became a philosopher. The speech he gave before the council veered from his usual approach. In synagogues, Paul would cite Old Testament prophecies to show how Jesus was the Messiah. But what did Greek philosophers care about the Hebrew Scriptures? He had to find the longings in their own culture, and while walking around town, he did. Paul came across a shrine "to an unknown god" (Acts 17:23). There are various theories as to the origin of this shrine. Perhaps this culture of many deities wanted to be sure no god was left out. But Paul found here a point of entry for the gospel. After commending the Athenians for being "extremely religious . . . in every way" (verse 22), he announced that this "unknown god" was the one he served. They were already worshipping him without knowing it.

Paul quoted two different popular poets (Epimenides and Aratus) to make his point that this God was not some quirky character thundering from Mount Olympus but a God who was involved in the very fiber of their being and who was intimately related to the human race. Indeed, God had demonstrated his involvement by sending his Son—a Savior, who rose from the dead.

Paul's teaching on the resurrection was a point of contention among the Greek philosophers, and some of Paul's listeners interrupted him. Others wanted to hear more. A few of them came to faith. The apostle's speech to the Areopagus has stood through the ages as a lesson in how to tailor the Christian message to a particular audience.

Cornelius

CORNELIUS WAS A ROMAN centurion stationed in Caesarea. He was the first recorded Gentile to convert to Christianity.

Judaism was somewhat popular among citizens of the Roman Empire. Many appreciated its rich traditions, its high moral standards, and its wise Scriptures. A category was created for Gentiles who respected the Jewish faith and even wanted to attend synagogue services. They were called "God-fearers." They didn't choose to go through the conversion process to become Jews, but they were interested in worshipping the God of the Jews.

Cornelius was a God-fearer. He also served in the Roman army and was responsible for 100 soldiers, who were posted at Caesarea, the new Roman-style city built on the Mediterranean Sea. Cornelius was known for his generosity and his prayer.

Once, in his regular time of afternoon prayer, he received a vision in which the Lord gave explicit instructions to send for the Apostle Peter, who was staying in Joppa, just down the coast. Immediately Cornelius did so.

The next day, God sent another vision to Peter. At this point, all Christians were Jewish. In fact, as a devout Jew, Peter would have considered it sinful even to visit the home of a Gentile like Cornelius. But God had another idea, unveiling a vision of a sheet let down from heaven bearing nonkosher animals. A voice said, "Kill and eat." Of course Peter protested, but God responded, "What God has made clean, you must not call profane" (Acts 10:15). As the vision vanished, the messengers from Cornelius were at the gate.

Prepped by his own vision, Peter visited Cornelius (joined by a few other Jewish Christians). He preached about Jesus to the assembled family and friends of Cornelius, and before he was finished, "the Holy Spirit fell upon all who heard the word" (verse 44). They spoke in tongues, glorified God, and were baptized in the name of Jesus. In Christ, both Jews and Gentiles were one.

This was a huge event in the life of the early Church, as a door was opened to the Gentiles. Peter faced some opposition for this groundbreaking activity, but he explained his vision at a Church council in Jerusalem and received their affirmation. Soon churches were actively sending missionaries (including Paul and Barnabas) into the Gentile world.

The Epistle to the Ephesians

MANY SCHOLARS DISPUTE Paul's authorship of Ephesians. Since Paul had spent three years in Ephesus, it seems strange to these scholars that he should introduce himself to the Ephesians (3:1–13) and that he sends no personal greetings to individuals, as he does in other letters. The extensive similarities between Ephesians and Colossians further suggest the possibility that a disciple of Paul composed Ephesians after the apostle's death, using Colossians as a model. We have difficulty thinking of such an act as anything more than a forgery. While people could write something in the name of another person with malicious intent (for example, to promote their own ideas or even to get the other person in trouble), the ancients recognized situations in which the practice was honorable and appropriate. Disciples writing what represented essentially the thought and teaching of their master would be one such situation.

On the other hand, the strangeness of the letter can be explained another way. The three most important ancient manuscripts of Ephesians lack the words "in Ephesus" in the opening greeting. This suggests to some scholars that Paul composed it as a circular letter to be read throughout the churches in Asia Minor at about the same time he wrote more personal and particular letters to the churches in Colossae and Laodicea (this letter having been lost). According to this theory, the similarities between Ephesians and Colossians are the result of each having been written at about the same time.

Unlike the other Pauline letters, there appears to be no pressing reason for writing and sending this letter—there is no mention of rival teachers, disagreements within the communities of readers, or renewed hostilities from outside. It is the closest thing to a "tract" in the New Testament. The first half celebrates the revelation of the mystery of God through Jesus' death. This mystery is the ability of Christ's death to reconcile human beings with God and human beings with each other. Ethnic barriers that have separated Jew from Gentile are, in Christ, no more (2:14).

The second half gives ethical instruction concerning how to live out this new life that reconciliation with God has made possible. The disciples are called to a radical commitment to nurture the virtues of love, peace, and kindness in thought, word, and deed in their relations inside and beyond the Church (4:25—5:1). And they are to mirror the relationship of Christ and his Church in their relationships within their households (5:21—6:4).

Ephesians provides a stunning vision for how the Spirit-led life transforms the individual believer, the Christian household, and the Christian community.

Samaria

JESUS SHOCKED EVERYBODY when, after stopping at a well in Samaria, he asked a local woman to draw him a drink. "Jews do not share things in common with Samaritans," the gospel tells us (John 4:9).

But why? What was the problem between these two peoples? There's a history to it, of course.

Under King Omri, Samaria became the capital of the northern kingdom, and the whole nation eventually became known as Samaria. On the whole, the northern kingdom had major problems with idolatry. Despite the warnings of God's prophets, Baal-worship was common in the north. In 722 B.C., the Assyrian military machine rolled through that kingdom, relocating much of its population to other lands and moving people from other countries into Israel's (Samaria's) territory.

An odd account in Second Kings 17:24–28 has lions attacking these new inhabitants of Samaria, "because they do not know the law of the god of the land" (verse 26). As a result of this incident, the king of Assyria sent back one of the captured priests, who set up shop in Bethel and taught the ways of the Lord. Still, we can see how the religion of this region would become a mixture of various faiths—that is, a hodgepodge of newcomers, the old Canaanites, and any idolatrous Israelites who remained. Naturally, purists in Jerusalem despised Samaritans as apostates.

The Samaritans would explain the rift differently. As they saw it, the original worship site of the Israelites was Mount Gerizim (see Deuteronomy 11:29; Joshua 8:33), but the southerners in Judah moved it. Holding to the Law of Moses, but not other Scriptures, they would say a faithful remnant stayed in the land after the Assyrian conquest and continued worshipping God on their mountain, as Moses had intended.

The enmity between Jews and Samaritans intensified when Jews refused Samaritan help in rebuilding the temple after the exile and when the Samaritans then hindered the reconstruction of Jerusalem (see Ezra 4:10). Later, when the Seleucid kingdom forced a Greek style on its cities, Jerusalem resisted. After their successful fight for independence, Jewish forces conquered Samaria and destroyed the temple on Mount Gerizim.

It is not surprising, therefore, that bad blood existed between the two groups. In Jesus' day, local Samaritans often harassed Jews traveling between the Jewish regions of Galilee and Judaea. Meanwhile, pious Jews would take the long way around to avoid being defiled by contact with the Samaritans.

The Last Supper

FEW EVENTS IN JESUS' life are remembered more frequently than the meal he shared with his closest disciples on the night when he was arrested. That meal is known by such names as the Last Supper, the Lord's Supper, the Eucharist, or communion.

That last evening, however, posed concerns other than food. Jesus realized that his death was imminent, and perhaps no act more appropriately represented his life and death than a meal. Gathered in the Upper Room with his disciples, Jesus took a loaf of bread, "and when he had given thanks, he broke it and said, 'This is my body that is for you. Do this in

remembrance of me.' In the same way he took the cup also, after supper, saying, 'This cup is the new covenant in my blood. Do this, as often as you drink it, in remembrance of me'" (1 Corinthians 11:24–25). Jesus took the ordinary food of his day and asked his followers to remember him as they ate. The one who ate with tax collectors, sinners, and prostitutes; the one who miraculously multiplied bread and fish in feeding the multitudes; the one who proclaimed the heavenly banquet in the future was the one who broke the bread, took the cup, and said, "Do this in remembrance of me."

It should also be recalled that Jesus linked this solemn meal with his signature act of humility when he washed the feet of his disciples (see John 13:1–20). Thus we are to remember not only the meal that symbolized his death, burial, and resurrection but also the character of the one we are to emulate in our daily walk with God. During this meal he promised the coming of the Holy Spirit and the assurance of eternal life with God; he talked about suffering for the faith and true joy in him; and he prayed to his heavenly Father. And throughout his act of humility and his words of comfort, Jesus expressed his deep love for all he would soon die to save.

POSTSCRIPT

■ The word *Eucharist* means "thanksgiving."

■ In the first centuries of the Church, communion, or the Lord's Supper, was celebrated within the context of a meal. That meal was an "agape meal" or "love feast." When the Apostle Paul describes this meal in the First Epistle to the Corinthians, chapter 11, it is clear that the various participants are each bringing food.

Elijah in the Whirlwind

Eᴸɪᴊᴀʜ ᴡᴀꜱ ᴀ ᴩʀᴏᴩʜᴇᴛ during one of the darkest periods in Israel's history. God raised up Elijah to confront the idolatry that pervaded Israel. God then performed miracles through him, the likes of which had not been seen for centuries.

But what makes Elijah unique is that he actually did not die. Scripture tells of only one other person whom the Lord took to heaven without seemingly experiencing death, and that is Enoch, about whom the Bible tells us very little (see Genesis 5:21–24). Elijah's story, however, is told with much more detail.

Elijah and his disciple Elisha were walking from Gilgal to Bethel when Elijah perceived that the Lord was preparing to take him "up to heaven by a whirlwind" (2 Kings 2:1). He told Elisha to stay behind, but Elisha refused, so they went on to Bethel together.

At the Jordan, "Elijah took his mantle and rolled it up, and struck the water; the water was parted to the one side and to the other, until the two of them crossed on dry land" (verse 8). Here was a third instance of the Lord miraculously parting water to allow humans to cross. On the other side, Elijah asked Elisha what he could do for him. Elisha asked for a "double share" of his spirit (verse 9). Elijah said he would receive this if he were able to witness his mentor being taken up into heaven.

While the two walked and talked, "a chariot of fire and horses of fire separated the two of them, and Elijah ascended in a whirlwind into heaven" (verse 11). Elisha called after him: "Father,

Elijah *by Edward von Steinle*

father!" (verse 12). He then tore his clothes in two, picked up Elijah's mantle, and used it to part the Jordan once more. The spirit of Elijah had obviously come to rest upon Elisha.

This episode is unparalleled in the Bible. It shows the special place that Elijah had in God's sight—so special that he was taken into heaven directly rather than suffering physical death. Elijah had endured much opposition and persecution, but God rewarded him with a spectacular exit from this earth.

Jezebel

JEZEBEL IS ONE of the few queens about whom the Bible says anything, and in her case, it's all bad. She was the daughter of Ethbaal, king of Sidon, a Phoenician city on the Mediterranean coast.

King Ahab of Israel was already known for his rebellion against the Lord, but his marriage to Jezebel took his apostasy to another level of spiritual corruption. As a result of her influence, he established the worship of Baal as the official state religion and built an altar for Baal in a temple in Samaria, Israel's capital city at the time. "Indeed, there was no one like Ahab, who sold himself to do what was evil in the sight of the Lord, urged on by his wife Jezebel" (1 Kings 21:25).

Jezebel's evil went even further. She ordered a massacre of all the true prophets of the Lord, though Obadiah, the brave overseer of Ahab's household, saved a hundred of them by hiding them in a cave and providing them with food and water. Then, after Elijah's victory over the prophets of Baal at Mount Carmel, she ordered that Elijah be killed, causing him to flee into the wilderness, where God protected him.

Such wickedness could not continue without comment from the Lord. God said through the prophet Elijah, "The dogs shall eat Jezebel within the bounds of Jezreel" (verse 23). Although Ahab was struck with guilt over his sins when Elijah reproached him, Jezebel became an even worse enemy of God. After Ahab's death, the prophet Elisha approached Jehu, an Israelite commander, and anointed him king over Israel. Elisha then told Jehu that he must destroy the entire house of Ahab and that "the dogs shall eat Jezebel in the territory of Jezreel, and no one shall bury her" (2 Kings 9:10).

Jehu obeyed and killed most of Ahab's household. When Jezebel heard that he was coming to the palace, she calmly "painted her eyes, and adorned her head, and looked out of the window" (verse 30). Even in the face of death, she was vain and sarcastic as she greeted Jehu, who called for her attendants to throw her out the window. Jezebel met her end when the attendants complied with Jehu's order. She also suffered the ignominy of being eaten by dogs; only her skull, hands, and feet remained.

Jehu's epitaph was fitting for this wicked woman: "The corpse of Jezebel shall be like dung on the field in the territory of Jezreel, so that no one can say, This is Jezebel" (verse 37).

Apollos Is Corrected

AFTER 18 MONTHS IN CORINTH, the Apostle Paul headed for home—that is, to Antioch of Syria and the church that had commissioned him. This was the last leg of his second missionary journey.

During his stay in Corinth, Paul connected with a couple who shared his tentmaking trade, Priscilla and Aquila. (These Jewish Christians had recently been forced to leave Rome when Emperor Claudius expelled the Jews from that city.) When Paul left, this couple journeyed with him across the Aegean Sea to Ephesus. Paul stopped briefly there to speak in the synagogue and then continued on his way home—but Priscilla and Aquila stayed.

Subsequently, a dynamic speaker by the name of Apollos arrived in Ephesus. He came from Alexandria, well known as a center for cutting-edge Jewish scholarship, and he knew the Scriptures extremely well. Somewhere along the line he had learned about Jesus, and this became part of his preaching, too. In fact, he "taught accurately the things concerning Jesus" (Acts 18:25), but there was something vitally missing. He knew only about "the baptism of John" (verse 25).

What does this mean? The next chapter gives us a clue. When Paul returned to Ephesus, where he had left Priscilla and Aquila, he found some believers who didn't know anything about the Holy Spirit, though they had experienced "the baptism of John." Paul explained to them, "John baptized with the baptism of repentance, telling the people to believe in the one who was to come after him, that is, in Jesus" (Acts 19:4).

We might wonder if Apollos had taught these people prior to his encounter with Priscilla and Aquila. Apollos had known about Jesus, and he might even have understood Jesus' atoning death. But did Apollos know about Christ's resurrection? We don't know, but it's fairly clear he knew nothing about Pentecost and the coming of the Holy Spirit.

When Priscilla and Aquila heard Apollos preaching his partial gospel in the synagogue, they did not engage him in public debate. Instead, they took him aside and filled him in on what he was missing. Apparently, he gladly accepted their counsel.

In the following years, he became a notable Christian speaker with a substantial following in Corinth. In his first epistle to the Christians in Corinth, the Apostle Paul speaks well of Apollos.

The Apostle Paul

PAUL PERSECUTED the early followers of Jesus without mercy, but then he encountered Jesus and became his greatest missionary. He planted churches throughout the Mediterranean world and mentored a new generation of Church leaders.

Paul began life as a Jewish boy named Saul in Tarsus, a city in Asia Minor (now Turkey). At some point in his youth, he went to Jerusalem to study under the great rabbi Gamaliel. There he became a Pharisee: "a Hebrew of the Hebrews," he said (Philippians 3:5 NIV). Employed by the high priest, he hunted down Christians and brought them to trial.

In an effort to widen the scope of his pursuit of Christians, he went to Damascus, but along the way a light from heaven blinded him, knocking him off his horse. He heard Jesus saying to him, "Saul, Saul, why do you persecute me?" (Acts 9:4). Thereafter he preached the faith that he once tried to destroy. At first, the apostles and other believers were skeptical of his conversion, but Barnabas brought him into their circle, and Saul (later known as Paul) was received as one of the faithful. When he became the object of death threats from his former Jewish allies, he retreated to his hometown for about a decade.

Later, Barnabas fetched him once again, bringing him into the church at Antioch of Syria. That church soon sent out Barnabas and Paul (now using his Roman name) on a missionary journey. Paul took three mission trips that we know of, establishing churches in Cyprus, Asia Minor, and Greece. Then, through a misunderstanding, he caused a riot in Jerusalem and was arrested. Declaring his Roman citizenship, he appealed to Caesar, an act that kept him imprisoned for a while but eventually got him to Rome to argue his case in an imperial court. Some believe that after years of house arrest he was probably freed and may have taken one more journey as far as Spain. Tradition says he was rearrested in Rome and beheaded in A.D. 64 during a persecution of Christians launched by Emperor Nero.

During his ministry for Christ, Paul preached in numerous cities and wrote numerous epistles. At least 13 of his letters are in the New Testament.

POSTSCRIPT

■ Paul worked as a tentmaker and generally paid his own way, not depending on collections from the congregations he established. Tentmaking was also a great way to meet travelers. If they accepted the gospel, they would spread it.

The Epistle to the Philippians

PAUL AND SILVANUS took their message to the Roman colony of Philippi around A.D. 49. They planted a congregation there thanks to the hospitality of householders such as Lydia, who opened her home for meetings of the new church. This congregation entered into a special partnership with Paul. He visited them at least twice more—the last time on his way to Jerusalem, where he was arrested in A.D. 57 or 58. They also sent emissaries to Paul to bring him financial support for his missionary endeavors, supplementing what he earned at tentmaking.

Paul's letter to the Philippians is written, in part, in response to another gift from the church, carried to Paul in prison by Epaphroditus. Given Paul's claim that his imprisonment had become an occasion to make the gospel known throughout the "whole imperial guard" (1:12–14), many scholars believe the letter was written during Paul's imprisonment in Rome (A.D. 60–62), when he was under house arrest awaiting a trial that resulted in a life-or-death verdict.

Epaphroditus had also brought some disturbing news about the congregation. Two leading figures within the church—two women, Syntyche and Euodia—were engaged in such a strong disagreement that the harmony of the church as a whole was threatened, perhaps because of people's tendency to take sides.

Paul uses this letter as an occasion to speak to this internal problem. He urges Syntyche and Euodia to place harmony above winning arguments or getting one's way (4:2–3). Putting the interests of others ahead of one's own interests is the main directive in the Church, which Jesus exhibited. Paul notes that this can also be seen in people whom the Philippians themselves have observed, such as Timothy, Epaphroditus, and Paul himself. They are examples who show that pursuing Christ means giving up one's claims to recognition and privilege. There are enough enemies outside the congregation—from false teachers to hostile neighbors. Christians must strive side by side, not against each other.

POSTSCRIPT

■ Philippians includes a lyrical passage about Christ humbling himself when he became human, taking the role of a servant and dying on the cross—an act of obedience that God rewarded by exalting his Son in the heavens (2:6–11). Many scholars believe Paul is reciting a hymn already in use in churches at this time, which would make it an early witness to Christian hymnody and worship.

Synagogue

THE WORD *SYNAGOGUE* MEANS "gathering." The synagogue has become the Jews' primary meeting place for worship, study, and social interaction. But it wasn't always this way.

The Law of Moses established the tabernacle as the religious gathering point for the ancient Israelites. Their interaction with God revolved around the sacrificial system, and they would bring livestock or grain to the altar in the tabernacle. Once the temple was built, this became the worship center. Songs and prayers became associated with the annual festivals.

We should note that the other religious focus of Israel was always the home. The Shema—Israel's powerful statement of faith in one God—instructs parents to teach God's words "to your children and talk about them when you are at home . . . write them on the doorposts of your house" (Deuteronomy 6:7, 9).

The Jews needed something in between the home and the temple, where the community could go to talk about God and pray together. It's not clear when synagogue services began. We know that the Babylonian destruction of the temple in Jerusalem in 586 B.C. forced a crisis of faith, and this might have prompted a healthy reconfiguration of Jewish religion. How can you come before God if you have no sacrifice, no altar, and no temple? The psalms provide one answer: "You have no delight in sacrifice," the psalmist wrote. "The sacrifice acceptable to God is a broken spirit" (Psalm 51:16–17). Other psalms equate sacrifice with the act of listening to God and doing his will (see Psalm 40:6–8) or prayers of praise and songs of joy (see Psalm 107:22). In other words, the temple and sacrifices were less important to God than a humble and godly spirit.

As a captive in Babylon, the prophet Ezekiel met with Israel's elders in something that might have been like a synagogue meeting, in which God's people came together to worship him (see Ezekiel 14:1; 20:1). Returning from captivity, Ezra gathered the people to read the law and explain it (see Nehemiah 8). Was *that* the first synagogue? It would make sense that synagogues began during the Babylonian Exile, among the exiles in Babylon and/or among those who remained in Judaea. It's possible that synagogues existed even earlier in remote regions of Israel or among early emigrants, but we have no record of that. An Egyptian note from the third century B.C. does mention a Jewish "place of prayer," which could have been a synagogue. In any case, synagogues were widespread by Jesus' day.

The Garden of Gethsemane

AFTER SHARING A MEAL with his disciples in the Upper Room, Jesus took them to the Garden of Gethsemane at the Mount of Olives. There he withdrew from the rest of the disciples with Peter, James, and John, telling those three to remain awake. He then left them so that he might pray alone.

Jesus prayed that he would not have to die—that the cup of death would be taken from him: "Abba, Father, for you all things are possible; remove this cup from me; yet, not what I want, but what you want" (Mark 14:36). The Gospel of Luke describes the intensity of his prayer in this way: "In his anguish he prayed more earnestly, and his sweat became like great drops of blood falling down on the ground" (Luke 22:44). Despite his deep distress, he committed himself to the path that his heavenly Father had planned for him.

When he returned from his prayer, he was disappointed to see that Peter, James, and John had fallen asleep. He said to Peter, "Keep awake and pray that you may not come into the time of trial; the spirit indeed is willing, but the flesh is weak" (Mark 14:38). Jesus again went to pray. When he returned to the disciples a second time, they were again asleep. He woke them up, went off to pray, and once more "he came a third time and said to them, 'Are you still sleeping and taking your rest? Enough! The hour has come; the Son of Man is betrayed into the hands of sinners. Get up, let us be going. See, my betrayer is at hand'" (verses 41–42).

Immediately Judas, accompanied by a crowd armed with swords and clubs, approached Jesus. Judas then betrayed Jesus with a kiss, which indicated to the temple officers whom to arrest. After Jesus rebuked Peter for using his sword against one of the slaves of the high priest, his disciples fled, leaving Jesus alone.

Although the disciples had the best of intentions, they had fallen asleep. They had come to the time of trial, but they had run away. The spirit was willing, but the flesh was weak. Conversely, however, although Jesus had prayed to be freed from death, he accepted it.

POSTSCRIPT

■ *Gethsemane* comes from an Aramaic word meaning "oil press." The Garden of Gethsemane today still has many very old olive trees.

Jonah and the Great Fish

JONAH IS WELL KNOWN for being swallowed by a "whale" and then being spit up on land three days later, alive. Yet the significance of his story lies more in his attitude than in his personal fortunes.

God told Jonah to go to Nineveh, capital of the mighty Assyrian Empire, and to preach against its wickedness. Instead, Jonah fled in a ship whose destination was in the opposite direction. A terrifying storm came up, and the sailors dumped their cargo and prayed to their gods, all to no avail. They finally awoke the sleeping Jonah, who, realizing that the storm was his fault, and told them to throw him overboard. When they did, the storm abated.

God then "appointed a great fish" (Jonah 1:17 RSV) to swallow Jonah. Miraculously, Jonah survived in the belly of that fish for three days and nights, and during that time he praised the Lord for delivering him from the depths of the sea. It seems he experienced a change of heart regarding God's command, and so he thanked God for his help.

When the fish spit him up on land, Jonah obeyed God and went to Nineveh, where he preached the Lord's message of doom. Incredibly, the city repented, from the king to the common citizens. So God spared the city.

Jonah, however, was not pleased. In fact, he was incensed, which revealed the true reason why he did not obey God at the start. "I knew that you are a gracious God and merciful," he complained, "relenting from punishing" (Jonah 4:2). He did not want these pagan people to repent, for he did not want God to be merciful toward them. And so he asked God to take away his life. In a way, he was challenging God to destroy either Nineveh or himself. In a huff, he built a booth outside the city and waited for the Lord to act, possibly thinking God would favor him—one of God's special people—over the pagans.

But as time passed, God did neither, and so Jonah became more sullen as he sat in the shade of a bush God had grown for him. But then the Lord appointed a worm to eat the bush and brought forth a hot east wind, which caused Jonah to suffer miserably. Jonah complained to God, and God turned it back on him, saying, "You are concerned about the bush ... which you did not grow; ... And should I not be concerned about Nineveh, that great city?" (verses 10–11). The lesson God wanted to teach Jonah and all Israelites was that even though they were his chosen people he was God over *all* the nations and wanted *all* nations to repent and turn to him, for his compassion was for *all* people.

Elisha

ELISHA WAS ELIJAH's designated successor as *the* prophet in Israel. When God told Elijah to anoint Elisha for this task, the prophet cast his mantle over Elisha as a sign of God's appointment. Elisha then bade his parents farewell and followed Elijah.

Elisha was with Elijah for a long time before God took Elijah to heaven in a whirlwind, accompanied by a fiery chariot and horses. When Elijah was gone, Elisha took up his master's mantle and parted the waters of the Jordan, just as Elijah had done, in the first of a series of impressive miracles.

Unlike most other prophets, Elijah and Elisha were miracle-workers, especially Elisha, and their reputation spread throughout the land. Elisha himself performed more miracles than anyone else in Old Testament times except Moses. These miracles served to legitimize his place as a prophet sent by God.

The Children
Devoured by Bears
by James Tissot

The strangest of all stories concerning Elisha is probably his encounter with a number of small boys recorded in Second Kings. While walking toward Bethel, a group of boys came out of the city and jeered at him, screaming, "Go away, baldhead! Go away, baldhead!" (2 Kings 2:23). In reaction, he cursed them, and then two bears came out of the woods and mauled the boys. What is the intention of this biblical passage? Perhaps it was to reveal more of Elisha's personality, or maybe it was to indicate how seriously God took the mocking of one of his servants. In any case, this incident warned people not to disrespect him.

Possibly the best-known miracle of Elisha is his healing of Naaman, who was commander of the army of the king of Aram. Although Naaman was a renowned soldier, he suffered from leprosy. When Naaman heard about Elisha and his power to heal, he received permission from his king to go to the king of Israel to be healed. Although the king of Israel fretted, thinking the king of Aram was searching for a reason to go to war, Elisha sent a message to the king of Israel to direct Naaman to him. When Naaman arrived in Israel, Elisha sent him a message to wash himself in the Jordan seven times, but Naaman became angry, thinking such an act was ludicrous. Nevertheless, his servants persuaded the commander to follow the prophet's instructions. Naaman's flesh was then healed, and so he went to Elisha and declared, "Now I know that there is no God in all the earth except in Israel" (2 Kings 5:15).

Paul in Ephesus

EPHESUS WAS A RELIGIOUS grab bag, famous for its magnificent temple to the local goddess Artemis, emperor worship, and an abundance of magic arts. When Paul briefly stopped there on his way home from his second missionary journey, he promised to return. Perhaps that first taste of Ephesian culture had convinced him that a major ministry was necessary there.

When Paul came back to Ephesus, he preached first in the synagogue, which was his customary routine. Some accepted his message; others rejected it. After three months, he was forced to speak at a lecture hall, where he held daily discussions. This ministry continued for two years.

During this time, we're told "God did extraordinary miracles through Paul" (Acts 19:11). Any miracle is extraordinary, of course, and the apostles had previously worked astounding wonders, but this display of spiritual power was probably more than what even Paul had done before. The Ephesians' love of magic created a situation where miracles were necessary to get their attention. Thus healings and exorcisms became a regular part of Paul's operation to the point that "when the handkerchiefs or aprons that had touched his skin were brought to the sick, their diseases left them" (verse 12).

A group of traveling exorcists tried to duplicate Paul's exploits, casting out a demon "by the Jesus whom Paul proclaims," but the demon attacked them, saying, "Jesus I know, and Paul I know; but who are you?" (verses 13, 15). Obviously Paul had a unique power, and that incident confirmed the divine origin of his message. The people were "awestruck" by these events (verse 17) and began to give up dabbling in magic, thus burning their books of divination. (Luke totals the value of the burnt books at 50,000 silver coins, a stupendous sum.)

About five years later, Paul wrote to the Ephesian believers from prison in Rome. He prayed that they would know "the immeasurable greatness of his power for us who believe" (Ephesians 1:19).

POSTSCRIPT

■ Archaeologists have dug up portions of the wealthy district of Ephesus. Some homes had heated bathrooms with running water. A brothel and casino were found in the center of town.

■ In his biography of Alexander the Great, the ancient historian Plutarch gives a passing reference to all the "Eastern soothsayers" who were gathered at Ephesus.

Ananias of Damascus

ANANIAS WAS A WELL-RESPECTED Christian living in Damascus. We know of him because he was instrumental in Paul's conversion. Not only did he restore Paul's vision, but he also conveyed the Lord's mission to Paul (see Acts 9:1–19; 22:12).

Paul, then known as Saul of Tarsus, was traveling to Damascus to arrest people such as Ananias. Paul worked for the high priest in Jerusalem, who was zealously trying to squelch the burgeoning Christian movement. But on the journey a light from heaven blinded Paul. After being knocked to the ground, he heard the voice of Jesus, which changed his life forever. The entourage around Paul was baffled. They heard a voice but saw no one, and now their leader was blind. They subsequently led him into Damascus.

Meanwhile, the Lord spoke to Ananias in a vision, giving him directions to Paul's location and telling him to heal his blindness. Ananias protested, "Lord, I have heard from many about this man, how much evil he has done to your saints" (Acts 9:13). *Is this really a man you want to heal?* Ananias must have been thinking. But the Lord assured Ananias that Paul was "an instrument whom I have chosen to bring my name before Gentiles and kings and before the people of Israel" (verse 15).

Years later, Paul retold the story of his conversion, calling Ananias "a devout man according to the law and well spoken of by all the Jews" (Acts 22:12). Ananias's excellent reputation among all Jews might have allowed him access to Paul that other Christians wouldn't have had. He was able to visit the blind apostle-to-be in a private home in Damascus and lay hands on him, speaking a word of healing. "Immediately something like scales fell from his eyes" (Acts 9:18). Paul's vision was restored.

But Ananias had a further message for Paul: "The God of our ancestors has chosen you . . . you will be his witness to all the world . . . Get up, be baptized, and have your sins washed away" (Acts 22:14–16). Paul's conversion was completed. He now had a new mission.

Paul stayed with Christians in Damascus after this, and we might guess that Ananias made living arrangements for him. Though Ananias had understandably felt some reservation about going to Paul, his first words to him were "Brother Saul" (Acts 9:17). Apparently Ananias had taken to heart Jesus' instruction to "love your enemies" (Matthew 5:44).

The Epistle to the Colossians

THE CHURCH IN COLOSSAE was founded by Epaphras, a coworker of Paul's. Paul was not a maverick evangelist; he worked at the center of an extensive network of missionaries and teachers. As many as 40 different people were part of Paul's team at some point during his two decades of missionary work. He names many of the same coworkers at the end of this letter to the Colossians and the letter to Philemon, suggesting the letters were sent from the same place, perhaps Ephesus, at the same time. Paul's public mention of Onesimus, Philemon's runaway slave, as a "faithful and beloved brother" (4:9) may have served to rally broader, local support for Philemon to free him

Colossians was written in response to some traveling teachers who were promoting their own "twist" on Christianity, combining elements of Jewish practice with elements of what would later develop into Gnosticism. They taught that human beings seeking God needed to interact with intermediary spirits such as angels and "elemental spirits," offering them the appropriate acknowledgment and worship as emanations of God's fullness. They kept a host of rules about what not to eat or drink, what not to touch, and what rituals to keep on special days of the week, month, and year, which they believed aided spiritual progress.

Paul argues that the disciples need to focus only on the one spirit-being, Jesus Christ, in whom all God's fullness dwells. Spiritual progress will not come through human-devised rules about food, drink, seasonal rituals, and interaction with angels and other spirit-beings. Rather, spiritual progress comes through the moral and personal transformation of laying aside our self-centered attitudes and behaviors and taking up the attitudes and behaviors that reflect Jesus Christ: dealing gently with one another, devoting ourselves to selfless outreach, and nurturing the harmony of the Christian community.

POSTSCRIPT

■ Philemon appears to have lived in Colossae and to have been a member of one of the house churches there. Paul converted Philemon personally, probably while Philemon was in Ephesus or some business or personal matter.

■ The letter of Paul to the Christians in Laodicea, a neighboring city, was not preserved, but awareness of its existence from the reference in Colossians 4:16 gave rise to two attempts to "restore" it. The first was a second-century forgery promoting Gnosticism. The second was composed slightly later and was compiled largely of verses taken from known Pauline letters.

Sanhedrin

THE SANHEDRIN WAS THE RULING council of the Jews. It included 71 men, who were leaders in the community. At times, it had substantial power, acting as a parliament or supreme court.

Jewish historian Josephus reports that a Sanhedrin was in place before the Maccabean Revolt, but Judas Maccabeus cleaned house and installed his own people, mostly friends and family members. Since the Maccabees (also known as *Hasmoneans*) established a royal dynasty, their relatives became the aristocracy—rich and powerful. The Maccabees were also of priestly lineage, so many Sanhedrin members were priests as well. These wealthy, well-born citizens became known as the Sadducee party and tended to be more open to worldly ways, giving up their old Jewish traditions for modern Greek styles. One of the later leaders of the Maccabean clan, Salome Alexandra, pushed a more traditional trend and placed some from the conservative Pharisee party on the Sanhedrin as well.

This was the makeup of the Sanhedrin in Jesus' time: a mixture of Pharisees and Sadducees, aristocrats and priests—as well as scribes and rabbis. When Rome took over, they left the Sanhedrin in place, though there were clear restrictions on its power. The high priest was the top "executive" in this government, with the Sanhedrin filling judicial functions—but all members answered to the Roman governor or procurator.

Jesus managed to alienate all the groups in the Sanhedrin. He challenged the hypocrisy of the conservative Pharisees and disputed the disbelief of the liberal Sadducees. While at least two council members—Nicodemus and Joseph of Arimathea—were secret disciples of Jesus, it's no surprise that the rest of the Sanhedrin quickly united to do away with him. In the following years, Peter and John, Stephen, and Paul would all stand trial before the Sanhedrin, which tried to check the growing Jesus movement.

POSTSCRIPT

▪ *Sanhedrin* means "seated together." The members sat in semicircular rows with a clerk at each end. The accused stood in the center. Behind the accused was a gallery of three rows for rabbinical students (this might have been Saul's place at the trial of Stephen).

▪ The Sanhedrin continued to meet even after the Roman destruction of Jerusalem in A.D. 70, holding an important convocation at Jamnia in A.D. 90.

The Trials of Jesus

AFTER JESUS WAS ARRESTED in the Garden of Gethsemane, he was taken before the Sanhedrin, the supreme religious counsel that consisted of key elders in the Jewish community in Jerusalem. The Sanhedrin, which comprised both Sadducees and Pharisees, called several witnesses to give testimony against Jesus during this first phase of his trials, but Jesus could not be condemned because their statements were not in agreement. Nevertheless, Jesus eventually acknowledged that he was the Christ. This apparent blasphemy enraged the high priest and the council. Whether the trial actually was held before the entire Sanhedrin (since it was held late at night in secret, they may not have had a quorum) is questionable. What is clear, however, is that Jesus' response is what led to his next trial.

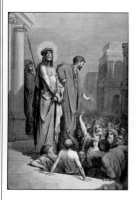

Early on Friday morning, after the priests completed their questioning, they bound Jesus and took him before Pontius Pilate. There they accused Jesus of blasphemy. In the Gospel of Luke, they say he is also guilty of sedition in order to persuade the secular authorities to execute him (the priests lacked the legal jurisdiction to put him to death under Roman law). Meanwhile, Pilate's concern was whether Jesus was a threat to public order.

Evidently, Pilate did not want to get entangled in this religious affair, for after he discovered that Jesus was from Galilee, which was in Herod's jurisdiction, he sent Jesus to Herod, who had come to Jerusalem. Herod was curious to meet this man who he hoped would perform signs for him. When Jesus did not comply, Herod tired of him and sent him back to Pilate, who had been warned by his wife not to have anything to do with this "innocent" man because of a dream that had troubled her.

After listening to the accusations of Jesus' detractors and reviewing the case further, Pilate determined that Jesus was not guilty of a crime deserving death. Nevertheless, Jesus' enemies continued to insist on his execution. Finally, Pilate offered the people a choice: They could pardon and free either Jesus or an insurrectionist and murderer named Barabbas. The loudest members of the crowd before Pilate yelled for Barabbas's release and for the crucifixion of Jesus. At this point, Pilate literally washed his hands before the crowd, who shouted, "His blood be on us and on our children!" (Matthew 27:25).

Sennacherib's Empty Boast

SENNACHERIB WAS KING of Assyria at the height of the empire's power. He ruled from 705 to 681 B.C., establishing the capital in Nineveh and launching several building projects after the death of his father, Sargon II, who had conquered the northern kingdom of Israel. He led his army in successive campaigns of conquest, destroying any resistance and recording his conquests for posterity in his royal annals. On his third campaign, he marched against the southern kingdom of Judah and lands nearby, capturing city after city with little or no resistance.

Hezekiah, king of Judah at the time, had paid an exorbitant tribute of 22,500 pounds of silver and 2,250 of gold to Sennacherib so that he would leave Jerusalem alone. Hezekiah had to plunder the treasuries of the temple and the palace to do this. Still, Sennacherib demanded the surrender of Jerusalem itself, which Hezekiah would not agree to do. In public negotiations conducted between Sennacherib's officials standing outside the walls of the holy city and Hezekiah's officials standing atop the walls—with the people of Judah observing and listening to the entire dialogue—Assyrian officials insulted Hezekiah and his God, threatening the listening people with complete annihilation unless they capitulated.

Isaiah the prophet heard of the predicament, and he prophesied that Sennacherib would return to Assyria of his own volition without taking Jerusalem and that he would be killed in his own land. He quoted God's words: "[Sennacherib] shall not come into this city... For I will defend this city to save it, for my own sake and for the sake of my servant David" (Isaiah 37:33, 35; see also 2 Kings 19:34).

That very night, God's words came true. The Bible says, "The angel of the Lord set out and struck down one hundred eighty-five thousand in the camp of the Assyrians; when morning dawned, they were all dead bodies" (Isaiah 37:36). And when Sennacherib returned home, two of his sons killed him, and their brother Esarhaddon succeeded their father on the throne. The exact means by which the Assyrians were killed is not known. Some speculate that it was a fast-acting plague, while others see a direct "act of God" accomplishing this mass slaughter.

POSTSCRIPT

■ Sennacherib's annals tell of this campaign, but they omit any mention of his defeat, which is not surprising, since the norm in ancient Near Eastern royal annals was to record only successes and to put the best spin on defeats.

Isaiah the Prophet

ISAIAH WAS THE GREATEST of the so-called "writing prophets." He addressed significant themes: the urgent need for repentance, the threat of exile, messages of comfort and hope for the future, and most importantly, prophecies of a coming messiah.

Isaiah was the son of Amoz, and he lived in Jerusalem. Isaiah was married to an unnamed prophet, who bore him two sons, Maher-shalal-hash-baz (see Isaiah 8:3) and Shear-jashub (see Isaiah 7:3). One interesting note concerning his prophetic ministry is that he walked around naked and barefoot for three years as a divine sign to shame the Egyptians and Ethiopians (see Isaiah 20:3–5). Otherwise, he often wore mourning clothes such as coarse linen, to express God's sorrow for his wayward people.

The Prophet Isaiah *by Michelangelo*

Isaiah was a prophet to the nation of Judah and to four of its kings (Jotham, Ahaz, Hezekiah, and Manasseh) from about 740 B.C. to 681 B.C. He preached several decades after Elijah and Elisha and was a contemporary of the prophets Amos, Hosea, and Micah. God called him in the year that King Uzziah died (740 B.C.) in a vision where he saw God himself seated on a throne, attended by six-winged seraphs who cried out, "Holy, holy, holy is the Lord of hosts" (Isaiah 6:3). Jewish tradition says he was sawed in two during Manasseh's reign (686–642 B.C.); if so, then his ministry spanned more than 50 years. (Incidentally, the writer of Hebrews is possibly making an allusion to Isaiah's death in chapter 11, verse 37.)

Isaiah uttered some of the greatest messianic prophecies in the Old Testament: "For a child has been born for us, a son given to us; authority rests upon his shoulders; and he is named Wonderful Counselor, Mighty God, Everlasting Father, Prince of Peace" (Isaiah 9:6), and "But he was wounded for our transgressions, crushed for our iniquities; upon him was the punishment that made us whole, and by his bruises we are healed" (Isaiah 53:5).

According to the Jewish historian Josephus, even Cyrus, the first great Persian king, was persuaded to liberate the Jews from captivity because of Isaiah's prophecies concerning Cyrus himself. This is one indication of how revered Isaiah was among both Jews and Gentiles.

Riot in Ephesus

THE CHRISTIAN FAITH can be bad for business, especially when you make idols for a living. That's what a silversmith named Demetrius discovered when Paul started preaching the gospel in Ephesus. The city was sacred to the goddess Artemis, with a temple that was one of the wonders of the ancient world. This was an earth-mother deity from the hinterland of Asia Minor who had been fused with the Greek hunting goddess of the same name (and whose Roman version was Diana). Ephesus did quite a tourism business with Artemis-worshippers, and the sale of small silver shrines was a major industry.

Demetrius was a leader in that industry, perhaps the head of the metalworkers guild. When Paul swept into town, convincing people to give up their magic and idolatry, Demetrius perceived a serious threat to his business. "This Paul has persuaded and drawn away a considerable number of people by saying that gods made with hands are not gods" (Acts 19:26). The silversmith stirred his fellow artisans into a frenzy, and they rushed downtown to the city's theater, gaining numbers on the way. "Great is Artemis of the Ephesians!" they shouted again and again (verse 34).

Archaeologists have found a theater structure in Ephesus right on a main street. Quite possibly it is the same building mentioned in Acts. Nearly 500 feet across, it would have held 24,000 people in three decks. We don't know that this crowd filled the place, but they created considerable confusion. Interestingly, "Most of them did not know why they had come together" (verse 32).

The rioters managed to grab two associates of Paul—Aristarchus and Gaius—and Paul wanted to enter the theater and address the crowd, but his friends feared for his life. You can imagine Paul's quandary. Certainly he was aware of the danger, but when would he have another chance to tell a stadium full of people about Jesus? Even some government officials who knew Paul begged him not to face the mob.

Within the amphitheater, a Jew named Alexander stepped forward, perhaps to clarify that the synagogue had ousted Paul some time earlier, but he was shouted down. For two hours, there was an impromptu worship service for Artemis until the town clerk (effectively, the mayor) quieted the people down, urging them to "do nothing rash" (verse 36). He reminded them that the Christians had broken no laws, and if there was a grievance, it could be settled in court. Meanwhile, the Romans might be concerned about a riot such as this, and "there is no cause that we can give to justify the commotion" (verse 40). The crowd then dispersed.

Gamaliel

A JEWISH RABBI in the time of Jesus, Gamaliel was also a respected scholar and leader. As a member of the Sanhedrin, the Jewish ruling council, he spoke up during a trial of Peter and John. His comments may have saved their lives.

In the first century, there were different schools of thought among rabbis. Among the Pharisees, the schools of Hillel and Shammai were most influential. Gamaliel was the grandson of Hillel, carrying on and developing his teaching, which valued traditional interpretations of the Scriptures over newer interpretations. While this generally resulted in a conservative lifestyle, Gamaliel remained open to non-Jewish ideas in his studies. Where other rabbis dismissed Greek philosophy, Gamaliel used it to enhance his own thinking. This is especially significant with regard to the Apostle Paul, who studied under Gamaliel, probably as a youth (see Acts 22:3). While Paul broke from Gamaliel's thinking on key points, he displayed a helpful knowledge of Greek thought, which enabled him to reason effectively in the Gentile culture.

Arrested once for preaching about Jesus in the temple, Peter and John were released with a slap on the wrist. But, of course, they resumed their ministry of preaching and healing, so they were arrested a second time and jailed. But an angel miraculously released them and told them to go back to the temple to preach.

When the council opened their session, they sent for the prisoners but were told, "The men whom you put in prison are standing in the temple and teaching the people!" (Acts 5:25). So they were arrested a third time; this time they preached to the council. While others in the council became incensed, Gamaliel arose and spoke calmly, reminding them of all the other rebel movements that had come and gone. "Keep away from these men and let them alone," he suggested, "because if this . . . undertaking is of human origin, it will fail; but if it is of God, you will not be able to overthrow them" (verses 38–39). The council was persuaded to release the disciples after having them flogged.

POSTSCRIPT

■ Rabbinic records give us further information about Gamaliel, who served as president of the Sanhedrin for a number of years. He died around A.D. 52.

The Epistles to the Thessalonians

PAUL AND HIS TEAM preached in Thessalonica around A.D. 49, just after moving on from Philippi, a city in the same province. Thessalonica was a Roman colony with a long history of loyalty toward the imperial family and active cults of the ancient gods. Paul proclaimed that a crucified revolutionary would return to end the Roman order in favor of the "kingdom of God," and he persuaded citizens to stop participating in the idolatrous rituals that showed their loyalty to the state and the ancient gods. The majority of the people did not welcome Paul's declarations, so Paul and his team were forced to leave the city, and their converts were left to face the disapproval of their neighbors.

Deeply concerned about his converts' perseverance in their newfound faith, Paul sent Timothy to encourage them. After Timothy returned with good news about their firmness, along with some questions they had, Paul wrote First Thessalonians to follow up on that visit. (This letter is probably the earliest of Paul's surviving letters.)

Much of the letter is devoted to insulating the converts from their neighbors' disapproval and hostility. Whatever honor they have lost in their local environment on account of their conversion, Paul asserts that they have regained many times over in the eyes of Christians and non-Christians alike in communities across Macedonia and Greece. The hostility they encounter is normal and not a cause for doubting: Jesus endured it; the churches in Judaea endured it; and now so do the Thessalonians. Paul also rekindles their mutual affection by reminding them of his love for them and his manner of life, using his own example of working to support himself as an encouragement to each member of the church not to rely on the charity of the group but to find ways to be productive and contribute to charitable work instead. He answers the church's questions about the return of Christ, assuring them that the possibility of dying before this event does not mean that they should lose hope. In light of Christ's return, Paul urges the believers to remain committed to pure, watchful lives.

Shortly after sending First Thessalonians, Paul wrote a second letter to this congregation to address two problems: a misunderstanding about the nearness of the "Day of the Lord" and the growing problem of believers quitting their livelihoods in anticipation of it, increasing the drain on the church's resources. He urges the Christians to maintain orderly, productive lives for the good of their witness, as well as for the reputation of the Church.

Pharisees

IT'S NOT EXACTLY CLEAR when the Pharisees first appeared. An unsupported Jewish tradition takes them back to the fifth century B.C., the time of Ezra the scribe. Many of the Pharisees were also scribes devoted to copying and studying Scripture, so it makes sense that their scribal tradition would start there. Other scholars place the genesis of this group at 250 B.C. or around the time of the Maccabean Revolt (168 B.C.).

Pharisee comes from a Hebrew word for "separate," and that seems to be the point. They wanted the Jews to separate themselves from corrupting influences by being extra scrupulous in obeying God's laws. Because the Pharisees believed that the future prosperity of Israel depended on its purity, they taught a strict code on sabbath keeping, tithing, and even hand washing.

An issue that separated the Pharisees from others, such as the Sadducees, was the value of the oral law. All agreed that the books of Moses (the first five books of the Bible) were sacred, but rabbis had been interpreting Mosaic law for centuries, and their teachings had been passed on. The Pharisees maintained that oral law was just as binding as the written law and that God had given oral law to Moses as well as the written law. Jesus, however, accused the Pharisees of "making void the word of God through your tradition that you have handed on" (Mark 7:13).

Jesus had many run-ins with the Pharisees, often regarding sabbath observance. The Law of Moses established the seventh day as a day of rest, and it gave a few examples of the "work" that shouldn't be done on that day. But the Pharisees had gathered a huge collection of interpretation on the subject, such as how many steps you can take on a sabbath before you're "traveling" and therefore "working." They severely criticized Jesus for healing on the sabbath, and they even set up traps so they'd catch him healing on this sacred day. They really didn't need to, because Jesus openly viewed it as a day of restoration, when healing was not just allowed but appropriate.

The Pharisees came in for scathing criticism from Jesus, who called them hypocrites (and worse). If the gospels were the only source of data on the Pharisees, we would consider them a terrible lot, but the historian Josephus writes about their noble intentions and their reputation as Bible scholars. Clearly something had gone wrong in Jesus' day. They were supposed to teach folks how to please the Lord, but instead they would "lock people out of the kingdom of heaven" (Matthew 23:13).

Taunted and Tortured

A FTER PILATE SENTENCED Jesus to death, he handed Jesus over to Roman soldiers to be crucified. They stripped him, put a purple cloak on him, twisted thorns into a crown, and shoved it on his head. "And they began saluting him, 'Hail, King of the Jews!' They struck his head with a reed, spat upon him, and knelt down in homage to him. After mocking him, they stripped him of the purple cloak and put his own clothes on him. Then they led him out to crucify him" (Mark 15:18–20).

Humiliating captives was not an unusual practice in ancient times. In Psalm 137, the Jewish author writes of being in exile "by the rivers of Babylon" (verse 1). He notes how his captors told him to sing songs for their entertainment in the midst of his grieving and sadness.

What is so striking about the Roman soldiers' mockery of Jesus, however, is that each action was laced with irony. They put royal colors on him—purple and scarlet. They took an instrument of torture—that is, thorns—and made a king's crown for him. They knelt down to him and even saluted him, saying, "Hail, King of the Jews!" The account in Matthew says they put a reed in his hand, representing a royal scepter.

At a certain point, when the mockery became particularly intense, there arose an increasing recognition that there was something unusual about this man. Clearly, it seemed, his kingship was not of this world. Pontius Pilate himself had an inscription written and placed on Jesus' cross. In Hebrew, Latin, and Greek, the inscription read, "Jesus of Nazareth, the King of the Jews" (John 19:19). When the chief priests said "Do not write, 'The King of the Jews,' but, 'This man said, I am King of the Jews,'" Pilate answered, "What I have written I have written" (verses 21–22).

The mockery acknowledges a much deeper literal truth than even the Roman soldiers and Pilate recognized.

POSTSCRIPT

- The acronym "INRI" frequently appears as a title on the cross in paintings that portray the Crucifixion. Those letters stand for the Latin words for "Jesus of Nazareth, the King of the Jews."

- Although INRI is a well-known expression, the term "ICHTHUS," the Greek word for "fish," may be the most famous acrostic from early Christianity. The letters come from the initial letters of the Greek words for "Jesus Christ, God's Son, Savior."

A Righteous King Reforms Judah

JOSIAH WAS ONLY EIGHT years old when he began his 31-year reign in the southern kingdom of Judah. Unlike many of his predecessors, he followed the Lord all his days. In fact, he was the last Jewish king to faithfully serve God.

One of his righteous acts as king was to repair the holy temple in Jerusalem. While this work was being done, an old copy of the book of the law was found and brought to Josiah. When the king heard it read to him, he tore his clothes realizing how far astray from its teachings the people of Judah had strayed. Thus he sent officials to the prophet Huldah, who foretold dire consequences for Judah after Josiah's death.

Josiah then set in motion a comprehensive set of reforms. The list of them illustrates how thoroughly the land had been corrupted and intertwined with pagan worship practices:

- They cleared the temple of all vessels used in the worship of Baal, Asherah, and other gods.
- They tore down the pagan shrines of worship on the high places throughout the land and removed all of their priests.
- They leveled the houses of the male cult prostitutes who practiced in the temple.
- They removed from the temple the wooden pole and woven hangings devoted to Asherah.
- They destroyed Topheth, the place where child sacrifices were offered to the god Molech.
- They took away the horses devoted to the sun god and burned their chariots.
- They got rid of the altars in the royal palaces and the temples dedicated to pagan gods.
- They demolished the shrines devoted to Ashtoreth, Chemosh, Milcom, and Asherah.
- They destroyed the altar at Bethel erected 300 years earlier by Jeroboam.
- They rid the land of all the mediums, necromancers, household gods, and idols of every king.
- They celebrated the full Passover feast for the first time since the days of the judges before the monarchies.

The Bible says Josiah was unique in his zeal and faithfulness to God.

Josiah

JOSIAH BECAME the 16th king of Judah when he was just an eight-year-old boy. He reigned in Jerusalem for 31 years (640–609 B.C.), and he was one of Judah's greatest kings. The Bible says of him: "Before him there was no king like him, who turned to the Lord with all his heart, with all his soul, and with all his might, according to all the law of Moses; nor did any like him arise after him" (2 Kings 23:25). Sadly, Josiah's successors to the throne all rebelled against the Lord.

King Josiah Cleansing the Land of Idols *by William Hole*

Josiah was the son of King Amon and Queen Jedidah. His grandfather was King Manasseh, one of the worst kings of Judah. Even though Manasseh's father, Hezekiah, was a godly king and a spiritual reformer, and although Manasseh's reign of 55 years was the longest according to the biblical record, Manasseh zealously brought idolatry back into the kingdom by rebuilding the altars to Baal and Asherah and turning the people to the worship of the gods of Ammon, Moab, and Edom. He also promoted Babylonian and Egyptian paganism throughout his kingdom. Moreover, Manasseh waged a ferocious persecution of any prophet who denounced his apostasy. He even brutally slaughtered the great prophet Isaiah. Although Manasseh repented at the end of his life, his son, Amon, continued to worship pagan idols until he was assassinated after only two years on the throne.

In this spiritual darkness, Josiah "began to seek the God of his ancestor David, and in the twelfth year he began to purge Judah and Jerusalem of the high places, the sacred poles, and the carved and the cast images" (2 Chronicles 34:3). He also repaired the house of the Lord, recovered the Law of Moses, and kept the Passover in Jerusalem. In fact, "No passover like it had been kept in Israel since the days of the prophet Samuel" (2 Chronicles 35:18).

Josiah met his end when he foolishly went out to engage Pharaoh Neco in battle; Neco was simply passing through his land on his way to fight the Assyrians, and he told Josiah that the God of Israel was with the Egyptian army and that they would not harm him or his people if they stood by. Nevertheless, Josiah disguised himself and joined in battle against the Egyptians in the plain of Megiddo. Egyptian archers fatally shot Josiah. At his burial, all of Jerusalem and Judah mourned his death, including the great prophet Jeremiah.

Paul Restores Eutychus

IT'S A STORY MANY CHURCHGOERS can relate to—that is, the dozing part. While the Apostle Paul was preaching late into the night, a teenage boy fell asleep. The problem was, he was sitting on a windowsill—and the window was open.

On a Sunday night, Paul was preaching to believers in Troas. This church was not one of the prominent churches mentioned in the New Testament. Where other congregations met in lecture halls or spacious homes, this group was meeting in someone's apartment. The description in this story suggests one of the tenement buildings that were common in the Roman world, especially in poorer neighborhoods. The room was packed, and a number of oil lamps were burning. You can imagine the close atmosphere of the apartment.

Eutychus, a young teenager whose name means "good luck," probably thought himself lucky to get a window seat. But the service seemed interminable. Paul had a sense that this was the last time he would see these people, and he wanted to get everything in. It was past midnight and Eutychus "began to sink into a deep sleep while Paul talked still longer" (Acts 20:9). Suddenly, he fell out the open window and plunged three stories to his death.

Of course, the worshippers rushed to him, frantic for his health yet probably knowing he could not survive such a fall. As grief swept through the crowd, Paul bent over the boy, took him in his arms, and said, "Do not be alarmed, for his life is in him" (verse 10). Indeed, the boy was alive again. He was taken home, and Paul continued the service—until dawn.

This story is not accompanied by much fanfare, so some have assumed that Eutychus just had the wind knocked out of him and that Paul did mouth-to-mouth resuscitation to revive him. Yet it was a three-story fall, and Luke, the physician who writes this account, says he was dead. Ultimately, it may not matter. The church understood that the healing power of Jesus went along with the impassioned proclamation of his name.

POSTSCRIPT

- Troas was named for the region around the ancient city of Troy, whose site was about ten miles up the coast.

- Paul's meeting in Troas involved communion ("breaking the bread") and was held on Sunday, the first day of the week. Most Christian services by this time were held on this day.

Silas

SILAS WENT ON MISSIONARY journeys with Paul. It's also possible that Paul dictated some of the letters that were accepted into the New Testament to Silas.

We first meet Silas at the end of a significant Church council that decided that Gentile Christians did *not* have to convert to Judaism—that is, they did not have to keep the Jewish law in order to be Christians in good standing. But, as an apparent compromise measure, the council also wrote a note, asking Gentiles to abstain from immoral behavior. This message was sent with Paul and Barnabas to the Antioch church. But just to make sure the message would be well received, the council also sent two of their most respected men. One of them was Silas (see Acts 15).

Because Paul and Barnabas decided to split and go on separate missions, Paul needed a new partner for his second missionary journey. Paul chose Silas. This second trip revisited churches in Asia Minor but also extended into Macedonia and Greece. So we find Silas singing hymns with Paul in jail at Philippi before an earthquake rattles their cell (see Acts 16:16–40). It seems that Silas stayed in the area of Philippi, Berea, and Thessalonica for a while after Paul moved on. Later he rejoined Paul in Corinth, where they stayed for more than a year. This suggests he was not just an assistant to Paul but an independent associate.

This itinerary also explains why Silas is mentioned in Paul's letters to the Corinthians and the Thessalonians, since Silas spent substantial time with both of those churches. In fact, some think Silas might have written a good portion of the two Thessalonian letters.

An acknowledgment in Peter's first epistle establishes Silas's writing credentials. Peter says he has written his letter "through" his faithful brother Silas (1 Peter 5:12). This commendation describes a relationship common in ancient literature, where a person of note dictates to a ghostwriter or secretary who has the ability to improve the author's writing. Peter had learned a great deal from Jesus, but as a fisherman by trade, he might have needed Silas to fix his grammar.

POSTSCRIPT

■ Silas the missionary was probably also Silvanus the writer. They are two forms of the same name, which in Hebrew is *Saul*. Where we know other New Testament characters by Hebrew and Greek names, the names *Silas* and *Silvanus* are Aramaic and Latin. That suggests Silas was more connected with Syria and Rome than with Jerusalem.

The Epistles to Timothy (First) and Titus

Together with Second Timothy, these letters are known as the "Pastoral Epistles," since they chiefly contain directions to pastors explaining how to shepherd a local ministry. They lay out the duties and qualities of local church officials, who must master themselves and manage their own households if they hope to be counted worthy of authority over the household of God. The letters stress the importance of teaching Christians to live in ways that will bear a good witness to the society around them, particularly by embodying the society's best values (such as self-control, justice, and modesty) and fulfilling society's expectations for certain groups of people (the young, wives, slaves). They also stress the importance of preserving solid teaching in churches rather than allowing popular ideas to lead the Church to drift from its moorings in the gospel of Jesus handed down by his witnesses.

Both Timothy and Titus figure prominently as important team members in other Pauline letters, and Timothy plays a significant supporting role in Acts, as well. The letter to Titus places Titus in Crete, overseeing the growth of a church that has been planted there and is developing local leadership. First Timothy places Paul's younger coworker in Ephesus. Neither of these situations is otherwise specifically mentioned in Acts—which never speaks of a mission to Crete—or the other Pauline letters. It is true, however, that Acts presents a very selective history.

The official and rather impersonal tone of these letters to Paul's longtime friends and partners, along with observations about the distinctive vocabulary of these letters when set beside other Pauline writings, has suggested to many that they were written by a disciple of Paul in his name. These letters, however, also resemble letters emperors would send to governors to be read in the hearing of the local population. These epistles had an official tone because they had an official purpose: to authorize delegates to act with authority and to lay out the scope of that authority. These letters of Paul would have been read aloud to the whole church, serving much the same function.

POSTSCRIPT

Polycarp, the bishop of Smyrna, used these letters extensively in his own letter to the church in Philippi, written around A.D. 113, attesting to the early acceptance of their value and authority.

Sadducees

THE SADDUCEES WERE A PARTY of Jewish leaders that emerged about 160 B.C., while the Maccabees were fighting for Jewish independence. When the historian Josephus first reports on them, he contrasts them with the Pharisees, and these two groups seem to be linked as opponents right on through Jesus' time. (It seems their opposition to Jesus was one of the few things they agreed on.)

Apparently the Sadducees were a party formed from the upper class. Because they were also of the priestly class, many of them served in the temple in Jerusalem. In many ways, however, their views were secular. They did not believe in an afterlife. They believed in self-determinism. Josephus described them this way: "They take away fate . . . they suppose that all our actions are in our own power, so that we are ourselves the causes of what is good." They also were comfortable speaking Greek and adopting Greek customs.

When the Maccabees succeeded in their revolt, they began a dynasty, with brothers and children serving as kings and priests over the next hundred years. The Sadducees were closely tied to the ruling family; some may have been family members themselves. Not surprisingly, this group assumed control of the Sanhedrin, the Jewish ruling council.

In Jesus' time, both the Sadducees and Pharisees served on the council. Rome held the political power, of course, but they allowed the high priest and the council to determine many local matters. The Sadducees would still have been the aristocracy of Jerusalem, closely tied to the high priests, who were mostly members of the corrupt Annas family.

Both John the Baptist and Jesus took issue with the "Pharisees and Sadducees," but that doesn't mean that the two groups had patched up their differences. Both groups had some measure of power in that society, and both viewed Jesus as a threat to the status quo.

POSTSCRIPT

▪ The Apostle Paul cleverly extricated himself out of a jam by using a disagreement between the Pharisees and Sadducees. His trial before the Sanhedrin wasn't going well, so he declared himself a Pharisee and said he was being tried for preaching about the afterlife (see Acts 23:6). That split the council.

▪ The name *Sadducee* seems to come from the Hebrew word for "righteous," which is odd, because they weren't known for their purity. It's possible that the Sadducees descended from the priest Zadok, from whom they might have received their name.

The Destruction of the Temple

FROM THE GOSPEL OF MARK comes this intriguing verbal exchange: "As he came out of the temple, one of his disciples said to him, 'Look, Teacher, what large stones and what large buildings.' Then Jesus asked him, 'Do you see these great buildings? Not one stone will be left here upon another; all will be thrown down'" (Mark 13:1–2).

Jesus' words would have been intensely offensive to most of the Jews of his day. The temple was deeply sacred to them. It was a place where sacrifices were offered, both for thanksgiving and atonement. It was a place where prayers were invoked and where special holy days such as Passover, Shavuoth, and Succoth were celebrated. The temple was the center of economic and commercial activity, and it housed the national treasury. Even more significantly, the temple was seen as the dwelling place of God, the place where the divine and the earthly came together in a special way.

Most Jews of Jesus' day would not have heard his words in a positive light. It would not be surprising if they misheard him—deliberately or not—and claimed that Jesus himself said that he would destroy the temple. It is, therefore, not surprising that later Jesus was mocked as one who claimed that he would destroy the temple and then raise it again in three days (see Mark 15:29).

After several years of civil war, rebellion, and famine in Jerusalem, the Roman army stripped the surrounding forests bare, piled the wood on the city buildings, and burned it, as well as the temple, to the ground. Meanwhile, the Jewish population in Jerusalem was obliterated. Again the words that Jesus spoke to the wailing women on his way to the cross were fulfilled (see Luke 23:27–31). And although the physical temple was not rebuilt—either in three days or in the subsequent two millennia—three days after Jesus was crucified, a different temple was raised.

POSTSCRIPT

■ The temple built by Herod was considered an architectural marvel. The Jewish author Josephus said that to approaching visitors the temple appeared as a "mountain of snow" as it glittered in the sunlight (Josephus's *War* 5.5.6).

■ In Jesus' day, the temple reached up to 90 feet. No part of the temple exists today, except for an outer wall that surrounded the courtyard of the temple. The Romans did not destroy this section of the wall in part because it was not part of the temple itself. Today it is known most frequently as the "Western Wall" or the "Wailing Wall."

The Fall of Jerusalem

THE BABYLONIANS under King Nebuchadnezzar captured and destroyed Jerusalem in 586 B.C., slightly more than 400 years after David had first seized the city from the Jebusites. Nebuchadnezzar had actually invaded and taken a first wave of captives to Babylon in 605 B.C., including Daniel and his friends. A second set of deportations occurred in 597 B.C. At this time, Nebuchadnezzar took Jehoiachin, king of Judah, back to Babylon as a captive, along with all the treasures of the temple and royal palace. He also took captive those citizens who formed the cream of society: officials, warriors, artisans, and smiths. He left only the poorest of the land and installed Jehoiachin's uncle, Mattaniah/Zedekiah, in his place as a vassal king.

A few years later, however, Zedekiah rebelled against Nebuchadnezzar, who returned and laid siege to the city. After two years, his army captured it. This time he utterly destroyed the city, including the temple, the royal palace, and all the great houses. He took captive most of the remaining citizens, including the king, and he left the poorest of the land to be vinedressers and plowmen. He dismantled the great bronze

Jews held captive in Babylon

pillars of the temple and carried away their bronze and all the temple utensils back to Babylon.

It is difficult to overstate the devastating impact that the destruction of their capital city had on God's people. For centuries, Jerusalem and its temple had stood as proud witnesses to God's favor upon them as his chosen people. Despite Judah's downward slide into increasingly corrupted worship through the centuries—interrupted only by occasional reforms and repentance under a few good kings—God nevertheless withheld the destruction of the city for the sake of his promises to David.

Finally, however, God would forgive no more, and he gave the city over to its enemies. Still, his grace shone through the prophet Jeremiah, who encouraged the people, saying they should settle in and around Babylon, build houses and plant gardens, and wait for the appointed time when God's elect would be restored to their homeland. In time, God did fulfill these promises, and his people returned to rebuild the city and the temple.

Jeremiah the Prophet

JEREMIAH, ALONG WITH ISAIAH and Ezekiel, is one of the "major prophets," so-called because of the length of their books. His name means "Jehovah will lift up." We know more about Jeremiah than about any other prophet, both because he was more transparent concerning his emotions and because roughly one third of his lengthy book consists of narrative accounts of the momentous events in which he was a participant. His prophetic ministry stretched over a 40-year period, 627 to 586 B.C., which climaxed with the destruction of Jerusalem.

Jeremiah was born in a village near Jerusalem and was the son of Hilkiah, a priest of Anathoth in the land of Benjamin. God called him as a young man, saying, "Before I formed you in the womb I knew you, and before you were born I consecrated you; I appointed you a prophet to the nations" (Jeremiah 1:5). Moreover, God told him not to marry, because conditions in the land were so terrible that any children would die of deadly diseases, unnoticed and unmourned.

The times were the last decades before the fall of Jerusalem and the exile of the people to Babylon. Much of Jeremiah's message consisted in warnings about the people's sins and calls to repent. But it soon was too late: God let the Babylonians under Nebuchadnezzar have their way with his people. Yet in his grace, God gave Jeremiah words for dealing with the impending doom.

One of Jeremiah's recurring themes is that God's people should not look to Egypt for help but rather they should submit to the coming punishment from Babylon, go quietly into exile, and settle down there. Jeremiah's message was not popular, even among his family (see Jeremiah 12:6). He was subjected to ridicule, death threats, and imprisonment. He was even thrown into a cistern, where he sank into the mud until he was rescued. Despite his warnings about *not* trusting in Egypt, in the end, when Jerusalem fell, some Jews took him against his will down to Egypt.

The plight of the Jews, nevertheless, had moved him to passionate outbursts such as: "My anguish, my anguish! I writhe in pain! Oh, the walls of my heart! My heart is beating wildly; I cannot keep silent; for I hear the sound of the trumpet, the alarm of war" (Jeremiah 4:19) and "O that my head were a spring of water, and my eyes a fountain of tears, so that I might weep day and night for the slain of my poor people!" (Jeremiah 20:14).

Jeremiah's personal sorrow and his grief for his nation, which the Babylonian army had devastated, are also expressed in the Book of Lamentations. He is thought to have died in exile in Egypt.

Turmoil in Jerusalem

IT WAS SOMETHING LIKE a "farewell tour" for the Apostle Paul. As he headed back from his third missionary journey, he made several stops along the way. The elders of the Ephesian church came to meet him at the seaport and heard an inspiring farewell address (see Acts 20:18–35). He was headed for Jerusalem, primarily to deliver the financial aid he had been raising for the drought-stricken and persecuted people of the mother church. But he heard grim warnings: Danger awaited him in Jerusalem. But, just as Jesus had purposefully stepped toward his Jerusalem destiny, Paul was ready to do the same.

Once in the city, he met with James and the elders of the Jerusalem church. (James, the brother of Jesus, had been leading this church for some time now.) Some brought up their old dispute with Paul. They said he was teaching Jewish Christians in the Gentile world to "forsake Moses" (Acts 21:21), telling them they didn't need to follow the Jewish law. It would ease matters greatly, they said, if he would publicly participate in a ritual of purification at the temple, showing everyone that he was still a devout Jew.

There were four men of the Jerusalem church who had just taken a purifying vow, shaving their heads and committing to an extra level of holiness for seven days. Paul was urged to go with them to the temple and to pay their expenses. Knowing the value of public imagery, Paul agreed. (It's unclear whether Paul himself took a vow at this time. Perhaps he would indicate his support merely by paying for the others.) But the plan backfired.

On the day the vow was completed, some Jews from Asia Minor saw Paul in the area of the temple complex reserved for Jews. Earlier that day, they had seen him in the city with Trophimus, whom they knew to be a Gentile from Ephesus, and it seems they now mistook one of the vow-takers with Paul at the temple for this man. Grabbing Paul, they cried for help, accusing the apostle of defiling the temple by bringing in a Gentile. A riot ensued, and the angry mob began beating Paul, but Roman soldiers intervened. Assuming that he was an Egyptian rebel, the commander had Paul bound and carried to the Antonia Fortress as the crowd yelled, "Away with him!" (verse 36).

Paul was stepping in his Master's footsteps. Jesus had been taken to the same fortress, where Roman soldiers had scourged him. A similar crowd now called for Paul's death. These events would allow Paul to stand before governors and a king as Jesus had, but eventually they would send him to Rome.

Luke the Physician

LUKE WROTE ONE of the four gospels as well as the Acts of the Apostles. He was also one of Paul's devoted companions during Paul's missionary trips and was especially valuable to the group as a physician.

St. Luke *by Edward Bannister*

In the account of Paul's second missionary journey, the text suddenly begins to use the pronoun *we* as the missionaries start out for Macedonia (see Acts 16:10). The obvious conclusion is that Luke joined the mission team at that point, which might mean that he lived in that area—that is, northwestern Asia Minor or Macedonia. Following the pronouns, we surmise that Paul traveled on without Luke but picked him up again when he came back to Philippi on his *third* missionary journey. This time Luke accompanied Paul back to Caesarea and Jerusalem and eventually to Rome. In what was probably his last epistle, written from a Roman prison, Paul wrote, "Only Luke is with me" (2 Timothy 4:11).

In an earlier letter, Paul calls Luke "the beloved physician" (Colossians 4:14). Could it be that, late in his ministry, Paul had health problems that required a doctor's care? (He did pray, "a thorn was given me in the flesh" [2 Corinthians 12:7].) In any case, Luke's medical profession falls in line with a number of observations we can draw from the gospel he wrote.

For one thing, Luke's gospel is especially good at describing the medical conditions of people who came to Jesus for healing. It also shows a concern for the poor and needy befitting a writer who spent his life caring for sick people. Yet even beyond these specific qualities, we can identify a broader scientific mind-set in this writer. In the introduction to his gospel, Luke talks about "investigating everything carefully from the very first, to write an orderly account" (Luke 1:3). Indeed, the gospel seems careful with its facts. The birth of Jesus, for instance, didn't happen "once upon a time." It was in the days of Caesar Augustus, "while Quirinius was governor of Syria" (Luke 2:2).

From time to time historians and archaeologists have set out to prove Luke wrong. They usually come back with a new appreciation for his research. Apparently Luke did his homework.

POSTSCRIPT

■ A comment by Paul in Colossians 4:11 would suggest that Luke was a Gentile. That would make him the only known non-Jewish writer of the New Testament.

The Second Epistle to Timothy

THOUGH PAUL'S SECOND EPISTLE to Timothy is grouped with his first letter to Timothy and his letter to Titus—collectively they are known as the "Pastoral Epistles"—such grouping obscures the significant differences between the more official instructions in the other two letters and this very personal letter to his protégé. The letter opens with personal remarks about Timothy's character, Paul's pride in him, and reminiscences about Timothy's mother and grandmother, as well as their contributions to Timothy's faith. The letter ends with a lengthy list of personal greetings from Paul and his companions to specific people around Timothy. Paul also includes personal instructions to bring the cloak and parchments that he had left in Troas. The vocabulary of this letter aligns better with the remaining Pauline epistles than do First Timothy and Titus, which has led many scholars to affirm that Paul himself wrote Second Timothy.

Paul writes from a Roman prison, where he is awaiting execution. The book is traditionally dated around A.D. 64, during the brief but fierce persecution of Christians in Rome under Nero. The chief purpose of the letter is to help prepare Timothy to carry on after Paul's death. Of paramount importance is Paul's charge to Timothy to guard the message about Jesus as it had been handed on to him; he is instructed to speak out regarding distortions of it. Having encountered enough religious charlatans during his own ministry, Paul expresses concern that Timothy continue to defend the flock against such wolves. He also urges Timothy to continue to look after his own soul's well-being, keeping himself rooted in the Scriptures and the teaching he has received from Paul. He is also told to keep his own passions and desires in check.

A second major theme concerns the inevitable experiences of persecution. Even though the Christian strives to live a virtuous life, he or she will often be treated as a deviant. Paul urges Timothy to show fortitude in the face of suffering, to refuse to allow the hostility or insults of non-Christians to make him feel ashamed of the gospel. He is also to stand beside those whom society targets for their beliefs rather than being embarrassed to be associated with them. This was the example Timothy observed in Paul, and it ultimately was the example of Jesus himself. Paul assures Timothy that by trusting in the reward that God guards for the faithful disciple, the victim of society's abuse becomes the victor.

Scribes

A T FIRST, SCRIBES WERE BASICALLY secretaries. A ruler would need a writer to handle official correspondence. A merchant might hire someone to write out bills of sale. But when the Jews returned from the Babylonian Exile, the role of the scribe took on a specialized meaning.

The scribe Ezra rewriting the sacred records

Ezra was the prototype. Though he was a priest, he was also called "a scribe skilled in the law of Moses" and "a scholar of the text of the commandments of the Lord" (Ezra 7:6, 11). We're told that "Ezra had set his heart to study the law of the Lord, and to do it, and to teach the statutes and ordinances in Israel" (verse 10). Immediately we see he's far more than a stenographer.

Most of the Jews returning to Judaea were rather ignorant of the Law of Moses. Ezra took on the task of teaching them. He also trained a team of teachers to help him (see Nehemiah 8:7, 13). Jewish tradition credits Ezra with gathering together the Hebrew Scriptures. If he didn't do it, then other scribes did. Over the next few centuries, scribes became the curators of God's Word. Long before the printing press, they still needed to copy the Scriptures by hand, but they also studied the text, interpreted it, and taught it.

"He seeks out the wisdom of all the ancients and is occupied with the prophets' writings," writes Ben Sirach about scribes in the Apocryphal book of Ecclesiasticus. "He is careful to remember the sayings of the famous, and he can perceive the subtle truths of parables. He searches out the hidden meanings of proverbs and is very familiar with the secrets of parables. His services are employed by the great, and he appears before the rulers" (39:1–4).

Scribes became well respected in Jewish society. Some scribes were included with priests and nobles in the Sanhedrin, the ruling council. Originally scribes *were* priests, or at least from priestly families (descendants of Aaron), but by Jesus' time any Jew could train to be a scribe.

The gospels link scribes with Pharisees, but these terms are separate designations. "Scribe" refers to a job; "Pharisee" to a party affiliation. Many scribes were Pharisees, upholding the oral tradition as well as the written Torah, but some weren't. And not all Pharisees were scribes. Jesus attacked both groups for their hypocrisy.

The Crucifixion of Jesus

To the Christians in Corinth, the Apostle Paul wrote, "For Jews demand signs and Greeks desire wisdom, but we proclaim Christ crucified, a stumbling block to Jews and foolishness to Gentiles" (1 Corinthians 1:22–23). What was Paul trying to convey to the Corinthians? Paul realized that preaching a crucified Christ was difficult for nonbelievers to accept.

Jews emphasized that anyone "hung on a tree" was "under God's curse" (Deuteronomy 21:23). Romans saw crucifixion as so horrific that it was used only on foreigners, slaves, and those who committed treason. The Roman philosopher Cicero called it the most extreme form of punishment. Because crucifixions were performed alongside the roads, frequently at the entrance to a city, people were familiar with this grisly form of death.

Christ on the Cross *by Diego Velasquez*

The death itself was intense, for the crucified expired slowly of asphyxia and severe cramps. Sometimes the corpses were displayed or left hanging on the crosses, where birds and wild beasts picked the bones clean.

Jesus probably carried only the crossbeam, not the entire cross, to Golgotha. Even then, we are told that Simon of Cyrene assisted him. Before his crucifixion, Jesus—like others—had been beaten, scourged, and humiliated. Such torture certainly increased his agony on the cross.

During his teaching ministry, Jesus had said, "If any want to become my followers, let them deny themselves and take up their cross and follow me" (Mark 8:34). Of course, what he meant could not fully be understood until after his ordeal on the cross. Meanwhile, it is not surprising that Jews and Greeks responded the way they did. For who can believe in someone who claimed to be the Son of God and yet died ignobly on the cross in such utter humiliation and anguish?

POSTSCRIPT

■ The oldest evidence of a crucifixion comes from Persia in the sixth century B.C., where Darius I is said to have crucified more than 3,000 political opponents.

■ Tradition says Peter was crucified upside down because he asserted that he was unworthy to be crucified as his Lord had been.

Ezekiel's Amazing Vision

G OD RAISED UP EZEKIEL as a prophet in extremely hard times for
the Jews during the years immediately preceding and following the
Babylonian destruction of Jerusalem. In order to impress upon Ezekiel
something of his awesome and glorious nature, God showed Ezekiel a
spectacular vision that formed the basis of his call to a prophetic ministry. That vision would also strengthen him during difficult times.

In this vision, he saw a raging storm with lightning flashing continually.
Out of the storm appeared four living creatures that had the bodies of
men, but each had four faces and four wings, with human hands under
each wing. The front face was that of a man; on the right, a lion; on the
left, an ox; and behind, an eagle. The creatures moved in unison, darting
to and fro like flashes of lightning, and burning coals of fire like torches
moved among them.

Ezekiel then saw four wheels, one for each of the four creatures. They
gleamed like beryl crystal, and their rims were full of eyes, and wherever
the creatures went, the wheels followed. The Bible says the creatures
would go "wherever the spirit would go" (Ezekiel 1:12). Given the context
of the vision, in which God was revealing to Ezekiel something of his
glory, "the spirit" was likely God's Spirit.

Above the creatures, Ezekiel saw something like a dome, shining like
crystal, and above that a sapphire throne. On it was seated a fiery creature
whose form was not discernible, and "there was a splendor all around"
(verse 27).

What was the significance of this vision? The details are impossible to
correlate specifically with prophecies or events, but the overall impres-
sion was what mattered. Ezekiel wrote that "this was the appearance of
the likeness of the glory of the Lord" (verse 28), and he fell on his face in
worship. He then heard the sound of a voice speaking. God wanted him
to go as a prophet to his people, who had "a hard forehead and a stubborn
heart" (Ezekiel 3:7). But God promised to make Ezekiel's forehead and
heart harder than flint in order to withstand the opposition he would face
as he brought harsh words from the Lord to his rebellious people.

In the years before the destruction of Jerusalem, Ezekiel's words were indeed
harsh warnings. But after the fall of that city, Ezekiel spoke gentler words
and assured the people of God's forgiveness if they would turn to him.

Ezekiel the Prophet

EZEKIEL AND HIS CONTEMPORARY, Jeremiah, were the two great prophets of the Babylonian Exile. The Lord raised up Ezekiel to warn the Jewish people about the coming judgment—that is, exile in Babylon—and also to give the people messages of hope concerning their restoration to their homeland.

Like Jeremiah, Ezekiel was a son of a priest. His prophetic ministry unfolded over 20 years, from 593 to 573 B.C., which included a searing, defining moment: the destruction of Jerusalem by the Babylonians in 586. He himself was taken captive in the second deportation to Babylon in 597 B.C. As a result, his early messages were indictments of God's people, whereas his later messages were messages of hope for a better future.

God called Ezekiel to confront a wicked and stubborn people, and he equipped Ezekiel for this difficult ministry. He told Ezekiel, "I have made your face hard against their faces, and your forehead hard against their foreheads. Like the hardest stone, harder than flint, I have made your forehead; do not fear them or be dismayed at their looks, for they are a rebellious house" (Ezekiel 3:8–9). In addition, God subjected Ezekiel to a very severe test: He took the life of Ezekiel's wife and then forbade him to mourn or weep as a sign to the Jews that they should do the same when trouble came.

Ezekiel was known for his many dramatic visions. For example, once, while sitting in his house by the River Chebar and entertaining the elders of Judah, he was transported in several visions to Jerusalem to "see" what was happening there. Furthermore, the final nine chapters of his book tell of his vision of a new temple and a new Jerusalem in richly textured detail.

Ezekiel also performed many "acted signs," which were mini-dramas that illustrated his prophetic message. For example, he ate a scroll with God's words on it to illustrate the point that he was to speak only God's words (see Ezekiel 3:1–3). He also laid on his left side for 390 days and on his right side for 40 days, "bearing" the punishment of the house of Israel during that time (see Ezekiel 4:4–6). Moreover, God told him to prepare "an exile's baggage" as a sign that God's people would soon go into exile (see Ezekiel 12:3–6).

Ezekiel was a distinguished prophet among his people, but nothing is known of his death and how the people reacted to his passing.

Appealing to Caesar

THE ROMAN SOLDIERS who arrested Paul in Jerusalem surely saved his life. When a mob mistakenly believed that Paul had brought a Gentile into the temple, they had started to beat him to death. At that point, a Roman commander intervened and took Paul into custody, thinking he was a rebel warlord. He soon learned Paul possessed Roman citizenship. That changed everything, for Roman citizens had legal rights that most residents of occupied territories lacked.

Nevertheless, the Roman commander convened a makeshift trial with the chief priests and Jewish council interrogating Paul. This soon became a shouting match, and nothing was resolved. Some council members then devised a plot to kill Paul. They would ask the commander to bring Paul to their meeting place for further questioning and do away with him along the way. But Paul's nephew overheard the conspirators and informed the commander, who secretly took Paul to Caesarea under armed guard.

Paul spent the next few years under minimum security in a Caesarean prison, meeting occasionally with the Roman governor, Felix, who had heard the case against Paul but kept wanting to hear more. Familiar with the Christian faith, he might have wanted some spiritual guidance, but he was also hoping Paul would bribe him. Two years later, Porcius Festus replaced Felix, and the process was repeated. The chief priests brought their charges to the new governor, petitioning that Paul be brought to Jerusalem to stand trial. Once again they planned to murder Paul in an ambush along the way. So Paul pulled out his trump card, announcing, "I appeal to the emperor" (Acts 25:11). As a Roman citizen in an occupied territory, he could demand a trial in a Roman court. Not only was this a lifesaving tactic for him, but it ensured that he'd be able to preach the gospel in Rome, something he had long wanted to do.

While waiting for the transport to Rome, Paul had another audience with the governor, who had also invited King Herod Agrippa and Queen Bernice. Festus called Paul insane, but the king and queen seemed more favorable. They commented afterward, "This man could have been set free if he had not appealed to the emperor" (Acts 26:32).

POSTSCRIPT

■ There are records of Roman citizens having their appeal to Caesar denied in the case of murder, banditry, or piracy. Festus did confer with the legal experts in his court before granting Paul's appeal.

Timothy

Timothy was the grandson of Lois and the son of Eunice—two women full of faith in Christ. He was also the spiritually adopted son of the Apostle Paul, who calls him "my loyal child in the faith" (1 Timothy 1:2) and "my beloved child" (2 Timothy 1:2).

Paul met young Timothy in the town of Lystra in Asia Minor (modern Turkey) on his second missionary journey. The boy was the product of mixed parentage: His mother was Jewish, and his father was Greek. Paul had already visited the town on his first trip, so it's possible that Timothy and his mother (and grandmother) had become Christians at that time. There is no further mention of Timothy's father, suggesting that he was dead or absent. Since he already had a good reputation among believers in a couple of towns, we might guess that Timothy was an older teenager.

The gospel, as Paul preached it, involved breaking down barriers between Jews and Gentiles. Timothy was the poster child for that. Still, to facilitate ministry among the Jews, Paul took the paternal role in having this "son" circumcised. Then Timothy joined Paul's mission team. And he wasn't just tagging along. Paul felt comfortable going alone to Athens, leaving Timothy to start the church in Berea with Silas.

Frequent references to Timothy in Paul's letters indicate that he was one of the apostle's most loyal and most active companions. When he wasn't with Paul, he was on assignment for him. Apparently Timothy was sent to Corinth on a troubleshooting mission ("to remind you of my ways in Christ Jesus," Paul writes in 1 Corinthians 4:17) and to Philippi for similar reasons. "I have no one like him," Paul wrote, "... like a son with a father he has served me in the work of the gospel" (Philippians 2:20, 22). Timothy also brought Paul encouraging news from Thessalonica (see 1 Thessalonians 3:6).

Timothy was pastoring the church at Ephesus when Paul wrote two epistles to him. These were penned late in Paul's life, and they have the feel of comments during the last days of his life. Paul urged Timothy to withstand false teaching, lead a pure life, and set up good leadership systems within the Church.

The Epistle to Philemon

THE SHORTEST OF PAUL'S letters is also his most personal letter. Paul writes from prison, this time probably in Ephesus. Acts does not mention such an imprisonment. Paul, however, speaks of being imprisoned several times before his final series of trials (see 2 Corinthians 6:5; 11:23) and of his facing severe hardships in Ephesus. In any case, he is prompted to write this letter after a visit from Onesimus, a slave from the house of Philemon, who has left his master under some difficult circumstances.

We do not know precisely what these circumstances are. It has been suggested that Onesimus stole something from Philemon and ran away, but this is based more on ancient prejudice against slaves than actual evidence. It is more probable that Onesimus was simply discontent being a slave, a life he had not chosen for himself. Paul knows that he did not perform his services well. Perhaps it was Philemon's anger at his slave's lack of enthusiasm that made him leave, or it could have been Onesimus's own desire to improve his situation.

In seeking out Paul, Onesimus did not behave like a runaway slave. Though his departure was unauthorized, by going to one of his master's friends for mediation, he technically did not leave his master's extended household. While with Paul, Onesimus became a Christian, even as Paul had previously led Philemon to Christ. Onesimus served Paul in a way that he had never served Philemon—with enthusiasm for his newfound faith. So Paul sent Onesimus home with a letter requesting that Philemon give Onesimus his freedom to help the apostle—as a personal favor to Paul, to whom Philemon owed his very soul. Paul made this request in a letter that would be read out loud to the church that gathered in his house, cleverly putting Philemon's reputation at stake in his decision. Even though Paul did not crusade against slavery, this letter is a witness to his conviction that two Christians cannot be master and slave to each other.

POSTSCRIPT

■ On the way to his martyrdom in Rome in A.D. 110, Ignatius of Antioch wrote seven letters, one of them to the Christians in Ephesus. In this letter, he speaks highly of their bishop, a man named Onesimus. While Onesimus was not an uncommon name, it is quite possible that we find here the "end" of the story of the slave who became Paul's coworker.

Hanukkah

IN A WAY, HANUKKAH is a Jewish celebration of independence from foreign tyrants. It celebrates a miracle that occurred in a pivotal time in Jewish history, when brave heroes stood up against cruel overlords and won.

The year was 165 B.C. For four centuries, the Jewish nation had been ruled by others—first Babylon, then Persia, then Alexander the Great and his generals. Most recently, they were part of the Seleucid Empire, the Asian part of Alexander's legacy. In general, the Jews had learned to cope with their servitude. In fact, they actually enjoyed peaceful relationships with Persia and with Alexander, but when Antiochus IV took power for the Seleucids, he made life miserable for devout Jews.

His aim was to unite the empire with Greek culture. Alexander had started this process, making Athenian (Attic) Greek the official language of the territories he conquered. But then Antiochus forcibly imposed Greek religion on the lands that resisted, such as Judaea. In 168 B.C., Antiochus commandeered the temple in Jerusalem and dedicated it to the worship of Zeus, defiling the holy altar.

That set a violent revolution in motion. It took three years of fierce fighting, but Judas Maccabeus finally retook Jerusalem in 165 B.C. He replaced the defiled altar and planned an eight-day festival to rededicate the temple, cleansing it from the sacrilege of Antiochus. The problem was that there was only enough consecrated oil to burn the sacred lamps for

one day. The Talmud speaks of a divine miracle, however, saying the oil lasted all eight days of the festival. That's why Jews today light eight candles for Hanukkah.

Hanukkah begins on the 25th of the Hebrew month of Kislev and lasts for eight days. This period usually comes in mid- to late December. It is not one of the more prominent Jewish holidays, such as Passover, Rosh Hashanah, and Yom Kippur, but it has gained attention in Christian nations because of its proximity to Christmas. A new candle is lit on the eight-branched menorah for each day of the festival (there's also a place for the "service" candle that lights the others). There are particular prayers and songs for this holiday, and sometimes other traditions are upheld, such as the spinning of a top known as a *dreidl* or the giving of coins or candy *(gelt)* to children.

Seven Statements from the Cross

E VEN AFTER ALL THAT JESUS had suffered and while he endured great
pain, his first words on the cross still expressed his compassion for
his tormentors: "Father, forgive them; for they do not know what they
are doing" (Luke 23:34). Indeed, it was because of mercy and grace that
he chose to die for the sins of the world. This was demonstrated when he
promised one of the thieves that he would be in Paradise (see verse 43)
and when he commended his mother into the care of the Apostle John
(see John 19:26–27).

According to the gospels of Matthew and
Mark, however, among Jesus' last words—
presented in Aramaic—were "Eloi, Eloi, lema
sabachthani?" (Mark 15:34; see also Matthew
27:46). At first, some bystanders wondered
aloud if Jesus was summoning the prophet
Elijah. Those Aramaic words, however, were
a prophetic prayer found in Psalm 22:1: "My
God, my God, why have you forsaken me?"

What might stand out even more than the
words themselves are the words Jesus did not
quote. He spoke the opening line of the psalm. Those familiar with the
psalm, however, would know that as this psalm develops, ultimately it
focuses on faith and trust. As it progresses, it acknowledges that even in
the midst of doubt, there is absolute trust in God's sovereign plan. And
even in the midst of the worst death imaginable, Jesus cried out "My
God," and that relationship is what sustained him in death and beyond.

According to the Gospel of John, Jesus continued to fulfill Scripture
(see Psalm 22:15) when he uttered, "I am thirsty" (John 19:28). And
then toward the end of his ordeal, he said, "It is finished" (verse 30). With
this statement, Jesus was acknowledging the larger purpose behind his
death. These words were a natural culmination of a life lived toward a
focused goal.

Finally, Jesus said, "Father, into your hands I commend my spirit" (Luke
23:46), and then he breathed his last. Jesus' last words on the cross almost
seem to point beyond him to the Acts of the Apostles, the second volume
written by Luke. The Spirit that strengthened Jesus on the cross is also
presented in Acts 2 as the same Spirit that empowers the disciples at Pentecost, inaugurating the Church in Jerusalem and throughout the world.

Shadrach, Meshach, and Abednego

S HADRACH, MESHACH, AND ABEDNEGO—along with Daniel—were among the Jewish youths "without physical defect and handsome, versed in every branch of wisdom, endowed with knowledge and insight" (Daniel 1:4), whom King Nebuchadnezzar brought to Babylon to be instructed in the language and learning of the Babylonians.

In the Fiery Furnace *by James Tissot*

While in Babylon, these four youths would not eat the king's rich food, opting instead for vegetables, which resulted in their looking much healthier than anyone else in the court. God also gave them "knowledge and skill in every aspect of literature and wisdom," and the king found them "ten times better" than all the magicians and enchanters in his kingdom (verses 17, 20). It is no surprise, then, that he kept them in his court to serve him. It is also not surprising that others in the court became extremely envious of their status with the king.

When Nebuchadnezzar erected a gigantic golden statue nine stories high and ordered all the people of the land to bow down to it, Shadrach, Meshach, and Abednego refused to obey, affording some jealous Chaldeans the opportunity to report this affront to the king, who became incensed. Nebuchadnezzar was so filled with rage against them that he ordered that the fiery furnace, which had been prepared for anyone who disobeyed the order, be heated seven times hotter. When it reached the desired heat, the three men were thrown into it. When this was done, the fire was so hot that it consumed those who threw the three Jewish youths into the furnace.

Shadrach, Meshach, and Abednego, however, were not consumed. The king was astonished to see that they were unhurt and walking around freely inside the furnace. Furthermore, there was a fourth person with them, who looked like a god. So the king ordered them brought out of the furnace, and he saw that no hair on their heads was singed, their clothes were not burned, and they did not even smell like smoke.

Nebuchadnezzar was astonished, but he recognized that the God of these three men had delivered them. Accordingly, he issued a decree that no one should speak against this God on pain of death. He testified that "there is no other god who is able to deliver in this way" (Daniel 3:29).

Nebuchadnezzar

NEBUCHADNEZZAR WAS KING of Babylon from 605 to 562 B.C., a critical time in the history of the southern kingdom of Judah. His father, Nabopolassar, had captured Nineveh, the capital of the Assyrian Empire, in 612 B.C., bringing vast, far-flung lands under Babylonian control. Nebuchadnezzar is important in the Bible primarily as the king who destroyed Jerusalem and deported the Jews.

Nebuchadnezzar invaded Judah and took captives back to Babylon three times: in 605, 597, and 586 B.C. Each time, he took the cream of society, leaving the land increasingly desolated. Daniel was among the exiles of the first deportation. In the second, Nebuchadnezzar carried off the treasures of the temple and the king's palace, as well as a thousand captives that included the highest officials, warriors, artisans, and smiths. He also exiled King Jehoiachin, who had rebelled against him, and installed Jehoiachin's uncle Mattaniah as a vassal king in his place.

The third deportation was the worst. This time, Nebuchadnezzar essentially razed the city to the ground, burning the temple, the king's palace, and all the great houses. He slaughtered the king's sons, then put the king's eyes out and exiled him. He dismantled the great bronze pillars in front of the temple and carried them away, along with all the remaining temple vessels. The impact of this devastation was incalculable. The Book of Lamentations gives voice to the grief over the destruction, as does Psalm 137.

In the Book of Daniel, however, Nebuchadnezzar appears as a much different man. The wisdom, skills and faith of Daniel and his friends impress him, and he utters words of praise to their God. When Daniel interprets his dream for him, he says, "Truly, your God is God of gods and Lord of kings and a revealer of mysteries" (Daniel 2:47).

Later, God humbles Nebuchadnezzar in his pride as he boasts of the magnificence of the royal capital he has built. He is then "driven away from human society, and . . . made to eat grass like oxen" until he learns "that the Most High has sovereignty over the kingdom of mortals and gives it to whom he will" (Daniel 4:32). After a period of madness during which his hair grows "as long as eagles' feathers" and his nails become "like birds' claws," and after his crown is restored to him, he praises God, declaring, "I, Nebuchadnezzar, praise and extol and honor the King of heaven, for all his works are truth and his ways are justice; and he is able to bring low those who walk in pride" (verses 33, 37).

Shipwrecked!

BY APPEALING TO CAESAR, Paul had won himself a trip to Rome—but in chains. He would get his opportunity to defend himself in a Roman court, but getting there was another matter. He was put in the custody of a centurion named Julius, a member of the esteemed Augustan Cohort, along with other prisoners. Two of Paul's colleagues, Aristarchus and Luke, also took this journey, either as fellow prisoners or free passengers.

It was most likely early autumn when their ship left Caesarea, hugging the coastline and making several stops. Paul was given an unusual amount of freedom: At the port of Sidon, he was even allowed to visit with supportive friends. Throughout his ministry, Paul connected well with Gentile authorities, gaining respect with his cosmopolitan knowledge. Combined with the fact that he seemed to embrace his prisoner status, this may have convinced Julius that Paul was not a flight risk.

At one port in Asia Minor, they caught a freighter bound for Italy. This was a large ship, carrying 276 people, plus a cargo of wheat. With the prevailing winds against them, the westward journey was difficult, and each delay made the trip more treacherous. As an experienced traveler, Paul predicted disaster, but the crew pressed on. When a storm threatened the ship, Paul couldn't resist an "I told you so," but he reassured the passengers by relating a dream. An angel had told him that all of them—but not the ship—would come through this crisis safely.

The ship hit rocks in shallow waters near the island of Malta. The crew jettisoned the cargo to get closer to land. The soldiers wanted to kill the prisoners, but the centurion, wanting to save Paul, prevented them. The passengers swam, floated, or were carried to land, where the islanders showed them "unusual kindness" (Acts 28:2).

As he put some brushwood into a bonfire, a viper bit Paul. Witnessing the snakebite, the locals assumed that he was a murderer being punished by the gods, and if a shipwreck couldn't kill him, a snake would. But Paul shook off the creature and suffered no harm, which altered their opinion of Paul: They now thought he was a god. Later, Paul had the opportunity to heal the father of the leading man of the island, and that led others to come to him for healing. We can assume that Paul healed in Jesus' name, but there is no record of any formal preaching. After three months in Malta, they caught another ship for Rome.

Titus

TITUS WAS A GOOD FRIEND of Paul's, as well as a coworker. He also became pastor of the struggling church in Crete, and he is the addressee of one of Paul's epistles in the New Testament.

Titus first appeared on the scene at the Jerusalem council detailed in Acts 15. Paul and Barnabas had just returned from their first missionary journey, during which they had preached to Jews and Gentiles alike. It's likely that Titus, a Gentile, became a Christian during this journey and accompanied the missionaries to the council meeting as Exhibit A. The apostles were debating not just *whether* Gentiles could become Christians but also *on what terms.* Paul and Barnabas won a general victory when the apostles agreed that Gentiles did not have to convert to Judaism (and be circumcised) to be Christians. This was certainly good news for Titus (see Galatians 2:1–3).

It seems likely that Titus traveled with Paul on his second journey, but the next time we hear about him is on the third. During a lengthy stay in Ephesus, Paul learned that the Corinthian Christians were revolting. There were factions in that church disputing Paul's authority and second-guessing his doctrine. He first sent Timothy to fix things, then Titus. Later, Titus reunited with Paul, reporting that his troubleshooting trip was a success and the Corinthians were feeling good about Paul once again (2 Corinthians 7:6–7). Titus carried the second Corinthian epistle back to that church and helped collect funds for famine relief in Judaea (see 2 Corinthians 8:16–19).

The Book of Acts ends with Paul under house arrest in Rome, but clues from the epistles point to what happened after this. It seems that Paul might have been acquitted and at some point traveled to the island of Crete, taking Titus with him. He left Titus there in a pastoral role.

It was difficult work, but Titus had stepped up to the challenge in Corinth, and he was ready for this one. Paul warned that Titus's new congregation had "many rebellious people, idle talkers and deceivers" (Titus 1:10). False teachers were plentiful in the early Church, and Crete had more than its share. "Exhort and reprove with all authority," Paul wrote. "Let no one look down on you" (Titus 2:15).

According to tradition, Titus served as bishop of Crete into his elderly years and died there.

The Epistle to the Hebrews

EARLY CHRISTIANS were often subjected to the indignities that unpopular groups suffer: insults, physical assaults, economic boycott, even prejudice within the legal system. A number of the Christians addressed by the letter to the Hebrews had experienced all of the above (10:32–34). They followed a crucified political dissident. They refused to honor the gods of their neighbors, families, and friends. But they also increasingly did not fit the profile of the devout Jew, since they did not follow the Jewish law. They did not "fit" any known category, and so they were regarded as something foreign, quite probably dangerous. Their neighbors tried to cajole and pressure them into finding a better way of life, while also trying to deter others from joining the Church.

The author writes to these Christians, who have lost not only their respect in society but also their property, to set before them all that they have gained as a result of their faith in Jesus. They now have a high priest who has made everything right between them and God. They have lasting possessions in a heavenly homeland that they will soon enter when Christ returns to shake the visible earth and heavens and open the way into God's realm. The author speaks of Christ in the most exalted terms, in part to remind them of the glory that follows the shame and suffering of the cross and in part to warn them not to choose friendship with the unbelieving society at the cost of insulting such a powerful benefactor as Jesus Christ.

Hebrews is actually more of a sermon than a letter. It begins with a grand, artfully composed declaration of the author's theme, not the typical salutation of a letter. The author of Hebrews never actually reveals his identity, only that he knows Timothy (13:23), suggesting that the author worked as part of Paul's rather large team. The Church fathers of the second and third centuries suggested many candidates, including Apollos and Barnabas. Some claimed that Paul wrote the letter, but most modern scholars believe that is unlikely. It was probably written before the destruction of the Jerusalem temple in A.D. 70, since the author refers to the sacrificial system as still currently in operation (10:2–3).

POSTSCRIPT

■ The writer of Hebrews quotes the Septuagint, the ancient Greek translation of the Old Testament, throughout the epistle—except possibly verse 30 of chapter ten.

The Maccabees

Aﬀer the death of Alexander the Great in 323 b.c., his empire was divided among his generals. Judaea became part of the Seleucid kingdom, which was based in Syria. In 168 b.c., the Seleucid ruler, Antiochus IV, decided it was high time that the Jews joined the rest of the kingdom in adopting a Greek way of life. He imposed strict policies against the worship of Yahweh and promoted the worship of Greek deities—even setting up an altar to Zeus in the temple at Jerusalem.

Many Jews complied with these policies, seeing no way to resist, but one aged priest named Mattathias refused to go along with the sacrilege. After he killed a royal officer who was coercing him to commit idolatry, he fled to the mountains with his sons. This was the beginning of the Maccabean resistance.

Shortly after his flight, Mattathias died and left the revolution in the capable hands of his third son, Judas, who led a guerrilla army against the Syrian forces. In 165 b.c., Judas managed to take control of Jerusalem, where he rededicated the defiled temple in an eight-day festival now celebrated as Hanukkah.

Judas was such a powerful general that he gained the nickname *Maccabeus,* "the Hammer." This name became connected with his whole family—father, brothers, and descendants. They were "the Maccabees."

Judas won recognition of religious freedom from the Syrians but kept fighting for political independence, as well. In 161 b.c., he perished in battle and was succeeded by his brothers Jonathan and then Simon, and then Simon's son, John Hyrcanus. All of these Maccabees (also known as *Hasmoneans,* from an earlier ancestor) served as both religious and political leaders. Independence was won, and the territory of Judaea was actually expanded. John Hyrcanus was succeeded by his sons—Aristobulus I and Alexander Jannaeus—and daughter-in-law, Salome Alexandra, who died in 67 b.c. Civil war followed, allowing the Roman general Pompey to conquer Jerusalem in 63 b.c., effectively ending the Jews' century of autonomy.

Something odd occurred, however, along the way. John Hyrcanus began to embrace Greek culture, even though his grandfather had started the fight against Hellenization. This led to the rise of the Sadducee party—aristocrats who rejected the rabbinic traditions. The Sadducees also opposed the Pharisees, who taught separation from Gentile ways.

Death on the Cross

THE GOSPEL OF JOHN says that after Jesus and two thieves were crucified, some of the Jewish rulers wanted to ensure that the bodies were
not left on the crosses on the sabbath. Since the sabbath was a special
time, a time of great solemnity, they approached Pontius Pilate and asked
him if the bodies could be removed.

To make certain that they were truly dead, Pilate
ordered that the legs of the three crucified men
be broken. Because the crucified often died by
asphyxiation, they used the strength of their
legs to push themselves up in order to breathe.
By breaking their legs (known as *crurifragium*),
the Romans perhaps were being humane, for
the painful and indeterminate length of time to
an eventual death was shortened.

Although soldiers broke the legs of the two
thieves who were crucified next to him, when
they came to Jesus, they found that he had
already died. It was therefore not necessary for them to break his legs.
"Instead, one of the soldiers pierced his side with a spear, and at once
blood and water came out" (John 19:34). The water could have come
from the lungs, or it could have been pericardial fluid (a kind of lubricant
characteristic of heart trauma).

What stands out even more than the mix of blood and water is John's explanation of why Jesus' legs were not broken and why his side was pierced:
"These things occurred so that the scripture might be fulfilled, 'None of
his bones shall be broken.' And again another passage of scripture says,
'They will look on the one whom they have pierced'" (verses 36–37).

John's first quotation—"None of his bones shall be broken"—is from
Exodus 12:46. That passage in Exodus refers to the Passover lamb. Since
John sees Jesus as "the Lamb of God" (John 1:29), he presents Jesus' death
as sacrificial. For John, the significance of Jesus' death is not understood
unless it is understood as a sacrifice—that is, as a death for others.

POSTSCRIPT

■ The blood and the water came to be understood in symbolic terms, with the
blood representing the Eucharist, or the Lord's Supper, and the water representing baptism. Not surprisingly, both the Eucharist and baptism are understood
today within the context of Jesus' death.

The Den of Lions

DANIEL WAS ONE of the Jewish youths taken into exile in 605 B.C. by the Babylonians. He quickly established himself as a man of great learning and wisdom. He also interpreted several dreams for King Nebuchadnezzar. And when King Belshazzar gave a great banquet, Daniel was able to interpret a strange message written on a wall of the palace by a disembodied hand when none of the king's magicians, enchanters, wise men, and astrologers could do so.

When Daniel was an old man in his eighties, King Darius appointed him as one of three presidents of the kingdom, ruling over 120 provincial governors. The Persian Empire had now toppled the Babylonian Empire, and Daniel became an esteemed sage in Darius's court. In fact, he distinguished himself above all others, some of whom became his political opponents. The other presidents and satraps tried to undermine him, but they could find no fault in him. Finally, they decided to plot his downfall on the basis of his devotion to his God.

They subsequently asked the king to issue a decree that whoever petitioned any other god or man except the king for a period of 30 days would be thrown into a den of lions. The king agreed and signed the decree, not realizing that the enemies of the Jewish people were plotting the death of their most esteemed prophet.

Even though Daniel knew of the decree, he nevertheless continued his practice of praying publicly three times daily toward Jerusalem from an open window in his house, and so he was promptly arrested and brought before the king. The king was very distressed and tried to find a loophole in the law that would spare Daniel, but there was none. Reluctantly, he ordered Daniel delivered to the lions, saying, "May your God, whom you faithfully serve, deliver you!" (Daniel 6:16).

The king could not sleep that night, and when the day broke, he ran to the den to see what had happened, crying out anxiously to Daniel, "O Daniel, servant of the living God, has your God whom you faithfully serve been able to deliver you from the lions?" (verse 20). "My God has sent his angel," Daniel answered, "and shut the lions' mouths" (verse 22). The joyful king ordered Daniel brought out of the pit and his accusers and their families thrown there in his place. He then issued a decree: "That in all my royal dominion people should tremble and fear before the God of Daniel: For he is the living God, enduring forever" (verse 25).

Daniel

DANIEL'S NAME MEANS "God is my judge," and in the court of Nebuchadnezzar, he received the Chaldean name *Belteshazzar*. It was an Eastern custom at the time to change one's name in a new cultural setting.

Although little is known of Daniel's parentage and family, it seems he was a member of Judah's noble class (see Daniel 1:3). In any case, Ashpenaz, a palace official in Nebuchadnezzar's court, brought Daniel to Babylon, where he was educated and became a favorite of Ashpenaz. Meanwhile, Daniel became an expert in interpreting visions and dreams.

After three years of training, Ashpenaz presented Daniel to the king, who became quite impressed with the Jewish youth after Daniel revealed and explained a vision Nebuchadnezzar had long forgotten. He interpreted several other dreams for Nebuchadnezzar when no one else in the king's court could do so. As a reward, the king promoted Daniel, giving him many great gifts and bestowing on him the office of chief prefect over the entire province of Babylon.

Daniel interprets the writing on the wall at Belshazzar's feast

After the 43-year reign of Nebuchadnezzar—during which time Babylon flourished—his son, Evil-merodach, became king for a few years (562–560 B.C.) until his brother-in-law, Neriglissar, assassinated him. Subsequently, Labashi-Marduk succeeded his father, Neriglissar, but he was also murdered in a conspiracy during his first year of rule. Nabonidus was then chosen to sit on the throne, becoming the last official king of Babylon, though his son, Belshazzar, was a co-regent for a time. Throughout all of this royal intrigue, Daniel remained a high official in the Babylonian court. He even played a key role in the fall of King Belshazzar, who gave a great banquet during which a strange message was written on a wall of the palace by a disembodied hand. After the king's advisors failed to explain the writing, Daniel came forward and interpreted the message, despite the risk of displeasing the king. Daniel foretold the end of Babylon and the king's life, and the Bible tells us: "That very night Belshazzar, the Chaldean king, was killed" (Daniel 5:30).

Even in his later days, Daniel became a governing administrator in the Persian court, serving both King Cyrus and King Darius. In fact, "Daniel distinguished himself above all the other presidents and satraps because an excellent spirit was in him" (Daniel 6:3).

More Than a Slave

THE APOSTLE PAUL wrote this epistle to his "dear friend and co-worker," Philemon (Philemon 1). He also addresses Apphia and Archippus, whom we might guess to be Philemon's wife and son. (The identity of Archippus, however, is a matter of some conjecture. Paul calls him a "fellow soldier" here [verse 2] and also mentions him in Colossians 4:17. Perhaps he was a pastor who led the church in Philemon's house? In any case, others would be reading this letter and noting the written request it contained.)

Good detective work can help pin down the time and setting of this letter. Paul mentions his imprisonment, which was probably his Roman house arrest from about A.D. 60 to 62. The previously mentioned cross-reference to Archippus puts Philemon in Colossae in west central Asia Minor.

If Philemon had a house big enough to host church meetings, he was affluent enough to own slaves. As objectionable as slavery is today, it was an accepted part of the Roman culture at this time. But one of Philemon's slaves, Onesimus, had run away. Onesimus found his way to Rome and became a Christian under Paul's guidance. Or perhaps he had known Paul in Ephesus, or maybe he just knew of Paul as a friend of his master and sought Paul's protection. In any case, Paul says he became the "father" of Onesimus (verse 10), probably meaning that Paul became his spiritual mentor. Paul wanted to keep Onesimus with him, since he was old and in prison and Onesimus could help care for him. But instead, he made a sacrifice by sending Onesimus home with a bold request. He wanted Philemon to welcome back the runaway slave as "a beloved brother" (verse 16).

We don't know the end of this story. Did Philemon agree to free Onesimus? We might reasonably guess that he did, since it would have been difficult to say no to the esteemed apostle, who had given Philemon his life in Christ—and especially when Philemon's church also received a separate, accompanying letter calling Onesimus "the faithful and beloved brother" (Colossians 4:9). And by the very fact that Philemon's letter entered the collection of Christian literature that became the New Testament, we might surmise that the story had a happy ending for all concerned.

Besides, Paul told Philemon to "prepare a guest room for me" (Philemon 22). Paul would see firsthand whether Philemon had received Onesimus as a slave or a brother in Christ.

Priscilla and Aquila

TENTMAKERS BY TRADE, Priscilla and Aquila worked and traveled with the Apostle Paul. They were among the great behind-the-scenes people of the early Church, hosting church meetings, providing encouragement, and even instructing an errant preacher.

Their story starts in Rome, where Emperor Claudius banished all Jews from the city in A.D. 49. Consequently, this couple, both Jewish Christians, had to leave. They settled in Corinth, where they met Paul at the tail end of his second missionary journey (see Acts 18:2). Since Paul was also a tentmaker, they were able to work together. (We might guess that they ran a business and possibly hired Paul, providing financial support but also giving him time off to preach.)

Paul stayed in Corinth a year and a half. Priscilla and Aquila joined him when he crossed the Aegean Sea and stopped in Ephesus. They remained there while he sailed back to Caesarea and ultimately traveled to Jerusalem.

In Ephesus, the couple encountered a preacher named Apollos, a Jew from Alexandria, "an eloquent man, well-versed in the scriptures. The Acts of the Apostles tells us that Apollos taught accurately the things concerning Jesus, though he knew only the baptism of John" (verse 25). When Priscilla and Aquila heard Apollos speak in the synagogue, "they took him aside and explained the Way of God to him more accurately" (verse 26).

On his third missionary journey, Paul returned to Ephesus and taught there for three years. Priscilla and Aquila were there at the time. In fact, during that period Paul wrote to the Corinthians, adding a greeting from this couple "with the church in their house" (1 Corinthians 16:19). Of course, the Corinthians would remember Priscilla and Aquila from their earlier stay there. This further indicates that the couple led a house church in Ephesus. The fact that they owned a house big enough for a group meeting might reflect their economic status.

But just a few years later, it seems, the couple lived once again in Rome. Claudius had been killed in A.D. 54, and presumably the ban on Jews was lifted. About A.D. 57, Paul wrote to the Romans, sending greetings to this faithful couple and "the church in their house." He compliments them highly, saying they "risked their necks for my life, to whom not only I give thanks, but also all the churches of the Gentiles" (Romans 16:4).

The Epistle of James

PETER EMERGED AS THE ACTING HEAD of the church in Jerusalem, which he led until Herod Agrippa's persecution drove him to relocate to Caesarea (see Acts 12:1–19). The leadership role was quickly and naturally filled by James, a half brother of Jesus (see Mark 6:3). Although James was a very common name, this letter, which purports to instruct (mainly) Jewish Christians throughout the known world, was probably written by Jesus' half brother.

The author is quite familiar with the sayings of Jesus, which influence the work at least in a dozen places, and with Jewish wisdom and ethical traditions that were common in Judaea (rather than, for example, in the Jewish center of Alexandria, Egypt). The author's grasp of Greek—quoting the Old Testament in ways reflective of its Greek translation (the Septuagint)—has suggested to some that the son of a Galilean carpenter could not have written the letter of James. James, however, spent nearly three decades as the leader of a religious movement in cosmopolitan Jerusalem, talking with Greek-speaking Jews and overseeing Greek-speaking Jewish communities living in Judaea and abroad.

The letter of James is essentially an example of Christian wisdom literature. James teaches about topics familiar from Jewish wisdom writings such as Proverbs. Principal topics in this letter include the source of temptation to sin (1:12–16); the importance of showing consistency between one's beliefs and one's choices and actions (1:19–27); the ethical dangers associated with thoughtless words and hurtful speech (3:1–12); the behaviors that contribute to harmony within the community (4:1–12); and the prejudice and hostility that exists between rich and poor (5:1–6). James is especially interested in the last topic. He instructs Christians not to show partiality toward the rich and against the poor when welcoming people into their congregations (2:1–7), and he calls for just practices on the part of the rich toward their poorer and more vulnerable employees (5:1–6)

POSTSCRIPT

■ At first glance, James's emphasis on doing good works seems to contradict Paul's teaching on grace (compare James 2:14–26 with Romans 3:21–31). Both James and Paul, however, would agree that genuine faith finds expression in acts of love and justice.

Jerusalem

FIRST-CENTURY GEOGRAPHER Strabo described Jerusalem's location as a rocky place, nothing "for which anyone would make a serious fight." History has proven him wrong. The place was settled long before the Jews dwelled there. Known as *Salem* in ancient times, it is mentioned in several ancient texts, including Genesis. When the Israelites conquered Canaan, they left this rocky hill in the possession of the Jebusites, whose city there seemed impenetrable. It was David who finally captured the city, around 1000 B.C., ordering his general to sneak in through the water supply and open the gates.

David renamed the city *Jerusalem* and made it his capital, since it was centrally located within his new Israelite nation. Under Solomon, Jerusalem rapidly became one of the greatest cities on earth with its magnificent temple and Solomon's luxuriant palace. But that all came crashing down in the following decades and centuries. After Solomon died, the kingdom split, and Jerusalem became the capital of the smaller nation of Judah, which foreign armies regularly threatened or invaded.

In 586 B.C., the Babylonians devastated Jerusalem, deporting most of its citizens. Some 50 years later, under Persian rule, Jews began returning to the city, rebuilding the temple and the city walls. When the Romans took over the city, they made Herod the Great ruler over the Jews.

Herod played both sides of the culture clash. He made Jerusalem a world-class city on the Greek model, but he also built an extravagant temple complex for Jewish worship, even larger than Solomon's. This was the first-century temple that Jesus visited.

In the late A.D. 60s, a Jewish revolt mounted against the Romans, whose response was swift and decisive. General Titus led the utter destruction of the city in A.D. 70, first by starving its citizens and then razing the city to the ground. After another brief rebellion in A.D. 135, Jews were forbidden to live there for a time.

Jerusalem has a major presence in the prophecy of both the Old and New Testaments. "I am about to create Jerusalem as a joy, and its people as a delight," the Lord says through the prophet Isaiah (65:18). The Book of Revelation echoes that sentiment with a vision of a "new Jerusalem, coming down out of heaven from God, prepared as a bride adorned for her husband" (21:2).

The Centurion's Confession

AFTER JESUS CRIED OUT from the cross and breathed his last, the Roman centurion who faced Jesus said, "Truly this man was God's Son!" (Mark 15:39). This statement is unusual because it comes from a minor character in the Gospel of Mark. He appears only in this verse, but he makes an incredible statement. His words are also unusual because Luke and Matthew present the centurion quite differently.

The Gospel of Luke has a strong concern with history and a sensitivity to legal concerns. It is not surprising, therefore, that Luke wrote, "When the centurion saw what had taken place, he praised God and said, 'Certainly this man was innocent'" (Luke 23:47). The centurion's statement matches Luke's own concerns, for the centurion recognizes the injustice that has been done to Jesus.

Meanwhile, the Gospel of Matthew has the centurion say the same words as Mark but within a different context. According to Matthew, when Jesus was crucified, the earth shook, tombs broke open, and those events inspired the centurion's response: "Now when the centurion and those with him, who were keeping watch over Jesus, saw the earthquake and what took place, they were terrified and said, 'Truly this man was God's Son!'" (Matthew 27:54). In Matthew, the centurion responds in awe to the miraculous events that accompany Jesus' crucifixion.

The Roman centurion in the Gospel of Mark, however, behaves in a strikingly different manner. His words seem like a genuine faith statement. He does not see Jesus as God's Son because of the miracles surrounding his crucifixion. Rather, the realization seems to grow out of the act of crucifixion itself.

In chapters 8, 9, and 10 of the Gospel of Mark, Jesus often told his disciples that he needed to suffer and die. Despite his assertions, they did not understand what it meant for him to suffer and die for others. What is also interesting in the Gospel of Mark is that no person recognizes Jesus as God's Son prior to his crucifixion. Demons are able to see the truth, but not so with Jesus' closest disciples. After Jesus is crucified, however, one Gentile does recognize who Jesus is. At Jesus' death, the Roman centurion understood what eluded even Jesus' disciples, and that is: "Truly this man was God's Son!"

Hosea Marries a Prostitute

ONE OF THE MOST STARTLING and powerful dramas in the Bible occurs when God tells the prophet Hosea to take a prostitute for his wife. Since the writers of both the Old and New Testaments condemn prostitution, God's command is especially perplexing.

Hosea himself was an esteemed prophet to the northern kingdom of Israel during the eighth century B.C., when King Jeroboam II ruled. Although Jeroboam II was one of the most wicked kings of Israel, he and his counterpart Uzziah in Judah were able to expand their kingdoms' borders to their greatest extent since the time of Solomon, two centuries earlier. It was a time of great prosperity. The people, however, were morally and spiritually bankrupt.

God's intent, using the life of Hosea, was to show the Israelites, his chosen people, how far they had wandered from him and how immoral their lives had become. So he said to Hosea, "Go, take for yourself a wife of whoredom and have children of whoredom, for the land commits great whoredom by forsaking the Lord" (Hosea 1:2). One of the most common images God uses in the Old Testament is that of Israel committing adultery against him by worshipping other gods; now he was making this even more dramatic by asking the prophet Hosea to live a life of marital pain through union with a prostitute.

Hosea obeyed God's bizarre command by marrying a prostitute named Gomer. Apparently she went back to her prostitution after she bore Hosea three children, because God told Hosea a second time to "Go, love a woman who has a lover and is an adulteress, just as the Lord loves the people of Israel, though they turn to other gods" (Hosea 3:1). Hosea did so, buying her out of prostitution and loving her as his wife. This message was one of grace and hope, indicating that God would again restore Israel to himself "in the latter days" (verse 5), though his relationship with his people would not be without pain before that time.

The imagery of prostitution is jarring, but it made two points: that Israel was like Gomer in its rejection of the Lord and that God was gracious and long-suffering with his people's repeated sins. Hosea's own personal life provided a powerful and poignant exclamation point to the Lord's message.

Mordecai

MORDECAI WAS A JEW living in Persian exile during the reign of Ahasuerus (Xerxes), who ruled from 486 to 465 B.C. He was the son of Jair and a descendant of Kish from the tribe of Benjamin. The southern kingdom of Judah comprised the tribes of Judah and Benjamin; when the Babylonians conquered Judah and deported the Jews, they took people from these two tribes, who then became residents in Persia after the Persians took over the Babylonian Empire.

Mordecai dwelled in Susa, one of the capitals in the Persian Empire. Susa was renowned for the gorgeous lilies that grew around the city. It was also a winter residence of Persian royalty. It's in this setting that officials of Ahasuerus discovered Mordecai's younger cousin, Esther, and inducted her into the king's harem because of her striking beauty. The Bible does not indicate how Mordecai and Esther reacted to her selection. As a pious Jew, he was probably dismayed at the thought of a pagan taking his cousin, who was like a daughter to him, into the king's harem. It seems, however, that he accepted the situation as God-ordained, which he became increasingly convinced of in time.

Meanwhile, Mordecai incurred the wrath of Haman, a pompous high official before whom Mordecai refused to bow. So Haman persuaded the king to issue an edict commanding all Jews to be killed. He even erected a gallows on which to hang his nemesis Mordecai, but Esther intervened with the king, revealing Haman to be the author of this treachery, and Haman was hanged on his own gallows.

Mordecai's advice to Esther was critical in this regard. He persuaded her to approach the king and advise him of the sinister nature of his edict which was directed at her and her people. This was a very risky step, and she faced possible execution if she did this and the king was not pleased. But Mordecai emphasized that hers was a strategic position: "For if you keep silence at such a time as this, relief and deliverance will rise for the Jews from another quarter, but you and your father's family will perish. Who knows? Perhaps you have come to royal dignity for just such a time as this" (Esther 4:14). Esther took the risk, the king approved her request, and she was able to save her people.

When the crisis died down, Mordecai was elevated to the second-highest position in the land. The Bible's final verdict on him is laudatory: "For Mordecai the Jew was next in rank to King Ahasuerus, and he was powerful among the Jews and popular with his many kindred, for he sought the good of his people and interceded for the welfare of all his descendants" (Esther 10:3).

Exiled to Patmos

THE FIRST CHAPTER of the Bible's most cryptic book states, "I, John . . . was on the island called Patmos because of the word of God and the testimony of Jesus" (Revelation 1:9). Evidently, the Apostle John was the author of this book, which we know as Revelation.

The Apostle John was one of Jesus' three closest disciples. He stood with Peter at the empty tomb and after Pentecost in those exciting early days of the Church. But after a fact-finding trip to Samaria (Acts 8), his trail goes cold. We hear nothing more about John in the Acts of the Apostles. Church tradition says he became a senior elder in the church at Ephesus until he died of old age around A.D. 100.

St. John the Evangelist *by Diego Velasquez*

John says he was on Patmos "because of the word of God" (verse 9). That makes sense, because Patmos was one of several Aegean islands used by the Romans for exile, especially for soothsayers and prophets. (The Romans may have been too superstitious to kill such visionaries, but they wanted to remove them from circulation.) If John's visions began before his exile, and if he talked openly about them, it would explain why he was sent to Patmos. There he wrote down his visions, so they could be sent back to his home church in Ephesus and to other neighboring churches.

The timing of his exile is open to question. It obviously occurred around a time of intense persecution. That would likely be either Nero's reign in the A.D. 60s or Domitian's reign in the 90s. Many Bible scholars favor the latter date. That would mean John was at least 80 years old at the time.

As a senior statesman, John would have had plenty to say, but he saw himself as merely the conduit for the Lord's message. This attitude continues through a series of visions in highly symbolic imagery of conflict, persecution, and worship (in heaven and on earth).

The interpretation of these visions is still hotly debated, but the overall message is clear: God defeats evil in the end. That would have been—and remains—a great comfort to believers under persecution, as John was on the island of Patmos.

Apollos

APOLLOS CAME FROM ALEXANDRIA, which was renowned for its literary scholarship. Alexandria boasted a large Jewish community, of which Apollos was a part. He was a gifted Christian evangelist, who had nevertheless preached an inadequate gospel message until Paul's colleagues Priscilla and Aquila tutored him in Ephesus.

He first appears in the New Testament preaching in Ephesus and is described as "an eloquent man, well-versed in the scriptures" (Acts 18:24). He had been taught in "the Way of the Lord"—that's a term used for Christianity. "He spoke with burning enthusiasm and taught accurately the things concerning Jesus, but he knew only the baptism of John" (verse 25). So what was his message missing?

John the Baptist had preached a message of repentance, and Jesus had shared that message. But Jesus also taught that with repentance and God's forgiveness comes the indwelling of the Holy Spirit, and that was what was missing in the message of Apollos. After Priscilla and Aquila conveyed the rest of the gospel message to Apollos, his ministry became even more fruitful.

Apparently Apollos connected with the Ephesian church at that point, and subsequently they sent him across the Aegean Sea to Corinth, where he proved to be a great debater and powerful defender of the Christian faith. He was received so well by the Corinthians that divisions arose within that church. When Paul wrote to them about these "quarrels," he described the situation like this: "Each of you says, 'I belong to Paul' or 'I belong to Apollos,' or 'I belong to Cephas [Peter],' or 'I belong to Christ'" (1 Corinthians 1:12). The church was splitting into factions, each one elevating one spiritual leader against the others.

Peacefully, Paul explained how the Church works, with individual leaders offering service to God. "I planted, Apollos watered, but God gave the growth" (1 Corinthians 3:6). Later, Paul criticized a group of "super-apostles," who were criticizing Paul for his lack of rhetorical style. Perhaps this was the "Apollos faction," and they merely claimed such a connection to him without his support. But, as dramatic as it might be to set up an Apollos-Paul showdown, it appears that Apollos was a faithful Christian preacher, whom Paul had urged to visit Corinth again to sort out the mess, "but he was not at all willing to come now," Paul wrote to them. "He will come when he has the opportunity" (1 Corinthians 16:12).

The First Epistle of Peter

FOR ALL HIS IMPORTANCE in the gospel story and the growth of the early Church, Peter has surprisingly little voice in the New Testament writings. Two letters claim to preserve his voice, although some dispute the authorship of both epistles. The author of First Peter does show an awareness of several teachings of Jesus but does not share any personal reminiscences. Meanwhile, he refers to Rome as "Babylon," a practice that only becomes common after the destruction of the second temple during the siege of Jerusalem in A.D. 70, when Rome repeated Babylon's destruction of the temple of Solomon. Such observations do not disprove Peter's authorship, but they do raise questions.

Peter writes to Christians throughout what is now western Turkey. These Christians have suffered a loss of honor and, in some cases, endured physical violence because of their identification with Jesus and his Church. The author pinpoints the source of the problem: The believers' change of lifestyle, including their withdrawal from idolatry, has alienated their neighbors (4:1–4). Peter is especially sensitive to the vulnerable position of wives and slaves in the homes of unbelieving heads of households. The way forward, he states, is to live lives of virtue, forgiveness, and love.

St. Peter in Penitence *by Jusepe de Ribera*

The author affirms that the believers enjoy favor in God's eyes as a result of their trust in Jesus, and he calls them to keep their focus on the honor and favor that will be theirs when Christ returns. He tells them that their disgrace and hardship give them the opportunity to demonstrate the virtue of faithfulness and to follow in the steps of Jesus, who also endured the hostility of nonbelievers on the way to glory. He calls them to support one another along this difficult way with all the love and mutual care of a well-functioning family.

POSTSCRIPT

■ The author speaks of Jesus preaching "to the spirits in prison" between his own death and resurrection (3:19). This verse came to be interpreted as an indication that Jesus preached his gospel to those who had died before his coming, giving them an opportunity to believe and be released from hell.

Palestine

ABOUT THE SIZE of New Jersey—just 150 miles north to south and about 60 miles wide—Palestine sits at the crossroads of the world. Three continents come together in this strip of territory. No doubt that explains—at least in part—why so many wars have been fought over it.

Early on, it was known as the land of Canaan. When Abraham followed God's calling to settle there, it became the "Promised Land." "I am the Lord, who brought you from Ur of the Chaldeans," God said to Abraham, "to give you this land to possess" (Genesis 15:7). That was the promise. Centuries later, Abraham's descendants would walk out of Egypt, across the dry bed of the Red Sea, around the Sinai wilderness for 40 years, and across the dry bed of the Jordan River to repossess it. When they established dominance in the land, it became known as Israel.

For a few decades in the tenth century B.C., Israel was possibly the most powerful nation on earth and probably the richest. Under King Solomon, the nation extended its borders across the Sinai and north into Mesopotamia. Diplomacy and trade linked Israel with partners on all three continents. But its glory faded when the nation split into north and south. Now the land had two names: Judah for the south and Israel (sometimes Samaria or Ephraim) for the north. In 722 B.C., the brutal Assyrian Empire essentially stamped the northern kingdom out of existence. Although the Babylonians also conquered and relocated the southerners, a remnant of the Jewish population returned to Palestine during Persian rule. The south became known as Judaea. Parts of the northern territory were called by various local names, including Galilee and Samaria.

The name Palestine emerged in 135 A.D., after the Romans put down a second Jewish revolt. In an effort to remove the Jewish identity from the land, they took the name from Israel's old enemies, the Philistines. The British brought back that name when they were given responsibility for the area after World War I. When Israel won its independence, Palestine became known as Israel again.

The land itself, though small in area, is geographically diverse. The Mediterranean shore rises to plains, then grassy foothills good for grazing the *Shephelah*), then a mountain ridge. The mountains have soil rich enough for terrace farming, especially on the seaside, which receives more rain. Heading east, the mountains drop off drastically into the canyons of the Judaean Desert and the geologic rift of the Jordan Valley and Dead Sea.

The Tomb of Jesus

IN THE ANCIENT ROMAN WORLD, individuals who were crucified sometimes would be left on the cross until their bodies either had decomposed or had been eaten by birds and dogs. Crucifixion was not only a painful way to die but also a shameful one.

Jesus' disciples did not seek permission to take down his body from the cross. Most of them had run away and were in hiding. All four gospels note that Joseph of Arimathea was the one to ask Pilate for the body of Jesus. Who was Joseph of Arimathea? Mark says he was a member of the council—that is, the Sanhedrin—and that he had been waiting expectantly for the kingdom of God (see Mark 15:43). Luke adds that although Joseph was a member of the council, he recognized that the council had acted inappropriately (see Luke 23:50). Both Matthew and John say Joseph was a follower of Jesus, with John noting that Joseph had followed Jesus in secret out of fear for how others might treat him (see Matthew 27:57; John 19:38).

After Pilate granted Joseph of Arimathea's request, Joseph wrapped Jesus' body in a linen cloth and put him into a tomb. Although today different religious groups in Jerusalem still debate the actual location of the tomb, the gospels only say it was cut out of the rock and that it had not been used before. Matthew says the tomb actually was Joseph's, and John notes that it was near a garden.

According to the Gospel of John, Nicodemus helped Joseph by bringing spices for the body of Jesus—a mixture of myrrh and aloes, about a hundred pounds' worth. Another important detail in this account of Jesus' burial is that a large stone was rolled in front of the entrance, probably with the thought that his disciples might steal his body and then claim that he had risen from the dead. Matthew even says that Roman guards were stationed in front of the tomb.

What happened next is described in a variety of ways. All four gospels note that women went to the tomb on Sunday morning, apparently either to mourn or to engage in burial rituals. Mary Magdalene was not only among those women but seemingly was also the first to encounter the resurrected Christ.

When the women found the tomb empty, they initially thought that Jesus' body had been taken away, but then they discovered a startling truth. The hundred pounds of spices that Nicodemus had brought to the tomb had been unnecessary, for—as Christians have said on Easter mornings throughout the centuries—"He is risen."

Ezra Returns to the Homeland

THE KINGDOMS OF ISRAEL and Judah suffered centuries of successive occupations by the Assyrians, Babylonians, and Persians. Of these, the Persians were the most humane. Under their 200-year rule, beginning with Cyrus the Great in 539 B.C., the Jews and other peoples were allowed to return to their lands and build temples to their own gods.

For the Jews, Cyrus's emancipation decree allowed them to return to Jerusalem and rebuild the temple that the Babylonians had destroyed. The first returnees immediately began by erecting an altar and laying the foundations of the temple under the leadership of Zerubbabel, a descendant of King David, and Jeshua, the high priest. Local opposition slowed the rebuilding for more than 15 years, but the prophets Haggai and Zechariah urged the people to resume the work, and during the reign of Darius, the work on the temple was completed. This was an occasion of great joy, although the elders who remembered the first temple wept, since the new one did not begin to reflect the former temple's glory.

In 458 B.C., another Persian king, Artaxerxes I, authorized Ezra to return to Jerusalem with a large company of followers. Ezra's was a religious commission: He was a scribe "skilled in the law of Moses," and he "set his heart to study the law of the Lord, and to do it, and to teach the statutes and ordinances in Israel" (Ezra 7:6, 10). In this, he had the king's blessing and encouragement; indeed, the king and his counselors gave him silver and gold as free-will offerings to "the God of Israel, whose dwelling is in Jerusalem" (verse 15).

Ezra took courage from the Persians' goodwill, and so he gathered leaders from Israel and many other Jews and led this entourage of exiles back to Jerusalem, where they fasted and gave thanks to the Lord for not having forsaken them. God's promise of restoration had come true.

POSTSCRIPT

Cyrus's decree that freed the Jews is mentioned in the Bible *and* in his own words on a clay cylinder discovered in the 19th century. In Cyrus's inscription, he mentions freeing all peoples so they can return to their homelands at the behest of Marduk, the high god of the Babylonians and Persians. The Bible's perspective is that Israel's God, Yahweh, influenced Cyrus to make this decree.

Esther

ESTHER WAS AN OBSCURE Jewish girl living in the Persian metropolis of Susa. *Esther* was probably her Persian name. In fact, her Hebrew name was *Hadassah,* which means "myrtle," a common and lovely evergreen shrub with white flowers and edible berries.

At this time, King Ahasuerus, known as Xerxes I among the Persians and Medes, had divorced his wife, Vashti, because she had refused to come to a banquet at which he ordered her presence. He then told his officials to bring before him the most beautiful women in his kingdom; from them he would choose a new queen. During a 12-month preparation period, women from all parts of his empire were treated with oils, perfumes, and cosmetics, and then brought to the king. Of all the women, Esther was the one who pleased the king most, and so he made her queen.

Esther kept her Jewish heritage hidden, however, until a plot to exterminate the Jews in the Persian Empire was disclosed to her. It is at this point that her faith and courage are revealed in Scripture. It was customary among the Persians that no person could approach the king unless he first asked that person to appear before him. A violation of such protocol often meant immediate execution. Only in rare instances did the ruler stay the executioner's hand. Since Esther would have to seek an audience with the king without his request—and knowing how easily a queen could displease him—she had to draw deep from within her faith to act courageously on behalf of her people, whom she had not acknowledged before.

Using her wits, Esther dressed herself in her royal robes and stood humbly in the inner court of the king's palace, where he could see her in this way. Such a humble display contrasted with the obstinacy of the former queen and no doubt had the desired effect on the king. Thus she found favor with Ahasuerus, who then held out the golden scepter to her, indicating that she could approach him. After she touched the top of the scepter, the king asked her for her request. She then invited the king and Haman, arch-conspirator behind the plot to massacre the Jews, to attend a banquet she wanted to prepare for them. It was at this dinner that she revealed Haman's treachery to the king.

Her courage saved her people, and Jews have celebrated her bravery through the centuries in a festival known as "Purim."

Jesus Returns!

As THE DISCIPLES WATCHED Jesus ascend past the clouds into heaven, they were joined by angels who announced, "This Jesus, who has been taken up from you into heaven, will come in the same way as you saw him go into heaven" (Acts 1:11). Jesus himself had talked about the Son of Man "coming on the clouds of heaven, with power and great glory" (Matthew 24:30, echoing Daniel 7:13).

Jesus had faithfully fulfilled many of the messianic prophecies, particularly those of Isaiah regarding the Suffering Servant. But there was another batch of predictions about a conquering king, a new "David" who would appear on high to establish a reign of peace over the whole world (see Isaiah 9:7). These prophecies awaited completion.

And so Jesus' disciples waited for his glorious return. As they began to preach the gospel, they noted that Jesus had to "remain in heaven until a time of universal restoration that God announced long ago" (Acts 3:21). Apparently some Christians were getting worried as they saw believers dying before Jesus returned. Would these folks miss out on the second coming? Paul reassured them in his first epistle to the Thessalonians that Jesus would return *with* those Christians who had passed away. That passage remains one of the most vivid prophecies about Jesus' return, depicting Jesus descending from heaven "with the archangel's call and with the sound of God's trumpet" (1 Thessalonians 4:16). Living believers will be "caught up in the clouds" (verse 17). From that idea of being "caught up" (*raptus* in Latin), we get the word *rapture*. Elsewhere, Paul talks about the "last trumpet" in connection with the transformation of our bodies from perishable to imperishable (see 1 Corinthians 15:50–54).

Some have tried to determine the time of Jesus' return with various prophetic signs. Jesus himself warned against overzealous predictions, saying "no one knows" the day and hour of his return (Matthew 24:36).

Despite all the disagreements, there is broad agreement on the basics: Jesus will return for his followers, and we should always be ready.

POSTSCRIPT

■ Some scholars suspect that some of the Thessalonian Christians took Paul's words about the "rapture" too far, quitting their jobs or taking other drastic measures to await the Lord's return. With this in mind, it makes sense that his second epistle to that church mentions signs that will precede Jesus' coming (see 2 Thessalonians 2:1–12). Paul also sets forth a basic rule: "Anyone unwilling to work should not eat" (2 Thessalonians 3:10).

Lydia

LYDIA WAS A MERCHANT from Thyatira, and she sold purple cloth. She was living in Philippi when she encountered the Apostle Paul and became the first European convert to Christianity.

Purple dye was expensive in the ancient world, which is why it became the color of royalty. One of the leading cities in this new industry was Thyatira, located in Asia Minor (modern Turkey). Thyatira was near the ancient Lydian territory, which suggests that Lydia might have been a nickname for the businesswoman in Philippi.

Apparently Lydia imported purple cloth from Thyatira and sold it in Philippi, which became a lucrative business. She owned a home and had a "household" (which probably means she had servants and possibly employees living there). No mention is made of a husband.

Philippi had been a Roman colony, and many army officers retired there. While Jews had migrated over the centuries to most other major cities of the Mediterranean, Philippi did not have much of a Jewish population. It was Paul's pattern to first preach in the synagogue of any new town he visited, but it seems that Philippi lacked the ten men necessary to start a synagogue. There was only a prayer meeting by the river, attended by women. That was where Paul met Lydia.

"The Lord opened her heart to listen eagerly to what was said by Paul" (Acts 16:14). She was baptized as a Christian, and she begged Paul and his team to stay at her home, which they did. (The team at this point included at least Silas, Timothy, and Luke.) It's likely that the Philippian church started in that home.

During their time in Philippi, Paul and Silas encountered trouble, having cast a demon out of a slave-girl and angering her masters. Paul and Silas were thrown into prison, where a sudden earthquake resulted in the conversion of the jailer. When they were released, they returned to Lydia's home, where they met with the church and then left.

There is no further mention of Lydia in the New Testament. But if that's just a nickname, she might be one of the women (Euodia or Syntyche) mentioned in Philippians 4:2.

POSTSCRIPT

■ Lydia is described as a "worshiper of God," identifying her as a Gentile who was attracted to Judaism. That's why she was meeting with Jewish women for prayer.

The Epistles of John

A CHURCH SPLIT CAN BE ONE of the most painful experiences in the life of a congregation or denomination. People who once held each other dear and relied on one another for support and encouragement can become the bitterest of enemies over doctrine. This is precisely the situation out of which the three letters of John were written. The same communities in which the Gospel of John took root endured a hurtful schism, and significant numbers of believers left the original church to form rival congregations.

The divisions probably centered on differing interpretations of John's gospel. Those who withdrew were deeply influenced by Greek thought concerning the inferiority of matter (including flesh) and the impossibility of any divine being truly becoming human. Hence they developed a teaching that kept the divine Word, or Son of God, separate from the man, Jesus. This line of thinking would eventually lead to the development of Gnosticism, a mystic doctrine and movement that posed a major challenge to apostolic Christianity and that drew extensively on John's gospel to support its system of belief.

The author of the three epistles of John writes to assure those who remain in the original congregation that their understanding of Jesus is the correct one; it is grounded in the witness of the apostles themselves. These believers have held onto what was passed on from the beginning of the Christian movement. Those who left—the "antichrists" and "children of the devil" (1 John 2:18; 3:10)—were the ones who developed dubious beliefs. The theological issue is important for the author because of what it says about God's love. A God made human who lays down his life for humankind says a lot more about the essence of God as love than does the belief that the divine spirit remained distant and insulated from the suffering of the man, Jesus. This makes a difference, in turn, on the level of love and care that disciples should show to others. In the wake of the pain of fractured relationships, the author urges above all else that those who remain in the community love and encourage one another.

These letters are, in fact, anonymous. The author calls himself only "the elder" (2 John 1; 3 John 1). Their connection with the fourth gospel, and the tendency to ascribe that book to John, "the Beloved Disciple," led to the naming of John as their author. The early churches, however, knew multiple Christian leaders named John and sometimes distinguished between John the apostle and John "the elder," who wrote these letters.

Galilee

T HE SEA OF GALILEE was where Jesus called several fishermen to be his disciples. He stood in a boat and preached to people on its shores. He stilled a storm while sailing on this sea. He walked on its water.

Galilee was one name for the sea that meant so much in Jesus' ministry. This sea was also known as Tiberias, Gennesaret, or Chinnereth. The name "Galilee" also referred to the region around the sea, especially its western shore. (In fact, the name comes from a word meaning "ring," a possible description of the territory around this roundish lake.) The towns of Capernaum and Bethsaida were on the lakeshore. Nazareth was farther west but was still in the region of Galilee.

To picture the geography in your head, think of the land of Canaan as a stoplight with three round lamps. The bottom lamp is Judah, or later, Judaea. The middle lamp is Samaria. The top is Galilee.

Historically, Galilee was part of the land allotted to the Israelite tribes of Naphtali and Zebulun, possibly also Asher, but these tribes never quite displaced the Canaanites who lived there. A major trade route, connecting Asia to Egypt, went through the region, so there was regular contact with people of many races. And at various times, Syria or Tyre ruled parts of Galilee.

The Israelite presence was removed from the area when the Assyrians conquered the northern kingdom in 722 B.C., repopulating it with foreigners. But Jews began resettling it, especially during the Maccabean period of independence. The Romans recognized Galilee's Jewish identity and included it in the territory ruled by Herod the Great and some later Herods.

All of this contributed to its reputation as "Galilee of the Gentiles" (Isaiah 9:1; Matthew 4:15). Jews from Jerusalem tended to look down on Jews from Galilee because of their inevitable contact with Gentiles. Olive oil from Galilee was not considered pure enough for use in the temple in Jerusalem. This is surely one reason why the religious elite in Jerusalem had such a hard time accepting Jesus the Galilean.

Raised in Nazareth, Jesus performed his first miracle in the Galilean town of Cana and preached often in Capernaum. The Sermon on the Mount and the feeding of the 5,000 happened in this area. In fact, the great majority of Jesus' ministry occurred in Galilee. He made a few trips to Jerusalem before the week of his crucifixion, and a few stops in Samaria, but he stayed mostly in the north.

The Resurrection

DURING THE FIRST CENTURIES of the life of the Church, Christians did not celebrate Christmas. Many of them claimed that only pagans celebrated the birth of their gods. Rather, Christians remembered with reverence the days on which martyrs died. "Death days" were more important than "birthdays."

With Jesus, however, Christians did not focus primarily on the day of his death (which came to be known as "Good Friday"). Rather, the day of his resurrection (which came to be known as "Easter") was the most important holiday in the Church. Frequently, individuals were baptized and brought into the membership of the Church on that day.

Also of significance, Christians viewed the days of the week in a manner different from their Jewish contemporaries. Although they still recognized the sabbath (i.e., Saturday) as the seventh day of the week, they came to worship on Sunday, the first day of the week and the day God raised Jesus from the dead.

On that very special day, the first people to discover the empty tomb were Mary Magdalene, Mary the mother of James and Joseph, Joanna, and Salome. After they arrived, an earthquake shook the ground, and an angel descended from heaven and rolled away the very large stone from the opening of the tomb. "Do not be afraid," the angel said. "I know that you are looking for Jesus who was crucified. He is not here; for he has been raised" (Matthew 28:5–6).

The Resurrection *by Carl Heinrich Bloch*

Mary Magdalene then turned and saw a man she thought was a gardener. When the man said to her, "Mary," she realized it was Jesus and cried out, "Rabbouni!" (John 20:16). She then ran to the apostles and announced, "I have seen the Lord" (verse 18). Note that Jesus' first resurrection appearance was not to men. Rather, after Mary Magdalene encounters the risen Jesus, she is presented in John as being the one who tells the disciples the good news. Thus she came to be known as "the apostle to the apostles."

The Jerusalem Wall Is Rebuilt

NEHEMIAH WAS CUPBEARER to King Artaxerxes I in Persia and was a contemporary of Ezra the scribe. As a cupbearer, he would have had the absolute trust of the king and unparalleled access to him. He would have been well trained in court etiquette, would have known how to select good wines for the king, and generally would have had to run the court efficiently.

Yet Nehemiah's heart was with his fellow Jews in Judah. When he heard that the wall of Jerusalem still lay in ruins more than a century after the city had been destroyed, he was deeply saddened, and the king noticed his sorrow. He asked Nehemiah what the trouble was, and Nehemiah seized the opportunity to convince the king to send him back with a commission to rebuild the Jerusalem walls. (The temple had been rebuilt 75 years earlier, but the city remained vulnerable without protective walls around it.) The king agreed and sent Nehemiah back with letters authorizing the rebuilding, as well as the means to obtain the timber and other raw materials needed.

The first thing Nehemiah did when he arrived was survey the walls on a secret night ride. Although he encountered opposition to his project from local officials, he persisted, mobilizing the people to help in the rebuilding. In an ingenious plan, everyone worked on the portion of the wall opposite where they lived. The local officials continued to oppose them, but Nehemiah combined spirituality ("we prayed to our God"; Nehemiah 4:9) and practical savvy ("and set a guard as a protection"; verse 9) to keep the project moving. Half the workers labored, and half stood guard with spears, shields, bows, and coats of mail.

Opposition continued in the form of various plots to kill Nehemiah and with letters written against him, but he avoided all troubles and continued with the work on the wall, which was finished in the amazingly short time of 52 days. When the Jews' enemies heard this news, they were greatly fearful and demoralized.

Nehemiah and Ezra joined together in a great day of celebration on which the law was read in public for the first time in many years, the Feast of Booths was celebrated, and the covenant with God was reaffirmed. Later, the wall was dedicated with a grand procession consisting of two great companies of people who circled the city atop the walls, culminating with sacrifices and celebrations at the temple.

Ezra

EZRA WAS A JEWISH PRIEST and a scribe who was a descendant of Phinehas, the grandson of Aaron from the tribe of Levi. He was the son of Seraiah, who was the grandson of Hilkiah, the high priest when King Josiah ruled the kingdom of Judah. Scripture not only says he was a skilled expert in the Mosaic law but also notes how King Artaxerxes described him: "the priest Ezra, the scribe of the law of the God of heaven" (Ezra 7:12). Interestingly, Ezra's name means "help," and he certainly lived up to his name as he helped the Jews come to know and follow the Word of God.

In 458 B.C., Ezra received permission from Artaxerxes, the Persian ruler, to take a company of Jews back to Jerusalem to revive and promote the Jewish religion. This was the second time a Persian king had sent exiled Jews back to their homeland, and Ezra's return followed the first return in about 80 years. The mandate Artaxerxes gave to Ezra was important in reestablishing proper religious observances, since the initial excitement and fervor of the first return had long since worn off and the people had drifted away from any strong loyalty to their God.

Ezra's commission was extraordinary: Artaxerxes sent him to Jerusalem with a letter authorizing him to take anyone willing to return with him, along with the vessels for the temple and whatever else was needed, all to be paid for out of the king's treasury, from which the king also made a large gift of silver and gold. Artaxerxes further authorized Ezra to appoint magistrates and judges "who know the laws of your God" (verse 25), and ordered that Israel's law and Persian law both be obeyed in the province "Beyond the River" (verse 25).

Ezra returned with a large contingent of Jews, including religious personnel who would attend to all matters of worship in the temple. In a great, festive public ceremony, he read and explained the Law of Moses to the people, and the people celebrated the Festival of Booths for the first time since Joshua's day.

Ezra deeply loved God's Word and diligently studied it. He had a passion for keeping God's people devoted to the law of the Lord, and that's why he publicly grieved whenever he saw God's people trespass God's statutes. It is not surprising, therefore, that tradition has credited Ezra as the probable author of several Old Testament books, including First and Second Chronicles, Ezra, and Nehemiah.

The Final Judgment

JESUS COMPARED the final judgment to a common scene in the fishing business. Nets bring up good and bad fish, which are sorted out. "So it will be at the end of the age," he explained. "The angels will come out and separate the evil from the righteous" (Matthew 13:49). Throughout Scripture, people of faith look forward to "the Day of the Lord."

Sure enough, in the majestic vision of the Book of Revelation, the final battles lead to a final judgment. "I saw the dead, great and small, standing before the throne, and the books were opened" (Revelation 20:12). The trial is conducted before the throne of the Lord. Death and hell themselves are thrown into the lake of fire, along with anyone "whose name was not found written in the book of life" (verse 15). Those who come through this judgment are welcomed into a glorious new heaven and earth to live with God forever.

This begs a question: On what basis is the judgment made? How can we pass this test? The common wisdom is that good actions will be rewarded in this final judgment and bad actions punished. We reap what we sow. At least one of these "books" the Lord opens is a ledger of our good and bad deeds.

Then there's that other book—the book of life. And we find another theme pervading Scripture: that life runs on more than a merit system. Sins can be forgiven. Hearts can be restored. The righteous will find life through their trust in God. It is the "pure in heart" who will see God, those who approach him honestly, humbly, with unmixed motives. We are saved by trusting in God's grace, not our own works. From the cross, for example, Jesus invited a thief into Paradise (see Psalm 32:1; 51:10; Habakkuk 2:4; Matthew 5:8; Luke 23:43; Ephesians 2:8–9).

In the fantastic imagery of Revelation, the book of life belongs to "the Lamb" (Revelation 13:8). That's Jesus, the sacrificial Lamb, slaughtered for us. One of the first things John ever wrote about Jesus was that he was "the Lamb of God who takes away the sin of the world!" (John 1:29). In light of New Testament theology, therefore, the final judgment needs both books. First, the grade book demonstrates that everyone has fallen short of God's holy standard (see Romans 3:23). No one passes that test. But the book of life contains the names of those who rely on God's mercy and the Lamb's sacrifice.

Philemon, the Slave Owner

PHILEMON WAS A WEALTHY householder who had become a Christian through Paul's ministry. When Paul encountered a slave who had run away from Philemon, he wrote his old friend a short letter that found its way into the New Testament.

This epistle is more like a postcard—one sheet of papyrus. The whole message is not much longer than this article, and that's all we know about Philemon. But, of course, we can do some detective work.

Where did Philemon live? We don't know for sure, but the letter is also directed to Archippus, who is also mentioned as a recipient of the epistle of Colossians. Quite possibly Philemon lived in Colossae, too—except we have no evidence that Paul had ever visited that town, and he speaks of Philemon as a "dear friend and co-worker." Possibly Paul had known Philemon during his lengthy stays in Ephesus, and Philemon had retired to a country villa near Colossae. Scholars tend to agree that the bearer of Paul's letter to the Colossians also carried this letter to Philemon, for Onesimus (the slave) is mentioned as in company of the bearer (see Colossians 4:9).

While this letter is a personal note, it is also addressed to Philemon's whole family and to "the church in your house." Thus Philemon's family and friends in Christ would have heard of Paul's request and undoubtedly remained attentive to Philemon's response. Evidently Onesimus became a Christian when he met Paul, and so now Paul was asking Philemon to receive him as "more than a slave, [but] a beloved brother" (Philemon 16). Would Philemon go against Paul's desire, which surely was known by many in his Christian fellowship?

It's hard for modern believers to understand the importance of slavery in the ancient world. We wonder why Paul didn't just free Onesimus himself and declare all slavery abhorrent. But this was the social and economic system on which the Roman Empire was based, and Paul knew how to pick his battles. If Christianity would reform the Roman Empire, it would do so from the inside out. Hearts would have to change.

That seems to be the step Paul asks of Philemon, a change of heart. "Welcome him as you would welcome me," Paul says. We don't know how Philemon reacted to this letter, but that this letter became a part of the New Testament canon indicates that Philemon's response was favorable to Onesimus. Indeed, Paul often preached that in Christ "there is no longer slave or free" (Galatians 3:28).

The Epistles of Jude and Peter (Second)

JUDE WAS ONE OF JESUS' younger half brothers (see Matthew 13:55) who, together with James, exercised a leadership role in the Jerusalem church and for Jewish Christians living around the Mediterranean. He wrote this letter (Jude) to combat the influence of traveling teachers who, claiming authority on the basis of visions and dreams, sought to "liberate" Christians from what they viewed as an old-fashioned and unenlightened morality (including the Law of Moses). Jude reminds the congregations that throughout history God has shown a commitment to punish those who disobeyed his moral standards. He points out that it will be no different in the case of these teachers and their followers. What perhaps stands out most in this letter is Jude's quotation of the extrabiblical book First Enoch as an authoritative witness to God's certain judgment upon the rebellious.

The author of Second Peter found Jude's letter to be a helpful resource in combating a new breed of teachers. These teachers sought to make Christianity more philosophically respectable, freeing it from the idea that human evil could so trouble God that he would feel angry and seek vengeance. The apparent delay of the return of Jesus provided further evidence against divine judgment, as these false teachers urged Christians to live free from superstitious fears, with moral laxity being the unfortunate side effect. The author of Second Peter responds by affirming the reliability of the prophecies of God's judgment, incorporating most of Jude in his assertion that God will punish the wicked and deliver the righteous. Christ's redemptive death in the past and the fiery dissolution of this world in the future provide the two compass points for a moral life.

POSTSCRIPT

■ The fact that Jude quotes First Enoch was used by some Church fathers as an argument against including Jude in the New Testament (since it draws so explicitly from an extracanonical book). Tertullian, however, used the same fact to argue that First Enoch was itself an inspired work.

■ Leadership can run in families: Jude's grandsons would still be found at the helm of Jewish Christianity in Judaea at the end of the first century.

Greek Culture

ATHENS WAS THE CAULDRON of Greek culture. Macedonia was the catapult. Athens had great philosophers, such as Socrates, Plato, and Aristotle. It also had great playwrights, such as Aeschylus, Sophocles, and Euripides. Athens had democracy and the great leader Pericles. Art, architecture, music, mathematics, and medicine also blossomed in Athens.

Alexander the Great

But it was Macedonia, perched north of the Greek peninsula that launched this culture into the wider world. First Philip of Macedon conquered Greece, then his son Alexander the Great expanded their empire to other continents. With brilliant new battle strategies, this young general took control of the sprawling Persian Empire and marched beyond its borders. And wherever he went, he brought Greek culture with him.

The preeminent philosopher Aristotle tutored the young Alexander, who adored Greek culture. As a result, he imposed the Greek language and culture on the nations he conquered. After his untimely death, his generals divided his territory—but they kept his vision alive. History knows this time as the Hellenistic Period (from *Hellas*, Greece's name for itself). Greek-style cities sprang up in Asia Minor, Mesopotamia, India, and Egypt. Public buildings were constructed with Greek architecture. For entertainment, people went to theaters, stadiums, and hippodromes (racetracks). Temples offered sacrifices to Greek gods (or at least some local version of the Greek gods). Citizens took Greek names and adopted the fashions and hairstyles of Athens. And from Sicily to Susa, business was conducted in the common Greek tongue.

This was a hard sell in Judaea, however. The Jews were called to be a separate people. Interaction with non-Jews would defile them. The adoption of Gentile customs was unthinkable. When the Syrian king Antiochus IV tried to force assimilation, the Jews rebelled, but the pressure to conform to these worldwide ways continued. In time, the Jews gave in, and the grandchildren of those Jewish rebels were even given Greek names. When Herod the Great became king of Judaea, he rebuilt the Jerusalem temple in a Greek style. The adoption of Greek culture continued to be a controversy in Judaea until the Roman army devastated Jerusalem in A.D. 70.

Doubting Thomas

JOHN 20 IS AN INTERESTING PASSAGE. Three times in this chapter the risen Jesus approaches his disciples and says, "Peace be with you." Perhaps he says it because he is concerned that they might panic when they see him. The Aramaic phrase "Peace be with you" wishes a person a sense of wholeness, confidence, and control without any fear.

When Jesus first came to his disciples after his resurrection, one of them—Thomas—was not present. Later, after these disciples told Thomas about meeting the Lord, Thomas said he would only believe Jesus had been raised from the dead if he could put his hand into Jesus' side. Thomas did not say he wanted to gingerly touch Jesus' wound. Rather, he said—in a macabre manner—that he would not believe that Jesus was risen unless he could put his hand right inside the wound.

Thomas subsequently encountered the risen Jesus. Stunned, Thomas uttered a deep faith statement, "My Lord and my God!" (John 20:28). Here we begin to see that the weight of this story is directed not to Thomas but to the reader. In fact, this incident is not particularly about Thomas at all.

Doubting of St. Thomas *by Caravaggio*

"Have you believed because you have seen me?" Jesus asked Thomas. "Blessed are those who have not seen and yet have come to believe" (verse 29).

All of us go through moments or prolonged periods of doubt. Yet in the midst of that doubt, if we have the ears to hear, we can hear Jesus say to us, "Peace be with you," and hopefully we will be able to respond by exclaiming with great joy, "My Lord and my God!"

POSTSCRIPT

■ The name *Thomas* means "the twin" in Aramaic. A natural question for us to ask is, the twin of whom? An unusual tradition in Syria said that this Thomas was actually the twin brother of Jesus. A more likely explanation seems to come from the third-century document known as the *Acts of Thomas,* which indicates that Jesus and Thomas looked alike and apparently were close.

Purim

THE JEWISH FESTIVAL of Purim finds its roots in the story of Esther. When she first became queen, her cousin Mordecai foiled a plot on the king's life. Soon thereafter, a Persian officer, Haman, was elevated to a high position, and he became infuriated when Mordecai the Jew would not bow down to him when he passed. So he developed a plan to exterminate the Jews. He even cast lots *(purim)* to determine the proper date for this genocide, and he built a gallows from which to hang Mordecai.

Through Esther's timely intervention, however, the king learned of Haman's treachery and ordered him hanged on the gallows intended for Mordecai. He then issued a decree allowing the Jews to defend themselves when attacked, which they did. The Jews had come close to being exterminated, victims of Haman's nefarious intentions. But through the strategically placed Esther and Mordecai, this tragedy was avoided.

Mordecai's Triumph
by James Tissot

The festival of Purim ("lots") celebrates the reversal of the Jews' fortunes. The Bible says it celebrates "the days on which the Jews gained relief from their enemies, and as the month that had been turned for them from sorrow into gladness and from mourning into a holiday" (Esther 9:22). Furthermore, the Jews are to make these "days of feasting and gladness, days for sending gifts of food to one another and presents to the poor" (verse 22).

In other words, to celebrate this great deliverance from the genocide planned for them, the Jews are to think of others less fortunate than themselves; they are to exchange presents and provide for the helpless.

POSTSCRIPT

▪ As Purim evolved over the centuries in Jewish tradition, more customs were added to the biblical instructions. The central feature, however, was still the reading of the scroll of Esther.

▪ The word *pur* was not known outside of the Book of Esther until recently, which led many Bible scholars to be skeptical of the historical value of this story. In the 1970s, however, an ancient small, six-sided clay die was found with the word *pur* on it, lending veracity to the biblical story.

Nehemiah

NEHEMIAH WAS A JEWISH cupbearer to King Artaxerxes of Persia. It was a dangerous position, for a cupbearer had to taste any drink or food before it passed to the lips of his rulers, thus precluding any assassination attempt through poison. In the ancient Middle Eastern courts, this was a position of honor, and the cupbearer was in no way regarded as simply a guinea pig. That's why the cupbearer was frequently selected for his handsome appearance and superior intelligence.

No doubt, Nehemiah probably possessed extraordinary influence with the king and was considered a person of rank and importance in the Persian court. Moreover, he was likely quite wealthy, so leaving Persia would have been a personal sacrifice for him in several ways. Nevertheless, after hearing about the deplorable conditions among his people in Jerusalem, Nehemiah yearned to travel there. Because he had the complete confidence of the king, when he asked the king to allow him to return to Jerusalem and rebuild its walls, the king readily granted his request.

Nehemiah returned to Jerusalem in 445 B.C. with a governor's commission from the king to rebuild the walls of the city. When Nehemiah arrived, he discovered a demoralized city with a wall in ruins. Since a city's security depended on its defense system in ancient times, this meant that Jerusalem was effectively a "non-city." So Nehemiah efficiently organized the Jews into groups to rebuild the walls.

The project encountered stiff opposition from non-Jewish residents in and around Jerusalem, who felt threatened by Nehemiah's plans. In his typical fashion, Nehemiah devised a practical solution that combined spiritual devotion and pragmatic execution. He records in his memoirs, "So we prayed to our God, and set a guard as a protection against them day and night" (Nehemiah 4:9). As a gifted administrator and leader, he was able to persevere and succeed.

When the walls were completed, Nehemiah took part (along with Ezra) in a celebration at which the law was read and the Festival of Booths was observed for seven days, during which the Jews confessed their sins. As governor, he led a ceremony of covenant renewal, in which the people rededicated themselves to God and to observing the Mosaic law. He led the dedication of the wall and called for many Jews who had resettled elsewhere to return to repopulate Jerusalem. Nehemiah also instituted other reforms, including evicting Tobiah who was his opponent and had taken up residence in the temple itself. He also commanded the people to separate from their foreign wives who still worshipped pagan gods.

The Kingdom of Heaven

T HE LAST TWO CHAPTERS of Revelation form the ultimate happy ending. The battles are over. Evil is defeated. Suffering is no more. Humanity returns to Eden, but actually it's better than Eden. John describes "a new heaven and a new earth" (Revelation 21:1). It's not clear whether this is a brand new creation or a makeover of the old model. In any case, it's amazing, brilliant, magnificent! What's most important is that God is fully present. He banishes death and wipes away every tear.

As in the rest of Revelation, there are echoes of the Old Testament throughout this description. As in Eden, rivers run through this land, nourishing the "tree of life." Yet here there is no curse (see Revelation 22:2–3). Ezekiel gave architectural measurements of the holy city he saw in his visions, and specifically for the temple, and John provides a blueprint as well, except no temple is necessary because the Lord himself is the Temple (see Revelation 21:11–22).

Let's pause in our vision of this new heaven to consider an important question: Is this a current picture of heaven, or is it the future? If it's the future, where do dead believers exist *now*? The questions are complicated by the concept of eternity. If this "future" kingdom exists outside the realm of time, wouldn't that be an eternal "now"? Does the believer wake up from death already transported to the future events of rapture, reign, and new heaven and earth? The Bible doesn't provide a lot of details, but we're told that being absent from the body is being present with the Lord (see 2 Corinthians 5:8), and the Lord's presence is the main component of the new heaven and earth. So we should be able to speak of a dying believer being received into heaven.

In John's vision, after a vivid description of golden streets and jeweled gates, an invitation is extended to those who "wash their robes" (Revelation 22:14). Earlier John had seen a multitude dressed in white, those who had washed their robes in the blood of the Lamb (see Revelation 7:14). Now these souls, cleansed by Christ's sacrifice, are invited to enter the city and partake of the tree of life (see Revelation 22:14).

The invitation becomes a song, one that rings through all eternity with a celebration of God's grace:

> "The Spirit and the bride say, 'Come.'
> And let everyone who hears say, 'Come.'
> And let everyone who is thirsty come.
> Let anyone who wishes take the water of life as a gift" (verse 17).

Onesimus

ONESIMUS WAS A RUNAWAY SLAVE when he encountered the Apostle Paul and became a Christian. Though Paul wanted to keep Onesimus on his own mission team, he sent him back to his owner, Paul's old friend Philemon. Onesimus carried a one-page letter from Paul that became part of the New Testament.

St. Paul in a Roman prison cell with Onesimus

Paul was in prison when Onesimus found him, but we're not sure where Paul was. Rome is our best guess. That's a long hike for a runaway slave from Asia Minor, but as they say, "All roads lead to Rome." If a fugitive wanted to get lost, Rome was the place to do so.

But as it turns out, Onesimus found Paul, who was imprisoned. (This was probably his "house arrest" in about A.D. 60, so he could receive visitors but couldn't travel.) After Paul led him to a conversion and a transformation of sorts, he sent Onesimus back to Philemon. It reveals Onesimus's deep trust in Paul and his great faith in Christ that he voluntarily returned.

Paul told Philemon that he wanted to keep Onesimus with him as a helper, but in the socioeconomic system of ancient Rome, the right thing to do was to send him home. Only Philemon could free this slave.

We don't know for sure how Philemon responded, though Paul's appeal would be hard to turn down. Onesimus is also mentioned in Colossians as a "faithful and beloved brother, who is one of you" (Colossians 4:9). Probably the two letters were delivered together by Tychicus and Onesimus, and together the letters were a strong inducement for all the Christians in Colossae to receive Onesimus with open arms. Indeed, how could they not when Paul says, "I am appealing to you for my child, Onesimus, whose father I have become during my imprisonment" (Philemon 10).

POSTSCRIPT

■ The name *Onesimus* means "profitable," and Paul played with this idea, telling Philemon that even though Philemon once considered him "useless" as a slave, Onesimus has become "useful" in Paul's ministry.

The Book of Revelation

Toward the end of the first century A.D., a Jewish Christian prophet named John, banished by the authorities to the island of Patmos for his apparent subversive activity, sent a circular letter to seven churches in the nearby province of Asia on the mainland. These churches faced a variety of challenges. Some were experiencing persecution or enduring poverty as a result of their witness to Jesus and their more radical withdrawal from society. Others were prospering in the local economy, unaware of how they were participating in the sins of a violent and economically unjust imperial system. Still others were listening to Christian teachers who justified some degree of idolatry so they could have better relationships with the non-Christians around them and become better integrated into the local economy and social networks.

John addresses these challenges by writing Revelation. Immersed in the Old Testament, he helps these seven congregations look at their situations—and the world of Roman imperialism—in the light of scriptural revelation. This vision shows a God who will not share worship with any other; who stands against every empire's violence, greed, and self-glorification; and who calls his people to stop cooperating with and bonding themselves to such empires. The government at this time energetically promoted a picture of Rome as a beneficent goddess and the emperors as benefactors and saviors of the world. John reveals Rome to be a bloodthirsty prostitute, corrupting the world through her rule, plundering at will. He reveals the emperors to be pawns of Satan, drawing people away from the worship of the true God, who is their only hope for a just peace.

John then creates a picture of things to come that resembles a cosmic version of the plagues sent to Egypt when God brought his people Israel out from slavery into the Promised Land. This picture is of the end times, which concludes with God receiving the faithful into the new Jerusalem. In light of the broader canvas that John paints, in which Christ returns in triumph to claim his own and to cast his enemies into a lake of fire, faithfulness at any cost emerges as the wisest course of action.

POSTSCRIPT

John does not refer to Rome by name, thus avoiding any charge of insurrection by the Roman authorities. Instead, he names Babylon, but readers during his day would comprehend the true identity of "Babylon."

The Roman Empire

HISTORIANS DON'T ACTUALLY refer to Rome before 27 B.C. (when Octavian was named Caesar Augustus) as an empire, but at this point it had already been acting imperial for two and a half centuries. The Roman Republic took control of Italy in 266 B.C. and quickly set its sights on North Africa and then Spain. In the second century B.C., it gobbled up Alexander's old territory to the east. Meanwhile, in 161 B.C., the Maccabees asked Rome for help in their revolt against the Syrians. The threat of Roman aid seemed to keep Syria at bay, but a century later, in 63 B.C., the Roman general Pompey conquered Palestine while besieging Jerusalem.

By then the Romans had most of the pieces of their empire in place, a ring of territory around the Mediterranean, the sea free of piracy, and a well-trained army deployed strategically. All they needed was an emperor, and a series of civil wars—involving Julius Caesar, Pompey, Marc Antony, and others—took care of that. The emergence of Caesar Augustus ushered in a period of two centuries of relative peace, the *Pax Romana*.

A good organizer, Augustus set up a system of local leadership with checks and balances. In general, the Romans allowed nations to govern themselves within certain parameters, but unrest was dealt with swiftly and often brutally. Herod the Great had already been installed as king in Palestine. After his death, his son Archelaus ruled badly, so the Romans rearranged the territory and inserted a Roman governor before matters became more unruly. While Jesus was growing up in Nazareth, a revolt arose in the nearby town of Sepphoris. The Roman army moved in and crushed it, killing many. This was the sort of swift retaliation the Jewish leaders feared if they let the Jesus movement get out of hand.

Tiberius succeeded Augustus, and he ruled from A.D. 14 to 37. The possibly insane Caligula (37–41) followed, and then Claudius (41–54), who expelled the Jews from Rome. Nero (54–68), however, is the Roman emperor who affected Christian history the most. In 64, a fire raged through Rome, which Nero blamed on the Christians. A vicious persecution ensued in which both Peter and Paul were executed.

Shortly after that, the Jewish Revolt broke out. As usual, the Roman army dealt forcefully with it. Vespasian led the army at first but returned to Rome to become emperor, leaving his son Titus to quell the uprising. Subsequently, Titus systematically destroyed Jerusalem. Vespasian served from A.D. 69 to 79, and his sons, Titus (79–81) and Domitian (81–96), ruled next. Domitian was a tyrant who liked to be called "Lord and God." It's likely that the Book of Revelation was written during his reign.

The Ascension

THE FOLLOWING WORDS are from the Apostles' Creed, which are mirrored from a passage from Mark 16:19: "The third day he rose from the dead, he ascended into heaven, and sitteth on the right hand of God the Father Almighty." Some regard this passage as a later addition to that gospel. Jesus' bodily ascension, however, is described in greatest detail through the writings of Luke, both in Luke 24:50–53 and in Acts 1:9–11. The passages address the question of what happened to the body of Jesus.

Acts 1 says that after Jesus rose from the dead, he was with the disciples for 40 days, speaking about the kingdom of God and telling them that the Holy Spirit would come upon them. Then, "they asked him, 'Lord, is this the time when you will restore the kingdom to Israel?' He replied, 'It is not for you to know the times or periods that the Father has set by his own authority. But you will receive power when the Holy Spirit has come upon you; and you will be my witnesses in Jerusalem, in all Judea and Samaria, and to the ends of the earth'" (Acts 1:6–8).

The Ascension by
Andreas Hunaeus

After Jesus spoke these words, he was lifted up and a cloud took him out of sight. The disciples looked upward while men in white robes stood by them and said, "Men of Galilee, why do you stand looking up toward heaven? This Jesus, who has been taken up from you into heaven, will come in the same way as you saw him go into heaven" (verse 11).

The focus of this passage ignores the speculation about the end times and the disciples' need to be concerned with the present state of Israel. Nor is the primary focus on the imminent return of Jesus. Rather, it is on the disciples' call to be filled with the Holy Spirit and to be Jesus' witnesses throughout the world. Thus this passage serves as a kind of commissioning for the disciples.

In that moment, Jesus was present and his teachings were clear. The men in white robes offered clear instructions. Even the continuum between heaven and earth was immediately apparent. The moment of ascension revealed to the disciples that their lives were going to be very different. Henceforth the power of God would strengthen them in a new way. Jesus ascended, and the Holy Spirit called them to be witnesses beyond Jerusalem, Judaea, and Samaria, indeed to the ends of the earth.

The Books of the Old Testament

Genesis	2 Chronicles	Daniel
Exodus	Ezra	Hosea
Leviticus	Nehemiah	Joel
Numbers	Esther	Amos
Deuteronomy	Job	Obadiah
Joshua	Psalms	Jonah
Judges	Proverbs	Micah
Ruth	Ecclesiastes	Nahum
1 Samuel	Song of Solomon	Habakkuk
2 Samuel	Isaiah	Zephaniah
1 Kings	Jeremiah	Haggai
2 Kings	Lamentations	Zechariah
1 Chronicles	Ezekiel	Malachi

The Books of the New Testament

Matthew	Ephesians	Hebrews
Mark	Philippians	James
Luke	Colossians	1 Peter
John	1 Thessalonians	2 Peter
Acts of the Apostles	2 Thessalonians	1 John
Romans	1 Timothy	2 John
1 Corinthians	2 Timothy	3 John
2 Corinthians	Titus	Jude
Galatians	Philemon	Revelation

INDEX

INDEX

INDEX

INDEX

Jezebel, 77, 189, 246, 269, 276, 277, 283, 284, 291
Jezreel, 175, 283, 291
Joab, 256, 263
Joanna, 110, 156
Job, 39, 112
Job (book), 39, 112
Joel (book), 182
Joel (prophet), 138, 182
John (gospel), 16, 19, 22, 26, 33, 75, 82, 89, 93, 97, 107, 117, 125, 139, 153, 177, 181, 191, 245, 357
John Hyrcanus, 337
John Mark, 257, 272, 279
John the Baptist, 13, 16, 19, 23, 27, 41, 85, 93, 97, 100, 118, 146, 153, 215, 217, 232, 277, 316, 349
  angel announces birth of, 43
  beheading, 33, 146
John (the Beloved), 40, 83, 121, 145, 155, 245
  exile in Patmos, 83, 348
  in Garden of Gethsemane, 75, 82
  responsibility for Mary, 13, 83, 96
  at Resurrection, 110
Jonah (book), 196
Jonah (prophet), 196, 225, 297
Jonathan, 197, 249, 337
Joppa, 194
Jordan River, 16, 29, 41, 42, 93, 108, 160, 172, 185, 232
Jordan Valley, 60, 67, 87
Joseph, Rabbi Akiba ben, 106
Joseph of Arimathea, 103, 110, 153, 237, 302, 352
Joseph (son of Jacob), 130, 136, 143, 176
Joseph (stepfather of Jesus), 12, 20, 51, 55, 72, 79, 118
Josephus (historian), 65, 93, 145, 216, 302, 305, 309, 317
Joshua, 42, 56, 172, 179, 185, 197, 239
Joshua (book), 49, 232
Josiah (king), 154, 311, 312
Jotham (king), 305
Judaea, 19, 55, 96, 146, 194, 201, 209, 215, 216, 252, 258, 264
Judah, 37, 77, 91, 116, 122, 123, 147, 154, 161, 189, 210, 214, 220, 242, 262, 267, 270, 274, 284, 304, 312, 333, 346
Judas Iscariot, 121, 139, 197, 244, 279
Judas Maccabeus, 302, 330
Jude (book), 364
Judges (book), 56, 186, 193, 200, 207
Julius Caesar, 48
Justin Martyr, 113

K
Kadesh, 35
Ketaubim, 64
Kings (books), 77, 84, 99, 175, 191, 210, 220, 241, 246, 262, 291, 312
Kirath-Arba, 179
Kish, 347

L
Laban, 95, 109, 115, 122
Labashi-Marduk, 340
Lake of Gennesaret, 114
Lamech, 66
Lamentations (book), 154, 225, 319
Last Supper, 22, 68, 82, 111, 139, 191, 279, 289
Latin language, 99, 134
Law of Moses, 79, 93, 137, 171, 175, 218, 283, 295, 309, 312, 323
Lazarus, 47, 125, 181, 188, 195, 202, 240, 245, 260
Leah, 116, 122, 123
Lemuel (king), 126
Lent, 268
Levi, 122
Levites, 49, 122, 190
Leviticus (book of), 15, 28, 42
Lord's Prayer, 142
Lot, 60, 67, 87, 239
Lucifer, 57
Lucius of Cyrene, 229
Luke (gospel of), 12, 13, 16, 27, 30, 41, 43, 48, 51, 57, 64, 65, 69, 93, 103, 117, 124, 149, 174, 209, 238
Luke, 229, 321
Lydia, 264, 271, 294, 356
Lystra, 272

M
Maacah, 263
Maccabean Revolt, 302, 309
Maccabees, 337
Macedonia, 259, 264, 314
Machpelah, 81
Magi, 12, 13, 37, 55, 58, 65
"Magnificat" (song of praise), 13, 27
Mahalath, 102
Mahershalal-hash-baz, 305
Mahlon, 63, 221
Malachi (book), 23
Malachi (prophet), 41, 217, 277
Malchus, 75
Malta, 334
Manaen, 229
Manasseh (king), 130, 305, 312

INDEX

INDEX

Daniel, 43
Elijah, 27, 40, 77, 85, 184, 197, 217, 232, 269, 276, 277, 283, 284, 290, 298
Elisha, 184, 232, 254, 277, 290, 298
Ezekiel, 50, 87, 295, 325, 326
false, 40
Habakkuk, 203
Haggai, 91, 210, 281
Hebrew, 12
Hosea, 305, 346
Isaiah, 12, 23, 40, 50, 175, 189, 258, 267, 304, 305, 312
Jeremiah, 61, 154, 197, 312, 319
Joel, 138, 182
John the Baptist, 41
Jonah, 196
Malachi, 41, 217, 277
Micah, 305
Nahum, 203
Nathan, 197, 234
Obadiah, 189
Samuel, 70, 206, 220, 235
Zechariah, 91, 217, 261
Zephaniah, 210
Proverbs (book), 126, 241
Psalms (book), 17, 31, 54, 60, 68, 70, 85, 100, 119, 126, 261, 295
Purim, 105, 367

Q
"Q" document, 238
Quirinius, 209, 321
Qumran, 85

R
Rachel, 109, 116, 122, 130, 228
Rahab, 30, 123, 185
Rebekah, 88, 95, 101, 102, 108, 109, 130
Red Sea, 21, 164, 169, 179
Rehoboam, 262
Resurrection of Christ, 43, 110, 117, 124, 156, 177, 355, 359
Revelation (book), 50, 52, 57, 83, 113, 348, 362, 369, 371
Rhoda, 222
Roman Empire, 372
Romans (book), 18, 177, 259
Rome
    Christianity in, 48
    occupation of Israel, 55, 223
    Peter in, 76
Rosetta Stone, 120
Rosh Hashanah, 330
Rufus, 230

Ruth, 30, 63, 214, 221
Ruth (book), 63

S
Sabbath, 17, 36, 110, 204
Sadducees, 132, 167, 209, 302, 303, 316, 337
Salome, 33, 110
Salome Alexandra, 302, 337
Salt Sea. See Dead Sea.
Samaria, 77, 173, 194, 201, 212, 252, 258, 264, 267, 284, 288, 291
Samaritans, 166, 173, 212, 254, 264, 267
Samson, 56, 192, 200, 253
Samuel (books), 70, 72, 197, 199, 206, 228, 234, 235, 253
Samuel (prophet), 70, 72, 199, 206, 220, 227, 235
Sanhedrin, 65, 180, 202, 302, 303, 307, 316, 323, 352
Sapphira, 152, 159
Sarah, 27, 46, 53, 74, 81, 88, 95, 101, 128, 130
Sargon (king), 267
Satan, 39, 52, 57, 100, 112
Saul (king), 70, 84, 206, 213, 220, 227, 234, 235, 249, 253
Saul of Tarsus. See Paul.
Sea of Galilee, 76, 79, 83, 89, 90, 97, 104, 167, 232
Semitic language, 71, 99
Sennacherib (king), 304
Septuagint, 44, 78, 113, 127, 134, 336
Seraphim, 43, 50, 305
Sermon on the Mount, 135
Seth, 66
Shabbat, 17
Shadrach, 332
Shalmaneser III (king), 284
Shamgar, 253
Shammai, 307
Shavuot, 317
Shear-jashub, 305
Shechem, 108, 262
Shelah, 123
Shem, 143
Shema, 36, 295
Sheol, 57, 260
Sheshbazzar, 281
Shiloh, 211, 228
Shinar, 80
Sidon, 246, 291
Sihon, 165
Silas, 257, 264, 278, 314, 328, 356
Silvanus, 294